The Princeton Review

MCAT*
Workout

Extra Practice to Help You Ace the Test

Matthew Patterson, M.D., Jennifer Wooddell,
and Jason Faulhaber, M.D.

PrincetonReview.com

Random House, Inc. New York

The Princeton Review, Inc.
2315 Broadway
New York, NY 10024
E-mail: editorialsupport@review.com

ISBN 978-0-375-76631-2
ISSN 1937-6375

MCAT is a registered trademark of the Association of American Medical Colleges (AAMC).

Editors: Melody Marcus, Mariwyn Curtin
Production Coordinator: Kim Howie
Production Editors: Heather Brady, Meave Shelton

Printed in the United States of America.

10   9   8   7   6   5   4   3   2

2008 Edition

Acknowledgments

The Princeton Review would like to thank James L. Flowers, M.D. and Theodore Silver, M.D. for their authorship of the two online tests provided with *MCAT Workout* as well as some of the practice passages inside the book. The online tests were originally published in a longer form in *Practice MCATs*, the book that *MCAT Workout* replaces. When the MCAT changed in January 2007, we edited the tests and put them online to mirror the format of the new exam.

Thanks to Brittany Winston for her contributions to the Introduction and parts of the Verbal Reasoning and Writing sections.

A book like this requires extensive accuracy checking. We are grateful to the following Princeton Review Master Trainers for their expert review of the content: Bethany Blackwell, Kristen Brunson, and Carolyn Shiau, M.D.

Thanks also to Tricia McCloskey, Liz Rutzel, and David Kelley for their hard work in preparing the online content, and to Mariwyn Curtin for freelance editorial work on all of the chapters.

Speical thanks to Adam Robinson, who conceived of and perfected the Joe Bloggs approach to standardized tests and many of the other successful techniques used by The Princeton Review.

Finally, many thanks to Judene Wright, Content Director for MCAT Program Development, without whose constant guidance and input this project would not be possible.

Contents

Foreword

In April 1991, the Association of American Medical Colleges (AAMC) first administered a substantially revised MCAT. At the same time, after two years of development, The Princeton Review introduced its comprehensive MCAT preparation course nationwide.

Since then, AAMC has made the MCAT progressively more difficult due to the drastically increased number of medical school applicants in the mid-1990s. During this time, The Princeton Review has taken steps to ensure that our course reflects this increased level of difficulty.

In 1996, The Princeton Review and Hyperlearning, California's premiere MCAT prep company, took MCAT preparation to new heights by merging their programs—the combined course was billed as a "Test Prep Utopia" for premedical students by the UCLA Daily Bruin. The combined MCAT program had the largest, most up-to-date collection of MCAT materials available, the equivalent of over 30 MCATs. In 2007, the program was further updated to reflect the MCAT's change to computer based testing (CBT), with nine online diagnostic exams, hundreds of practice passages online, and unlimited access to the eight AAMC online Practice Tests.

Today, one out of every three applicants to medical school prepares for the MCAT with us. Students who take our course improve their MCAT scores by an average of 10 points, with the top half averaging a total score of over 30 points. We are proud of our program and of the accomplishments of our students.

This book is not a replacement for a full MCAT course; no book is. Instead, it is a valuable resource for students just beginning the MCAT preparation process who wish to diagnose their areas of strength and weakness. It is also a useful tool for students who have already invested the time required to master MCAT topics and are now looking for more practice materials and that extra edge.

Good Luck!

More Review, More Strategy, More Ways to Learn

There's more to this book than just this book. *MCAT Workout* includes exclusive access to the following online tools designed to enhance your studies:

- Two full-length, online practice tests with detailed performance analysis available on completion

- Optional essay scoring with our exclusive LiveGrader℠ service

- Links to important information about the MCAT

To access your online tools, go to: **PrincetonReview.com/cracking** and register the serial number at the bottom left corner of the inside back cover of this book. You will promptly receive an e-mail with confirmation of your registration and additional instructions.

Part I
Introduction

Chapter 1
Introducing the MCAT and MCAT Workout

WHAT IS THE MCAT?

The Medical College Admissions Test (MCAT) is now an exclusively computer-based test (CBT) offered multiple times a year at professional testing centers. The test itself is four hours and twenty minutes long (with check-in and breaks you should expect to be at the testing center for well over five hours), and almost all American and Canadian medicals schools use it to help decide whether to admit or reject applicants. If you are planning to attend medical school, you will most likely need to take the MCAT. It can determine where you go—or whether you go at all.

HISTORY OF THE MCAT

The MCAT is produced, administered and scored under the auspices of the Association of American Medical Colleges (AAMC). Since 1991, the MCAT has been, in part, a passage-based test, rather than a test that depends wholly on rote memorization of facts. This has not been altered with the 2007 change to a computer-based test format. The MCAT now takes less time and has one-third fewer questions. This change will allow you to receive your scores in nearly half the time as examinees did on the old, paper-based tests because there are no answer sheets to process or paper essays that need to be physically handled. The structure, content, and scoring system are the same as they were on the old, paper-based test. Reading comprehension, critical thinking, and application of knowledge to new situations are tested throughout the exam in Physical and Biological Sciences as well as Verbal Reasoning and in a Writing Sample.

HOW IMPORTANT IS THE MCAT?

When to Take the MCAT
You should try to take the MCAT on one of the April test dates, at least one year prior to the date you wish to begin medical school.

Source: *Best 168 Medical Schools,* 2008 Edition

Medical schools use an MCAT score for three main reasons: First, it gives admissions officers a sense of whether the applicant is likely to succeed academically in the face of challenging med school curriculum. Second, it gives a picture of an individual's particular strengths and weaknesses over the range of content encountered in med school. Lastly, it backs up the information provided with the rest of the application, such as personal statements, letters of evaluation, and transcripts.

The weight that a particular medical school gives to an applicant's MCAT scores varies from school to school. Furthermore, the range of scores considered acceptable may be very different for each school or even for the programs within a school. The MCAT is just one aspect among a set of criteria that med schools use to compare qualifications of applicants. The admissions committee will also examine many other aspects of your prior academic and extracurricular history as they weigh one candidate against another. Some of the factors considered important are as follows: grade point averages for all undergrad, postgrad, and graduate study; the content of your course of study and its difficulty; and letters of evaluation. Additionally, non-academic aspects are considered, such as involvement in extracurricular activities, medical school interview results, and participation in and quality of health-related work and research, among other factors.

WHAT IS THE FORMAT OF THE MCAT?

The MCAT is divided into four sections:

- Physical Sciences (Physics and General Chemistry)
- Verbal Reasoning
- Writing Sample
- Biological Sciences (Biology and Organic Chemistry)

The science sections of the MCAT apply first-year, college-level topics in Physics, General Chemistry, Biology, and Organic Chemistry to new, perhaps unfamiliar situations.

Except for the writing sample, the exam is entirely multiple choice. All questions are followed by four choices (A, B, C, and D), and there is no penalty for guessing. Your score is based only on the number of correct responses, so you should never leave any question blank. No study aids of any kind (books, notes, formula sheets, or calculators) are permitted. The test center will provide you with scratch paper and pencil or possibly a dry erase board and marker.

The following table represents the current structure of the test.

Test Section	Questions	Time
Tutorial (optional)		5 minutes
Physical Sciences	52	70 minutes
Break (optional)		10 minutes
Verbal Reasoning	40	60 minutes
Break (optional)		10 minutes
Writing Sample	2	60 minutes
Break (optional)		10 minutes
Biological Sciences	52	70 minutes
Survey		10 minutes
Total Test Content Time		4 hours, 20 minutes

Physical Sciences

According to the AAMC, the Physical Sciences section presents anywhere from seven to nine passages, each pertaining to physics and/or general chemistry. All recent test administrations have contained seven passages. A science passage is a description of some physical situation or experiment, often accompanied by diagrams of experimental apparatus, data tables, graphs, and/or formulas. Each passage is followed by five to seven multiple-choice questions that concern the passage and the relevant science. In addition, the section includes about ten questions that do not relate to any passage. We call these "freestanding" questions. Recent test administrations included thirteen freestanding questions. Altogether, the Physical Sciences section has 52 questions with a time limit of 70 minutes.

Verbal Reasoning

The Verbal Reasoning section consists of 40 questions with a 60-minute time limit. This section is composed of seven reading passages (about 600 words each), with an average of five to seven questions after each one. The passages come from books or articles published in magazines, journals, or newspapers. The potential subject matters are diverse and include history, sociology, psychology, political theory, social and literary criticism, anthropology, and general science. Most questions require recognition of the author's main idea and tone, as well as an understanding of the arguments used to establish and support his or her position. Simple retrieval of factual information contained in the passage makes up only a small percentage of the questions.

Writing Sample

The Writing Sample section requires the test taker to write two essays (each with a time limit of 30 minutes) based on a philosophical or social statement. Successful essays must address three specific writing tasks based on the topic provided: Explain the meaning of the statement, provide a counterexample to the statement, and discuss criteria for determining when the statement is true and when the statement is false. There is no specific answer that the test writers are looking for. The AAMC holds that each essay will be scored "holistically"—i.e., essays will be viewed in their entirety and not given separate scores in areas such as grammar or organization. Now that doesn't mean you can be sloppy with language, spelling, or punctuation! Demonstration of good, basic writing skills is always a plus. Your focus, however, should be on creating essays that are clear, focused, and reflect complexity of thought.

Biological Sciences

The Biological Sciences section has 52 questions with a time limit of 70 minutes and is structured exactly like the physical sciences section, except the topics of the passages and questions are from Biology and Organic Chemistry.

HOW IS THE MCAT SCORED?

Approximately four weeks after your test date, you will receive a score report in the mail. You can also get your scores online from the AAMC's official MCAT website: **www.aamc.org/students/mcat**. Online scores are available sooner than the scores sent by mail. The score report contains four scores—one for each section, plus the total numerical score for the three multiple-choice sections. The three multiple-choice sections are scored on a 1 to 15 scale (whole number scores only), with 15 as the highest possible score for a section. Scores of 10 or above are considered very good. The overall national average is about an 8. The scores for the writing sample are averaged and translated into a letter score scaled from J through T, with T being the highest. The most common scores are M and Q; the average score is O.

MCAT Score Reporting
The AMCAS (American Medical College Application Service) and the medical schools to which you're applying will automatically receive your MCAT scores for any MCAT taken in 2003 or later.

Source: *Best 168 Medical Schools*, 2008 Edition

THE COMPUTER-BASED EXAM FORMAT

Unlike some computerized, standardized tests, the MCAT CBT is not an adaptive test. Briefly, this means that the questions on the MCAT CBT are predetermined; they are not selected based on the test taker's performance, and all questions are weighted equally.

CBT MCAT Tools

The MCAT CBT requires test takers to use basic mouse and keyboard commands to answer questions and navigate through the test. A brief tutorial is available at the start of the exam that provides information about the MCAT computer interface, but you can skip it if you wish. Many people find that the five-minute tutorial does not provide enough time to try out all of the tools, so here is an overview of your powers in the CBT universe.

Tools You Can Use on Every Question

You can click a button to access a **Periodic Table**. A **Highlighting** feature lets you mark important pieces of the text so that they stand out when you look back at the passage to answer a question. However, be aware that your highlights will not be retained throughout the duration of the exam, only for as long as you are looking at that particular passage. The **Strikeout** capability is your key for the Process of Elimination (POE) strategy. It lets you cross out answers you know must be wrong so that you can make an educated guess among what's left.

Speaking of guessing, if you've begun work on a question, but you think you might want to come back to it, guess and use the **Mark** button to flag it to come back to if you happen to have time at the end of the test. There's more specific advice about using the highlighting feature in Chapter 10: Mastering Verbal Reasoning that is useful for all passage-based questions, even in the scientific content sections.

Previous and Next Buttons and the Review Screen

These are your tools for skipping around from passage to passage and question to question within a section. The **Previous** and **Next** buttons will advance you through the section linearly backward or forward, respectively. It is somewhat faster for most students to navigate using the **Review** screen. The Review screen is incredibly helpful and easy to use—all you have to do is double-click on a question you want to go back to, and you jump to the question immediately. The questions are clearly indicated as unanswered or marked, and you can easily choose to review just the marked questions, just the incomplete questions, or review all. You only have the ability to review questions for a section as long as you are still working in that section. You cannot return to a section once you have exited it.

Remember, you do not have to do the passages and questions in the order they are presented within a given section. The MCAT provides easy-to-use tools that allow you to quickly skip past passages and question sets that have unfamiliar or tough topics. Use these tools to focus your time and effort on answering the questions that are easiest for you first, then go back to complete the more time-consuming or difficult ones. Use the Review screen to make sure you fill in an answer for every question in the section. Remember—there is no penalty for guessing!

Word-Processing Tools for the Writing Sample

In the Writing Sample section, basic word processing tools such as cut, copy, and paste are available. That's about it. There is no "undo" feature, so be careful what you delete. You can review and change answers within a section as long as you are still working in that section. You are given 30 minutes for each essay, and you cannot return to the first essay once you have exited it. For the best preparation, use the skills and techniques discussed in this book in conditions that are similar to those of the actual computer-based test. For additional practice with a simulated interface, visit **PrincetonReview.com** or **www.e-mcat.com**.

Important Differences between AAMC's Practice Tests and the Real Thing

It helps immensely to use computer-based practice tests to get used to taking a CBT, because that's how you will encounter the exam on test day. The AAMC has several practice tests available; most are for a fee, though at least one free exam is available. These tests come straight from the source. But beware! As of this writing, there are significant differences between the tool set on the practice exams and those made available on the actual MCAT. First of all, as mentioned earlier, Highlighting in the passage is not maintained from passage to passage. On the other hand, strikeouts of answer choices do persist, even though in the practice tests they disappear when you move to the next passage.

Some tools that appear on the practice test are simply absent altogether on the real thing: There is no **Search** feature, so you have to scan with your eyes to find a word or phrase in a passage. Furthermore, there is no **Notes** feature, so you are not able to insert electronic text notes within a passage. You do have scratch paper or a white board on the real test, however, so you will be able to utilize the strategy of annotating the passage (described in more detail in Mastering Verbal Reasoning). Finally, there is no **Guess** box for each question, but instead, there is a **Mark** button to flag the questions you might want to reconsider later.

REGISTRATION INFORMATION

The Association of American Medical Colleges administers the examination and provides a wealth of information about the test structure, content, scoring, and administration. The most reliable and up to date information on these topics can be obtained directly from the AAMC.

Registration for the MCAT is available online at the AAMC website: **www.aamc. org/students/mcat**. The MCAT is administered during seven sessions a year, and for each session, there are multiple dates for a total of 22 administrations a year. Morning, afternoon, and weekend administrations are available. Information regarding deadlines, fees, and testing locations is available on the MCAT website. In order to ensure that you get the most convenient location at which to take the test, you should register as soon as possible. The exam is delivered by Thompson-Prometric testing centers, on behalf of the AAMC. Contact information for the MCAT program/AAMC is as follows:

Association of American Medical Colleges
MCAT Program Office
2450 N Street, NW
Washington, DC 20037
tel: 202-828-0690
fax: 202-828-1125
www.aamc.org/mcat
e-mail: **mcat@aamc.org**

HOW THIS BOOK IS ORGANIZED

Following this chapter, you will encounter the subject areas of the exam in the order in which you will see them on the test: Physical Sciences, Verbal Reasoning, Writing Sample, and Biological Sciences. Each content area begins with an Overview to give you a general picture of what you will encounter on that section on the test and some ways to best manage the section. All sections with the exception of the Writing Sample will have more specific information and techniques in the "Mastering" chapter. You'll put this into use in the practice section called "Mastery Applied."

Finally, the "Answers and Explanations" chapter will provide you with complete explanations for all questions and guidance on how to use the techniques presented to maximize your score when applied to similar questions.

The two Science chapters are further broken down into the two main areas of content in each: General Chemistry and Physics for Physical Science, and Biology and Organic Chemistry for Biological Sciences. Each of these four specific science areas will have its own set of Mastering, Mastery Applied, and Solutions chapters.

The Writing Sample chapters are structured somewhat differently than those for the other sections. Remember, there are only two Writing Sample questions on the MCAT. "Overview of the Writing Sample" contains the best techniques for answering the essay prompts. The chapter titled "Practice MCAT Essays" provides six prompts much like those you will see on test day, a high- medium- and low-scoring response to each, and an analysis of each essay explaining its strengths and /or weaknesses. This will allow you to see the differences between essays that receive higher and lower scores and where your response falls among them. Don't forget, with your purchase of this book, you also have access to two online tests, with the option to have your essays scored by Princeton Review's professional essay graders.

Applying to Med School
Due to intense competition, most premed advisors recommend you apply to at least 10 schools. If your grades are below average or you live in a state with competitive, state-affiliated schools, you should apply to as many as 30 schools. Talk to your advisor to figure out which schools are right for you.

Source: *Best 168 Medical Schools,* 2008 Edition

USING THIS BOOK

The focus of this book is to illustrate MCAT test-taking techniques and provide practice items and full-length computer-based tests for the application of both content knowledge and techniques. This book is *not* designed to be a complete content review of the scientific concepts encountered on the MCAT. You'll have the opportunity to put your practice into action in the same way as taking a real MCAT by utilizing the two computer-based tests provided online. Detailed explanations are provided to enable you to learn from your mistakes.

Accessing the Online Tests

The inside back cover of this book includes a long serial number at the bottom left corner. You need to register this number at **PrincetonReview.com/cracking**. Be sure to type the number exactly as it appears, including all dashes and using all caps for the letters. Once your number is accepted, you will be asked to complete a brief registration form. When that's done, a confirmation message will be sent promptly to your registered e-mail account. Keep that confirmation message, as it contains important information about accessing the MCAT Workout site and contact information for any problems you experience.

FURTHER REVIEW

Want more? For complete mastery of all concepts covered on the MCAT, it is strongly recommended that you use this book in conjunction with a thorough MCAT test preparation guide such as *Cracking the MCAT CBT* by The Princeton Review. Additional materials and practice tests are available from the AAMC at **www.aamc.org,** and one free practice test (besides the ones that come with this book) is available at **PrincetonReview.com**. Finally, comprehensive preparation in both content review and strategy is provided by The Princeton Review MCAT preparatory course. To learn more, visit **PrincetonReview.com** or call **800-2Review.**

By picking up this book, you are already on track to increase your score on the MCAT. We wish you all the best as you engage in study and practice for this step in your medical career. Good luck!

Part II
Physical Sciences on the MCAT

Chapter 2
Overview of Physical Sciences

PHYSICAL SCIENCES STRUCTURE AND SCORING

Physical Sciences is the first section on the MCAT. There are 52 total questions with a time limit of 70 minutes. According to the AAMC, on any given administration of the examination, there will be approximately 7 to 9 passages with associated questions and approximately 10 freestanding questions with no associated passage. Recent test administrations, however, have been consistent in presenting 7 passages and 13 freestanding questions. In general, the freestanding questions are distributed throughout the section in small groups between passages. Passages typically contain between 5 and 7 associated questions.

The Physical Sciences section is scored on a scale of 1–15. Each individual question is associated with a level of difficulty. The raw score is the number of individual questions answered correctly. This raw score is converted into a scaled score taking into account the difficulty level of the questions on the test form, which varies between test-takers. There is no penalty for guessing. Not all of the items on a particular test form will be scored. Those items not scored likely include questions that are problematic for scaling or are in the exam for test development purposes. As it is not possible to accurately predict these items, treat all questions as if they will be scored. Because there is no penalty for guessing, no item should be left blank in any section of the test.

PHYSICAL SCIENCES IN A CBT

Navigating the MCAT CBT requires basic keyboard and mouse computer skills. The short tutorial at the beginning of the test covers the functions available to the test taker. Specifically, you can highlight sections of the passage, cross out answer choices, mark specific questions for later review, and navigate to individual questions from a review screen. As you work through the section, passages can be skipped and returned to later within the 70-minute time block for the Physical Sciences. Likewise, answers can be changed within this time period. The test center supplies either scratch paper or a white board to use during the test. A periodic table with atomic number and atomic mass is available in a pop-up window by pressing an onscreen button.

Given the limited time for the introductory tutorial and the unique nature of taking a test on a computer, it is highly recommended that you practice working through an MCAT CBT. This essential practice can be obtained by taking the online practice tests that come with this book and by purchasing tests at **www.e-mcat.com**. After gaining mastery of the CBT format, it is still necessary to work through the opening tutorial, as actual test features may be different on the day of the exam.

PHYSICAL SCIENCES THEMES

The unifying theme for the MCAT Physical and Biological Science sections is the application of *basic* scientific principles to novel situations through reasoning and problem solving. Individuals beginning their preparation for the MCAT are often surprised and bewildered by the apparent complexity of the scientific passages presented on practice tests. It would be a mistake to set out and learn this advanced content. In time, the smart test taker learns to look beyond the distracting information and see the underlying fundamental principles at work. Success is driven by the application of a core foundation of basic knowledge to a seemingly complex situation. Therefore, preparation must involve a balance of basic content mastery and the refinement of test-taking skills.

New Information

One of the things that can be guaranteed on the MCAT is that the test taker will eventually encounter unfamiliar territory. This is by design and can take the form of a novel concept, experimental data, complex diagrams or graphs. Even when a passage details a familiar concept in depth, the questions will often ask about the effects of a modification or new situation. Therefore, a useful study method is to draw diagrams or graphic representations of important concepts. Detail how everything is supposed to work correctly and then systematically change each variable to understand how the system will respond.

Problems

Problem solving can range from the basic application of a formula to understanding the nature of a broad physical science phenomenon. As the MCAT evolves, it focuses more and more on conceptual understanding, even when the situation is quantitative in nature. Number crunching, even in the Physical Sciences section, is surprisingly sparse given the nature of physics and general chemistry. Understanding the meaning behind a formula (i.e., the proportionality between two of the several variables within the equation) or how to apply the formula to a particular situation is often the focus of problems. This reflects the unifying theme of MCAT science—the application of basic principles to novel situations.

The Painful Reality
Each year, there are about 40,000 applicants to medical school for approximately 18,000 spots.

Source: *Best 168 Medical Schools,* 2008

Experiments

At some point on the MCAT, you will encounter an experiment. Frequently, the results of an experiment are presented in a table or graph. Therefore, basic data interpretation and graph skills are very important to this section. In addition, concepts of experimental design, data collection, and the validity of conclusions can be addressed. A question may ask if a particular conclusion is supported by the data presented or if an experiment was designed appropriately to address a particular phenomenon. Again, it is essential to focus on the basic principles addressed and not become overwhelmed by the specifics of the content involved. Experimental reasoning questions are simply another way of asking the test taker to apply knowledge to a new situation.

Evidence

Based on information presented in the passage, is it appropriate to draw a certain conclusion and why? Just as medicine is becoming more and more evidence based, the MCAT seeks to assess the ability of a test taker to evaluate the effectiveness of an argument. Although it seems that these questions would be very open-ended, the answer will always come back to basic principles of physics and general chemistry and reflect the central theme of information provided in the passage.

PHYSICAL SCIENCES CONTENT

The content of the Physical Sciences section of the MCAT is more or less equally divided between physics and general chemistry. On some passages, it may be difficult to see a strict distinction, and concepts from both disciplines may be combined. In addition, physics and general chemistry phenomena are often presented in the context of biological systems, particularly the human body. The level of content corresponds to a year-long, undergraduate, freshman year, introductory course with laboratory for both sciences. Advanced coursework is not required and potentially counterproductive given the reasoning focus of the test.

As detailed knowledge of the concepts is not expected, a surprising level of detail about a particular phenomenon may be presented in the passage itself. The questions are focused much more on the practical application of the concepts to various problems. A solid content foundation will save a tremendous amount of time when tackling these types of passages, as known facts can be quickly skimmed. The specific physics and general chemistry topics that can appear on any given test are provided in an outline by the AAMC on its website. These will be explored in the Mastering Physical Sciences chapters that follow.

PHYSICAL SCIENCES TEST-TAKING SKILLS

The most efficient approach for MCAT preparation is to address both content and technique. Working through passages and taking practice examinations periodically is the best way to gauge progress. Careful and introspective review of performance on practice items will often reveal if a deficiency is based more on content or technique. Weaknesses in either area can be addressed with further study or practice as appropriate. Specific techniques for particular passage and question types are covered in the Mastering Physical Sciences chapters. However, there are several skills that apply to the Physical Sciences section as a whole.

Attack the Section in Your Order

Do not allow the test to dictate the order in which you approach the passages and questions. For most people, the CBT will actually make this easier, as there is a **Mark** button that lets you flag questions for later review. The **Review** screen lets you jump directly to blank and marked questions, and there is no separate bubble sheet that can get out of sync with a test booklet.

The easiest way to practice taking control of the test section is to treat each passage or group of freestanding questions as a single chunk. Beginning with the first passage, make a decision rapidly about whether or not to tackle it. With practice, you will be able to quickly identify those topics that are more comfortable for you. On the first pass through the section, skip over any passages that contain content in which you are weak or feel less confident. The goal of the first pass is to address comfortable passages and all freestanding questions. This way, you focus your best energy on questions you are most likely to get right, and you eliminate the possibility that you will run out of time without addressing later questions on well-known content.

On your second pass, tackle the remaining material in an order from least to most difficult for you. Before you exit, carefully review the section to be sure that all questions are answered. If you are running out of time, be sure to answer every question, guessing as needed, to maximize your score. There is no penalty for guessing.

Although you may be the type of student that always takes a test in order from beginning to end, practice approaching the MCAT in multiple passes. There are several reasons for this. If time is an issue, this ensures that you do not miss an easier question that you know well. The computer-based navigation is well-designed to get you to the questions you want to review, and it's easy to discern where in the test you are. Most importantly, comfort at skipping around gives you confidence. On the actual test day, if that first passage is something terrible to lay eyes on, you can confidently and efficiently move on to a better passage. Having practiced this before, you will be well prepared to maximize your score under potentially stressful situations.

Attack the Questions in Your Order

Similar to the approach for the entire section, the items within each passage or group of freestanding questions should be done in the order that plays to your strengths. This varies for each person. You may find yourself gravitating to graphing and quantitative questions and away from broad experimental reasoning items. Feeling comfortable moving around from question to question allows you to maintain momentum. Sometimes it can be very tempting to persist on a particular problem for too long. This can have dramatic consequences on the amount of time you have left for the remaining items. Working on the questions within a passage from easiest to hardest makes it less likely that you will miss points on something you know well.

Process of Elimination (POE)

While this may seem obvious, it is important to point out the method and importance of POE on this multiple-choice test. When evaluating answer choices, it is typically easier to eliminate items that are known to be incorrect than to immediately search for the correct answer. Remember to focus only on evaluating if an answer choice is absolutely wrong. If you are trying to assess each answer choice as either right or wrong, then you are essentially just looking for right answers, and this is not the best approach for the MCAT. Eliminate what is clearly wrong and use the strikeout feature on the computer to focus your eyes on what remains. Sometimes, a problem can be effectively answered by confidently eliminating three answer choices without having to really assess the correct choice. Also, eliminating answer choices will improve odds when guessing is necessary.

When in Doubt, Guess and Move On

Spending too much time on a problem or two can significantly affect your ability to address the remainder of the test calmly. Purely on the basis of the number of questions, you have approximately 80 seconds per question. When you include the time necessary to approach each passage and navigate between passages on the test, however, the actual time is more like 75 seconds. The best approach on a question that is giving you difficulty is to confidently eliminate anything you can and then guess, marking in your answer. Do not leave any item blank.

If you want to revisit the question later, time permitting, use the Mark tool to tag this question as a guess. You are most likely to answer the question correctly when you are working on it initially in the context of the other questions in the passage. Left blank and returned to 30 minutes later, it will be much more challenging. If you have time at the end of the section, you can always return to a marked question and change the answer if you arrive at a different conclusion. Remember—never leave any item blank on the test. There is no penalty for guessing. Feel like you've heard this before? Good! That means we're getting through to you.

Figures, Tables, and Graphs

Refrain from spending too much time interpreting a figure, table, or graph before you are required to do so. If you are scanning the passage before addressing the questions, simply note the location and general content of the graphic. Unless you have a photographic memory, you are certain to return to the table or graph to retrieve a specific data point or trend when the question asks you to. Therefore, don't waste time on an item that you either may not use at all or that you have to return to later anyway to answer the question.

Stay Inside the Box

Keep your focus on core principles, and do not be tempted to stray into any advanced concepts or creative reasoning that the passage is presenting. Remove the fancy distractions and apply the fundamental concept. This can be difficult to do if you have any advanced experience in the topic presented. Resist the urge to hold the passage to the standards of the cutting edge and stick to the basics.

The Quantitative Toolbox

Although pure calculation problems are by far the minority in this section, a strong foundation in basic mathematical concepts is required to perform well on the test. Facility in all of the following is recommended:

- **Arithmetic:** proportions, ratios, square root, percentage, exponents, basic logarithms, scientific notation
- **Algebra:** manipulation of equations, variables, shapes of graphs, direct and indirect proportions, slope
- **Trigonometry:** basic trigonometric functions of right triangles (sine, cosine, tangent) and common angles
- **Unit analysis:** familiarity with common SI and metric units
- **Estimation and proportional analysis:** simplification of numbers, fractions, and complex equations
- **Statistics:** mean, probability, conceptual understanding of standard deviation, and correlation
- **Vectors:** addition, subtraction, resolution, and right-hand rules

Particular emphasis is placed on algebraic manipulation of equations, proportional analysis, and estimation. Often, answer choices are given in the form of a properly set up equation without the need to solve the equation. Similarly, a novel and complex equation can typically be reduced to the relationship of two of the variables within it. Finally, when calculations of numbers are involved, estimation and looking carefully at the answer choices before completely solving the problem can often allow you to effectively answer the question. Specific examples of these concepts will be addressed in the following chapters.

The Qualitative Toolbox

The key skills required for success on the Physical Sciences section of the MCAT reflect the themes of the test.

But Here's What You Can Make!
Once in practice, physicians are among the most highly paid professionals. In 2005, a typical family practitioner made $156,000, while the average for all specialists was close to $300,000.

Source: *Best 168 Medical Schools*, 2008

Information Recall

Although the application of reasoning to novel situations is the name of the game, nothing beats being able to recall an equation or concept that solves the problem. In fact, as your content foundation grows, you will find that your reliance on the passage decreases dramatically. The goal is to eventually get to a point where you only require information from the passage when it is absolutely necessary, and you are able to readily identify when this is the case. Many questions associated with a passage actually do not require any information in the passage itself.

Reading Comprehension

Even though this is the Physical Sciences section and not Verbal Reasoning, efficient and accurate reading comprehension plays a very important role in today's MCAT. This is particularly true if the concepts presented are totally foreign or unfamiliar to you. In addition, when asked about experimental reasoning, it will be necessary to understand the problem addressed and the steps taken to address it. At the most basic level, there are times when simple but important facts are contained within the passage that dramatically affect an otherwise straightforward question.

Data Interpretation

The MCAT will require you to pull data from a table or graph. More than simply retrieving a number, you will often be required to assess the shape or trend of the data. Data interpretation can also involve making conclusions based on results provided. Other times, you will be asked if the conclusions within a passage are appropriate based on the data presented. Finally, new data can be introduced in a question and you will be asked to apply that to the findings or concepts presented in the passage.

Concept Application

Application of concepts is one of the most frequently required skills on the Physical Sciences section of the MCAT. Assuming a basic understanding of the scientific principles at work, how can they be used to solve a particular problem? Questions can be very concrete, such as providing a formula with data and requiring a calculation. Other times, the question will require you to choose which concepts are appropriate to apply to a particular problem without actually performing any specific operation or calculation.

Scientific and Experimental Reasoning

Given a problem, are you able to suggest potential methods and concepts that would determine an answer? Given experimental methods, results, and conclusions, are you able to apply fundamental concepts to evaluate the accuracy and validity of what is presented? Although this may sound complex or broad, the questions will be very focused on basic underlying principles. Staying current on the scientific literature is not a prerequisite for excelling on the MCAT. The basic issues of experimental error, data collection, data reporting, and conclusions encountered in a freshman chemistry or physics laboratory provide more than enough background. Practicing passages with these concepts will provide all the preparation that is needed.

Chapter 3
Mastering Physical Sciences: General Chemistry

This chapter expands on the principles outlined in the overview of physical sciences. The major areas of general chemistry that may appear on the MCAT are briefly outlined. A thorough content review from other resources, such as The Princeton Review's *Cracking the MCAT CBT*, will address these topics in detail.

The primary purpose of this text is to present test-taking techniques and sample test items for putting both content and technique into practice. A detailed and comprehensive approach for attacking general chemistry passages and questions follows. In addition, a bag of tricks is introduced. Sounds interesting, eh? Who said studying for the MCAT wouldn't be fun? The physical sciences techniques discussed here can be put into play under specific test circumstances and often prove useful if all else fails in your systematic approach.

GENERAL CHEMISTRY CONTENT

Some Current Trends in Medicine
- New technology
- Increased health care costs
- An aging patient population
- Greater reliance on primary and preventive care

Source: *Best 168 Medical Schools*, 2008

The AAMC provides an outline of all the potential general chemistry topics that can appear on the MCAT. This can be found on its website under the category "Preparing for the MCAT Exam." The emphasis of particular concepts may be different than what is presented in a first-year college course. Given the vast amount of topics that can be drawn upon, it is not practical or advisable to attempt to master this material at the level that is presented by the test itself. The MCAT is designed to present novel situations, and there is no way to predict the specific topics that will appear on any given administration. That said, there are fundamental concepts that are particularly relevant to the practice of medicine that are more likely than others to find their way to the test.

Keep in mind the following goals when reviewing content. First, the review should be taken only to a level of detail sufficient for mastering basic, fundamental concepts that can then be applied to new situations. For example, practicing the calculation of final concentrations of compounds when an equilibrium system is disturbed is not likely to yield much for the examination. However, a solid understanding of the general concept of how an equilibrium system responds to stresses of concentration change, pressure change, temperature change, and the addition of a catalyst is very important. Concepts are more important than details.

Second, focus more on application than memorization. A surprising number of formulas that you think you need to memorize may be explained in detail in a passage. The test will be more concerned with how you apply that formula to a new situation. That said, the better you know core concepts and some core formulas, the more time you will be able to spend on the questions themselves and not the passage. If you do enough practice passages and tests during your MCAT review, you will find that certain key formulas come up again and again. Essentially, you will not be able to help memorizing equations like $c = \lambda f$ and $PV = nRT$.

Finally, during your study, consider how the MCAT would ask about the topic you are reviewing. The test has common patterns when presenting material. One trend is a straightforward description of a scientific principle followed by questions that place that principle in unique situations or with changed variables. For example:

What would happen to the kinetics of a reaction if the temperature changed?

Another approach is the presentation of an experiment that explores a key concept.

What is suggested by the data?

What would happen if a different reagent were used?

Finally, think about how the topic you are studying could be presented in a diagram, table, or graph. Your content mastery should be at a level sufficient for effective problem solving on the test and nothing more. Do not delay practice items until the end of your study, as it is essentially impossible to "finish" studying for this test given how broad it is. Test yourself frequently to assess areas of study that need the most attention. Is it content or technique where you need to improve? If content, in which areas are you weak?

GENERAL CHEMISTRY TOPIC OUTLINE

Basic Concepts

These topics are typically not the focus of passages but are nonetheless essential to the foundation of general chemistry knowledge. Topics include the following:

- molecular formulas
- moles
- stoichiometry
- balanced equations
- dimensional analysis
- limiting reagent
- oxidation states

As mentioned at the beginning of this chapter, the AAMC provides a list of General Chemistry concepts that you need to understand for the MCAT on their website. At a length of ten pages, the list is rather intimidating; just think how smart you're going to get while you're studying for this exam!

Atomic Structure

The number of protons, neutrons, and electrons within a particular atom define its physical properties and chemical reactivity. The basics of quantum numbers, electron configurations, and nuclear chemistry can all appear on the test. Of all the concepts in this area, nuclear transformations and half-life problems deserve thorough review and are typically easy points to pick up. The key players of radioactive decay should be learned, and a simple percentage technique for solving half-life problems is more than sufficient for the types of questions on the MCAT.

Periodic Trends and Bonding

Periodic trends and intermolecular forces are high yield topics for the MCAT. By understanding the concept of nuclear shielding, you can determine essentially all of the periodic trends (atomic radius, electronegativity, etc.) without having to memorize them. Increases in intermolecular forces, especially by hydrogen bonding, have dramatic effects on the physical properties of compounds by increasing melting point, boiling point, and viscosity while decreasing vapor pressure. Covalent bonding, ionic bonding, and molecular geometry are also frequently encountered topics.

Phases

For the most part, this section comes down to two graphs and two formulas. The graphs are the pressure vs. temperature phase diagram and the temperature vs. heat phase change diagram. In particular, understanding how water is different from all other molecules by favoring the liquid phase under increased pressure at certain temperatures is a frequently tested concept. Another issue addressed here is how a substance can change phase *or* change temperature but not do both at the same time. The two formulas that deal with the increase in temperature of a substance with applied heat and the energy associated with phase change are $q = mc\Delta T$ and $q = n\Delta H$ respectively.

Gases

Unfortunately, $PV = nRT$ is probably not enough to carry you on gases for the test. Deviations from this formula under non-ideal situations (high pressure and low temperature), partial pressure, and effusion are other topics that present excellent MCAT problem solving situations.

Solution Chemistry

As many reactions occur in the liquid or aqueous environment, a thorough understanding of basic solubility and concentration measurement is required for the test. In addition, colligative properties on both a qualitative and quantitative level are important to learn and apply to problem-solving situations.

Kinetics

For the MCAT, you must know what kinetics are and what they are not. Kinetics are *not* thermodynamics. By clearly understanding the variables that play a role in the kinetic realm (temperature, catalysis, concentration, rate), you will often be able to use POE to arrive at correct answers. A key concept for the MCAT is the very different manner in which kinetics and thermodynamics drive a reaction. Understanding what a catalyst does (lowers energy of activation) and does not do (change thermodynamics) is another vital concept. Finally, rate laws and rate constants are frequently tested material.

Equilibrium

Equilibrium is one of the most important and unifying concepts in general chemistry and on the MCAT. Understanding what an equilibrium constant means and not just how to set one up will open many doors on the test. These constants are applied in reaction yield, solubility, thermodynamics, electrochemistry, and extensively in acid base chemistry. Le Chatelier's principle, solution precipitation, and the reaction quotient are all related to equilibrium.

Acid Base Chemistry

Along with equilibrium, acid base chemistry is among the most important topics for the Physical Sciences section. From basic definitions to estimated calculation of pH, neutralizations, buffers, and titrations, this is a high yield topic for review. Titrations and buffers are particularly amenable to graphic representation.

Thermodynamics and Thermochemistry

Conceptual topics include the laws of thermodynamics, enthalpy, entropy, and the basics of defining a system and its surroundings. Terminology of various processes such as isothermal, isobaric, and adiabatic comes into play. Gibbs free energy, spontaneity, and equilibrium are topics that are intimately connected and deserve ample study.

Electrochemistry

There are certain aspects of an electrochemical cell that are always the same no matter what kind of cell it is. These should be memorized (anode is site of oxidation, cathode is site of reduction, etc.), or better yet, understood. The first step is to focus on oxidation and reduction. Once the basics of oxidation and reduction are mastered, it is easy to construct an appropriately labeled galvanic or electrolytic cell because each aspect (flow of current, charge of each electrode, etc.) follows from the previous one.

Again, this is a brief outline of the major categories of general chemistry topics that appear on the MCAT and is in no way meant to be exhaustive. For most people, reviewing college texts and revisiting class notes is not the most efficient manner to obtain the particular kind of mastery required for excelling on the MCAT. The value of effective content review materials that specifically target the way the MCAT asks about these topics cannot be overstated. By combining this knowledge foundation with the systematic approach and techniques presented in *MCAT Workout*, you will be well on your way to success.

Trends in Medical School
- Less time spent in lecture
- More clinical problem solving during first two years
- Greater emphasis on health economics, health care management, and public health.
- Better training in outpatient medicine

Source: *Best 168 Medical Schools*, 2008

ATTACKING GENERAL CHEMISTRY FREESTANDING QUESTIONS

According to the AAMC, there will be approximately 10 freestanding questions in the Physical Sciences section. The number may vary from test to test, but MCAT administrations throughout development of this book included 13 freestanding questions. About half of these are likely to cover concepts in general chemistry, but again, the exact ratio can vary among test forms and administrations. Free-standing questions are not associated with any passage and tend to be presented in groups. For example, there may be three groups of 3 to 4 questions placed between every few passages.

Focus on Freestanding First

Taken as a whole, the freestanding questions tend to be easier to manage than passage-based questions. The degree of difficulty may actually be harder, but a relatively straightforward question presented in the absence of complex text, graphs, and experiments lends itself to efficiency. These questions should be considered opportunities to maximize your score. For this reason, it is absolutely essential that you attempt every freestanding question and do not run out of time before doing so.

As these questions can appear at the end of the section, doing the test questions in the order presented is not the best approach on the MCAT for most people. Referring to the techniques outlined in the Overview of Physical Sciences chapter, all freestanding questions should be done on the first pass through the section. Some may find it effective to go through the entire section and do all of these questions first. Others may prefer to have the occasional break in having to do passage-based items. Whatever your approach, do not leave these for the end!

Don't let any one question suck up too much of your time. If you have eliminated as many answer choices as you can, just pick one of the remaining answers and move on. Without a penalty for guessing, you are always doing yourself a disservice in not answering a question, but to not answer a question after you have invested time and work on it is an even bigger mistake. Your time is valuable. Make the most of it. If you feel uncertain that the answer you select is not the best one, or if you have guessed, you can use the Mark tool to select it for review at the end of the test.

Given the typical brevity of the questions, the technique(s) necessary for solving them is/are usually readily apparent. Often these are short quantitative problems that require the recall of a core formula, such as $\Delta T = kim$ for freezing-point depression. These questions also provide opportunities for the test to address topics that do not merit the devotion of an entire passage, such as stoichiometry or molecular geometry. POE and the effective recall of information provide the solutions, as in the following examples.

1. In a galvanic cell, which of the following correctly describes the signs of Gibb's free energy ($\Delta G°$) and electric potential ($E°$)?

   A. $\Delta G°$ is positive, $E°$ is positive
   B. $\Delta G°$ is positive, $E°$ is negative
   C. $\Delta G°$ is negative, $E°$ is positive
   D. $\Delta G°$ is negative, $E°$ is negative

These two-part answer choices are common on the MCAT. The best approach is to choose the variable with which you are more comfortable and then eliminate the two answer choices you know are wrong. For example, you may recall that a galvanic cell is spontaneous, and therefore $\Delta G°$ must involve the release of free energy and be negative. Answers A and B can be eliminated, leaving you with C and D. Alternatively, you may recall that electric potential is positive in a spontaneous galvanic cell and eliminate B and D first. Finally, even if you do not remember any of this, you can reason that anything that gains energy ($\Delta G°$ is positive) cannot start at a high potential ($E°$ is positive). Therefore, $\Delta G°$ and $E°$ must have opposite signs, eliminating A and D. The answer is C.

Studying for the MCAT, Part II
Most students find it easier to raise their science scores than their verbal scores. Unfortunately, most students start out with higher scores in science than in verbal.

Source: *Best 168 Medical Schools*, 2008

2. When 500 J are applied to a 2 kg sample of silver, the temperature of the metal increases by 1.06°C. What is the specific heat of silver?

   A. 0.17 J/g°C
   B. 0.24 J/g°C
   C. 0.48 J/g°C
   D. 0.63 J/g°C

This question illustrates some important techniques. Solving the problem involves the use of the formula $q = mc\Delta T$, where q is heat in J, m is mass in g, and T is temperature in °C or K. The specific heat, c, is obtained by rearranging the equation to $c = q/m\Delta T$. Note that even if you cannot recall this equation, the units of all the answers are the same and essentially provide the formula for solving the problem. This is intentionally obvious in this example and may be subtle on the actual exam. However, the point is to use all of the information available, including that from the answer choices. The answer is **B**.

The second point demonstrated here is estimation. It is not necessary to perform long division using 1.06. Setting ΔT at 1 is sufficient because the answer choices are so different from each other. In fact, once the equation is set up as $c = (500\ J)/((2\ kg)(1))$, it becomes clear that the first digit after the decimal point in the answer must be a 2. There is no need to carry the calculation any further given the answer choices. These techniques will be expanded later in the book.

ATTACKING GENERAL CHEMISTRY PASSAGES

As recommended in "Overview of Physical Sciences," approach the passages in the section in the order that makes sense for you, not necessarily the order in which they are given to you. Always maximize your effort on topics that you know best. For example, you may be much stronger in physics than general chemistry and decide to do all of the physics passages and all freestanding questions first and then do the general chemistry passages last. Take advantage of practice tests to experiment with approaches to the test that work well with your skills. You never want to be in a situation on the actual MCAT where you run out of time before you get to the passages and questions that play to your strengths.

Now or Later

The first step is to decide if a passage should be approached at all or left for later. Practice making this decision in a matter of seconds. As you study, you will be amazed at how easy it becomes to recognize topics. Typically, the subject is mentioned in the first paragraph, or a large figure in the passage will give it away. If acid-base chemistry is not your forte and you run smack into a giant titration curve, perhaps it is time to click the Next button and come back later. Otherwise, continue to the next step.

Scan the Passage

An average general chemistry passage can be scanned effectively in less than one minute. The two goals of this are to identify main ideas and the *location* of information. Appraise the passage one paragraph, figure, or table at a time. It is not important to understand or memorize details at this point. Do not spend unnecessary time on tables or figures to which you will almost certainly have to return if a question addresses them. In fact, you may not be asked about them at all. Identify the location of unfamiliar terminology or equations that may be required from the questions. You can use the highlighting tool to help you. It is faster to scan the passage and then do the questions one by one, referring back to the passage as needed, than it is to read through all of the questions first and then approach the passage. In addition, if you go back to the passage for each question individually, you will be less likely to exclude a key piece of information for certain questions. Remember that even in the Physical Sciences section, reading comprehension can still come into play for many questions.

Get to the Questions!

Points are awarded for answering questions correctly, not for understanding the nuances of a particular passage. Spend the bulk of your time where the points are—the questions. Do the questions in the order that works best for you. Typically, it is more effective to do the easier questions first and the more difficult questions last. Again, with experience, you will be able to identify the level of difficulty by appearance and pattern recognition. By handling 2 or 3 easy questions first, you gain momentum, confidence, and a greater understanding of the passage at large that helps you with the more difficult items. As you work from question to question, look for common themes. The MCAT has a way of asking the same question over and over again in a manner that seems different. Unlocking this can make the passage much easier.

Keep Moving, but Leave Nothing Blank

Once you commit to doing a general chemistry passage, do not leave anything blank! That's right. Do not skip items to come back to at the end of the test. Use POE, cross out what you know is wrong, and then answer with your best guess. Use the Mark tool to annotate this question as a guess. At the end of the test, if you have time, you can always return to the question. However, if you run out of time, at least you can feel confident that you answered the question at the point when you were most focused on the themes of the passage. This is typically better than returning 30 minutes later and having to re-familiarize yourself with the details. Remember also that you should fill in an answer for every question on the MCAT because you lose no points for incorrect answers. Sorry, we just can't help reminding you of this once again!

If you find yourself bogged down on a particular question, you must resist the urge to stick with it for an excessive amount of time. This can be one of the most challenging skills for an MCAT test taker. Typically, those in the premedical field are adept at testing and tend not to shy away from a challenge. It is helpful to look at the scales provided by the AAMC practice tests to realize that you can miss many questions on the Physical Sciences section and still score very high. Do not let one tough question prevent you from getting ten correct answers at the end of the section. Leave the hard questions for last. If you move quickly through the other questions, you might be able to afford a little extra time on those that are more difficult. Given the time needed to scan all the passages in a Physical Sciences section, you have about 75–80 seconds per question.

When to Apply

As early as possible, because a majority of medical schools engage in some type of rolling admissions.

Source: *Best 168 Medical Schools*, 2008

Passage Based or Not?

Although the questions follow a passage, it does not mean that information in the passage is required to solve them. This is when having a solid content foundation can be the most helpful. The more you understand the fundamental concepts of general chemistry, the less reliant you will be on the passages for background information. When you are doing practice passages, take the time to ask yourself directly if each question is passage based or not. The answer will be different for each person depending on how much you know. This is a helpful exercise, because it reinforces the correct approach to solving the problem and is time efficient. Do not waste time looking for information in a passage if the question is really just asking if you know a fundamental concept. For example, take a look at the following passage-based question:

3. In experiment 3 in the passage, if the canister was insulated so that no heat could escape, the process would become:

   A. isothermal.
   B. isochoric.
   C. adiabatic.
   D. isobaric.

The answer is **C**, regardless of what is in the passage. Processes where no heat is exchanged are adiabatic. The information in the passage will not change this.

With time and practice, you will not need to ask yourself overtly if a question is based on the passage or not because it will come to you naturally. As your content knowledge grows, be cautious not to become too independent of the passage. Sometimes, an important piece of information in the passage can change your approach. Usually, this will be obvious. In addition, if you are effectively scanning the passage before doing the questions, you will be less likely to overlook these points. Overall, the goal on the MCAT is to spend as much time as possible on the questions and answers and little time on the passage whenever feasible.

Uncover the Fundamentals

Somewhere in the passage is a fundamental concept trying to find you. Your job is to cut through all the distractions and allow it to emerge. For example, to be successful on the MCAT, you do not need to know the pharmacodynamic properties of aspirin absorption. However, if you were told the pK_a of aspirin, you should know that it is a weak acid. In addition, you should be able to use reasoning to determine the effects of changing stomach pH on the absorption of aspirin by understanding how the dissociation equilibrium of aspirin would shift according to Le Chatelier's principle. With practice, you will gain confidence with passages that appear very complex at first glance.

Use Techniques

Most questions on the MCAT can be answered in multiple ways. The obvious approach taken on most questions is to apply the appropriate scientific principle to the information provided and solve the problem. However, there may be times when this would be inefficient or you have forgotten the principle or formula. POE and answer analysis can often present a logical solution that is not necessarily scientific. At the very least, perhaps one or two answer choices can be eliminated and your guess will be more effective. Two drills can be used to practice these techniques.

First, pick a random practice passage and eliminate all wrong answer choices from all of the questions without looking at the passage. Second, try to answer the questions without looking at the passage. Even if you get many of them wrong, it is a useful exercise to see how much you can accomplish without using your test time to read the passage. Mastery of content is the most important tool in your skill set for the MCAT. However, there are others, and you must exercise these techniques regularly to be effective on the day of the test. When you run out of options, remember your bag of tricks presented at the end of this chapter and the similar chapter on physics.

Use the CBT Tools Provided

The CBT format has improved many aspects of the test taking experience. It is very easy to navigate from passage to passage. You can review everything you have answered on one screen and see where you have blank questions or marked questions that were guesses. Within a passage, you can highlight information, and for each question, you can cross out wrong answers. All of these tools allow you to take more control of your test-taking experience, but only if you use them effectively.

Highlighting and striking out are both done by left clicking, and clicking a second time removes the highlight or strikeout. As of press time, there are some differences in tool functionality between the AAMC's online practice tests and the actual exam. In the actual MCAT, the highlights do NOT persist when moving from passage to passage, but the strikeouts DO persist. Note that this is exactly opposite to what AAMC's online practice tests do. Also notably absent are the Search function and the Notes feature, both of which are available on AAMC's online practice tests. This may change by your test date, but be prepared for differences between the online practice tests and your real MCAT.

INTRODUCING THE PHYSICAL SCIENCES BAG OF TRICKS

Tricky is not a good word to describe the MCAT. Unfortunately, it is more challenging than tricky. The questions tend to require fairly straightforward applications of fundamental scientific concepts to novel situations. The variety of topics that can appear on the test combined with the reasoning required to answer the questions can make it difficult. The MCAT is not a test marked by obvious patterns that once recognized can be exploited with cookie-cutter methods. However, given the challenging nature of the test, it is likely that you will encounter situations where your knowledge is lacking or your systematic techniques have broken down.

The bag of tricks presented here and expanded in the Mastering Physical Sciences: Physics chapter are simply additional tools that may help in tough circumstances. When faced with a situation where you are running out of time or have to guess, you may find yourself using these effectively. They may not work in every situation. A sample general chemistry passage is presented here followed by solutions for each question that illustrate the techniques in the bag of tricks.

Passage I (Questions 1–5)

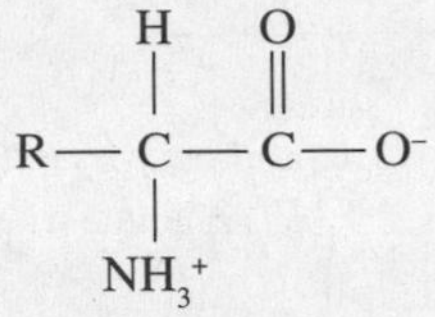

$$R - C - C - O^-$$

with H, O, and NH$_3^+$ substituents

Figure 1 Amino acid structure

Amino acids have the general structure shown in Figure 1. The molecule has acid-base properties at the carboxylic acid group (–COOH) and amine group (–NH$_2$). In addition, some amino acids have these groups on their side chain (–R). The molecule is a *zwitterion* when it has a neutral charge with a protonated amine group and deprotonated carboxylic acid group. The pH at which the molecule exists as a zwitterion is the *isoelectric point* (pI). When the pH of the environment changes from this point, the amine group loses a proton or the carboxylic acid group gains a proton in a proportion predicted by the Henderson Hasselbalch equation:

$$pH = pK_a + \log_{10} \frac{[A^-]}{[HA]}$$

A research scientist is investigating the role of amino acid availability on the upregulation of a gene product *mjn*, a protein. In prior studies, the amount of *mjn* that could be produced by a colony of cells was related to the concentrations of various amino acids in the extracellular space. The amino acids are taken into the cells and used for the synthesis of *mjn*. Those molecules with a neutral or positive charge were taken into the cell more readily than negatively charged molecules. This new study involves changing the pH of the extracellular space and measuring the resulting uptake of various amino acids and *mjn* production.

Table 1 Amino Acids

Amino Acid	pK_a – COOH	pK_a – NH$_3^+$	pI
Alanine	2.35	9.87	6.0
Aspartic Acid	2.10	9.82	2.9
Cysteine	2.05	10.25	5.1
Glycine	2.40	9.8	6.1
Histidine	1.77	9.18	7.6
Phenylalanine	2.58	9.21	5.5

1. In the experiment, which of the following is the expected relationship between amino acid uptake (R), K_a, and pK_a at constant pH?

   A. As K_a increases, R increases.
   B. As K_a increases, R decreases.
   C. As pK_a decreases, R increases.
   D. As pK_a increases, R decreases.

2. Which of the following is true of the side chain of histidine?

   A. It contains a basic functional group.
   B. It contains an acidic functional group.
   C. It is linear.
   D. It is nonpolar.

3. For an amino acid placed in a solution with a pH lower than its isoelectric point, the surrounding [H$_3$O$^+$]:

   A. decreases and the amino acid will be negatively charged.
   B. decreases and the amino acid will be positively charged.
   C. increases and the amino acid will be negatively charged.
   D. increases and the amino acid will be positively charged.

4. At a pH of 5.0, the ratio of positively charged molecules to zwitterions will be the largest for:

   A. aspartic acid.
   B. cysteine.
   C. glycine.
   D. histidine.

5. Approximately what percentage of glycine is in the zwitterion form when placed in human plasma (pH = 7.4)?

   A. 1%
   B. 25%
   C. 50%
   D. 99%

No Right Answer is Created Equal

1. In the experiment, which of the following is the expected relationship between amino acid uptake (R), K_a, and pK_a at constant pH?

   A. As K_a increases, R increases.
   B. As K_a increases, R decreases.
   C. As pK_a decreases, R increases.
   D. As pK_a increases, R decreases.

On the MCAT, as on any multiple-choice test, whenever two answer choices are essentially equivalent to each other, they must both be wrong. The first question can be answered without any information from the passage at all. Going into the MCAT, you should know that K_a and pK_a are inversely related for an acid. Therefore, as K_a increases, pK_a decreases. Answer choices A and C are equivalent, and both must be wrong. Without knowing anything about R, it is clear from the answer choices that it changes in some direction relative to K_a or pK_a. Answer choices C and D both describe an inverse relationship, and therefore, they are equivalent and are both wrong. While this question is purposely designed to illustrate this concept, often times this skill can be used on the MCAT to at least eliminate two answer choices. The correct answer is **B**.

Acids with a high K_a have a low pK_a, and according to the Henderson Hasselbalch equation, as pK_a decreases, the difference between pH and pK_a will increase, favoring the deprotonated form of the acidic group (the ratio of $[A^-]/[HA]$ increases). The passage states that neutral and positively charged molecules are favored for absorption. At relatively low pH, as pK_a of the COOH group decreases, it is more likely to be deprotonated, favoring the zwitterionic form of the amino acid over the positively charged form. R is unaffected. At neutral to high pH, the COOH group will already be deprotonated. As pK_a of the NH_3^+ group decreases, it is more likely to be deprotonated, favoring the negative form of the amino acid over the zwitterion. This will therefore decrease R. The rate of absorption would be expected to decrease for amino acids with smaller pK_a values (larger K_a values) when pH is constant. Because of all the variables involved with this question, it is probably more efficient to answer it based on a limited knowledge of K_a and pK_a and some logic rather than formally solving it according to the principles involved.

Opposites Attract

2. Which of the following is true of the side chain of histidine?

    A. It contains a basic functional group.
    B. It contains an acidic functional group.
    C. It is linear.
    D. It is nonpolar.

Unlike the rule of equals, when two answer choices on the MCAT are essentially opposites of each other, it is often *but not always* the case that one of them is correct. At times, it is easier to disprove one of these answer choices, thereby supporting the opposite choice. Exercise some caution, however, as opposite answer choices can both be incorrect if they do not effectively relate to the question, but if you are guessing or running out of time, this skill can be helpful.

Answer choices A and B are opposites of each other. Therefore, guessing between these two options is better than guessing among all the options. Histidine has a cyclic, polar side chain with basic functional groups. As this knowledge is not needed for the MCAT, the answer must be within the passage. Looking at Table 1, histidine is the only amino acid with a pI greater than 7. Therefore, when histidine is a zwitterion, it produces a net base effect that must originate in the side chain. The correct answer is **A**.

Two for One

3. For an amino acid placed in a solution with a pH lower than its isoelectric point, the surrounding $[H_3O^+]$:

    A. decreases and the amino acid will be negatively charged.
    B. decreases and the amino acid will be positively charged.
    C. increases and the amino acid will be negatively charged.
    D. increases and the amino acid will be positively charged.

Answer choices often take the form of two variables acting in all possible combinations. Although it is tempting to work with one complete answer choice at a time, it is easier to pick one variable at a time and eliminate two answer choices at the start. The nice part is that either variable can be used, so pick the one that is easier to deal with.

For this question, if an amino acid is placed in a highly acidic environment, its functional groups will be protonated, removing hydronium ions from the solution. Therefore, C and D are wrong. Even if you knew nothing else about this question, at least you would have a 50 percent chance when guessing. At a pH lower than the pI, the carboxylic acid group begins to be protonated and the overall molecule will have a positive charge, because the amine group is already protonated at the isoelectric point. The correct answer is **B**.

To the Extreme

4. At a pH of 5.0, the ratio of positively charged molecules to zwitterions will be the largest for:

    A.   aspartic acid.
    B.   cysteine.
    C.   glycine.
    D.   histidine.

When the MCAT asks about something that is the *most, greatest, least*, etc., the two answer choices with middle values of the operative variable will both be wrong. The MCAT deals with indirect and direct relationships, and it would be extremely rare to see a parabolic mathematic relationship. In other words, when some x goes up, y goes down or up, either linearly or at some exponential rate.

This question is asking you to compare pH and pI for a group of amino acids. Without knowing anything else about chemistry, you can safely eliminate answers B and C because their values for pI are in the middle of the pack. If you are unsure of the relationship beyond this, at least a guess would have a 50 percent chance of being correct. For this problem, when surrounding pH is below the isoelectric point, the molecule is protonated and has a positive charge. The larger the pI relative to pH, the larger the proportion of positively charged molecules there will be. **D** is the correct answer.

In the Ballpark

5. Approximately what percentage of glycine is in the zwitterion form when placed in human plasma (pH = 7.4)?

 A. 1%
 B. 25%
 C. 50%
 D. 99%

Quantitative problems on the MCAT can often be answered on the basis of order of magnitude without having to perform any specific calculations. For example, answer choices in scientific notation may differ by the sign or magnitude of the exponents only. Answers that are out of the ballpark can be eliminated.

This may not seem as obvious for this problem, until you remember we are dealing with a logarithmic scale. For every difference of 1 between pH and the appropriate pK_a, the ratio of $[A^-]/[HA]$ changes by a *multiple* of 10. At a pH of 7.4, the titration curve of glycine is between pI and the pK_a of the $-NH_3^+$ functional group. Therefore, only the $-NH_3^+$ and its pK_a (9.8 from Table 1) need to be considered. Rearranging the Henderson Hasselbalch equation gives $pH - pK_a = \log_{10}([A^-]/[HA])$, where HA is the zwitterion ($^-OOC-R-NH_3^+$) and A^- is the negatively charged form of the amino acid ($^-OOC-R-NH_2$). The left side of the equation becomes $7.4 - 9.8 = -2.4$ for this problem. From there you can stop. Think about what -2.4 means on a logarithmic scale. The ratio favors the denominator of $[A^-]/[HA]$ by over 2 orders of magnitude. Therefore, the ratio must be smaller than 1/100, and over 99 percent of the solution will contain the zwitterion form of the amino acid. Even if you were unsure of the difference between a negative and positive logarithm, answers B and C could be eliminated because they are out of the ballpark. D is the correct answer.

Chapter 4
Mastery Applied:
General Chemistry Practice

This chapter provides several passages and freestanding questions on which you can practice the strategies discussed previously and determine those topics that require additional study. The number of general chemistry passages and freestanding questions is intentionally greater here than that which you will encounter on the actual MCAT in order to give you comprehensive practice. Are you ready for a workout?

Passage I (Questions 1–5)

Although ethanol is often consumed in many beverages, several commonly used industrial alcohols are toxic for human ingestion. Without treatment, accidental or intentional poisoning from these compounds can be fatal. Table 1 lists some of these poisons along with their physical properties.

Table 1 Physical Properties of Toxic Alcohols

Compound	Formula	Melting Point (°C)	Boiling Point (°C)
Ethylene glycol	$C_2H_6O_2$	−12.9	197.3
Diethylene glycol	$C_4H_{10}O_3$	−10.5	244.5
Methanol	CH_3OH	−97.0	64.7
Isopropanol	C_3H_8O	−89.0	82.3

Ethylene glycol by itself is a relatively harmless molecule, but it is converted in the liver to toxic metabolites. The metabolism is a four-step process depicted below. In the first and rate-determining step, ethylene glycol is converted to glycoaldehyde by the enzyme alcohol dehydrogenase (ADH). Glycoaldehyde is then rapidly converted to glycolic acid by aldehyde dehydrogenase. The third step is relatively slow and involves the transformation of glycolic acid into glyoxylic acid. The final step is the metabolism of glyoxylic acid into oxalic acid. The oxalate anion readily precipitates with calcium, forming crystalline deposits in the kidneys.

Step 1 $HO-CH_2-CH_2-OH \xrightarrow{ADH} H-\overset{\displaystyle O}{\overset{\|}{C}}-CH_2-OH$

Step 2 $H-\overset{\displaystyle O}{\overset{\|}{C}}-CH_2-OH \longrightarrow HO-\overset{\displaystyle O}{\overset{\|}{C}}-CH_2-OH$

Step 3 $HO-\overset{\displaystyle O}{\overset{\|}{C}}-CH_2-OH \longrightarrow HO-\overset{\displaystyle O}{\overset{\|}{C}}-\underset{\underset{\displaystyle O}{\|}}{C}-H$

Step 4 $HO-\overset{\displaystyle O}{\overset{\|}{C}}-\underset{\underset{\displaystyle O}{\|}}{C}-H \longrightarrow HO-\overset{\displaystyle O}{\overset{\|}{C}}-\underset{\underset{\displaystyle O}{\|}}{C}-OH$

1. Treatment of ethylene glycol poisoning likely includes giving the affected person:

   A. calcium.
   B. ethanol.
   C. acetic acid.
   D. alcohol dehydrogenase.

2. Mixing 10 g of which of the following alcohols with 500 mL of water will result in a solution with the highest boiling point?

   A. Ethylene glycol
   B. Diethylene glycol
   C. Methanol
   D. Isopropanol

3. The effects of ethylene glycol poisoning on the bloodstream include:

   A. increased osmolality and increased pH.
   B. increased osmolality and decreased pH.
   C. decreased osmolality and decreased pH.
   D. decreased osmolality and increased pH.

4. Which compound would be expected to have the lowest pK_a?

   A. Glyoxylic acid
   B. Glycoaldehyde
   C. Oxalic acid
   D. Glycolic acid

5. Additional diethylene glycol is added to a 0.3 m aqueous solution resulting in a 0.18°C change in boiling point. What is the approximate change in osmolality of the resulting solution ($k_b = 0.5$°C/m)?

   A. 0.06 m
   B. 0.09 m
   C. 0.21 m
   D. 0.36 m

Passage II (Questions 6–11)

Arsenic, element 33, has been used for a variety of medicinal and industrial purposes but is most widely known for its use as a poison. Inorganic forms are more toxic than organic forms, and trivalent forms are more toxic than both zero-valent or pentavalent forms.

Trivalent arsenic inhibits pyruvate dehydrogenase, an important enzyme used to create energy in cells, by binding to critical sulfhydryl groups on the molecule. One result is that fewer high-energy molecules (such as ATP) are created, resulting in widespread organ damage. Pentavalent arsenic resembles inorganic phosphate and thus can become incorporated into ATP, resulting in a molecule that does not deliver energy to critical body processes.

Treatment of acute arsenic poisoning requires consultation with a toxicologist experienced in the use of chelation therapy. Dimercaprol is an effective chelating agent that is administered intramuscularly in an oil suspension. It binds to arsenic-containing compounds and renders them inactive, as illustrated in Reaction 1:

$$
\begin{array}{c}
\text{SH} \\
|\\
\text{HOCH}_2\text{CHCH}_2\text{—SH} \quad + \quad \text{AsO}_2^-
\end{array}
$$

↓

$$
\begin{array}{c}
\text{CH}_2\text{—S} \\
|\qquad\qquad \text{As—O}^- \quad + \quad \text{H}_2\text{O} \\
\text{HOCH}_2\text{CH—S}
\end{array}
$$

Reaction 1

Arsenic compounds in soil are a contamination threat to water supplies. The acidity and oxidation state of soil are important considerations when assessing arsenic contamination. Acidity of soil is measured by a standard pH scale, while the oxidation state of soil is measured on an Eh scale. Soils under reduced conditions have a high Eh value, and oxidized soils have a low Eh value. Figure 1 shows the Eh-pH diagram for arsenic in soil.

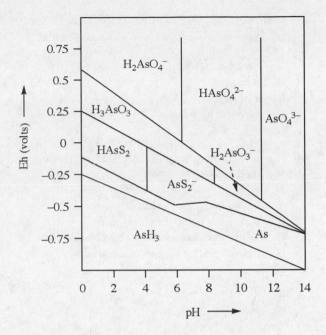

Figure 1 Eh-pH diagram of As in soil

6. Of the following, which is likely to be the *least* toxic?

   A.
   $$\begin{array}{c}\text{Cl}\diagdown^{\text{As}}\diagup\text{Cl}\\ \;\;|\\ \text{Cl}\end{array}$$

   B.
   $$\begin{array}{c}\text{O}\\ \|\\ \text{HO—As—OH}\\ |\\ \text{OH}\end{array}$$

   C.
   (arsenic oxide cage structure)

   D.
   $$\begin{array}{c}\text{H}\\ |\\ \text{O}\!=\!\text{As}\!=\!\text{O}\end{array}$$

7. Which of the following best describes the bond formed by dimercaprol to compounds of arsenic?

   A. Network covalent
   B. Ionic
   C. Coordinate covalent
   D. Metallic

8. Methylarsonic acid, $CH_3AsO(OH)_2$, is isolated in a laboratory analysis. What is its molecular shape?

A. Square planar
B. Seesaw
C. Tetrahedral
D. Trigonal bypyramidal

9. The role of dimercaprol in chelation therapy is best described as a:

A. ligand that donates electron pairs.
B. ligand that accepts electron pairs.
C. Lewis acid that donates electron pairs.
D. Lewis acid that accepts electron pairs.

10. Which of the following molecules are most likely to be appropriate for chelation therapy to treat toxic metal poisoning?

A. I and II only
B. I and III only
C. II and III only
D. I, II, and III

11. A sample of soil with suspected arsenic contamination has an Eh of 0.25 V and pH 6. Which of the following steps would be most effective in limiting potential toxicity?

A. Alkalinizing the soil
B. Aerating the soil
C. Acidifying the soil
D. Removing reducing agents from the soil

Passage III (Questions 12–17)

A danger of mining operations is the collapse of tunnels or underground chambers, resulting in closed atmospheres for trapped workers. Significant efforts are made to provide emergency equipment that can sustain breathable air, focusing on oxygen generation and carbon dioxide removal.

Normal air at sea level (760 torr) contains 21% oxygen and 0.03% carbon dioxide. A typical human consumes about 2.7 L/hr of O_2 and generates about 2.3 L/hr of CO_2 during regular breathing. Maintaining O_2 partial pressure above 130 torr and CO_2 partial pressure below 30 torr is critical for survival. O_2 and CO_2 percentages in a closed atmosphere change over time according to the following formulas:

$$O_2\% = (\text{Initial } O_2\%) - \frac{NRt}{V}$$

Equation 1

$$CO_2\% = (\text{Initial } CO_2\%) + \frac{NRt}{V}$$

Equation 2

where $R = O_2$ consumption or CO_2 generation rate (in L/hr), t = time (in hr), V = floodable volume of compartment (in L), and N = the number of people in the compartment.

Oxygen candles can be burned to generate about 300 L/hr (1 atm) of emergency oxygen by the following reaction:

$$NaClO_3 + Fe \rightarrow NaCl + Fe_xO_y + O_2$$

Reaction 1

Carbon dioxide can be removed from a closed atmosphere with lithium hydroxide canisters by the following reaction:

$$2\,LiOH + CO_2 \rightarrow Li_2CO_3 + H_2O + heat$$

Reaction 2

Each canister can absorb approximately 40 kg of CO_2. Figure 1 shows the average absorption rate for one LiOH canister.

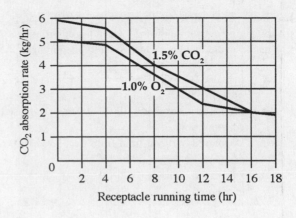

Figure 1 Average absorption rate for one LiOH canister

Experiment

A researcher investigates the effectiveness of oxygen candles and LiOH canisters on an experimental, enclosed mining shaft with the following characteristics:

P = 1 atm

Normal initial air composition

Floodable volume = 5.4×10^2 L

Number of trapped workers = 4

Regular breathing

Two LiOH canisters operating at a time

1 O_2 candle operating at a time

12. Which of the following would the researcher be *least* likely to observe as temperature and humidity increase in the experiment described in the passage?

   A. Decreased O_2 generation from candles
   B. Increased CO_2 clearance by LiOH canisters
   C. Increased compartment pressure
   D. Increased partial pressure of $H_2O(g)$

13. In the experiment, if each worker generates 1.5 kg/hr of CO_2, how often must the LiOH canisters be changed to maintain ambient CO_2 at 1.0%?

   A. Every hour
   B. Every 2 hours
   C. Every 7 hours
   D. Every 10 hours

14. Tachypnea (increased breathing rate) results from breathing air with elevated CO_2 in the environment. What result would tachypnea have on a trapped miner?

    A. Increased survival time from increased O_2 partial pressure
    B. Increased survival time from decreased O_2 consumption
    C. Decreased survival time from decreased CO_2 partial pressure
    D. Decreased survival time from increased O_2 consumption

15. If all the emergency atmosphere equipment in the experiment described in the passage were unavailable, about how long would the miners have before reaching a critical O_2 level?

    A. 4 days
    B. 6 days
    C. 8 days
    D. 10 days

16. Of the following actions, which one would likely be the most advantageous for survival in the experiment?

    A. Spreading the LiOH on blankets on the ground
    B. Digging to expand the floodable volume
    C. Burning the oxygen candles in a fire
    D. Partially flooding the compartment to raise compartment pressure

17. Suppose that after three days of being trapped in a shaft without emergency equipment, a miner is able to dig a very small hole that opens to the outside air. Which of the following will happen to the gases in the shaft?

    A. CO_2 will escape more rapidly than O_2, because it has a greater kinetic energy.
    B. CO_2 will escape more slowly than O_2, because it is moving against its concentration gradient.
    C. O_2 will escape more rapidly than CO_2, and the mole fraction of O_2 will increase.
    D. O_2 will escape more slowly than CO_2, and the mole fraction of CO_2 will decrease.

18. If conditions are established that increase the magnitude of ΔG for a reaction, what other observation can be expected?

    A. The reaction proceeds faster.
    B. The reaction releases more energy.
    C. The reaction proceeds at a higher temperature.
    D. The difference in concentration of reactants and products is increased.

19. Compounds with relatively stronger intermolecular forces are expected to have:

    A. higher specific heats and higher heats of fusion.
    B. higher specific heats and lower heats of fusion.
    C. lower specific heats and higher heats of fusion.
    D. lower specific heats and lower heats of fusion.

20. What is the molecular shape of XeF_4O?

    A. Trigonal bipyramid
    B. Octahedral
    C. Square pyramid
    D. Square planar

21. In which compound does manganese have the lowest oxidation state?

    A. $KMnO_4$
    B. $CaMnO_4$
    C. K_2MnO_4
    D. MnO_2

22. A molecule of ^{93}Rb undergoes two beta decay cycles. What isotope is formed?

    A. ^{95}Br
    B. ^{93}Br
    C. ^{95}Y
    D. ^{93}Y

Passage IV (Questions 23–28)

The rate of a reaction is defined as the change in concentration per unit time. Usually, the disappearance of the reactants is monitored; however, it is also possible to quantify the reaction rate by measuring the appearance of products. Reaction rate must be experimentally determined. The rate of the reaction depends on the concentrations of reactants and products; as the reaction proceeds to completion, the rate slows, so that at equilibrium, the apparent rate of reaction is zero—the concentrations of all species remain constant.

Reactions physically occur when the reactants collide with sufficient energy to change their chemistry. The high-energy state of the reactants is called the activated complex. The higher the energy input required to bring about chemical change, the more slowly the reaction occurs. Two things can increase the rate of reaction. Increasing the temperature of the reactants or adding a catalyst increases the rate constant and the rate of the reaction. If the temperature of the reactants is increased, less energy is required to form the activated complex and the reaction proceeds more quickly. (The energy of the activated complex is a constant, but less energy input is required to raise the reactants to that energy level.) It is also possible to add a substance that will hold the reactants in a favorable configuration that encourages interaction resulting in chemical change, thereby lowering the activation energy. Such a substance is known as a catalyst.

Reaction order expresses the number of species involved in the activated complex of the rate-limiting step. First-order reactions have only one species involved in the activated complex. In this case, the activated complex is a high-energy form of the reactant, such as a radical or ion, which is formed upon collision with another reactant molecule or the walls of the reaction container.

An example of a first-order reaction is the thermal decomposition of dinitrogen pentoxide:

$$2 \, N_2O_5 \, (\text{in } CCl_4) \rightarrow 4 \, NO_2 \, (\text{in } CCl_4) + O_2(g)$$

Reaction 1

This reaction is carried out in CCl_4 because both N_2O_5 and NO_2 are soluble, but O_2 is not. The reaction progress is monitored by measuring the volume of O_2 evolved. One hundred mL of a 2.0 M solution of N_2O_5 in CCl_4 is placed in a flask in a constant-temperature bath maintained at 45°C. The evolving gas is captured in a volumetric, mercury-filled manometer attached to the cork of the flask. Data collected at 200-minute intervals are plotted in Figure 1.

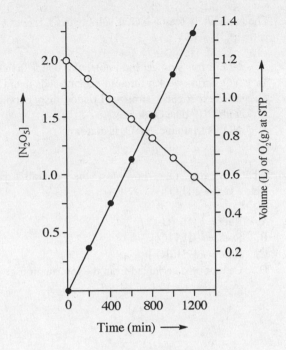

Figure 1 Gas data

23. Which one of the following is NOT a possible Lewis dot structure for N_2O_5?

A.

C.

B.

D.

24. What is the average rate of Reaction 1, the thermal decomposition of N_2O_5?

A. 4.2×10^{-4} M/min
B. 5.5×10^{-4} M/min
C. 8.4×10^{-4} M/min
D. 1.1×10^{-3} M/min

25. The most likely reason NO_2 is soluble in CCl_4 but O_2 is not is that:

A. NO_2 forms stronger intramolecular bonds than O_2.
B. NO_2 forms weaker intramolecular bonds than O_2.
C. NO_2 experiences stronger London dispersion forces with CCl_4 than O_2 does.
D. NO_2 is triatomic, but O_2 is diatomic.

26. What is the rate law for the overall reaction $2 H_2 + O_2 \rightarrow 2 H_2O$?

A. Rate $= k [H_2][O_2]$
B. Rate $= k [H_2]^2[O_2]$
C. Rate $= k [2H_2][O_2]$
D. Cannot be determined from the information given

27. Monitoring which one of the following quantities would be *least* helpful in calculating the number of moles of NO_2 produced in Reaction 1?

A. Temperature of the system
B. Pressure of the system
C. Volume of reactant
D. Volume of products

28. What is the half-life of N_2O_5?

A. 580 min
B. 720 min
C. 1,180 min
D. 2,430 min

Passage V (Questions 29–34)

The decay of a radioactive sample releases energy that can affect human tissue. Human tissue may be made to absorb radiation intentionally for diagnostic purposes, such as the use of radioactive iodine to study thyroid or kidney function or technetium to scan for a brain tumor. However, the exposure of human tissue to radiation may also be nondeliberate, such as that caused, for example, by naturally occurring sources such as cosmic rays impacting the atmosphere, radioactive elements in the ground, potassium-40 in the diet, or by artificial sources in laboratories and nuclear power facilities. Radiation ionizes the atoms absorbing the energy, which can directly damage DNA strands in a cell; damage to DNA strands can also be caused by the attack of hydroxyl radicals produced by the ionization of water molecules in the cell.

If N_0 denotes the number of radioactive nuclei at time $t = 0$, then the number at any later time t is given by

$$N(t) = N_0 e^{-\lambda t}$$

Equation 1

The parameter λ is the *decay constant*, equal to $1/\tau$, where τ is the average lifetime (approximately 1.4 times the half-life) of a nucleus in the sample. The number of decays per unit time, called the *activity* and denoted by $\mathcal{A}$, is

$$\mathcal{A} = \lambda N(t)$$

Equation 2

The energy deposited by ionizing radiation per unit mass of body tissue is called the *absorbed dose*, D; the unit of absorbed dose is the *rad*. By definition, 1 rad is equal to 100 ergs per gram, where 1 erg is a non-SI unit of energy equal to 10^{-7} joule. Since 1.6×10^{-19} J = 1 eV, 1 rad is equivalent to 6.25×10^{10} MeV per kilogram.

The biological effect of radiation is not simply a matter of measuring the absorbed dose, however. Different types of radiation have different effects and are therefore assigned different *radiation weighting factors*. For example, β particles and γ-rays deliver their energy over a long path and thus deposit a relatively small amount over any small region; the radiation weighting factor, w_R, for these radiations is only 1. By contrast, the value of w_R for α particles is 20. So, to determine the overall effect of radiation on body tissue, the absorbed dose is multiplied by the weighting factor to give the *dose equivalent*:

$$DE = w_R D$$

Equation 3

When D is expressed in rads, the dose equivalent is given in *rems*.

The average dose equivalent due to naturally occurring background radiation averages about 0.2 rem per year. It is recommended that the general public limit their dose equivalent to 0.5 rem per year.

Table 1 Radiation Weighting Factors

Radiation	w_R
β^- particle, β^+ particle, X-ray, γ-ray	1
proton (> 2 MeV)	5
neutron (10–100 keV)	10
α particle	20

Table 2 Data for Selected Radioisotopes Used in Medical Diagnosis

Radioisotope	Half-life	Decay mode(s) and energies (in MeV)
^{18}F	2 hr	β^+ (0.6 MeV)
^{42}K	12 hr	β^- (3.5 MeV) γ (1.5 MeV)
^{58}Co	72 days	β^+ (0.5 MeV) γ (0.8 MeV)
^{99m}Tc	6 hr	γ (0.1 MeV)
^{131}I	8 days	β^- (0.6 MeV) γ (0.08 MeV)

29. After ^{131}I decays, what is the daughter nucleus?

A. ^{130}Te
B. ^{131}Te
C. ^{130}Xe
D. ^{131}Xe

30. A physician injects a patient with a small sample of $^{42}KCl(aq)$ in order to help her detect a tumor. How long must the patient wait until the activity drops to 5% of its initial value?

    A.   32 hr
    B.   40 hr
    C.   52 hr
    D.   64 hr

31. It can be inferred from the passage that compared to β particles, α particles of the same energy are:

    A.   less harmful, because they travel a shorter distance due to their greater mass.
    B.   less harmful, because they carry a smaller electric charge.
    C.   more harmful, because they deliver a greater absorbed dose.
    D.   more harmful, because they deposit larger amounts of energy over small regions.

32. If a sample of $Na^{18}F$ has an approximately constant activity of 10^9 decays/sec over a time interval of 1 minute and all of the emitted radiation energy is absorbed by 2 kg of body tissue, what is the dose equivalent?

    A.   0.3 rad
    B.   0.3 rem
    C.   0.6 rad
    D.   0.6 rem

33. If all of the following radiations deposit 10^{12} MeV of energy to human tissue, which one would be most likely to cause the greatest harm?

    A.   10 kg of tissue absorbing 50-keV neutrons
    B.   40 kg of tissue absorbing α particles
    C.   2 kg of tissue absorbing γ-rays
    D.   10 kg of tissue absorbing 3-MeV protons

34. Compared to that of ^{58}Co, the decay constant λ of ^{131}I is:

    A.   smaller by a factor of 9.
    B.   smaller by a factor of (9/1.4).
    C.   larger by a factor of (9/1.4).
    D.   larger by a factor of 9.

Questions 35 through 39 are NOT based on a descriptive passage.

35. Which of the following occurs at the equivalence point of a titration of a weak base with a strong acid?

    A.   An acidic salt is formed.
    B.   A buffer zone is reached.
    C.   The pH is > 7.
    D. $[H_3O^+] = [OH^-]$

36. What is the ground state electron configuration for Cr?

    A. $[Ar]\ 4s^1 3d^5$
    B. $[Ar]\ 4s^2 3d^5$
    C. $[Ar]\ 4s^1 3d^4$
    D. $[Ar]\ 4s^2 3d^4$

37. In an adiabatic process, the change in total internal energy of a system is equal to the:

    A.   heat absorbed by the system.
    B.   heat released to the environment.
    C.   work performed on or by the system.
    D.   change in pressure per unit volume.

38. If human blood is buffered by H_2CO_3 ($pK_a = 6.4$) to a pH of 7.4, what is the ratio of $[H_2CO_3]/[HCO_3^-]$?

    A.   0.01
    B.   0.1
    C.   1.0
    D.   10

39. $Pb^{4+} + 2e^- \rightarrow Pb^{2+}$ ($E^\circ = 1.83$ V)
$Pb^{2+} + 2e^- \rightarrow Pb$ ($E^\circ = -0.13$ V)
When the two half-reactions above are combined in a galvanic cell:

    A. Pb^{2+} is reduced at a positively charged electrode.
    B.   Pb is oxidized at a negatively charged electrode.
    C. Pb^{4+} is oxidized at a positively charged electrode.
    D. Pb^{4+} is reduced at a negatively charged electrode.

Passage VI (Questions 40–44)

The dissolution of a substance in a solvent affects the physical properties of the solvent, most notably the colligative properties: vapor-pressure depression, boiling-point elevation, freezing-point depression, and osmotic pressure. Knowledge of these properties can be used to determine the molar masses of unknown substances such as proteins and other biologically relevant molecules.

When a nonvolatile solute is added to a volatile solvent, the relative amounts of solvent molecules in contact with the surface decrease and fewer solvent molecules escape into the gaseous phase. This lowers the vapor pressure. For an ideal solution, the vapor pressure, P', is given by Equation 1, where X is the solvent mole fraction and P is the vapor pressure of the pure solvent:

$$P' = XP$$

Equation 1

One can use Equation 2 below to determine the free energy change ΔG associated with the transfer of a volatile solute to an ideal solution:

$$\Delta G = nRT \ln X$$

Equation 2

where n is the number of moles of solute being added, R is the universal gas constant (8.314 J/mol-K), and T is the temperature.

Since the presence of a solute lowers the vapor pressure, the boiling point is elevated. Equation 3 relates this new boiling point, T_b', to the solvent mole fraction, X:

$$\Delta H_{vap}\left(1 - \frac{T_b'}{T_b}\right) = nRT_b'\ln X$$

Equation 3

where ΔH_{vap} is the enthalpy of vaporization and T_b is the boiling point of pure solvent. Based on this equation, the boiling-point elevation constant, k_b, can be determined:

$$k_b = \frac{RT_b^2 M}{1,000\Delta H_{vap}}$$

Equation 4

where M is the molar mass of the solvent.

An equation of the same form as Equation 4 can be applied to determine k_f, the freezing-point depression constant. Table 1 lists the freezing points and freezing-point depression constants for a number of solvents.

Table 1 Solvent Data

Solvent	T_f (°C)	k_f
Benzene	5.5	5.12
Camphor	179.5	37.7
Carbon tetrachloride	–22.3	29.8
Chloroform	–63.5	4.68
Ethanol	–114.6	1.99
Naphthalene	80.5	6.90
Water	0.0	1.86

The last of the colligative properties, osmotic pressure, is also dependent on the number of dissolved particles and not on their nature. Osmotic pressure is defined as the pressure necessary to prevent the flow of solvent particles across a semipermeable membrane from a region of higher solvent concentration to a region of lower solvent concentration.

40. Which of the following best characterizes the process of vaporization?

   A. Increase in entropy, increase in enthalpy
   B. Increase in entropy, decrease in enthalpy
   C. Decrease in entropy, increase in enthalpy
   D. Decrease in entropy, decrease in enthalpy

41. Intravenous solutions must be isosmotic to blood (approximately 300 mM) to prevent damage to red blood cells. What mass of calcium chloride must be added to water to create 1 kg of solution isosmotic to blood?

   A. 11 g
   B. 33 g
   C. 37 g
   D. 111 g

42. Destructive distillation involves heating an organic substance in a closed container in the absence of oxygen. The destructive distillation of wood produces acetic acid (T_b = 117.9°C), methanol (T_b = 65.0°C), and acetone (T_b = 56.2°C). Which of these will be the first to be vaporized?

    A. Acetic acid
    B. Methanol
    C. Acetone
    D. It cannot be determined from the information given.

43. A hypertonic solution, *X*, separated from a hypotonic solution, *Y*, by a semipermeable membrane (permissive to water only) will result in all of the following after equilibration EXCEPT:

    I. An increase in the melting point of Solution X.
    II. An increase in the volume of Solution Y.
    III. An increase in the vapor pressure above Solution Y.

    A. I only
    B. I and II only
    C. II and III only
    D. I, II, and III

44. Of the following substances, which will provide the greatest protection against freezing?

    A. 1 m ethanol (C_2H_6O)
    B. 1 m potassium acetate ($KC_2H_4O_2$)
    C. 1.5 m sucrose ($C_{12}H_{22}O_{11}$)
    D. 0.5 m calcium chloride ($CaCl_2$)

Passage VII (Questions 62–67)

The treatment of many gastrointestinal diseases was revolutionized by the development of drugs that block acid secretion in the stomach. Parietal cells in the stomach normally secrete protons in exchange for potassium ions as depicted in Figure 1. This maintains a pH of approximately 1.5 in the stomach lumen.

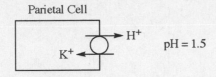

Figure 1 Proton-potassium exchange

Omeprazole is a medication that is a potent inhibitor of the H^+/K^+ exchange pump. The drug is a weak base with a pK_a of 1.6. After oral administration, it is absorbed primarily from the small intestine into the bloodstream. The properties of this compound cause it to accumulate in low-pH spaces, and it shows great organ specificity.

Following widespread use of omeprazole, it was discovered that many other oral medications, when used in conjunction, were less effective. Many oral medications are either weak acids or bases. When weak base medications reach the stomach, the amount of drug that is non-ionized or ionized can be predicted from the Henderson-Hasselbalch equation:

$$pH = pK_a + \log\frac{[B]}{[BH^+]}$$

Equation 1

where B denotes a weak base and BH^+ is its conjugate acid. Some drugs are absorbed in the stomach mostly in the non-ionized form, while others are only absorbed when dissolved in aqueous solution in the ionized form.

Ketoconazole is a powerful, oral, antifungal antibiotic absorbed into the bloodstream in the stomach. It is a weak base with a pK_a of 3, and it is only able to be absorbed in the ionized form. A researcher explores the relationship between stomach pH and ketoconazole absorption. The results are summarized in Figure 2.

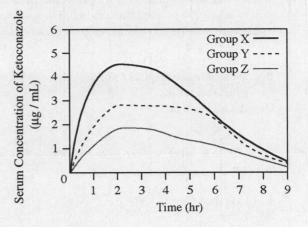

Figure 2 Experiment results

45. Under normal conditions, the value of $[H_3O^+]$ in the stomach is most nearly equal to which of the following?

A. 1×10^{-2} M
B. 3×10^{-2} M
C. 1×10^{-1} M
D. 3×10^{-1} M

46. Which of the following best explains why omeprazole specifically targets the stomach and not most other organs?

A. The non-ionized form of the drug predominates in parietal cells.
B. The ionized form of the drug becomes trapped within parietal cells.
C. After ingestion, it is ionized in the stomach where it remains trapped.
D. It effectively raises stomach pH, resulting in more of the drug becoming ionized for absorption.

47. What is the correct order of stomach pH values for the experimental groups in the passage?

A. Group X > Group Y > Group Z
B. Group Y > Group Z > Group X
C. Group Z > Group Y > Group X
D. Group X > Group Z > Group Y

48. A patient requiring oral therapy with ketoconazole is found to have achlorydia (neutral stomach pH). The most helpful intervention would be to administer ketoconazole:

   A. with ginger ale (pH = 2).
   B. with baking soda (NaH$_2$CO$_3$).
   C. with omeprazole.
   D. at a higher dose.

49. Approximately what percentage of omeprazole is ionized in blood (pH = 7.4)?

   A. Less than 1%
   B. 10%
   C. 50%
   D. Greater than 99%

50. Comparing ketoconazole and omeprazole, all of the following are true EXCEPT:

   A. both are partially ionized in the stomach.
   B. omeprazole has a weaker conjugate acid.
   C. ketoconazole is a stronger base.
   D. omeprazole has a higher K_a value.

Passage VIII (Questions 51–55)

With regard to their electrical properties, solids are generally classified into one of three categories: conductors, insulators, or semiconductors. It is well known that metals, the prototype conductors, have a very high electrical conductivity because one or more electrons per atom in the crystal lattice of positive ions are not attached to any one ion; instead, they are free to roam through the lattice. These electrons, known as conduction electrons, are then free to respond to an applied electric field and drift through the metal; the result of this drift is electric current.

If we look at the situation more closely, we can understand not only why certain materials conduct electricity so easily but also why other materials do not. When atoms are separated, any interaction between the electrons of one atom and those of the others is negligible. As a result, the electron energy levels are undisturbed, and we have the familiar case of discrete, quantized energy levels. However, as the atoms are brought closer together, the electrons interact and their energy levels split into many very closely spaced levels—so many, in fact, that even in a tiny crystal, the levels can be considered to be made up not of discrete values but of a continuous band of values.

The energies of the innermost electrons form completely filled energy bands. The valence electrons, however, are in an energy band—known as the valence band—which may be filled or partially filled. In addition, a conduction band is formed, consisting of energy levels available to electrons that are free to drift and conduct electricity. In a conductor, the conduction band and valence band overlap. As a result, there are some valence electrons which are automatically in the conduction band, as is the case with metals.

However, if the conduction band is empty and separated from the filled valence band by an energy gap, then valence electrons need to acquire sufficient energy to "jump" into the conduction band before the material can conduct electricity. The gap consists of energies which the electrons are forbidden to have; the size of this gap—the difference in energy between the top of the valence band and the bottom of the conduction band—is known as the gap energy, E_g. Table 1 lists the value of E_g for several different materials.

Crystal	E_g (eV)
PbSe	0.3
InAs	0.4
Si	1.1
GaAs	1.4
AgCl	3.2
ZnS	3.6
Diamond	5.4

Table 1 Energy Gap Values

In general, a material is called an insulator if the energy gap is greater than 3 eV and a semiconductor if the energy gap is less than 3 eV. Semiconductors become more conducting as the temperature increases, since the electrons can acquire enough energy to jump the energy gap into the conduction band. At temperature T, the average kinetic energy of an electron is approximately kT, where k is the Boltzmann constant, 8.6×10^{-5} eV/K. Therefore, at room temperature, $T = 300$ K, the average energy of an electron is only about 0.025 eV, so there is insufficient energy to jump into the conduction band. At higher temperatures, however, electrons can acquire enough extra energy to jump the gap. In fact, at temperature T, the concentration of electrons in the conduction band is given by the equation

$$c(T) = Ae^{-T^*/T}$$

Equation 1

where A is a constant and $T^* = E_g/(2k)$.

51. A crystal composed of atoms of which of the following elements would be expected to have a partially filled conduction band, even at very low temperatures?

   A. Carbon
   B. Silicon
   C. Sodium
   D. Silver chloride

52. By how much would the temperature of a sample of zinc sulfide need to be increased to expect that virtually all of the electrons near the top of the valence band would jump to the conduction band?

    A. 700 K
    B. 2,100 K
    C. 4,200 K
    D. 42,000 K

53. If a constant electric field E were applied to a metal, what would be the change in velocity of a conduction electron (charge magnitude = e, mass = m) in the time t between collisions with the lattice ions?

    A. eE/m
    B. eEt/m
    C. $2eE/m$
    D. $2eEt/m$

54. Which one of the following statements concerning metals, insulators, and semiconductors is most likely true?

    A. As the temperature is increased, the resistivity of a metal increases but the resistivity of a semiconductor decreases.
    B. As the temperature is increased, the resistivity of a metal decreases but the resistivity of a semiconductor increases.
    C. Insulators typically have a smaller energy gap than semiconductors.
    D. Electrical conduction in insulators is due to the drift velocity of electrons while in the valence band.

55. Which of the following graphs best illustrates how the concentration of electrons in the conduction band of a semiconductor depends on temperature?

    A.

    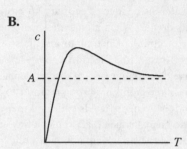

    B.

    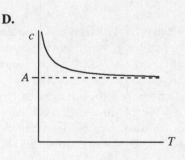

    C.

    D.

56. The ideal gas law is violated most under conditions of:

    A. high temperature and low pressure.
    B. high temperature and high pressure.
    C. low temperature and low pressure.
    D. low temperature and high pressure.

57. Of the following, which has the smallest atomic radius?

    A. Sodium
    B. Oxygen
    C. Calcium
    D. Silicon

58. The specific heat of copper is 0.39 J/g°C. If 400 J of heat are applied to a 50 g sample of copper, what is the approximate change in temperature?

    A. 2°C
    B. 15°C
    C. 20°C
    D. 40°C

59. The rate constant, k, is dependent on all of the following factors EXCEPT:

    A. catalysis.
    B. temperature.
    C. activation energy.
    D. enthalpy.

60. Compared to a SCUBA diver on the surface, a similar diver breathing compressed air at the same rate deep in the water will run out of air faster because the surrounding pressure increases the:

    A. temperature of the air supply.
    B. gas law constant.
    C. effective volume of the lungs.
    D. moles of air consumed.

Chapter 5
General Chemistry Practice:
Answers and Explanations

Passage I (Questions 1–5)

1. **B** According to the passage, the toxic effects from ethylene glycol come from its metabolites. Therefore, effective treatment should prevent the production of these metabolites. Because ethanol is also metabolized by alcohol dehydrogenase, it will compete with this enzyme, thereby decreasing the formation of the toxic metabolites. Giving calcium will result in more precipitation of calcium oxalate in the kidney (A is wrong). Giving acetic acid could reduce the pH of the blood, which is already lowered by the acidic metabolites of ethylene glycol (C is wrong). Increased alcohol dehydrogenase will only lead to the formation of more toxic metabolites (D is wrong).

2. **A** In the presence of a nonvolatile solute, boiling point is elevated. Therefore, both choices C and D (methanol and isopropanol) should be eliminated, because according to the passage, they are more volatile than water; they will decrease the boiling point of the solution. The boiling point change can be quantified according to the equation: $\Delta T = k_b im$, where ΔT is the change in boiling point, k_b is the boiling-point elevation constant of the solvent, i is the van't Hoff factor, and m is the molality of the solution. The k_b is constant, and all of the answer choices are nonelectrolytes with a theoretical van't Hoff factor of 1. Therefore, the compound that forms the highest molality solution will have the greatest impact on boiling point. If 10 g of each compound is used, the compound with the smallest molecular weight will yield the most concentrated solution.

3. **B** Ethylene glycol and its metabolites will result in more solute in the bloodstream, increasing osmolality (C and D are wrong). Nearly all of the metabolites of ethylene glycol are carboxylic acids and therefore, the pH will decrease (A is wrong).

4. **C** The compound with the lowest pK_a is the most acidic. All of the carboxylic acids will be more acidic than glycoaldehyde (B is wrong). Among the rest, oxalic acid has two carboxylic acid functional groups, each with strong resonance stability that make it the most acidic compound listed.

5. **A** Boiling point is elevated according to the equation: $\Delta T = k_b im$, where ΔT is the change in boiling point, k_b is the boiling point elevation constant of the solvent, i is the van't Hoff factor, and m is the molality of the solution. Diethylene glycol is a nonelectrolyte and therefore has a theoretical $i = 1$. The ΔT and k_b are provided. Solving for molality gives:

$$m = \frac{\Delta T}{k_b i} = \frac{0.18°\text{ C}}{(0.5°\text{ C/m})(1)} = 0.36\text{ m}$$

This is the final molality. Because the question started with a 0.3 m solution, the change is 0.06 m.

6. **B**   The passage states that trivalent compounds are more toxic than pentavalent compounds. The oxidation state of As in compounds A, C, and D is +3, making them all trivalent. However, the oxidation state of As in compound B (arsenic acid) is +5, making it pentavalent and thus less toxic.

7. **C**   The bond between S and As is covalent, so eliminate choices B and D. Network covalent bonds are connected in a lattice of covalent bonds such as diamond or quartz. Dimercaprol is a chelator (Lewis base) that donates full electron pairs to form coordinate covalent bonds, so C is the best choice.

8. **C** · In this compound, As has no lone pairs and is surrounded by four electron groups, as indicated by the structure shown below.

$$H_3C-\underset{\underset{OH}{|}}{\overset{\overset{O}{\|}}{As}}-OH$$

Because the central atom has no lone pairs, the shape cannot be square planar or see-saw (eliminating choices A and B). And since the central atom is surrounded by four electron groups, not five, the shape must be tetrahedral (choice C), not trigonal bipyramidal (choice D).

9. **A**   Lewis bases, or ligands, donate electron pairs and Lewis acids accept electron pairs, so eliminate choices B and C. Dimercaprol donates electron pairs to effectively bind arsenic compounds, so A is the best choice.

10. **A**   Compound I, succimer, has two S moieties with lone pairs of electrons available to donate and form a stable ring around a metal compound. Compound II, penicillamine, has an S moiety and N moiety, each with a lone pair of electrons available for donating to form a stable ring around a metal compound. (In fact, both I and II are compounds used in chelation therapy.) Compound III, sildenafil, has an S and N moiety, but the S has no lone pairs to donate. This would be an ineffective chelator.

11. **A**   At this Eh and pH, the most likely form of arsenic, according to Figure 2 in the passage, would be $H_2AsO_4^-$. This is a pentavalent form. Adding oxygen via aeration (lowers Eh), acidifying the soil (lowers pH), or removing reducing agents from the soil (lowers Eh), would all steer conditions toward H_3AsO_3. This is a trivalent and thus more toxic form of arsenic. Alkalinizing the soil would maintain pentavalent forms.

12. **B** Oxygen candles are self-sustaining from the exothermic oxidation of Fe. Both H_2O and increased temperature would not favor the forward reaction (eliminates A). Likewise, increased T and H_2O will not favor the forward reaction of LiOH canisters (B is correct). In a closed container with constant V, as T increases, P increases (eliminates C). H_2O is generated from LiOH and respiration, increasing the partial pressure of H_2O vapor (eliminates D).

13. **D** The CO_2 generated by four workers is (4)(1.5 kg/hr) = 6 kg/hr. If two canisters are in operation, then each is responsible for half the load, or 3 kg/hr. At this rate, the canisters must be changed every 10 hours (according to Figure 1) to maintain ambient CO_2 at 1.0%.

14. **D** Anything that increases breathing rate in a closed atmosphere will be bad for survival (eliminates A and B) because more O_2 is consumed (D is correct) and more CO_2 is generated. The partial pressure of CO_2 will rise with time (eliminates C).

15. **C** Rearranging Equation 1 in the passage to solve for critical O_2 time gives

$$t + \frac{V}{RN}(O_2\%_{initial} - O_2\%_{crit})$$

From the passage, a partial pressure of 130 torr is critical for O_2, which corresponds to (130 torr/760 torr)(100%) = 17% at 1 atm. So, plugging in this value of $O_2\%_{crit}$, along with the values of $O_2\%_{initial}$, V, R, and N given in the passage, we find that

$$t = \frac{V}{RN}(O_2\%_{initial} - O_2\%_{crit})$$

$$= \frac{5.4 \times 10^2 \, L}{2.7\dfrac{L}{hr} \cdot 4}(21\% - 17\%)$$

$$= 200 \, hr$$

$$\approx 8 \, days$$

16. **A** Spreading LiOH increases surface area, rate, and efficiency of CO_2 removal (A is best). Changing V would slightly change both O_2 and CO_2 partial pressures (not one preferentially) and require increased exertion (B) or risk of exposure (D). Fires in enclosed spaces consume valuable O_2, negating the use of candles (C is wrong).

17. **C** At the same temperature, CO_2 and O_2 have the same average kinetic energy (A is wrong). Graham's law states that relative escape velocities of gas molecules are inversely proportional to the square root of their masses: $v_1/v_2 = \sqrt{m_2/m_1}$. CO_2 escapes more slowly but moves down its concentration gradient to the outside air where $CO_2\%$ would be lower (B is wrong). O_2

escapes more rapidly, but relatively more O_2 will come into the chamber to establish equilibrium, thus raising the mole fraction of O_2 inside the shaft (C is correct). Although the mole fraction of CO_2 decreases with time, O_2 escapes more rapidly (D is wrong).

Freestanding Questions (18–22)

18.   **D**   Changing ΔG, the free energy of a reaction, does not reveal information about the kinetics of the reaction because reaction rate is a kinetic factor (A is wrong). Without knowing the sign, it is not possible to tell if the reaction will absorb (+) or release (–) more energy, or whether an increase in magnitude of ΔG will occur at a higher or lower temperature according to the equation $\Delta G = \Delta H - T\Delta S$ (B and C are wrong). D is the best answer, because a larger difference between reactants and products in a reaction will change the value of Q for the reaction. According to the equations below, the magnitude of ΔG will always change regardless of the way the reaction quotient changes:

$$Q = \frac{[products]}{[reactants]}$$
$$\Delta G = \Delta G^\circ + RT \ln Q$$

19.   **A**   Intermolecular forces determine the strength of interactions between molecules. The stronger these forces, the less likely they are to pull apart or move faster (average kinetic energy is related to the temperature). Therefore, physical properties such as melting point, boiling point, and viscosity tend to increase with increasing intermolecular forces. It will take more energy to raise 1 g of a substance by 1 degree Celsius (specific heat), and it will take more energy per mole to melt a substance (heat of fusion) with strong intermolecular forces.

20.   **C**   Xe has 6 bonding groups surrounding it, putting it in the octahedral family (A is wrong). Of the 6 available positions, 5 are occupied by atoms and 1 is occupied by a lone pair of electrons. Therefore, the shape is a square pyramid.

21.   **D**   The oxidation state of manganese can change with its bonding. However, the oxidation states of all the remaining elements are constant. Calculating the contributions from these elements first (K = +1, O = –2, Ca = +2) gives the following manganese oxidation numbers for answers A (+7), B (+6), C (+6), and D (+4).

22.   **D**   The reaction proceeds as:

$$^{93}_{37}\text{Rb} \rightarrow\; ^{0}_{-1}\beta +\; ^{0}_{-1}\beta +\; ^{93}_{39}\text{Y}$$

Passage IV (Questions 23–28)

23.   **B**   The structure shown in B cannot be correct because the net charge on the structure is –2, but N_2O_5 is a neutral molecule.

24.   **A**   The concentration of N_2O_5 drops from 2.0 M to 1.0 M in approximately 1,200 min. Since the coefficient of N_2O_5 in the balanced reaction is 2 (see Reaction 1),

$$\text{rate} = -\frac{1}{\text{coeff of } X} \cdot \frac{\Delta[\text{reactant } X]}{\Delta t}$$

$$= -\frac{1}{2} \cdot \frac{(1.0 - 2.0)\text{ M}}{1,200\text{ min}}$$

$$= 4.2 \times 10^{-4}\,\text{M/min}$$

25.   **C**   Recall that solubility depends on intermolecular associations between solute and solvent; therefore, choices A and B are eliminated since they refer to intramolecular (covalent) bonds. Choice D can be eliminated because the number of atoms is not important. Choice C must be correct since it is the only statement that discusses intermolecular forces.

26.   **D**   The passage states that reaction rate laws must be empirically determined. Without empirical data, it is not possible to determine the rate law.

27.   **C**   Since the oxygen produced is a gas and its volume is being measured in a manometer, the number of moles can be calculated using the ideal gas law: $n = PV/(RT)$. Therefore, it is important to measure the pressure, volume, and temperature of $O_2(g)$ but not the volume of reactant.

28.   **C**   The half-life is the time required for half of the substance to disappear. Looking at the graph in Figure 1, the time required for N_2O_5 to drop from a concentration of 2.0 M to 1.0 M is approximately 1,200 min.

Passage V (Questions 29–34)

29.   **D**   According to Table 2, ^{131}I decays by β^- emission; that is, the nucleus transforms a neutron into a proton and an electron (and an antineutrino, which is of no concern here) and then emits the electron. As a result, the daughter nucleus has 1 more proton but the same mass number. Therefore, the daughter is ^{131}Xe. The nuclear reaction is

$$^{131}_{53}\text{I} \rightarrow {}^{131}_{54}\text{Xe} + {}^{0}_{-1}e^-$$

30. C   Equation 2 tells us that the activity is proportional to the number of radioactive nuclei present at any time, and according to Table 2, the half-life of ^{42}K is 12 hours. Therefore, since the number of radioactive nuclei present drops by 1/2 every 12 hours, so will the activity. Consider the sequence 100% → 50% → 25% → 12.5% → 6.25% → 3.125%, where each arrow represents the passage of one half-life. Since 5% is between 6.25% and 3.125%, a time interval of between 4 and 5 half-lives—that is, a time interval between 48 hours and 60 hours—will be required for the activity to drop to 5% of its initial value. Only choice C falls in this range.

31. D   Because α particles have a much greater radiation weighting factor than β particles do, α particles are intrinsically more harmful to biological systems; this eliminates choices A and B. (Choice B could also be eliminated since α particles carry a *greater* electric charge than β particles.) Choice C is a trap: all things being equal, α particles would deliver the same *absorbed dose*, but it's the *dose equivalent* that most directly measures the biological effect of radiation. The passage states that "β particles . . . deposit a relatively small amount [of energy] over any small region," and β particles have the lowest weighting factor. Since α particles have the highest weighting factor, we can infer that, in contrast to β particles, α particles deposit *larger* amounts of energy over small regions.

32. B   First, eliminate choices A and C; the question asks for dose equivalent, which is expressed in rems, not rads. Since Table 2 tells us that each decay of ^{18}F emits a β^+ particle with an energy of 0.6 MeV, the total energy delivered in 1 minute by this sample is

$$\frac{10^9 \text{ decays}}{\text{sec}} \cdot \frac{0.6 \text{ MeV}}{\text{decay}} \cdot \frac{60 \text{ sec}}{\text{min}} \cdot 1 \text{ min} = 3.6 \times 10^{10} \text{ MeV}$$

Dividing this by 2 kg gives the absorbed dose:

$$D = \frac{3.6 \times 10^{10} \text{ MeV}}{2 \text{ kg}} = \frac{1.8 \times 10^{10} \text{ MeV}}{\text{kg}}$$

Converting this to rads, we get

$$(1.8 \times 10^{10} \tfrac{\text{MeV}}{\text{kg}}) \cdot \frac{1 \text{ rad}}{(6.25 \times 10^{10} \tfrac{\text{MeV}}{\text{kg}})} = \frac{1.8}{6.25} \text{ rad} \approx 0.3 \text{ rad}$$

Finally, since $w_R = 1$ for β^+ particles, the dose equivalent of 0.3 rad by β^+ particles is 0.3 rem, choice B.

33.   **A**   Here we use the data given in Table 1. The radiation most likely to cause the greatest harm is the one that delivers the greatest dose equivalent. In each case, the absorbed dose D is equal to the total absorbed energy, $E = 10^{12}$ MeV, divided by the appropriate mass of body tissue; then, multiplying this result by the weighting factor gives the dose equivalent, $DE = w_R \cdot D$. We find that

choice A: $DE = 10 \cdot E/10\quad = E$
choice B: $DE = 20 \cdot E/40\quad = E/2$
choice C: $DE = 1 \cdot E/2\quad\ \ = E/2$
choice D: $DE = 5 \cdot E/10\quad\ = E/2$

Clearly, then, the radiation described in choice A delivers the greatest dose equivalent.

34.   **D**   According to Table 2, the half-life of ^{131}I (8 days) is 9 times less than the half-life of ^{58}Co (72 days). Because we're told that the average lifetime τ is proportional to the half-life, it follows that the value of τ for ^{131}I is also 9 times less than that of ^{58}Co. But the decay constant λ is the *reciprocal* of τ, so the value of λ for ^{131}I is 9 times greater than that of ^{58}Co.

Freestanding Questions (35–39)

35.   **A**   The products at the equivalence point of any acid-base titration are a salt and water. The relative acidity or basicity of the salt formed determines the pH of the solution at the equivalence point. The combination of a weak base and strong acid will form an acidic salt, making A the best answer. This resulting acidic solution will have a pH < 7 (C is wrong). The buffering region occurs around the half-equivalence point (B is wrong). At the equivalence point of the titration in question, the number of moles of H_3O^+ added should equal the number of moles of OH^- originally present in solution, but unless both a strong acid and strong base are used in the titration to form a neutral salt, the pH at the equivalence point will not equal 7, which is the only way $[H_3O^+]$ can equal $[OH^-]$.

36.   **A**   Chromium has 24 electrons, which is 6 more than the argon shell (B and C are wrong). Using the traditional vector method of assigning electrons, answer choice D would be obtained. However, the atom achieves greater stability by shifting an electron from the 4s orbital to the remaining empty 3d orbital. When an atom can achieve a half-full or completely full d subshell, it becomes more stable.

37.   **C**   An adiabatic process is a theoretical process that is thermally insulated. Therefore, no heat is exchanged between the system and surroundings (A and B are wrong). Given that total internal energy (U) is the sum of heat transfer (q) and work (w), $U = q+w$, the equation reduces to $U = w$. The work done is also equal to the area under a pressure vs. volume curve, $w = -P\Delta V$, or the *product* of pressure and volume changes (D is wrong).

38.   B   The Henderson-Hasselbalch equation is used:

$$pH = pK_a + \log_{10} \frac{[A^-]}{[HA]}$$

$$pH\text{-}pK_a = \log_{10} \frac{[A^-]}{[HA]}$$

$$pH\text{-}pK_a = \log_{10} \frac{[HCO_3^-]}{[H_2CO_3]}$$

$$7.4 - 6.4 = \log_{10} \frac{[HCO_3^-]}{[H_2CO_3]}$$

$$1.0 = \log_{10} \frac{10}{1}$$

Therefore, the ratio of acid to conjugate base is the inverse, or 1/10.

39.   B   A galvanic cell is spontaneous, so the two half-reactions must add to a positive value of $E°$. Therefore, the first reaction remains as the reduction, and the second reaction will reverse and become the oxidation (A and C are wrong). Pb^{4+} is reduced at the cathode, where electrons are received. In a spontaneous cell, the cathode will be positively charged (D is wrong). Pb is oxidized at the negatively charged anode, where electrons are generated.

Passage VI (Questions 40–44)

40.   A   Vaporization is the process of transforming a liquid into a gas. Molecules are going from a more ordered liquid state to a more disordered gaseous state, increasing entropy (C and D are incorrect). Heat must be added to the system to break the intermolecular forces that keep the substance in the liquid state. Adding heat, an endothermic process, increases the enthalpy of the system (B is incorrect).

41.   A   Blood is mostly water (ρ = 1,000 kg/L), so molarity is roughly equal to molality (0.3 M). Osmolarity is determined by the number of osmotically active particles. $CaCl_2$ has three osmotically active particles per molecule dissolved. To produce a 0.3 M solution, we need to make a 0.1 M calcium chloride solution. The molecular mass of $CaCl_2$ is about 111 g/mol. To make a 0.1 M solution in 1 kg of solution ($\approx$ 1 liter), we need 0.1 mol (Molarity = moles/liter); 0.1 mol multiplied by 111 g/mol is approximately 11 grams (choice A).

42.   C   Boiling point is the temperature at which vapor pressure is equal to external pressure. Since external pressure will be the same throughout the destructive distillation process, the substance to vaporize first will be the one that has the lowest T_b. A low T_b indicates that the intermolecular attractive forces in the liquid state are relatively weak, which creates a relatively high vapor pressure at any given temperature. Since acetone has the lowest boiling point, it will vaporize first, making C the correct answer.

43. C   A hypertonic solution has a higher osmotic pressure than the surrounding solution; a hypo-
          tonic solution has a lower osmotic pressure. To reach equilibrium, there will be a net flow of
          water from the hypotonic (Y) to the hypertonic (X) solution. This decreases the concentration
          of solute in X and increases it in Y. A lower solute concentration in X will increase the melting
          point (I is true and thus eliminated). Since water is flowing from Y to X, the volume of Y will
          decrease (II is false and thus correct here). As water leaves Y, the solute concentration increases
          and the vapor pressure decreases (III is false and thus correct here).

44. B   The best protection against freezing will be given by the substance that lowers the T_f by the
          greatest amount. This is determined by the number of dissolved particles. One molal etha-
          nol gives 1 molal of dissolved particles. One molal potassium acetate gives 2 molal particles
          (one K^+ and one acetate). Sucrose does not dissociate and therefore yields 1.5 molal particles.
          Finally, 0.5 molal calcium chloride will produce a 1.5 molal solution (one Ca^{2+} and two Cl^-).
          Therefore, the highest molality of dissolved particles is found in choice B.

Passage VII (Questions 45–50)

45. B $[H_3O^+]$ can be approximated from the pH of the stomach, given in the passage as 1.5. Since
          pH $= -\log [H_3O^+]$, if pH $= 1.5$, then $[H_3O^+]$ must be between 10^{-2} and 10^{-1}, so the answer
          must be B. In general, if the pH is between n and $n + 1$, where n is a whole number, then
          $[H_3O^+]$ will be between $10^{-(n+1)}$ and 10^{-n}.

46. B   The passage states that omeprazole is primarily absorbed in the small intestine (eliminating C).
          The pH of the stomach is 1.5 and the pK_a of omeprazole is 1.6. Using the Henderson-Hasselbalch
          equation (Equation 1 in the passage), we get

$$\text{pH} - \text{p}K_a = \log \frac{[B]}{[BH^+]} \quad \Rightarrow$$

$$1.5 - 1.6 = \log \frac{[B]}{[BH^+]} \quad \Rightarrow$$

$$-0.1 = \log \frac{[B]}{[BH^+]}$$

Because the left side of the equation is negative, the ratio $[B]/[BH^+]$ must be less than 1, so
$[BH^+]$ is slightly greater than $[B]$. The ionized form of the drug predominates at low pH (eliminates A and D), and it is unable to passively diffuse out of the low pH environment of the
parietal cell.

47.   C   If absorption of ketoconazole is related to pH, then the pH order from the graph must be X > Y > Z or Z > Y > X (eliminates B and D). Ketoconazole has a pK_a of 3 and is absorbed only in the ionized form. From Equation 1, we find that

$$pH - pK_a = \log \frac{[B]}{[BH^+]}$$

So, to maximize the ionized form, pH must be as low as possible. If absorption in Group X is the best, that means the stomach is most acidic or has the lowest pH (eliminates A).

48.   A   As in the preceding question, the absorption of ketoconazole is maximized when stomach pH is minimized. NaH_2CO_2 is a base, and omeprazole will also raise pH (eliminates B and C). A is a better choice than D because it will lower stomach pH.

49.   A   Again, using Equation 1, we can calculate that

$$pH - pK_a = \log \frac{[B]}{[BH^+]} \quad \Rightarrow$$
$$7.4 - 1.6 = \log \frac{[B]}{[BH^+]} \quad \Rightarrow$$
$$5.8 = \log \frac{[B]}{[BH^+]}$$

This shows that [B] is about 6 orders of magnitude higher than [BH$^+$], so far less than 1% will be ionized in the blood.

50.   B   Both omeprazole and ketoconazole have pK_a values greater than the pH of the stomach, so they will get ionized there (eliminates A). Choice C is eliminated because the higher the pK_a, the stronger the base. Because $pK_a = -\log K_a$, the higher the K_a, the lower the pK_a (eliminates D). The answer must be B: The weaker the base, the stronger its conjugate acid.

Passage VIII (Questions 51–55)

51.   C   A crystal with a partially filled conduction band, even at very low temperatures, must be a conductor. Choice C, sodium, is a metal and thus an excellent conductor, so this is the best answer here. Diamond is a crystal of carbon, and according to Table 1, it has an energy gap of 5.4 eV and thus is definitely an insulator, eliminating choice A. Choices B and D are also listed in Table 1, with energy gaps which classify them as a semiconductor and insulator, respectively.

52.   D   The passage states that the average energy of an electron at temperature T is kT. Therefore, to acquire enough energy to jump into the gap, the temperature would need to be high enough to ensure that $kT \geq E_g$. According to Table 1, the energy gap for zinc sulfide (ZnS) is 3.6 eV, so the minimum temperature necessary would be $(3.6 \text{ eV})/(8.6 \times 10^{-5} \text{ eV/K}) = 42,000$ K.

53.   B   The electric force on the electron would have magnitude eE and thus impart an acceleration a of eE/m. Since $\Delta v = at$, the change in velocity in time t would be eEt/m. Note that choices A and C have units of acceleration, not velocity, so they can be eliminated immediately.

54.   A   As the temperature is increased, the conductivity of a semiconductor increases, so its resistivity decreases; this eliminates choice B. The passage states that the energy gap for insulators is more than 3 eV while for semiconductors it is less than 3 eV; therefore, insulators have a larger energy gap than semiconductors, eliminating choice C. Finally, D is wrong, since it is the drift of conduction electrons—that is, electrons in the conduction band, not the valence band—that account for electrical conduction. Therefore, by process of elimination, the answer must be A. (Note: Metals have a practically "infinite" supply of conduction electrons, and as the temperature is increased, the greater, random thermal motion of these electrons and the lattice ions produce more and more frequent collisions, reducing the drift velocity and thus the conductivity.)

55.   C   The concentration of electrons in the conduction band is given by Equation 1, $c(T) = Ae^{-T^*/T}$. Note that as T increases, $e^{-T^*/T}$ approaches $e^0 = 1$, so c approaches (but never equals) the value A. This eliminates choices A and B. Since the number of electrons in the conduction band must increase as the temperature increases (because the electrons in the valence band can eventually acquire enough thermal energy to jump the gap), the graph of $c(T)$ must increase to A; this eliminates choice D.

Freestanding Questions (56–60)

56.   D   The ideal gas law applies when the assumptions of kinetic molecular theory are met. These assumptions are that the gas molecules have no effective volume and that all collisions are perfectly elastic. Gases behave ideally when they are at high energy and spread very far apart. At very low temperatures and high pressure, the effective volume of the molecules becomes a considerable factor on total volume and molecules tend to stick together.

57.   B   Atomic radius decreases from left to right across a period and increases from top to bottom within a group. Therefore, it is a minimum in the top right corner of the periodic table. Both silicon and oxygen are above and to the right of calcium and sodium respectively (A and C are wrong). Between silicon and oxygen, oxygen is further to the top right and is the correct answer.

58.   C   The problem is solved with the relationship between heat (q), mass (m), specific heat (c), and temperature change (ΔT):

$$q = mc\Delta T$$

$$\Delta T = \frac{q}{mc} = \frac{400 \text{ J}}{(50 \text{ g})(0.39 \text{ J/g}^\circ \text{ C})} \approx \frac{1{,}000}{50}\,^\circ \text{ C} = 20^\circ \text{ C}$$

59.   D   The mathematical expression for k is:

$$k = Ae^{-E_a / RT}$$

where A is the Arrhenius factor (related to the collision efficiency of the molecules), E_a is the activation energy, R is the gas law constant, and T is the temperature. Temperature and activation energy are explicitly shown in the equation, and catalysts lower the activation energy of a reaction affecting k (A, B, and C are wrong). Enthalpy is a thermodynamic factor not involved in reaction kinetics.

60.   D   As a diver descends in the water, ambient pressure increases. The temperature may increase or decrease, but this will not affect the amount of air consumed (A is wrong). The gas law constant does not change (B is wrong). The same volume of air is required to fill the lungs at the surface or at depth (C is wrong). However, when ambient pressure is increased, the number of moles required to achieve that volume in each breath is dramatically increased.

Chapter 6
Mastering Physical Sciences: Physics

This chapter is similar in presentation and content to Mastering Physical Sciences: General Chemistry. Many, if not all, of the techniques demonstrated in that chapter are applicable to the physics passages and freestanding questions on the MCAT. In fact, some passages may appear to be a blend of both of these important sciences.

The content outline presented here is a framework for further in-depth study based on a topic list provided on the AAMC website. Again, as the focus of this book is on technique and practice, a systematic approach for physics freestanding questions and passages is presented here. Many of the ideas are shared with the general chemistry chapter; they are repeated here for your convenience. The bag of tricks is expanded with more techniques that can be used throughout the Physical Sciences section of the MCAT.

PHYSICS CONTENT

The AAMC provides an outline of all the potential physics topics that can appear on the MCAT. As mentioned in Chapter 3, this document can be found on the AAMC website under the category "Preparing for the MCAT Exam." At press time, the link to the PDF was called "Physical Sciences—General Chemistry Topics," but don't let that dissuade you from clicking on it! The list of physics topics follows the list of general chemistry topics.

Given the nature of the test and the physics involved, passages and questions often present very visual scenarios. Figures, tables, graphs, and experimental reasoning are common. As in general chemistry, the focus will be on fundamental concepts. The MCAT does not contain questions requiring long, laborious mathematical solutions. Formulas and quantitative analysis are done in a conceptual manner.

The goals for physics content review are similar to those for general chemistry. In terms of the level of detail and complexity presented on the MCAT as compared to a freshman college course, the most striking difference is in quantitative problem solving. Questions requiring calculations to arrive at a numerical answer are relatively rare on the MCAT. The test still asks about quantitative issues, but often the solutions are conceptual or algebraic in nature. For example, you may be asked to solve for the final velocity of an object after a collision, and the answer will be an algebraic expression of the corresponding masses and their velocities before and after the collision.

Formulas are an essential aspect of physics. It may be tempting to compose a list or create a stack of cards to memorize as many formulas as possible before the test. This is not a necessary or advisable strategy. The MCAT is likely to provide many of the formulas necessary for solving problems. What the test does differently is it requires you to use those formulas in a non-computational manner. Do you understand what the formula really means? Do you understand the relationship between the variables as they are changed or affected by different factors?

The formulas that you will be required to recall from memory are the intuitive ones, such as $v = d/t$ and $F_{net} = ma$, but the MCAT has an uncanny ability for asking you about these concepts in a way that is not obvious. For example, when solving for the distance between a sound emitting source and something off of which the sound echoes, you must remember that the time it takes for the sound to travel to the object and back corresponds to twice the distance between the source and object. As with general chemistry, if you study and practice enough, the formulas that are impossible to forget tend to be the only ones you need.

Even more so in physics than in general chemistry, as you become more familiar with how the MCAT tests content, you need to use the effective strategy of predicting how a topic will appear on the test. Practice diagramming concepts using figures and graphs. Understand how a system works from top to bottom, and then systematically change all the variables involved to see how the system will respond. Facility with vectors and free-body diagrams is an important skill for the test. Physics is fascinating because it explains what we observe and helps us predict

Science Passages on the MCAT

They are intentionally designed to test your ability to see beyond unfamiliar subject matter. Most of them are rather arcane and complex. No set of questions will draw on *all* of the information in an associated passage.

Source: *Cracking the MCAT*, 2006

how things will behave in the future under similar or different circumstances. The physics of the MCAT for the most part focuses on these applications of physics content knowledge, not the page-long mathematical derivations that you may have encountered in a college course.

PHYSICS TOPIC OUTLINE

Basic Concepts

Although the physics questions on the MCAT may not involve complex calculations, they are still quantitative. A solid understanding of basic mathematics and trigonometry is essential. Arithmetic and algebraic concepts include the following:

- scientific notation
- exponents
- radicals
- proportions
- percentages
- algebraic manipulation of equations
- graphing
- logarithms

The basic trigonometry functions of sine, cosine, and tangent along with their inverse need to be understood. These values should be understood in terms of a right-angle triangle and for specific values such as 0, 30, 45, 60, 90, and 180 degrees. Facility with vectors and free-body diagrams is necessary.

Kinematics

The movement of objects in two dimensions in terms of velocity, acceleration, and displacement will appear on the MCAT. Examples of uniformly accelerated motion that are frequently tested include free fall and projectile motion. The kinematic equations are generally not provided in a passage. The concepts remain more important than the ability to solve an equation for a specific variable. For example, in projectile motion, the horizontal component of velocity stays constant, the vertical acceleration is due to gravity and directed straight down, and the time to the top of the parabolic path is equal to the time to come back down to the same initial height.

Forces

The MCAT will have questions related to various forces and Newton's laws. Most often, it is necessary to understand the concepts around equating different types of forces in a system at translational equilibrium. For example, a mass that floats in a fluid experiences an upward buoyant force and a downward gravitational force that are equivalent in magnitude. These situations provide endless opportunities for setting various formulas equal to each other and solving for one variable in terms of all the others. In addition, classic situations involving inclined planes, pulleys, and frictional forces are common on the test.

Circular Motion

Topics in this section include center of mass, torque, rotational equilibrium, and uniform circular motion. Regarding uniform circular motion, it is important to note that although the magnitude of velocity is constant, the object is accelerating because the direction of velocity is constantly changing. Another important concept is that although the instantaneous velocity is tangent to the circular motion, centripetal acceleration and force are always directed toward the center of the circle.

Work, Energy, Power, and Momentum

The concept of conservation of energy is essentially guaranteed to appear on the MCAT. Although work is typically recalled as the product of force and distance, thinking about work in terms of the change in energy of something is often more useful for the test. The formulas for potential and kinetic energy are those that will be used often and impossible to forget. For collisions, momentum is always conserved but kinetic energy is only conserved for perfectly elastic collisions. When dealing with power, the basic understanding that it is a rate with a factor of time is a core concept that can be tested in a variety of ways that are not necessarily intuitive.

Fluids and Solids

On the MCAT, fluids can be at rest or in motion. At rest, buoyancy and gauge pressure are the most frequently tested concepts. For floating objects, the relative density of the object to the fluid determines the proportional volume of the object submerged. Understanding that buoyant force is a function of the mass of the fluid displaced is fundamental. Likewise, gauge pressure is a function of the surrounding fluid density and not of the object submerged. In motion, the continuity equation that dictates constant flow is the most important concept. Bernoulli's equation should be provided if necessary, and it is clearly more important to understand the relative effects of the variables than to be able to come up with numerical solutions. For example, as the velocity decreases in a system at constant height with constant flow, the pressure will increase by the Bernoulli effect. Solid mechanics concepts include stress, strain, and Hooke's law.

Electrostatics

Electric charges, fields, forces, potential, and potential energy can all appear on the MCAT. Many analogies can be made between the electrostatic variables and the mechanics variables (mass and charge, gravity and electric field, height and potential), and the equations are comparable as a result. Regions of positive charge are always defined as high electric potential. Electric field lines are always drawn from positive to negative charges. Forces acting on positive charges act in the direction of the electric field, and those on negative charges act in the opposite direction of the electric field.

Dealing with Science Passages

The questions are readily answerable by applying

- knowledge of basic science
- logical thought
- a careful review of illustrations, graphs, or tables

Source: *Cracking the MCAT*, 2006

Electricity and Magnetism

Basic DC electric circuits will appear on the MCAT with voltage sources, currents, resistors, and capacitors. Ohm's law and Kirchoff's rules should be understood. Breaking down resistors and capacitors in either parallel or series circuits may be necessary. Capacitors provide a context to ask about many fundamental physics principles. Mechanics, electrostatics, circuits, and energy should be well understood. Again, knowing how to use the electricity formulas is more important than rote memorization of as many formulas as possible. Moving charges can create magnetic fields, and moving magnets can create electricity. The right-hand rules that govern the relationship between electricity and magnetic fields should be understood for the test.

Oscillations and Waves

The features of transverse and longitudinal waves, differences between them, and examples of both are potential topics on the MCAT. Examples of simple harmonic motion including springs and pendulums represent situations where a wide variety of topics can be incorporated, such as conservation of energy, momentum, forces, friction, etc. Although impossible to forget, the wave equation, $v = \lambda f$ is likely to come up on the MCAT.

Sound

The high-yield topics for sound are likely to be intensity and the Doppler effect. The logarithmic scale for sound intensity level should be understood in a conceptual manner. For example, every 10 dB step in intensity level represents a multiple of 10 changes in sound intensity. Complex calculations are not required. Situations involving apparent changes in frequency from the Doppler effect can appear on the MCAT. It is important to keep the relative contributions of the observer and the source separate when working out any calculations, if required. Typically, a qualitative judgment of a net increase or decrease in observed frequency is all that is asked.

Light and Geometrical Optics

While it may be tempting to focus on complex ray diagrams of mirrors and lenses when reviewing these topics, it is far more important to understand the fundamental concepts and behavior of electromagnetic radiation. Conceptual questions on reflection, refraction, and light behavior are likely to be more common than solving the lens equation. That said, it is still important to know the basics of convex and concave mirrors and lenses and to have a functional understanding of where images appear relative to objects in various situations.

ATTACKING PHYSICS FREESTANDING QUESTIONS

Of the approximately 10 freestanding questions in the Physical Sciences section, roughly half will be physics related and they will be scattered in two to three groups throughout the section. Again, it is absolutely essential to attempt all of these questions, as they tend to be easier places to pick up points. Given that freestanding questions can appear at the end of the section, doing the Physical Sciences section in more than one pass will ensure you get to these questions without running out of time. Hopefully you read the previous chapters, because all of this has been covered there in more detail. If not, go back and read them!

Freestanding physics questions are likely to be marked by short conceptual questions and proportional analysis. This is the primary reason why memorizing a hundred formulas is not necessary to do well on the test. For every formula you encounter, it is more important to understand why the variables relate to each other the way they do. Why is buoyant force directly proportional to the density of the fluid displaced? Which variable has the greatest effect on Newton's law of gravitational force and why? These stand-alone questions also provide opportunities for short and sweet calculation problems. Always estimate and evaluate your answer choices carefully when doing computations. The following are examples of freestanding physics questions.

1. If the distance between the plates of a capacitor with initial capacitance of C_0 were reduced by a factor of x, what would be the resulting capacitance?

    A. C_0
    B. C/x
    C. xC
    D. C^x

The question is referring to the relationship between capacitance (C), charge (q), and voltage ($V = Ed$). $C = q/V = q/Ed$. Therefore, C is indirectly proportional to d. The answer is **C**. The relationship between capacitance, charge, and voltage as well as the formula for voltage should be understood for the MCAT. This question requires you to combine these two concepts. Aside from the effective recall of this information, there are not any other approaches that can eliminate any of the other answer choices.

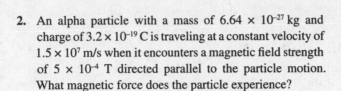

2. An alpha particle with a mass of 6.64×10^{-27} kg and charge of 3.2×10^{-19} C is traveling at a constant velocity of 1.5×10^7 m/s when it encounters a magnetic field strength of 5×10^{-4} T directed parallel to the particle motion. What magnetic force does the particle experience?

   A. 0 N
   B. 2.4×10^{-15} N
   C. 4.8×10^{-15} N
   D. 5.8×10^{-30} N

This question illustrates a couple of important techniques for physics questions on the MCAT. A person who has blindly memorized a hundred physics equations may be tempted to plug in numbers to $F_B = qvB$ and come up with answer choice B. This is why understanding the equation and its context is more important for the MCAT. Only the component of magnetic field that is perpendicular to the velocity of the moving particle will generate a magnetic force. Because B is parallel to v, the angle between them is 180° and there is no component of B perpendicular to v, so there is no magnetic force experienced by the particle. The answer is A. One feature of this question is that zero is an answer choice. If ever in doubt or running out of time, answering zero is not a bad choice, as will be explained later.

ATTACKING PHYSICS PASSAGES
All of the steps for general chemistry passages covered in Mastering Physical Sciences: General Chemistry are valid for physics passages. The steps are outlined here in less detail for your convenience, along with additional information that is particularly relevant for physics.

Now or Later
Make a quick decision about the passage in front of you to either do it now or save it for your second pass through the test. This decision may be made broadly based on general chemistry versus physics passages or may be related to specific topics within each area. The result of this technique is ensuring that all freestanding questions are attempted and your best effort is put forth on topics you know well.

Scan the Passage

Physics passages can be scanned in less than one minute for main ideas and the *location* of information. Take things one paragraph, figure, or table at a time. Physics passages are most likely to contain diagrams of vectors or an experimental apparatus. Outline where things are in the passage for reference later. Consider highlighting new terminology or formulas that are verbally described in the text, such as "...the magnetic field is directly proportional to the magnetic flux density."

Get to the Questions!

Always maximize your time where points are awarded. Do the questions from the least to most difficult whenever possible.

Keep Moving but Leave Nothing Blank

After scanning a passage, you should spend no more than an average of 75 seconds on each question. Because some questions will be relatively easy, doing those first will allow you to feel more comfortable spending a little extra time on the tough items. However, do not devote several minutes of time to any one problem, as it could result in you missing several easy questions later in the test if you run out of time.

Do not leave any items blank in a passage once you commit to it. Use POE and your bag of tricks to guess on anything you do not know and flag those questions using the Mark tool. It is better to answer everything in the event you do not have time to return to it. Your best guess at this point is likely better than your best guess when you are running out of time at the end of the test.

Passage Based or Not?

As your physics knowledge advances, you will find less need for the passage. In general, you will likely get to a point when the only time you use information in the passage is to retrieve a novel formula, extract data from a graph or chart, or understand an experiment. Many questions associated with a passage can be answered without referring to the passage at all. The ability to identify when and when not to use the passage is a skill that will reward you with precious time. As a drill when you take practice tests, attempt to answer all the questions for a passage without looking at the passage. This will give you an excellent sense of when it is truly necessary to refer to the passage, and it will give you extra time to rack your brain for the prior knowledge you need to arrive at an answer to the question.

Uncover the Fundamentals

For many people in a college physics course, the majority of effort is spent learning how to get the right answers through a series of formulas and equations. Even when professors try to reinforce conceptual understanding, the examinations by nature tend to reward computational prowess. For success on the MCAT, the focus should shift to understanding concepts. Learn the basic meaning behind the equations and challenge yourself to be able to explain in words why certain variables in a formula are related to each other the way they are. The best way to get used to the way physics is presented on the MCAT is to do a large number of practice items. When you review your work, try to determine the minimum level of content that, when combined with excellent technique, would get every question in a passage correct. This is where you should aim in your studies. Otherwise, it is nearly impossible to comprehensively study every topic that the AAMC lists as a possibility for the test.

Use Techniques

Techniques must be practiced to become effective. Rather than timing yourself on every practice passage, try doing some passages with no time limit while forcing yourself to come up with two or more ways to solve each question. The more options you have on the day of the test, the more confident you will be. When doing a passage under time constraints, you are most likely to fall back on using a content-only approach. It can be surprising to look back on the same question and see that other alternatives were available to solve the problem that were potentially much more efficient.

Use the CBT Tools Provided

The CBT format offers easy navigation, the ability to review skipped and marked questions, highlighting, and a cross-out function for POE. Do not forget that the periodic table is a click away. Take a few CBT format practice tests to get used to the interface and to build up the endurance needed to stare at a computer screen for several hours in one sitting if that is unfamiliar to you. As previously mentioned, the tools available on test day at the testing center may vary from the online practice tests available at the AAMC's website.

ADDITIONS TO THE PHYSICAL SCIENCES BAG OF TRICKS

Below you will find a sample physics passage followed by questions that illustrate more techniques for the bag of tricks. When combined with a solid scientific understanding of the question, these techniques tend to be useful to reduce the time needed to solve the problem or as guessing tools when you are out of ideas or out of time. Although valuable in most instances, you may encounter some questions in which the techniques may not be as useful. Practice using these techniques on a wide variety of questions before the test to develop a sense of when to pull which tools out of your bag of tricks.

Passage I (Questions 1–5)

A weapons manufacturer tests a new canon prototype on a large outdoor range. The canon fires 155 mm diameter (caliber) shells at a muzzle velocity of 827 m/s. The range (R) of the canon is given by:

$$R = \frac{v\cos\theta}{g}\left(v\sin\theta + \sqrt{(v\sin\theta)^2 + 2gy_0}\right)$$

where v is the initial velocity in m/s, g is the acceleration of gravity in m/s^2, θ is the angle of inclination of the canon relative to the ground, and y_0 is the initial height of the projectile in m. When $y_0 = 0$, the formula reduces to:

$$R = \frac{v^2}{g}\sin 2\theta$$

During testing, maximum range was determined to be approximately 30 km. The primary factor limiting range was the drag force given by:

$$F_D = \frac{1}{2}\rho v^2 C_d A$$

where ρ is the air density (1.293 kg/m^3), v is the initial velocity in m/s, C_d is the coefficient of drag for the shell (0.18), and A is the cross sectional area of the shell in m^2.

1. In the absence of air resistance, which of the following graphs represents the horizontal velocity of the canon shell after being fired?

A. v
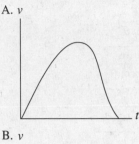

B. v
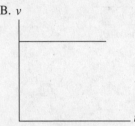

C. v
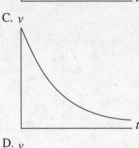

D. v
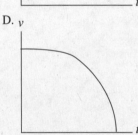

2. If the caliber of the canon were changed to 100 mm, the resulting drag would be reduced by a factor of:

   A.   [(0.05)/(0.0775)].
   B.   [(0.1)/(0.155)]^2.
   C.   [(0.0775)/(0.05)].
   D.   [(0.155)/(0.1)]^2.

3. What is the theoretical maximum range of the canon in the passage when fired from the ground in the absence of lift or resistance from air?

   A.   36 km
   B.   47 km
   C.   68 km
   D.   112 km

4. Which of the following gives the magnitude of the velocity of a cannon shell at a horizontal displacement of x from its initial firing point?

    A. $\sqrt{v^2 - 2gx\tan\theta(\dfrac{gx}{v\cos\theta})^2}$

    B. $\sqrt{v^2 - 2gx\tan\theta + (\dfrac{gx}{v\cos\theta})^2}$

    C. $\sqrt{v^2 - 2gx\tan\theta + (\dfrac{g}{xv\cos\theta})^2}$

    D. $\sqrt{v^2 - 2gx^2\tan\theta + (\dfrac{gx}{v\cos\theta})^2}$

5. The canon in the passage obtained a range of R_0 when fired at an angle of 30°. What is the range when the canon is fired again with an angle of 60°?

    A. $R_0/2$
    B. R_0
    C. $2R_0$
    D. $R_0\cos(30°)$

    _____

The Oddball

1. In the absence of air resistance, which of the following graphs represents the horizontal velocity of the canon shell after being fired?

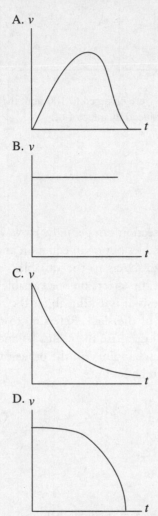

A. v

B. v

C. v

D. v

Sometimes one answer choice stands out as being significantly different than the rest. In this case, choice B represents a graph that is a linear proportion with a slope of 0. Every other graph represents some kind of exponential function. Whenever you see a similar pattern, pay particular attention to the oddball. Even if you have a solid understanding of the science involved, spend your initial time on that answer choice and go from there. If you are able to eliminate it, so be it. It is still a good place to start. If you are running out of time or have no idea whatsoever how to approach the question, pick the oddball. It will not always work, but it does represent a good guess that is likely to be better than chance.

In this case, this question is driving at a fundamental principle of projectile motion. The horizontal component of velocity remains constant throughout the entire flight, because in the absence of air resistance, there is no net force in the horizontal plane. The correct answer is **B**.

Proportions

2. If the caliber of the canon were changed to 100 mm, the resulting drag would be reduced by a factor of:

   A. $[(0.05)/(0.0775)]$.
   B. $[(0.1)/(0.155)]^2$.
   C. $[(0.0775)/(0.05)]$.
   D. $[(0.155)/(0.1)]^2$.

Novel formulas in the Physical Sciences section can get ugly. However, the MCAT tends to test your ability to pull two variables out of an equation and demonstrate how they are related. Always simplify formulas to the variables, and when possible, plug in easy numbers to determine the effects on one variable when another variable is changed. In this case, the question is asking about the relationship between drag force (F_D) and the diameter of the shell. Referring to the formula in the passage, decreasing the diameter will decrease the radius (r) and subsequently decrease the F_D. As r is the only variable changing, all the other variables can be considered constant and a proportion can be set up:

$$F_D = \frac{1}{2}\rho v^2 C_d A$$
$$F_D \propto A$$
$$F_D \propto \pi r^2$$
$$F_D \propto r^2$$

Consider that $r_1 > r_2$ and are related by the factor shown below:

$$r_1 = \left(\frac{0.155/2}{0.100/2}\right)r_2$$
$$r_1 = \left(\frac{0.155}{0.100}\right)r_2$$

Because it is a proportion, the step of converting diameter to radius by dividing by 2 is not necessary but included for clarity. Using this relationship between the two radii and the fact that $F_D \propto r^2$, we have that the factor relating the initial drag force, F_{D1}, and the new drag force, F_{D2}, is $(0.155/0.100)^2$. The correct answer is **D**.

MCAThematics

3. What is the theoretical maximum range of the canon in the passage when fired from the ground in the absence of lift or resistance from air?

    A. 36 km
    B. 47 km
    C. 68 km
    D. 112 km

Fortunately, strict calculation questions on the MCAT are rare. When you do encounter a problem requiring a mathematical calculation, do not expend any more effort than is required to get a correct answer. Always analyze the answer choices first. Do they differ by orders of magnitude? Are they sufficiently spaced apart so that estimation is a reasonable strategy? Is the first number of each answer choice different? The point is that once an equation is set up, it is usually possible to predict the answer or at least eliminate some choices without doing any significant math. In this problem, each answer choice starts with a different number. Let's see how we can use this to our advantage.

The question is about the theoretical maximum range of a projectile in the absence of air resistance. Therefore, no drag force or lift force is present. The fundamental concept required for this problem is that 45° represents the ideal angle at which to fire a projectile because it results in equal amounts of velocity dedicated to the vertical and horizontal components of velocity ($v\sin45° = v\cos45°$). This combined with the fact that the canon is fired from the ground simplifies the range equation in the passage dramatically:

$$R = \frac{v^2}{g}\sin 2\theta$$

$$R = \frac{v^2}{g}\sin 2(45°) = \frac{v^2}{g}\sin 90° = \frac{v^2}{g}$$

$$R = \frac{(827 \text{ m/s})^2}{(10 \text{ m/s}^2)} =$$

At this point, you should stop. Squaring 827 and dividing it by 10 can only result in an answer choice starting with the number 6, and only one choice is possible. The answer is **C**.

Are You a People Person?
With the exception of a few fields, medicine involves working with people. If science interests you but working with people does not, you may wish to consider a Ph.D rather than an M.D., or an M.D. that allows you to do only research.

Source: *Best 168 Medical Schools*, 2008

Check the Units

4. Which of the following gives the magnitude of the velocity of a cannon shell at a horizontal displacement of x from its initial firing point?

A. $\sqrt{v^2 - 2gx\tan\theta(\frac{gx}{v\cos\theta})^2}$

B. $\sqrt{v^2 - 2gx\tan\theta + (\frac{gx}{v\cos\theta})^2}$

C. $\sqrt{v^2 - 2gx\tan\theta + (\frac{g}{xv\cos\theta})^2}$

D. $\sqrt{v^2 - 2gx^2\tan\theta + (\frac{gx}{v\cos\theta})^2}$

Unit analysis can play a huge role in the Physical Sciences section. Given a very complex question or set of answer choices, starting with the units will help eliminate possibilities and sometimes provide the correct answer. This is the case for this question. Although it may seem daunting at first, you will get better at this with practice, and the MCAT is unlikely to contain an example quite as complex as this.

The question is asking for a velocity, so the units must work out to m/s. Let's take a look at each answer choice by unit analysis:

A. $\sqrt{v^2 - 2gx\tan\theta(\frac{gx}{v\cos\theta})^2} \rightarrow \sqrt{\frac{m^2}{s^2} - \left(\frac{m}{s^2}\right)(m)\left(\frac{(m/s^2)(m)}{m/s}\right)^2} \rightarrow \sqrt{\frac{m^2}{s^2} - \left(\frac{m^4}{s^4}\right)}$; NO

B. $\sqrt{v^2 - 2gx\tan\theta + (\frac{gx}{v\cos\theta})^2} \rightarrow \sqrt{\frac{m^2}{s^2} - \left(\frac{m}{s^2}\right)(m) + \left(\frac{(m/s^2)(m)}{m/s}\right)^2} \rightarrow \sqrt{\frac{m^2}{s^2} - \frac{m^2}{s^2} + \frac{m^2}{s^2}} \rightarrow \frac{m}{s}$; YES

C. $\sqrt{v^2 - 2gx\tan\theta + (\frac{g}{xv\cos\theta})^2} \rightarrow \sqrt{\frac{m^2}{s^2} - \left(\frac{m}{s^2}\right)(m) + \left(\frac{(m/s^2)}{m^2/s}\right)^2} \rightarrow \sqrt{\frac{m^2}{s^2} - \frac{m^2}{s^2} + \frac{1}{m^2s^2}}$; NO

D. $\sqrt{v^2 - 2gx^2\tan\theta + (\frac{gx}{v\cos\theta})^2} \rightarrow \sqrt{\frac{m^2}{s^2} - \left(\frac{m}{s^2}\right)(m^2) + \left(\frac{(m/s^2)(m)}{m/s}\right)^2} \rightarrow \sqrt{\frac{m^2}{s^2} - \frac{m^3}{s^2} + \frac{m^2}{s^2}}$; NO

Again, the example here is complex for a reason. The MCAT will provide opportunities to use a similar analysis on a much smaller scale to eliminate answers. If you can follow this example, you will have no problem using unit analysis as a technique on the MCAT. The correct answer is **B**.

Zero or No Change

5. The canon in the passage obtained a range of R_0 when fired at an angle of 30°. What is the range when the canon is fired again with an angle of 60°?

   A. $R_0/2$
   B. R_0
   C. $2R_0$
   D. $R_0\cos(30°)$

Physics can be especially enlightening when it provides simple explanations of phenomena that seem counterintuitive. For example, consider two jets, each of which carries a cargo box with a mass of 1,000 kg. The first jet is flying horizontally at a velocity v and altitude h. The second jet is flying directly upwards or vertically at the same velocity v toward an altitude h. Both jets drop their cargo at altitude h. Which cargo box will hit the ground with a greater magnitude of velocity?

When the cargo box is released from the second jet, it initially goes a little higher before starting free-fall, but the box from the first jet immediately falls. You may think that because the second box essentially falls from a higher altitude, it will have a greater impact speed. However, they both have the same magnitude of impact velocity. Both boxes start with the same potential and kinetic energy and therefore end with the same kinetic energy at impact.

Now what if we replaced the box in the second jet with one that had a mass of 2,000 kg? In this case, the second cargo box starts with more potential and kinetic energy, so it must land with a greater impact speed, right? Wrong. They will be equal yet again. Free-fall velocity is independent of mass. Work out the conservation of energy formulas and you will see.

These conceptual situations and problems are common on the MCAT. For this reason, anytime you see 0 as an answer choice, you should pay close attention to it. Likewise, anytime you see an answer choice that is the same thing or implies the same thing as what you started with, look carefully at that too. Even if you know all of the science behind the question, it is usually easier to start with these choices and work through the problem. If the answer works out to something different, that is fine. However, if you are running out of time, or if you are guessing because you have no idea how to solve the problem, answering 0 or the choice that implies no change is a great way to go. Note: This is not always going to work, but when all else fails, it is a reasonable strategy for both working through a problem and guessing. Ask yourself if there is anything special about a question that would make the answer 0 or no change. You may be surprised. Also, note that this is not the same as selecting an answer choice that states, "The answer cannot be determined by the information given." In general, this is not a good choice for either POE or guessing.

The question here is asking about range in terms of the angle of inclination. One approach would be to use the formula for the passage and plug in numbers to compare the sin of 60° and 120° to see that they are equal. Another approach is simply to focus first on choice B because it represents no change. Is there anything about this question that would result in no change? Yes. You remember that the ideal angle for a projectile is 45°, because it maximizes both v_y and v_x. Both 30° and 60° differ from 45° by the same amount and therefore will go the same horizontal distance. The 60° shot goes higher and spends more time in the air but has less momentum in the horizontal direction. The 30° shot goes lower and spends less time in the air but has greater momentum in the horizontal direction. A final approach is to see choice B as no change and guess, if you did not know how to approach the problem or were running out of time. The correct choice is **B**.

Chapter 7
Mastery Applied:
Physics Practice

As with Chapter 4, Mastery Applied: General Chemistry Practice Questions, this chapter provides several passages and freestanding questions that give you an opportunity to try out the strategies discussed in this book and determine those topics on which you need to spend additional time studying. The number of passages and freestanding questions presented here for physics exceeds that which you will encounter on the actual MCAT in order to give you comprehensive practice. Are you ready for another workout?

During a life-threatening cardiac dysrhythmia, a defibrillator passes an electrical current through the heart, causing it to stop and hopefully restart in a normal rhythm. Capacitors are essential to defibrillators, allowing a rapid delivery of stored charge. The capacitor is charged by a direct current source in one part of the circuit. When paddles are applied to a patient's chest, a second component of the circuit is available for the capacitor to discharge when a switch is activated. Figure 1 is a simplified schematic of a defibrillator.

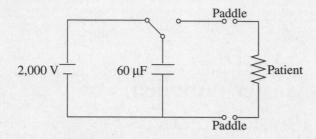

Figure 1 Defibrillator schematic

Early defibrillators delivered current in a monophasic wave that traveled in one direction, from one electrode to the other. Devices were then developed to deliver a biphasic wave of current, where current initially travels in one direction and then reverses. Biphasic devices require less energy to deliver equivalent total current compared with monophasic defibrillators. Figure 2 depicts examples of the different waveforms.

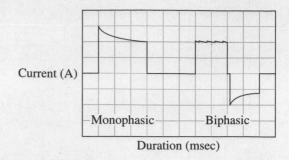

Figure 2 Monophasic vs. biphasic current waveforms

In addition to selecting a monophasic or biphasic mode, the only other variable that can be set on a defibrillator is the energy level of each shock. Energies between 50 and 360 J are typically used. One significant variable that cannot be controlled is the electrical resistance of the patient, which can be between 25 to 175 ohms and change during the delivery of the shock. Some defibrillators incorporate a resistance sensing mechanism to actively adjust and shape the current waveform before and even during each shock to maximize effectiveness.

1. The energy stored on the capacitor in Figure 1 is:

   A. 12 J.
   B. 60 J.
   C. 120 J.
   D. 240 J.

2. A biphasic defibrillator set at a constant energy delivers an equivalent charge to patients with different resistance by adjusting which variable?

   A. Time
   B. Voltage
   C. Capacitance
   D. Impedance

3. The defibrillator in Figure 1 is charged and the paddles are in place on a patient's chest. When the switch is activated, current will flow:

   A. clockwise from low to high electrical potential.
   B. clockwise from high to low electrical potential.
   C. counterclockwise from low to high electrical potential.
   D. counterclockwise from high to low electrical potential.

4. Which of the following is a likely feature of a biphasic defibrillator compared with a monophasic device?

   A. Smaller capacitor area
   B. Higher peak current
   C. Decreased battery life
   D. Longer charge time

5. An insulator is placed between the plates of the capacitor in Figure 1 that doubles the dielectric constant. What is the resulting potential difference across the capacitor plates when fully charged?

   A. 1,000 V
   B. 2,000 V
   C. 4,000 V
   D. 16,000 V

6. Adjusting the energy level of a defibrillator from 300 J to 75 J reduces the:

   A. voltage requirement by a factor of 2.
   B. charging time by a factor of 4.
   C. capacitance by a factor of 2.
   D. total charge available by a factor of 4.

Passage II (Questions 7–12)

When traveling at an angle to the wind, a sailboat will lean to one side or *heel*. This rocking motion is counteracted by a shift in buoyant force that results in a torque called the *righting moment* that acts to keep the boat upright. The ability to resist heeling is one measure of a sailboat's stability.

When upright, a sailboat's center of gravity (*G*) and upright center of buoyancy (*B*) are in vertical alignment. As the boat heels to one side from the wind, the center of buoyancy shifts laterally (B_1). The horizontal displacement of the center of buoyancy from the center of gravity is *GZ*, as depicted in Figure 1. The result is a coupling of two forces, gravity and buoyancy, about a *righting arm*, *GZ*, tending to rotate the boat back to an upright position.

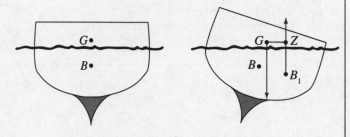

Figure 1 Righting moment of a sailboat

A designer measures *GZ* as a function of heel angle for 2 different sailboats. The resulting *GZ* curves are graphed in Figure 2.

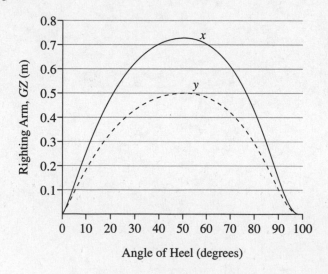

Figure 2 *GZ* Curve: Righting arm vs. angle of heel

7. Which of the following gives the magnitude of the righting moment of a heeled boat with mass *m* displacing a volume of water *V* with density *ρ*?

   A. $mg(GZ) + \rho Vg(GZ)$
   B. $mg(GZ) - \rho Vg(GZ)$
   C. $mg(GZ)$
   D. $mg + \rho Vg$

8. What will lengthen the period of time it takes a sailboat to rock from side to side as it travels?

   A. Shortening the *GZ* line
   B. Lengthening the *GZ* line
   C. Adding mass to the bottom of the boat
   D. Increasing width of the boat

9. What can be concluded about boat *x* compared to boat *y* from the passage and results in Figure 2?

   A. Boat *x* has a lower center of gravity
   B. Boat *x* is more stable to the wind
   C. Boat *x* has a greater width
   D. Boat *x* has a narrower hull

10. Based on the passage, which of the following is true about a boat sailing with a heel angle greater than 0?

    A. Shifting mass to the lower side of the boat will increase buoyancy
    B. Shifting mass to the higher side of the boat will lengthen *GZ*
    C. Decreasing wind will cause an increase in *GZ*
    D. Increasing wind will cause an increase in *GZ*

11. A sailboat is anchored in an enclosed pool. When the anchor is pulled off the bottom of the pool and into the boat:

    A. the water level stays constant and buoyant force on the boat increases.
    B. the water level rises and buoyant force on the boat increases.
    C. *G* is elevated and *B* is lowered.
    D. *G* is lowered and *B* is elevated.

12. The designer in the passage repeated his analysis of boats *x* and *y* in water of increased density. All of the following would be expected EXCEPT:

    A. a decrease in displacement.
    B. a decreased distance between *B* and the waterline.
    C. an increased buoyant force at *B*.
    D. an increased distance between *G* and the waterline.

Passage III (Questions 13–18)

Fiber optic cables are capable of highly efficient transfer of light down flexible pathways. They are composed of an inner core surrounded by a cladding layer that results in total internal reflection of propagated rays.

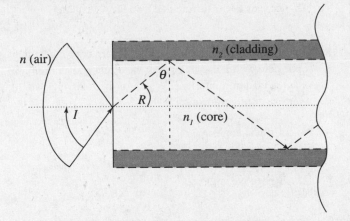

Figure 1 Fiber optic cable

The receiving end of a fiber optic cable will accept light rays at angles within a cone-of-acceptance. Only these light rays are capable of undergoing total internal reflection once they are within the core. The *numerical aperture* (*NA*) measures the openness of the receiving end of the cable and is calculated by:

$$NA = \sin I = \sqrt{n_1^2 - n_2^2}$$

where *I* is one-half of the cone-of-acceptance angle, n_1 is the core index of refraction, and n_2 is the cladding index of refraction. The light-gathering power is equal to the square of the numerical aperture.

Table 1 Fiber optic cable materials for core or cladding

Material	Index (n)	Attenuation (% per km)
DZ-9	1.50	8
ZJ-7	1.50	8
L-3	1.55	3
BR-6	1.60	1

A ray of light traveling through a 50 micron diameter cable may be reflected 10,000 times per meter of fiber. Therefore, the *attenuation*, or degree of intensity loss per unit distance, is an important factor in selecting materials.

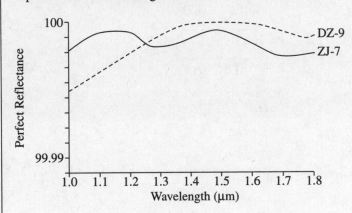

Figure 2 Percent reflectance vs. wavelength

13. What is always true for a fiber optic cable similar to the one in Figure 1?

    A. $n > n_1 > n_2$
    B. $n_1 > n_2 > n$
    C. $n > n_1 = n_2$
    D. $n_2 = n_1 > n$

14. At what angle from the normal would the light ray in Figure 1 be expected to exit the other end of the cable into the air?

    A. θ
    B. R
    C. $90 - R$
    D. I

15. What is the minimum value of θ in Figure 1 for total internal reflection to occur?

    A. $\sin^{-1}(n_2/n_1)$
    B. $\sin(n_2/n_1)$
    C. $\cos(n_2/n_1)$
    D. $\cos^{-1}(n_2/n_1)$

16. What is the theoretical cone of acceptance angle of a fiber optic cable with $n_1 = 1.5$ and $n_2 = 1.2$?

    A. $\sin^{-1}\sqrt{(1.5)-(1.2)}$

    B. $2\sin(\dfrac{1}{\sqrt{(1.5)^2-(1.2)^2}})$

    C. $\sin^{-1}\sqrt{(1.5)^2-(1.2)^2}$

    D. $2\sin^{-1}\sqrt{(1.5)^2-(1.2)^2}$

17. According to information in the passage, the optimum cable to transmit 1.6 µm wavelength signals would consist of a:

    A. core of DZ-9 surrounded by a BR-6 cladding.
    B. core of L-3 surrounded by a ZJ-7 cladding.
    C. core of L-3 surrounded by a DZ-9 cladding.
    D. core or BR-6 surrounded by a DZ-9 cladding.

18. A researcher studies a radially graded refractive index fiber optic core with a maximum n at the center and a minimum n at the cladding interface. Which of the following would increase during transmission?

    A. Critical angle
    B. Dispersion
    C. Frequency of reflections
    D. Reflective angles

19. Which of the following correctly orders the relative velocity of sound (v) in various phases of matter?

    A. $v_{liquid} > v_{solid} > v_{gas}$
    B. $v_{gas} > v_{liquid} > v_{solid}$
    C. $v_{solid} > v_{liquid} > v_{gas}$
    D. $v_{liquid} > v_{gas} > v_{solid}$

20. If an object is moving to the right along a straight line and at a constantly decreasing speed, then which one of the following must be true?

    A. The object's velocity is directed the same way as its acceleration.
    B. The net force on the object is directed to the right.
    C. The object's momentum is directed to the left.
    D. The total work performed on the object is negative.

21. What will happen to the electrostatic force between two protons when the distance between them increases by a factor of 4?

    A. It will decrease by a factor of 1/16.
    B. It will decrease by a factor of 1/4.
    C. It will decrease by a factor of 4.
    D. It will decrease by a factor of 16.

22. A Ping-Pong ball floats on water in a closed container.

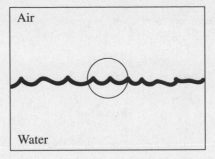

If the air in the container is replaced with oil that is less dense than water, what will happen to the ball?

    A. The ball will move up.
    B. The ball will move down.
    C. The ball will change position.
    D. The ball will spin.

23. A wooden block with mass m is positioned on an inclined plane at an angle θ that is just at the point where the block begins to slide. At this point, the coefficient of static friction, μ_s, is approximately equal to:

    A. $g\cos(\theta)$.
    B. $g\sin(\theta)$.
    C. $\tan(\theta)$.
    D. $\cos(\theta)/\sin(\theta)$.

Passage IV (Questions 24–29)

Flywheels represent a way to power a zero-emission vehicle. The rotational energy of a flywheel of radius R is given by the equation

$$KE_{rot} = \tfrac{1}{2}I\omega^2$$

Equation 1

where I is the flywheel's moment of inertia and $v/R = \omega$ is its angular speed. The moment of inertia, which quantifies an object's tendency to resist a change in its angular velocity (by analogy with mass, which quantifies an object's tendency to resist a change in its translational velocity), depends not only on the object's mass but also on how that mass is distributed about the axis of rotation. In particular, the more mass (on average) that is located farther from the axis, the greater the moment of inertia. For a cylindrical flywheel of uniform density with mass M and radius R (see Figure 1), the moment of inertia about the axis of symmetry through its center is given by the formula

$$I = \tfrac{1}{2}MR^2$$

Equation 2

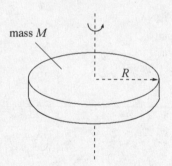

mass M

R

Figure 1 Flywheel

For a flywheel of a given size and shape, the amount of stored energy depends on its angular speed and the density of the material that the wheel is composed of. The density used is limited by the strength of the material, since more force is needed to move a material of greater density around its circular path. In theory, the amount of energy that can be stored is maximized when the ratio of the material's tensile strength, σ, to its density, ρ, is maximized, because then the flywheel could be "spun up" to higher angular speeds than could be tolerated by flywheels composed of weaker materials. (In practice, tiny defects in materials make the optimal design of flywheels a much more complex problem.) Currently, the largest σ/ρ ratios can be achieved by bonding together woven carbon fibers, which have tensile strengths greater than steel. Table 1 lists the tensile strengths and densities of some common materials.

Table 1 Tensile Strengths and Densities

Material	Tensile Strength σ (PA)	Density ρ (kg/m³)	σ/ρ (m²/s²)
Aluminum	2.2×10^8	2.7×10^3	8.1×10^4
Brass	4.7×10^8	8.6×10^3	5.5×10^4
Carbon fibers	6.9×10^9	1.7×10^3	4.1×10^6
Glass	1.0×10^9	5.0×10^3	2.0×10^5
Iron	3.0×10^8	7.8×10^3	3.8×10^4
Steel	1.9×10^9	8.0×10^3	2.4×10^5

Energy is stored in the wheel as it is first "spun up" using an electric motor connected to an electric power source. After disconnecting from the power source, the rotating flywheel can then be used to turn the same motor in the reverse direction, thereby generating electricity that can be used to power other electric motors that drive the car's wheels.

24. Four flywheels with the same dimensions are spinning with the same angular speed. According to Equation 1, the flywheel composed of which one of the following materials has the greatest rotational kinetic energy?

- **A.** Aluminum
- **B.** Brass
- **C.** Carbon fibers
- **D.** Steel

25. If all of the following wheels have the same mass and outer radius, which one has the greatest moment of inertia?

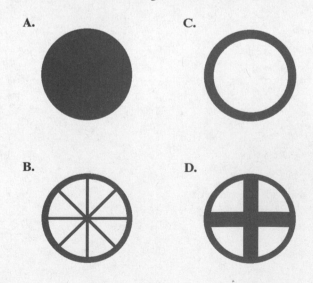

A.

B.

C.

D.

26. When compared to flywheels made of lower density materials, flywheels made of higher density materials tend to break apart at high angular speeds because:

    A. the centrifugal force on any portion of the wheel is smaller.
    B. the centripetal force on any portion of the wheel is smaller.
    C. the inertia of any portion of the wheel is larger.
    D. the radius of any portion of the wheel is smaller.

27. In theory, a flywheel constructed of which of the materials listed in Table 1 would be able to store the *least* amount of energy?

    A. Aluminum
    B. Brass
    C. Glass
    D. Iron

28. Which of the following best describes the energy transfers that take place starting at the power source and ending with the motion of a car powered by a flywheel system?

    A. Chemical, electrical, kinetic
    B. Electrical, kinetic, electrical
    C. Chemical, kinetic, electrical, kinetic
    D. Electrical, kinetic, electrical, kinetic

29. A flywheel of mass 400 kg and radius 0.5 m is rotating at an angular speed ω of 20 rad/s. What is the magnitude of the centripetal acceleration of a point on the outer rim of this wheel?

    A. 100 m/s^2
    B. 200 m/s^2
    C. 400 m/s^2
    D. 800 m/s^2

A dynamic loudspeaker produces sound from the movement of current in a magnetic field. Alternating current from an amplifier is passed through a wire coil that is suspended in a permanent magnet as shown in Figure 1. The coil is attached to a paper cone, and vibration of the assembly moves air to create sound. The cone and coil assembly must be mounted so it is free to vibrate. Therefore, speakers have an inherent resonant frequency at which vibratory amplitude is a maximum.

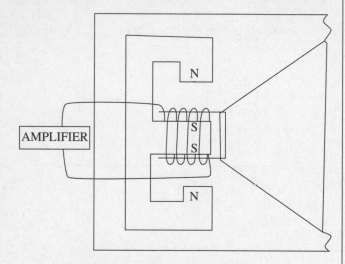

Figure 1 Dynamic loudspeaker

As current enters the speaker coil, a magnetic force (F_B) is generated on the movable parts of the speaker:

$$F_B = ILB$$

where I is the current (amperes), L is the length of wire (meters) in the magnetic field and B (teslas) is the magnetic field. In addition to making sound, movement of the speaker creates an induced electromotive force in the coil known as back-EMF that counteracts the initial magnetic force. This back-EMF results in an electrical impedance, Z, which is a measure of the loudspeaker's resistance (ohms) as a function of frequency. The impedance curve of a typical loudspeaker is shown in Figure 2.

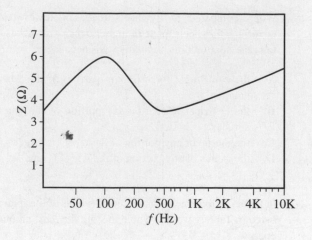

Figure 2 Impedance of a loudspeaker

30. Which of the following is/are true about Figure 2?

    I. The resonance frequency is 500 Hz.
    II. Back-EMF is a maximum at 100 Hz.
    III. Vibratory amplitude decreases between 100 and 200 Hz.

    A. I only
    B. I and II only
    C. II and III only
    D. III only

31. Doubling loudspeaker output from 40 to 80 W/m² corresponds to an intensity level increase of:

    A. 3 dB.
    B. 10 dB.
    C. 40 dB.
    D. 80 dB.

32. What will cause the speaker cone in Figure 1 to move toward the left of the diagram?

    A. Current flowing clockwise out of the amplifier
    B. Current flowing counterclockwise out of the amplifier
    C. Increased back-EMF
    D. Decreased back-EMF

33. Which of the following represents the power associated with operating a dynamic loudspeaker for 100 seconds with a 50 V direct current amplifier?

A. $\dfrac{F_B}{2LB}$

B. $\dfrac{50F_B}{LB}$

C. $\dfrac{LB}{50F_B}$

D. $\dfrac{5000F_B}{LB}$

34. When current passes through the following coil, what is the resulting vector of the magnetic field generated within the coil?

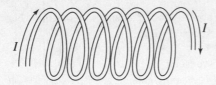

A. ↑
B. ↓
C. →
D. ←

35. All of the following will decrease the back-EMF magnitude in a loudspeaker EXCEPT:

A. increasing the number of loops in the coil.
B. decreasing B of the permanent magnet.
C. increasing the mass of the speaker cone.
D. decreasing I through the coil.

Questions 36 through 40 are NOT based on a descriptive passage.

36.

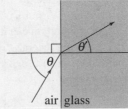

The figure above shows a ray of light in air striking the surface of a piece of glass. If n is the index of refraction of the glass, then which of the following equations is true?

A. $\sin \theta = n \sin \theta'$
B. $\cos \theta = n \cos \theta'$
C. $n \sin \theta = \sin \theta'$
D. $n \cos \theta = \sin \theta'$

37. A converging lens telescope focused on an object far out in space that is moving rapidly away from the earth will produce a:

A. virtual image in front of the focal point.
B. real image in front of the focal point.
C. virtual image on the focal point with a blue shift.
D. real image on the focal point with a red shift.

38. An object starts at rest and reaches a velocity of 25 m/s in 5 seconds. What is the magnitude of displacement?

A. 12.5 m
B. 25 m
C. 62.5 m
D. 125 m

39. What is the current traveling through each of 3 equivalent resistors (4 Ω) connected in parallel to a 12 V voltage source?

A. 1 A
B. 3 A
C. 6 A
D. 12 A

40. Which of the following decreases when a light wave passes from air into a pool of water?

A. Frequency
B. Speed
C. Wavelength
D. Index of refraction

Simple harmonic motion occurs when the acceleration of an oscillating object is proportional to and opposite in direction to the displacement from equilibrium. When set in motion at a very small angle, a simple pendulum can model simple harmonic motion. If one plots only the lateral displacement of such a pendulum, a graph similar to that in Figure 1 is obtained.

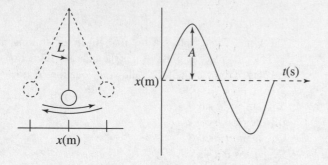

Figure 1 Pendulum in simple harmonic motion

The horizontal displacement (x), velocity (v_x), and acceleration (a_x) with respect to time (t) are governed by the following formulas:

$$x(t) = A\sin(2\pi ft + \gamma)$$

$$v(t) = A(2\pi f)\cos(2\pi ft + \gamma)$$

$$a(t) = -A(2\pi f)^2\sin(2\pi ft + \gamma)$$

where A is the horizontal amplitude in meters, f is the frequency of motion in hertz, and γ is the phase ($\gamma = 0$ if there is no displacement at $t = 0$). The period (T) defines the time of one complete wavelength or cycle of pendulum motion and is calculated by:

$$T = 2\pi\sqrt{\frac{L}{g}}$$

where L is the length of the pendulum arm and g is the gravitational acceleration.

An experiment is performed where a gun fires a bullet with mass (m_b) and velocity (u_b) at a ballistic pendulum. The pendulum consists of a wooden block with a mass (m_p) centered at a distance (L) from a pivot on the ceiling where it is suspended by a rigid wire of essentially no mass. After the bullet collides with the block, the pendulum is set into simple harmonic motion with an initial velocity (v_p).

41. In one trial of the experiment in the passage, a perfectly inelastic collision results. What is the maximum height the pendulum will obtain?

   A. $v_p^2/2g$
   B. $m_b v_p^2/2g$
   C. $m_p v_p^2/2g$
   D. $(m_b+m_p)v_p^2/2g$

42. If T represents the tension in the string of a simple pendulum in motion at an angle (θ), what is the centripetal force on the suspended mass (m)?

   A. $mg\cos\theta$
   B. $mg\sin\theta$
   C. $T - mg\cos\theta$
   D. $T - mg\sin\theta$

43. The acceleration of a pendulum in simple harmonic motion is best described as:

   A. constant.
   B. constantly changing.
   C. equal to g.
   D. tangent to the arc of motion.

44. During a trial of the experiment in the passage, a perfectly elastic collision results in a final bullet velocity of v_b and the pendulum obtaining a maximum height of h. What was u_b?

A. $\sqrt{2gh}$

B. $\dfrac{m_b v_p}{m_p}$

C. $\dfrac{m_b v_b + m_p \sqrt{2gh}}{m_p}$

D. $\dfrac{m_b v_b + m_p \sqrt{2gh}}{m_b}$

45. Based on information in Figure 1, which of the following is true?

A. f increases with increasing A
B. $a(t)$ is a maximum when $x(t)=A$
C. The units of γ are degrees
D. $a(t)$ is always in the opposite direction as $v(t)$

46. If the pendulum in Figure 1 had a length of 2.5 m and was initially pulled to a lateral displacement of 0.1 m, what maximum velocity will it reach?

A. 0.1 m/s
B. 0.2 m/s
C. 1.0 m/s
D. 2.0 m/s

Passage VII (Questions 47–53)

The properties of sound in the underwater environment are significantly different than in the air. The speed of sound (v) in the ocean is approximately 1,500 m/s but varies with depth as illustrated in Figure 1. The speed of underwater sound is given by:

$$v = \sqrt{\frac{K}{\rho}}$$

where K is the bulk modulus or resistance to compression and ρ is the water density. The intensity level of underwater sound is measured in dB sound pressure level (dB SPL) with a reference pressure (P_{ref}) of 1 µPa:

$$\text{dB SPL} = 20 \log_{10} (P/P_{ref})$$

Underwater, the threshold for human hearing is about 70 dB SPL with a maximum sensitivity at 1,000 Hz.

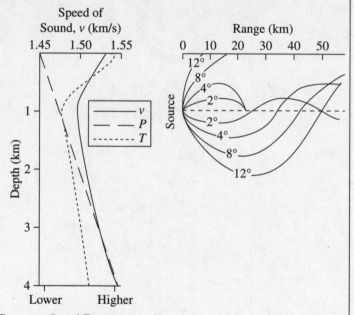

Figure 1 Speed of sound in water

The refraction of sound waves in water tends to bend their path from regions of high sound speed to regions of low sound speed. Sound emitted from a point at depth y can travel along several different paths. These paths tend to maximally intersect at depth y every 50–60 km in convergence zones. Between these areas at depth y are regions of low sound pressure level called shadow zones.

Inverted echo sounders are devices placed on the ocean bottom at a known depth that emit sound waves to the surface. The time for the sound wave to return can be used to calculate the temperature of the water column.

47. Which of the following is true about the propagation of sound waves underwater?

    A. Intensity increases with distance.
    B. Amplitude is parallel to displacement.
    C. Velocity is independent of water density.
    D. Waves can refract but not reflect.

48. An inverted echo sounder receives a sound signal after 3.0×10^2 msec. What is the approximate depth?

    A. 100 m
    B. 225 m
    C. 450 m
    D. 900 m

49. Compared to freshwater, sound in saltwater will travel faster due mostly to which variable?

    A. bulk modulus
    B. intensity level
    C. density
    D. frequency

50. What is the approximate minimum sound pressure detected by humans underwater?

    A. 100 µPa
    B. 700 µPa
    C. 3000 µPa
    D. 12000 µPa

51. A distant underwater explosion is detected at a depth of 1,000 m as a series of increasingly loud, intermittent signals. What was the most likely initial propagation angle of the loudest signal?

    A. 2°
    B. 4°
    C. 8°
    D. 12°

52. Based on information in the passage, the speed of sound in water is:

    A. constant above a depth of 3,000 m.
    B. directly proportional to the density of water.
    C. mostly temperature dependent up to 1,000 m depth.
    D. a maximum near the surface.

53. A submarine with constant velocity sends out an active sonar sound directly ahead that reflects off a whale. Which of the following is known?

    A. The whale is at the same depth as the submarine.
    B. The return sonar sound will be observed at a higher frequency.
    C. The distance between the submarine and whale is decreasing.
    D. The whale is in a convergence zone of the sonar sound.

Passage VIII (Questions 54–60)

Bone has physical properties allowing it to resist both stretching and squeezing forces. Collagen fibers provide tensile strength and calcium salts provide compression strength. However, given enough longitudinal pressure known as stress (σ), bone will undergo strain (ε), a change in length divided by its initial length. These changes are reversible up to a point known as the elastic yield (y). Beyond this point, the bone enters a zone of plasticity where changes in structure are permanent. The bone will withstand these changes up to the ultimate yield (u) point where it breaks apart. Hooke's law governs the elastic properties of bone:

$$\sigma = (E)(\varepsilon)$$

where E is the elastic modulus. When graphed, the area under this function represents work.

An experiment subjects a series of bones to various longitudinal compressions and records the findings. The data are presented in Table 1.

Table 1 Stress and strain on bone

Bone	σ_y (MPa)	ε_y (%)	σ_u (MPa)	ε_u (%)
1	100	.75	175	3
2	100	1	150	3
3	75	.75	150	2.5
4	75	1	125	2

54. What is the value of E for bone 3?

- A. 10 MPa
- B. 60 MPa
- C. 10 GPa
- D. 60 GPa

55. For a circular long bone, stress is:

- A. indirectly proportional to the length of the bone.
- B. directly proportional to the cross sectional diameter.
- C. inversely proportional to the square of the cross sectional radius.
- D. directly proportional to the volume.

56. Which of the following best describes the elastic region of a plot of stress vs. strain?

- A. Linear with a negative slope
- B. Linear with a positive slope
- C. Nonlinear with a negative slope
- D. Nonlinear with a positive slope

57. What are the units of E?

- A. Nm
- B. Nm^2
- C. Nm^{-1}
- D. Nm^{-2}

58. Which of the following represents a comparison of bone 1 and bone 3 from the experiment in the passage?

A.

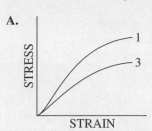

B.

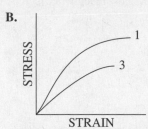

C.

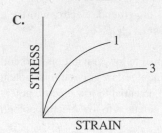

D.

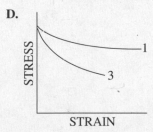

59. Which bone from the passage requires the most energy input to reach the elastic yield point?

A. 1
B. 2
C. 3
D. 4

60. What is the maximum compression force that bone 2 can withstand before permanent structural changes occur if the cross sectional diameter is 4 cm?

A. $(4 \times 10^4)\pi$ N
B. $(2 \times 10^4)\pi$ N
C. $(4 \times 10^2)\pi$ N
D. $(2 \times 10^2)\pi$ N

61. Which of the following is true when lift acts on an airplane wing?

    A.   Volume of airflow is lesser beneath the wing.
    B.   Velocity of airflow is greater beneath the wing.
    C.   Distance of airflow is greater on top of the wing.
    D.   Rate of airflow is greater on top of the wing.

62. What is the direction of magnetic force acting on the electron passing through the magnetic field (B) directed into the plane below?

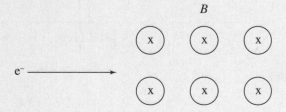

    A.   ↑
    B.   ↓
    C.   →
    D.   ←

63. Modifying all of the following will increase gauge pressure EXCEPT:

    A.   density of the surrounding fluid.
    B.   density of the submerged object.
    C.   gravitational acceleration.
    D.   depth.

64. A 4,000 kg vehicle traveling at 25 m/s decelerates to a stop over a distance of 100 m. How much work is done on the car by the brakes?

    A. 1.25×10^3 kJ
    B. 2.5×10^3 kJ
    C. 5.0×10^3 kJ
    D. 1.25×10^4 kJ

65. When lightning strikes the ground, electrons in the cloud move spontaneously from a region of:

    A.   low electric potential to low gravitational potential.
    B.   high electric potential to low gravitational potential.
    C.   high gravitational potential to low electric potential.
    D.   low gravitational potential to low electric potential.

Chapter 8
Physics Practice:
Answers and Explanations

1.   **C**   The potential energy stored in a capacitor (PE) can be calculated by:

$$PE = \frac{1}{2}CV^2$$

$$PE = \frac{1}{2}(6.0 \times 10^{-5} \text{ F})(2 \times 10^3 \text{ V})^2$$

$$PE = \frac{1}{2}(6.0 \times 10^{-5} \text{ F})(4 \times 10^6 \text{ V}) = 120 \text{ J}$$

2.   **A**   Since the same defibrillator is being used in both patients, the capacitance does not change (C is wrong). The question states the energy is constant, so the voltage required to achieve this energy is also constant (B is wrong). Impedance is resistance of alternating current, and this is a factor of the patient and not the device (D is wrong). The device adjusts the length of the shock. If charge (q) and voltage (V) remain constant but resistance (R) changes, then current (I) and therefore time (t) must change according to Ohm's law:

$$V = IR = \left(\frac{q}{t}\right)R$$

3.   **B**   As the capacitor in Figure 1 is charged, positive charge builds on the upper plate and negative charge builds on the lower plate. The plate with positive charges will have higher electric potential. The capacitor discharges when the switch is activated. Current flows spontaneously from high potential to low potential (A and C are wrong). As current is the direction that positive charge flows, it will be clockwise in the diagram (C and D are wrong).

4.   **A**   The passage states that biphasic defibrillators are able to produce equivalent current at lower energy levels. Therefore, the capacitor in such a device could be smaller (A is correct), and would take less time to charge (D is wrong), thereby increasing battery life (C is wrong). Biphasic devices would be expected to have lower peak currents, as seen in Figure 2, because they operate at lower energy levels (B is wrong).

5.   **B**   Although the capacitance (C), charge (q), and potential energy (PE) of the capacitor would double with a doubling of the dielectric constant, the potential difference or voltage across the plates would not change. Provided there is no dielectric breakdown, the voltage of a fully charged capacitor will equal the voltage of the direct current source that supplies it. Voltage does not change in this scenario.

6. A   The potential energy stored in a capacitor (*PE*) can be calculated by any of the following:

$$PE= \frac{1}{2}QV = \frac{1}{2}\cdot\frac{Q^2}{C} = \frac{1}{2}CV^2$$

A change in the energy level of the capacitor has no effect on the capacitance (C is wrong). Since capacitance does not change, we can see the effect on *V* using the formula $PE = (0.5)CV^2$. Decreasing energy by a factor of 4 decreases the voltage required to achieve that energy by a factor of 2.

Passage II (Questions 7–12)

7. C   The passage describes the force of gravity ($F_G = mg$) and buoyant force ($F_B = \rho Vg$) actions upon a lever arm, *GZ*, to produce a righting moment (torque) that tends to rotate the boat upright. Looking at Figure 1, both F_G and F_B act upon *GZ* to rotate the boat upright. The magnitude of the torque, $\tau = F \times$ (lever arm) can be calculated using any point along the lever arm as the axis of rotation:
Axis at the center of *GZ*: $\tau = \rho Vg(GZ/2) + mg(GZ/2)$
Axis about *G*: $\tau = \rho Vg(GZ)$
Axis about *Z*: $\tau = mg(GZ)$

8. A   The passage states that wind causes a sailboat to rock to the side, and the righting moment (torque) acts to rock the boat back upright. Any effect that increases the righting moment will cause the sailboat to return toward a neutral position faster. Decreasing the lever arm *GZ* will decrease this torque and *increase* the time it takes the ship to roll back upright (A is correct and B is wrong). Adding mass to the bottom of the boat will lower *G* in the neutral position and subsequently increase the length of *GZ* when the boat is heeled, thus increasing righting moment and decreasing the time of the roll (C is wrong). Widening the boat without changing *G* will shift B_1 further lateral when the boat is heeled and also increase *GZ* (D is wrong). Intuitively, things that are wide and bottom heavy tend to turn upright faster when placed in water.

9. B   According to Figure 2, the slope of the *GZ* curve is greater for boat *x* than boat *y*. For any given angle of heel, a longer righting arm (and thus a stronger righting moment) is generated in boat *x* to help return to an upright position. Another way of saying this is that it requires more wind to push boat *x* over to any particular angle of heel. Both concepts dictate that boat *x* is overall more stable to the wind. Stability can come from a variety of factors (including either a low *G* or greater width), but there is not enough information to chose one over the other (A and C are wrong). A narrow hull would be expected to decrease stability by limiting maximum *GZ* distance (D is wrong).

10. **B** Shifting mass will have no effect on the magnitude of buoyancy because overall displacement will not change (A is wrong). Increasing wind will tend to increase the angle of heel and vice versa. According to Figure 2, *GZ* might be increased by either an increase or decrease in wind depending where on the *GZ* curve the boat is at the time of the wind change (C and D are wrong). Shifting mass to the high side of a heeled boat will shift the center of gravity toward the high side, increasing *GZ* and stability. Intuitively, if wind were pushing a boat over on its side, one would climb toward the higher side to attempt to turn the boat back upright.

11. **B** An anchor sinks, so its mass is greater than the mass of water it displaces when it is thrown in the water. When the anchor is removed from the pool and placed into the boat, it floats as part of the overall new mass of the boat. Therefore, buoyant force on the boat increases as a result of an increased amount of water displaced. The increased displacement will cause the water level in the pool to rise (A is wrong and B is correct). When the anchor is placed in the boat, the positions of *G* and *B* cannot be predicted without knowing where the anchor is placed relative to the initial *G* (C and D are wrong).

12. **C** The mass and centers of gravity (*G*) of the boats are constant and they will still float. Therefore, the force of gravity ($F_G = m_{boat}g$) is still equal to buoyant force ($F_B = \rho_{water}V_{water}g$), and both do not change (C is correct). Since ρ_{water} increases and F_B is constant, then only the displacement V'_{water} must decrease (A is wrong). The boats both sit higher out of the water, causing *B* to approach the waterline (B is wrong) and *G* to move higher from the waterline (D is wrong).

Passage III (Questions 13–18)

13. **B** The index of refraction for air is essentially 1, the same as a vacuum. All other materials have a higher *n* (A and C are wrong). Total internal reflection can only happen when light attempts to go from a medium of higher to lower *n* (D is wrong and B is correct).

14. **D** Theoretically, light rays are transmitted down a fiber optic cable without changing their angle of reflection. When the ray in Figure 1 reaches the end of the cable, it will strike the core-air interface with an incident angle of R to the normal. As it passes from n_1 back to the *n* of air, it will be refracted away from the normal at an angle *I*, the same angle as it entered.

15. A   Light passing into a medium with a different n refracts according to Snell's law of refraction:

$$n_1 \sin\theta_1 = n_2 \sin\theta_2$$

The light ray in Figure 1 strikes the interface between n_1 and n_2 at the minimum angle required for total internal reflection, just beyond the *critical angle*. At the critical angle, no light passes into the cladding (n_2) and it is refracted along the surface of the interface such that $\theta_2 = 90°$. As the reflected angle θ must be larger than the critical angle (in order to achieve total internal reflection), Snell's law can be used to approximate its value:

$$n_1 \sin\theta = n_2 \sin(90)$$
$$\sin\theta = \frac{n_2}{n_1}\sin(90) = \frac{n_2}{n_1}(1) = \frac{n_2}{n_1}$$
$$\theta = \sin^{-1}\frac{n_2}{n_1}$$

16. D   The passage states that I equals one-half the cone of acceptance angle. Therefore, the acceptance angle is found by solving the numerical aperture formula for I and multiplying it by 2:

$$\sin I = \sqrt{n_1^2 - n_2^2}$$
$$I = \sin^{-1}\sqrt{n_1^2 - n_2^2}$$
$$\text{Acceptance Angle} = 2I = 2\sin^{-1}\sqrt{n_1^2 - n_2^2}$$
$$\text{Acceptance Angle} = 2\sin^{-1}\sqrt{(1.5)^2 - (1.2)^2}$$

17. D   Fiber optic transmission depends on total internal reflection, so the index of refraction of the core must exceed the index of refraction of the cladding (A is wrong). Figure 2 shows that for a wavelength of 1.6 μm, DZ-9 demonstrates the highest percent reflectance. Therefore, DZ-9 is the best cladding for this wavelength (B is wrong). BR-6 is a better core material than L-3 because it has less attenuation according to Table 1 (C is wrong and D is correct).

18. D   The core has a high n in the center that gradually decreases toward the cross-sectional circumference. Therefore, as a light ray travels from the central axis toward the cladding, it will bend *away* from the normal as it encounters a lower n. This will act to bend or focus the rays over time toward the center, reducing dispersion (B is wrong), decreasing the number of reflections off the cladding (C is wrong), and gradually increasing the angles of reflection (from the normal) of the rays that strike the cladding (D is correct). The critical angle is a function of the two indices of refraction at their interface and this will not change during transmission (A is wrong).

19. C The speed of sound depends on the compressibility and density of the medium. The speed of sound increases with increasing resistance to compression and decreasing density of the medium. In general, the resistance to compression will be most important when considering media of different phases, and density is typically considered between two media of the same phase. There are exceptions. However, in general, sound travels much faster in solids than liquids or gases.

20. D The velocity of the object is to the right, but since it is slowing down, there must be some component of acceleration to the left (A is wrong). Likewise, some component of net force must be pointing to the left as well for the object to slow down (B is wrong). Momentum ($p = mv$) is always in the same direction as velocity (C is wrong). Total work represents the change in total energy. Since the object is slowing down, kinetic energy is decreasing and work must be negative.

21. D Electrostatic forces are governed by Coulomb's law:

$$F_E = k\frac{q_1 q_2}{r^2}$$

where k is a constant, q is charge, and r is the distance between the charges. In this case, distance is increasing by a factor of 4, so the force will decrease by a factor of 16.

22. A Initially, the Ping-Pong ball is submerged in both water and air. The initial buoyant force is from both water and air and equal to the displaced weight of both of these media. When air is replaced with oil, the weight of displaced oil will exceed that of air. Therefore, overall buoyant force will increase and the ball will move up.

23. C For an object with mass m on an inclined plane at an angle θ, the gravitational force is mg straight down, the component down the plane (F_P) is $mg\sin(\theta)$, and the normal force (F_N) is $mg\cos(\theta)$. At this point, the force of static friction (F_f) just opposes F_P.

$$F_f = F_P$$
$$\mu_s F_N = mg\sin\theta$$
$$\mu_s mg\cos\theta = mg\sin\theta$$
$$\mu_s = \frac{mg\sin\theta}{mg\cos\theta} = \frac{\sin\theta}{\cos\theta} = \tan\theta$$

Passage IV (Questions 24–29)

24. **B**   Since all the wheels have the same ω, the wheel with the greatest I will have the greatest kinetic energy, because $KE_{rot} = (1/2)I\omega^2$. Since all the wheels have the same dimensions, the equation $I = (1/2)MR^2$ implies that the wheel with the greatest mass will have the greatest I. But again, because the dimensions are the same, the wheel with the greatest mass will be the one with the greatest density. This is brass, according to Table 1.

25. **C**   The passage states that "the more mass on the average that is located farther from the axis [of rotation], the greater the moment of inertia." Since each wheel has the same overall mass, Wheel C has the most mass located farther from the axis (which, as in Figure 1, is perpendicular to the face of the wheel, through its center).

26. **C**   The greater the density of the material, the greater the mass (or, equivalently, the inertia) of any portion, or "chunk," of the wheel. If the molecular bonds are not strong enough to provide the necessary centripetal force to move the "chunk" in a circular path, the material breaks. (Each "chunk" has the tendency to move in a straight line due to its inertia.)

27. **D**   The passage states, "In theory, the amount of energy that can be stored is maximized when the ratio $[\sigma/\rho]$ is maximized...." Therefore, it is reasonable to conclude that the amount of energy that can be stored is *minimized* when this ratio is *smallest*. Of the materials listed in Table 1, iron has the smallest σ/ρ ratio.

28. **D**   Because the end of the transfer is the motion of the car, the sequence must end with kinetic energy, so eliminate choice B, and since the transfer begins at the power source (which is an *electric* power source, as stated in the last paragraph of the passage), eliminate choices A and C. The answer must be D, consistent with the description in the last paragraph of the passage.

29. **B**   Centripetal acceleration is $v^2/R = (\omega R)^2/R = \omega^2 R$. Therefore, $a_c = \omega^2 R = (20 \text{ rad/s})^2(0.5 \text{ m}) = 200 \text{ m/s}^2$.

Passage V (Questions 30–35)

30. **C**   The peak at 100 Hz corresponds to the resonance frequency of the speaker. The cone vibrates most readily at this point which will cause a maximum vibratory amplitude. The result of this is an increase in the *induced* potential created by moving a wire through a magnetic field. This is the back-EMF, and it generates an increased impedance (I is wrong and II is correct, so only C can be correct). As frequency increases from the resonance frequency, vibratory amplitude decreases (III is correct).

31.   A   According to the formula for sound intensity level (β):

$$\beta = 10\log_{10}\frac{I}{I_0}$$

every multiple increase of 10 W/m² in sound intensity (I) results in an addition of 10 dB of intensity level (β). In this case, the sound intensity is multiplied by 2. Therefore, the intensity level increase must be less than 10.

32.   A   Focusing on the top part of the speaker coil, current will flow into the plane of the page when it flows clockwise. The magnetic field is directed straight down from the N to S pole of the permanent magnet. Using the right-hand rule with the thumb in the direction of current and the fingertips in the direction of magnetic field, the palm will point in the direction of F_B—in this case, left (A is correct and B is wrong). The back-EMF will increase or decrease only when the current from the amplifier increases or decreases, so this cannot be predicted (C and D are wrong).

33.   B   Information from the passage and the problem should be substituted into a familiar formula for electric power:

$$P = IV \text{ and } F_B = ILB$$
$$P = \frac{F_B}{LB}V$$
$$P = \frac{F_B(50 \text{ V})}{LB}$$
$$P = \frac{50F_B}{LB}$$

Note that the factor of 100 seconds is not needed to determine power, which is a rate.

34.   C   A current generates a surrounding magnetic field. The direction is determined using the right-hand rule. The thumb goes in the direction of current, and the fingers curl around an open palm to show the direction of magnetic field. If this is done on each ring of the coil, overall the magnetic fields will form a net movement from left to right within the coil itself.

35.　A　Back-EMF is an induced potential caused by the movement of a wire through a magnetic field. Even when disconnected, a loudspeaker can generate electricity by manually moving the coil back and forth across the permanent magnet. When the loudspeaker is plugged in, current flows through the coil resulting in some F_B. As the coil moves in response to F_B, back-EMF will be induced and produce a current in the opposite direction. Therefore, anything that increases F_B or the movement of the cone itself will increase back-EMF. Decreasing B and I will decrease F_B and back-EMF (B and D are wrong). Increasing the mass of the speaker cone will make it harder to move back and forth, thus decreasing back-EMF (C is wrong). Increasing the loops in the coil will increase F_B by increasing L and therefore increase back-EMF (A is correct).

Freestanding Questions 36–40

36.　B　Note that the angles θ and θ' are not defined with respect to the normal of the surface; instead, θ is the complement of the angle of incidence and θ' is the complement of the angle of refraction. By Snell's law, with $n = 1$ for air, we have $\sin \theta_1 = n \sin \theta_2$, where θ_1 is the angle of incidence and θ_2 is the angle of refraction. Because $\sin \theta_1 = \cos \theta$ and $\sin \theta_2 = \cos \theta'$, Snell's law in this case becomes $\cos \theta = n \cos \theta'$.

37.　D　For a converging lens, the focal length (f) and object distance (o) are positive. Using the lens equation to solve for the image distance (i) on a very distance object yields:

$$\frac{1}{o} + \frac{1}{i} = \frac{1}{f}$$
$$\frac{1}{\infty} + \frac{1}{i} = \frac{1}{f}$$
$$0 + \frac{1}{i} = \frac{1}{f}$$
$$i \approx f$$

The image forms on the focal length (A and B are wrong). Since i is positive, it is a real (A and C are wrong), inverted image. Since the object is moving away from the Earth, the effective wavelength of light will be lengthened, shifting the frequency to the red end of the visual spectrum (C is wrong).

38.　C　The problem is best solved with a kinematic equation for displacement:

$$x = \frac{1}{2}(v_0 + v)t$$
$$x = \frac{1}{2}(0 + 25 \tfrac{m}{s})(5 \text{ s}) = 62.5 \text{ m}$$

39.   **B**   First, solve for the total resistance by adding the inverse of the resistors in parallel:

$$\frac{1}{R_T} = \frac{1}{R_1} + \frac{1}{R_2} + \frac{1}{R_3}$$

$$\frac{1}{R_T} = \frac{1}{4\ \Omega} + \frac{1}{4\ \Omega} + \frac{1}{4\ \Omega}$$

$$\frac{1}{R_T} = \frac{3}{4\ \Omega}$$

$$R_T = 4/3\ \Omega$$

Next, solve for the total current in the circuit using Ohm's law. One third of this total current will travel through each of the equivalent resistors in parallel:

$$V_T = I_T R_T$$

$$I_T = V_T / R_T = 12\ \text{V}/(4/3\ \Omega) = 9\ \text{A}$$

$$I_{3\Omega\ \text{resistor}} = 3\text{A}$$

40.   **B**   The index of refraction of all media other than a vacuum is greater than 1, with air being very close to 1. The result is that the speed of light decreases when traveling into media with a greater index of refraction, like water (D is wrong). Although the speed changes, the frequency, and hence the wavelength, stay the same (A and C are wrong).

Passage VI (Questions 41–46)

41.   **A**   In a perfectly inelastic collision, the two masses stick together. Momentum is conserved, but the law of conservation of momentum is not needed in this problem because the initial velocity of the pendulum after the collision is given. Total mechanical energy is always conserved, so the initial kinetic energy of the block will equal the potential energy at maximum height:

$$KE_i = PE_f$$

$$\frac{1}{2}(m_b + m_p)v_p^2 = (m_b + m_p)gh$$

$$\frac{1}{2}v_p^2 = gh$$

$$h = \frac{v_p^2}{2g}$$

42.   C   At any given time in motion, the force of gravity (mg) can be broken into two components:

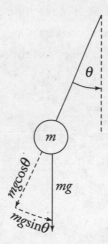

Centripetal force is always directed toward the center of the circular motion. In this case, it will be the vector addition of the tension on the string and the component of gravitational force that is perpendicular to the tangent of motion, $T - mg\cos\theta$.

43.   B   Simple harmonic motion involves the oscillation of an object where acceleration is proportional to and in the opposite direction of the displacement from an equilibrium point. The more the object is brought from this equilibrium point, the greater the magnitude of acceleration. Therefore, it cannot be constant (A and C are wrong). For a pendulum, acceleration comes from the center of gravity, which has components that are parallel and perpendicular to the tangent of arc motion (D is wrong).

44.   D   In a perfectly elastic collision, the objects bounce apart after hitting each other and both momentum and total kinetic energy are conserved. After being hit by the bullet, the wood will obtain a kinetic energy allowing it to reach height h. The initial velocity of the bullet can be found using a combination of conservation of energy and momentum. First, the conservation of momentum (note the initial velocity of the wood $u_p = 0$):

$$p_i = p_f$$
$$m_b u_b + m_p u_p = m_b v_b + m_p v_p$$
$$u_b = \frac{m_b v_b + m_p v_p}{m_b}$$

Next, apply conservation of energy:

$$KE_{p\ initial} = PE_{p\ final}$$
$$\frac{1}{2} m_p v_p^2 = m_p g h$$
$$v_p = \sqrt{2gh}$$

Finally, substitute in for v_p:

$$u_b = \frac{m_b v_b + m_p v_p}{m_b}$$
$$u_b = \frac{m_b v_b + m_p \sqrt{2gh}}{m_b}$$

Note that once it is realized that masses will not cancel, immediate attention to the location of m_b in the denominator would solve the problem.

45.   B   When x(t) = A, the pendulum is at maximum displacement from its equilibrium point and this results in the maximum tendency to return there. As long as the angle is small enough, a pendulum will approximate simple harmonic motion where the only factor determining f is the length of the pendulum (A is wrong). The units of γ are radians (C is wrong) based on the factor of π in the equations; radians = (degrees)(π/180). Finally, a(t) is always in the opposite direction as x(t), not v(t) (D is wrong). When the pendulum is returning to equilibrium from maximum displacement, a and v are in the same direction.

46.   B   First, solve for f as the inverse of T:

$$T = 2\pi\sqrt{\frac{L}{g}}$$

$$f = \frac{1}{T} = \frac{1}{2\pi}\sqrt{\frac{g}{L}}$$

$$f = \frac{1}{2\pi}\sqrt{\frac{10}{2.5}} = \frac{1}{2\pi}\sqrt{4} = \frac{1}{\pi}$$

Looking at figure 1, velocity will be a minimum whenever it is at greatest displacement, $x(t) = A$, and a maximum at the equilibrium point, $x(t) = 0$. Since this is simple harmonic motion, any $x = 0$ point can be used to find the maximum magnitude of velocity. The simplest point is when $t = 0$, because according to the passage, this makes $\gamma = 0$ and simplifies the formula for $v(t)$:

$$v(t) = A(2\pi f)\cos(2\pi ft + \gamma)$$
$$v(t) = A(2\pi f)\cos(0)$$
$$v(t) = A(2\pi f)(1)$$
$$v(t) = (0.1\ \text{m})(2)(\pi)(1/\pi\ \text{sec}^{-1}) = 0.2\ \text{m/s}$$

Passage VII (Questions 47–53)

47.   B   Sound traveling in a gaseous or fluid medium is a longitudinal compression wave. Therefore, amplitude is parallel to displacement (B is correct). Intensity of sound will always dissipate with displacement (A is wrong). According to the equation in the passage, the speed of sound is inversely proportional to the square root of density (C is wrong). Given that an inverted echo sounder functions the way it does, sound can refract and reflect underwater (D is wrong).

48.   B   Using the speed of sound in water as approximately 1,500 m/s:

$$v = \frac{d}{t}$$
$$d = vt = (1{,}500\ \text{m/s})(0.3\ \text{s}) = 450\ \text{m}$$

This is the distance to travel to the surface and back to the ocean floor. Therefore, the depth is half of this, or 225 m.

49. **A**   According to the first equation in the passage, sound is directly proportional to the square root of bulk modulus and inversely proportional to the square root of density. If sound travels faster in saltwater, than the salinity must increase K more than it increases ρ (C is wrong). Intensity level and frequency do not determine velocity (B and D are wrong).

50. **C**   The passage states that the threshold of underwater human hearing is about 70 dB. Therefore,

$$\text{dB SPL} = 20\log_{10}\frac{P}{P_{ref}} = 70$$

$$\log_{10}\frac{P}{P_{ref}} = \frac{70}{20} = 3.5$$

$$\log_{10}\frac{P}{1\,\mu\text{Pa}} = 3.5$$

$$P = 10^{3.5} \cdot 1\,\mu\text{Pa} = 10^{3.5}\,\mu\text{Pa}$$

Because $10^{3.5}$ must be between 10^3 and 10^4, the only possible answer choice is 3,000 µPa, corresponding to 69.5 dB SPL. Note that the answer must represent 3 orders of magnitude difference over baseline, and only one answer choice is then possible.

51. **A**   As illustrated in Figure 1, sound can travel along many different paths. The various angles refract and bend to a region of lower sound speed. This phenomenon is responsible for a column at a depth of approximately 1,000 m called the SOFAR channel, where sound can be efficiently transmitted for thousands of kilometers and is possibly used by humpback whales to communicate. Although the sound path closest to the axis of depth represents the shortest distance, it is the region of slowest speed. Therefore, it will arrive last. Note that without any math, the answer must represent one of the extremes of the choices (B and C are wrong).

52. **C**   The speed of sound increases with increasing pressure, temperature, and salinity. According to Figure 1, the effect of pressure does not overcome the primary temperature dependence until about 1,000 m depth (C is correct). The speed of sound increases past a depth of 3,000 m (A is wrong) and is inversely proportional to density (B is wrong). Finally, according to Figure 1, the speed of sound eventually exceeds near-surface speeds given enough depth (D is wrong).

53. **B**   Regardless of how the whale is moving, the submarine will run into the reflected sonar signal waves, giving them a higher observed frequency due to the Doppler effect. As sound waves refract considerably, the whale does not have to be at the same depth (A is wrong) and does not have to be at a maximum constructive interference zone to be hit by some of the sonar sound waves (D is wrong). Not enough information is provided to determine the relative distance between the submarine and whale (C is wrong).

54.   C   Elastic modulus, or Young's modulus, is the ratio of stress to strain. This can be derived from Hooke's law in the passage. Stress is given in units of pressure in Table 1, but strain is given as a percentage. This percentage must be converted to a ratio of change in length over initial length. Elastic modulus governs stress and strain up to the yield point, so the values of σ_y and ε_y are used.

$$\sigma = E\varepsilon$$
$$E = \frac{\sigma}{\varepsilon} = \frac{F/A}{\Delta L/L_0}$$
$$E = \frac{75\text{ MPa}}{0.75\text{ \%}} = \frac{75\text{ MPa}}{0.75/100} = \frac{75\text{ MPa}}{7.5 \times 10^{-3}}$$
$$E = 10 \times 10^3\text{ MPa} = 10\text{ GPa}$$

55.   C   Stress is a pressure, which is force divided by area. Therefore, stress is inversely proportional to cross sectional area, which in this case is a circle. Since the area of a circle is given by $A = \pi r^2$, stress is also inversely proportional to the square of the cross sectional radius of the bone.

56.   B   The initial compression or tension on a substance is the elastic phase governed by Hooke's law: $\sigma = E\varepsilon$. This is a linear relationship (C and D are wrong), and the slope will be E. The change in length will always be in the same direction as the force causing the stress, so the ratio is positive (A is wrong).

57.   D   Elastic (Young's) modulus is the ratio of stress (a pressure) to strain (ratio of change in length to original length):

$$E = \frac{\sigma}{\varepsilon} = \frac{P}{\Delta L/L_0} = \frac{F/A}{\Delta L/L_0} = \frac{\text{N/m}^2}{\text{m/m}} = \text{Nm}^{-2}$$

58. **B** Bone 1 has higher elastic yield (y) and ultimate yield (u) points. Bone 3 has a shorter plasticity region. Plotting (ε_y, σ_y) and (ε_u, σ_u) for each bone gives:

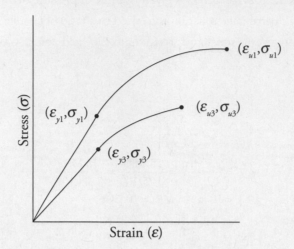

59. **B** The passage states that the area under the graph of stress vs. strain represents work, and work is defined as the change in energy of a system. The question asks only about the elastic portion, which will be a linear relationship according to Hooke's law. The area under this line will be a triangle:

$$Area = \frac{1}{2}(base)(height)$$
$$Area = \frac{1}{2}(\varepsilon_y)(\sigma_y)$$

Therefore, the bone with the largest value of $(\varepsilon_y)(\sigma_y)$, bone 2, will require the most energy to reach the elastic yield point.

60. **A** The elastic yield point defines when permanent changes in bone structure will occur. For bone 2, this requires a stress of 100 MPa. The cross sectional diameter is 4 cm, which gives a cross sectional radius (r) of 2 cm or 0.02 m.

$$\sigma = \frac{F}{A}$$
$$F = \sigma A = \sigma \pi r^2$$
$$F = (100 \text{ MPa})(\pi)(0.02 \text{ m})^2$$
$$F = (100 \times 10^6 \text{ Pa})(\pi)(4 \times 10^{-4} \text{ m}^2)$$
$$F = (1 \times 10^8 \text{ N/m}^2)(\pi)(4 \times 10^{-4} \text{ m}^2)$$
$$F = (\pi)(4 \times 10^4 \text{ N})$$

61.   C   In laminar fluid motion, flow (Q) is constant and is equal to the volume of fluid flow per unit time (A and D are equivalent answers and both wrong). A wing is curved presenting an angle of attack to the wind with convexity on the top of the wing and concavity on the bottom. Therefore, air must travel further over the wing than under the wing. If flow ($Q = Av$) remains constant, then velocity must increase over the wing (B is wrong) compared to under the wing. This creates a region of high pressure under the wing and low pressure over the wing and lift occurs.

62.   B   The direction of magnetic force generated from a magnetic field acting on a moving charged particle is obtained from the right-hand rule. The fingers are placed in the direction of the magnetic field (B) and the thumb is placed in the direction of a positively charged moving particle. The palm will point in the direction of magnetic force. The question asks about an electron, so either use the left hand in the same fashion or reverse the finding for a positive particle.

63.   B   Gauge pressure is given by: $P_g = \rho_{fluid}gD$, where D is depth. Therefore, the pressure is independent of the density of the object submerged.

64.   A   When the vehicle is moving along the earth, its only energy is kinetic energy. When it is stopped, its total energy is zero. Because work represents the change in total energy, it will be equivalent to the starting kinetic energy:

$$KE = \frac{1}{2}mv^2$$
$$KE = \frac{1}{2}(4 \times 10^3 \text{kg})(25 \text{ m/s})^2$$
$$KE = (2 \times 10^3 \text{kg})(625 \text{ m/s}) = 1.25 \times 10^3 \text{kJ}$$

65.   A   For gravity, higher potential means higher off the ground. For electricity, higher potential is always defined as the area of positive charge. When lightning strikes, electrons move spontaneously from a region of high gravitational potential to low gravitational potential (D is wrong). In addition, because it is spontaneous, the electrons travel naturally toward a region of positive charge. In this case, the ground is at a higher electric potential.

Part III:
Verbal Reasoning
on the MCAT

Chapter 9
Overview of
Verbal Reasoning

VERBAL REASONING STRUCTURE AND SCORING

Verbal Reasoning is the second section of the MCAT. There are 40 total questions with a time limit of 60 minutes. There will be 7 passages accompanied by related questions. Passages typically contain between 5 and 7 associated questions.

The Verbal Reasoning section is scored on a scale of 1–15. Each individual question is associated with a level of difficulty. The raw score is the number of individual questions answered correctly. This raw score is converted into a scaled score taking into account the difficulty level of the questions on the test form. You should note that while the scaled score is based on the difficulty of the questions, this doesn't mean that the difficult ones are worth any more than the easier ones. As on the science sections of the test, you should first do all questions on which it is easiest for you to scoop up raw points. Then do the questions that are more difficult for you, and be sure to fill in an answer for every question. There is no penalty for guessing. Not all of the items on a particular test form will be scored. Those items not scored likely include questions that are problematic for scaling or are in the exam for test development purposes. As it is not possible to accurately predict these items, treat all questions as if they will be scored.

All Scores are Not Created Equal

When you decided you might like to be a doctor and embarked on the premed path, you probably did so out of a love of science, not the written word. But apparently, the AAMC feels that reading comprehension, in addition to all that science knowledge, is pretty important. In fact, most medical colleges consider Verbal Reasoning to be the most important of the sections and thus weight the Verbal Reasoning score more heavily. To make this point more concrete, let's briefly examine two hypothetical students, both scoring a composite of 30.

Student A:	Physical Sciences	10
	Verbal Reasoning	10
	Biological Sciences	10
Student B:	Physical Sciences	11
	Verbal Reasoning	7
	Biological Sciences	12

All else being equal, the majority of medical colleges will select student A. So, if you happen to be in the minority of premed students who also loves to read on topics beyond the medical and scientific spheres, then consider yourself lucky. However, if you would rather study the nephron than read the novels of Dostoevsky,

Loans for Med School, Part I

There are many different kinds of loans available:

- Federal
- State
- Private
- Charitable
- Institutional

Source: *Best 168 Medical Schools*, 2008

do not despair. There are good readers and there are smart readers; this book is designed to get you on the path to being a smart reader who can get a respectable verbal score on the MCAT.

The first thing to incorporate into your mindset about the MCAT is that you do not have to be inherently skilled at the Verbal Reasoning section; there is a rhyme and reason behind what the MCAT folks do, and with a little methodology and some hard work, you can get a handle on the Verbal section. Let's analyze some reasons why the AAMC considers this section important.

VERBAL REASONING BASICS

Verbal Reasoning is rather vague terminology for the myriad skills the AAMC is actually testing. In reality, they are looking for three specific skills: comprehension, retention, and application. To be more explicit, they want you to be able to read a passage to which you have had no previous exposure, separate the relevant information from the irrelevant, and then apply the significant information to relevant situations. All of this still begs the question "Why is this so important?" As it turns out, you will in fact spend a great portion of your time in medical school, as well as in your career as a doctor, just reading. The medical colleges want to make sure that you can take those piles and piles of books and articles, understand them, weed out the relevant information from the muck, and apply that knowledge where appropriate. In fact, the Verbal Reasoning section was added to the MCAT in 1991 for explicitly this reason—to figure out how a student handles brand new information without the safety net of formulas and past knowledge.

Pick and Choose your Passages

The Verbal Reasoning section truly is an open-book test. The entire point of this section is to see how well you extrapolate information from the passages. There are no freestanding questions in Verbal Reasoning, only the seven passages mentioned earlier, each of which has a set of five to seven questions. The passages' order of difficulty is random, with a few harder passages among some less strenuous ones. One of the passages is likely to be a killer, so don't be afraid to skip around to find more comfortable passages. Your personal interests can also dictate which passages you attempt first. If the first passage is on a subject that bores you to tears or that you just can't wrap your head around, then move on. That's what that Next button is for. Check out all of the passages first, and then start with the one that is most engaging or makes the most sense.

What will the passages be about? According to the AAMC, the Verbal Reasoning section evaluates your ability to understand, evaluate, and apply information and arguments presented in prose style. Each of the passages is about 600 words long, from areas such as humanities, social sciences, and natural sciences. You could see topics as varied as politics, religion, biology, history, literary criticism, economics, law, animal behavior, and philosophy. Few of the passages will be science-based,

Loans for Med School, Part II
Be wary of commerical financial aid search services. They often charge hefty fees for information that you can find for free in your public, undergrad, and med school libraries.

Source: *Best 168 Medical Schools,* 2008

maybe two at most. Part of why this section is on the test at all is to see how you do with topics that are outside of your decided passion of science and medicine.

A Quick Word on the Sciences

As pointed out at the beginning of this book, some of the questions in the science sections of the test are based on passage information. Briefly, this means that some of the questions in Physical Sciences and Biological Sciences can be answered with little or no prior science knowledge, just some smart reading and test-taking skills. This bit of information is extremely significant for you, because most of the skills and techniques you practice in the Verbal section are just as applicable to the science sections and can, in fact, boost your overall scores. So now you have yet another reason not to blow off the Verbal Reasoning section!

The Good News

Precisely because you have no prior knowledge on which to rely, the Verbal section may seem rather daunting. Be encouraged, however, as there are some perks here! Four major benefits are described below:

1) Everything you need to know is right in front of you

There is no danger of forgetting facts and formulas; all the questions deal with the words on the screen. Finding the information may indeed be a tedious process, but never forget that it is a doable task. You should consider this a plus rather than a minus. It's just like an open-book test!

2) The multiple-choice format makes finding the answer easier

The best thing about multiple-choice tests is that you do not have to know the correct answer; you just have to find and eliminate bad answers. In fact, if you spend your time searching for the right answers on the MCAT, you will be terribly disappointed much of the time. The MCAT is infamous for its less-than-desirable answer choices. It is not always about finding the "right" answer; it is often about eliminating the most egregious nonsense presented to you and picking the best from whatever is left.

3) You get to choose the passages on which you spend your time

There is a lot about the test that you cannot control—the time constraints, the passage content, the format, etc. Don't let the AAMC control everything though. What you do have power over is the order in which you choose to approach the passages. The AAMC does not have your best interests at heart and certainly does not order the passages to your advantage, so be prepared to skip around. You should quickly decide if a passage is doable or ridiculously complex and decide to do it or postpone it accordingly.

If the structure or subject matter is dense and convoluted within the first couple of sentences, it is probably a bad passage on which to spend your time in your first pass through the section. If the questions and answer choices for a given passage are long, again, it is probably not the best passage to tackle first. But be careful and be flexible—a complex passage may be paired with not-so-awful questions and vice-versa. The bottom line is this: Skipping around is to your advantage. You don't want to be in a position in which you run out of time before you have a go at an easy passage that can earn you valuable points. One last note on this topic: You may find through practice that you struggle with a particular type of passage, such as philosophy or literary criticism. Learn about your strengths and weaknesses as you gain experience with different types of passages, and use this knowledge to guide your order of tackling passages on the actual exam.

4) You get to choose the questions on which you spend your time

The question difficulty varies a great deal on the MCAT. Some questions you can answer quite quickly; others can take three minutes of serious contemplation just to eliminate a couple of answer choices. The only consistency is that all the questions are worth the same amount. The bottom line is this: Do not waste three minutes of your time working through a ludicrously tough question that you are just as likely to get right as wrong when you could have spent that time doing three other questions or reading a whole other passage. It takes a little time and practice, but learn to identify tough questions quickly, and then give yourself a gold star for mastering this technique that helps you avoid wasting time.

Practice, Practice, Practice

Okay, so there are no facts or formulas you can memorize to help you through this section of the test, but you can improve with some time and patience. Verbal is typically the hardest section for which to study because it requires more practice, but it's not impossible. If you do enough passages and questions, eventually patterns emerge, trends become clearer, and MCAT's peculiar logic becomes more predictable. Keep an eye on your progress. Know the kinds of passages and questions at which you tend to excel and with which kinds you struggle so that you can pick your battles wisely.

The best conditions for practice are those that are most like the test itself. For additional practice with a simulated CBT interface, visit **PrincetonReview.com** or **www.e-mcat.com**. Get used to the tools that are available online that make your test-taking experience easier, such as the Review screen function, the Highlighting feature that enables you emphasize important pieces of the passages, and the Strikeout option that allows you to cross off incorrect answer choices. You can also use the Mark button to flag questions on which you guessed so that you can return to those questions at the end of the test, if time allows.

Online practice is very effective, but don't forget that some of the tools in the tests at **www.e-mcat.com** do not appear in the actual MCAT, so don't get too attached to your practice-test toolbox. For example, there is no Search feature on the real

Scholarships and Grants
Visit the "Scholarships & Aid" section of **PrincetonReview.com** to find out about any private, state, and institutional scholarships for which you may be eligible.

Source: *Best 168 Medical Schools*, 2008

test, so you have to scan with your eyes to find a word or phrase in a passage. Also, you are not able to insert electronic text notes within a passage. At the actual exam, you will be given scratch paper or a white board so that you will be able to utilize the strategy of annotating the passage (described in more detail in the next chapter, Mastering Verbal Reasoning: Passages and Questions). Finally, there is no Guess box for each question, but instead there is a Mark button to flag the questions you might want to reconsider later.

Timing

It would be convenient if there were a uniform number of questions per passage. Unfortunately, this is not the case. The number of questions varies from passage to passage (typically, 5–7 questions each), presenting a challenge when deciding how to allocate your time. How you attack this section will largely depend on your particular strengths and weaknesses. We have thus presented two possible timing schemes depending on your personality.

1) You perform better when you push yourself through all of the passages and don't over think things too much

Aim for three minutes to read the passage and a little less than one minute per question. A good rule of thumb is number of questions plus two. For example, if a passage has six questions, give yourself approximately eight minutes—three for reading the passage and the remaining five for the questions. It will probably take some time to get down to three minutes for reading the passage, so be prepared to work at it and reduce your time slowly (over weeks, not days).

2) You perform better if you slow down and think things through

Aim for finishing six passages and guessing on one of them. This works out to approximately four minutes to read the passage and about one minute per question. The idea is that the improvement in accuracy will make up for the questions on which you have to guess. If you find that particular questions impede your accuracy (strengthen and weaken questions are typical troublemakers), as an alternative, you may want to attempt all seven passages but skip the questions that tend to pose problems for you.

Both timing schemes are guidelines, of course, not ironclad unbreakable rules. Difficult passages/questions will take longer to get through and easier passages/questions will go faster. Be flexible and treat the timing guidelines as a general structure to keep you in line so that you don't spend twenty minutes on a passage.

Don't hold yourself to unreasonable expectations. Change takes time. You may not intuitively or immediately recognize which scheme is best for you. You may feel somewhat uncomfortable pushing through all seven passages, but it may yield you a better score than slowing down. Conversely, you may feel uneasy letting an entire passage go, but it is all about what gets you the greatest number of points in the end. The point is to do some experimenting before you settle on a system that works for you.

Whichever method you choose, remember that you get to decide the order of the passages and the questions that accompany them. Don't get locked into going through the test in order. The next chapter, Mastering Verbal Reasoning: Passages and Questions, will give you the information you need to be able to choose the passages and questions that play to your strengths.

Chapter 10
Mastering Verbal Reasoning:
Passages and Questions

HANDLING THE PASSAGE

You have two important tools at your disposal when reading the passage—highlighting and annotating. Both tools are intended to enhance your reading of the passage. Before we get into too much detail with those, let's discuss reading in and of itself. You have a limited amount of time to read the passage; you certainly don't have the fifteen or so minutes it would require to completely analyze each detail of the passage, so don't even try. If you find that you read the passage with an eye to understanding every little nuance (for example, you re-read paragraphs if you feel you didn't entirely get them), then you should adjust your approach; you do not have that kind of time. You are reading only to get the main idea of each paragraph and of the passage as a whole. You can come back for the subtleties if and when you are asked a question about them.

The Main Idea

When reading for the main idea, consider the structure of the passage. There are three ways passages are structured:

1) Some authors write exactly the way you and I were taught to write essays, by setting out the thesis at the beginning, then following it up with supportive explanations or details.

2) Other writers like to begin their essays with a lot of examples or explanations that culminate in a main idea at the end.

3) Some authors are less structured, and their main idea is strewn throughout the passage.

If you can identify the author's particular structure, or lack thereof, it will help you decide where to concentrate your efforts in your search for the main idea of the passage.

A final word on the main idea: You may wonder why we stress the main idea so much when there aren't all that many main idea questions on the MCAT. This is true, but many questions are so much easier to deal with if you keep an eye on the big picture. The primary reason for the emphasis is that an understanding of the main idea is indispensable to POE. For most question types, the correct answer will support the main idea of the passage, while answers that give the opposite of the main idea or don't address it are usually incorrect. When in doubt (except on a weaken question), pick the answer that resembles the main idea. Now, let's examine the tools that augment your reading of the passage.

Highlighting

This is a CBT tool available in the testing interface. The primary use of the Highlighting function is to emphasize important pieces of information. So, the relevant question is: What constitutes an important piece of information? The kind of details, evidence, or facts about which the MCAT tends to ask questions should be considered important information, not just anything that happens to be interesting to you personally.

Before we dig deeper into how you will be best served by highlighting, we want to stress that the point of highlighting is not to decorate the passage. Premed students in particular have a penchant for overemphasizing the details and thus over highlight. If you find that after completing a passage, you often have half the screen highlighted, then you are not letting this potentially helpful tool do its job. In other words, you cannot emphasize the crucial information if everything is emphasized. Highlights should be fairly sparse. A good rule of thumb is that if you consistently highlight more than two to three lines per paragraph, then you are overdoing it. So, let's discuss what you should highlight. This falls into four categories.

Words of Emphasis

If the author himself is emphasizing a point, the MCAT folks like to ask a question about it. Here is a comprehensive, but by no means complete, list of words that signal an emphasis.

aim	essential	paramount
basis	fundamental	primary
big (and words like it, such as enormous, giant, etc.)	goal	profound
	important	strong
central	main	valuable
chief	necessary	vital
crucial		

Consider, for example, the following section of a passage and the appropriate highlights:

> Official or state religion consisted in the main of an organisation of popular ritual. There was no priestcraft in Greece, no exclusive caste to whom the worship of the gods was assigned, although, of course, the right to practise certain cults belonged to particular families. But priesthood, as a rule, was a political office like any other magistracy, and there was no exclusive tradition in the case of the chief cults of any Greek states to keep the point of view of the priests different than that of the people generally. The tendency of state religion was, as a rule, conservative, for reasons that we have already noticed; innovations in the matter of ritual are dangerous, for the new rite might not please the gods as well as the old;
>
> Source: *Religion and Art in Ancient Greece* by Ernest A. Gardner

This paragraph is densely packed, but the only really important piece of information is that state religion was all about rituals of the people. The other pieces of information, such as the detail that the priesthood was like any other part of the state, is just to reinforce the original argument.

Let's look at another section from the same source:

> Public commissions of this sort are common of all times, but commonest in the years immediately succeeding the Persian Wars, when the spoils of the Persians supplied ample resources, and in many cases the ancient temples and images had been destroyed; and at the same time the outburst of national enthusiasm over the great deliverance led to a desire to give due thank-offerings to the gods of the Hellenic race, a desire which coincided with the ability to fulfil it, owing to the rapid progress of artistic power. Such public commissions, and the popular feeling which they expressed, offered an inspiration to the artist such as rarely, if ever, found a parallel. But any great victory or deliverance might be commemorated by the setting up of statues of the gods to whom it was attributed; and in this way the demands of official religion offered the sculptor the highest scope for the exercise of his art and his imagination.

There are a lot of long, convoluted sentences, but as long as you identify that public commission to the gods gave sculptors most of their opportunities, the rest of the details should fall into the background, and you have isolated the important (by important, we mean the MCAT will likely ask a question about it) piece of information.

Words of Conclusion

Words of conclusion alert you to the fact that an author is making an important point, and again, the MCAT people like to ask questions about the author's main arguments. Words of conclusion include:

as a result	in conclusion
consequently	therefore
hence	thus

Consider the following portion of a passage:

> Such a formalism implies a very firm belief in the existence of the gods. The dealings of a man with the gods are quite as really reciprocal as his dealings with his fellow citizens. But on the other hand though the existence of the gods is never doubted for a moment, the gods themselves are an unknown quantity; hence out of the formal relationship an intimacy never developed, and while it is scarcely just to characterise the early cult as exclusively a religion of fear, certainly real affection is not present until a much later day. The potentiality of the gods always overshadowed their personality.
>
> Source: *The Religion of Numa* by Jesse Benedict Carter

Though the author goes back and forth a bit, if you can identify the main point, that people didn't feel affectionately toward their gods at this point in time, then you can focus your attention more effectively and not get lost in the minutiae.

Words of Transition

Spotting these words is instrumental in giving you more control over the passage. Transition words help you predict what the author is going to do.

If the author begins a paragraph with a word of "same direction" transition such as one of the following, then she will probably continue to express thoughts in the same vein as in the previous paragraph.

also	in fact
furthermore	moreover
in addition	similarly

Humanities and Social Science Passages
These sometimes call for an understanding of the author's tone or attitude. Frequently, they require an understanding of the sense of a word or phrase that appears in the passage.
Source: *Cracking the MCAT,* 2006

If, on the other hand (see how it works?), she begins a paragraph with a "change direction" transition such as one of the following, then she will most likely reverse or amend the argument she has just made:

although	however
but	still
conversely	yet

There may be too many transitions within any one passage for you to highlight all of them. However, you do want to highlight those that indicate contrasts or a logical shift in the author's argument. Words of transition can help you effectively maneuver between paragraphs. Consider this transition between two paragraphs in a passage:

> The Renaissance, in truth, put forth in France an aftermath, a wonderful later growth, the products of which have to the full that subtle and delicate sweetness which belongs to a refined and comely decadence, just as its earliest phases have the freshness which belongs to all periods of growth in art, the charm of ascêsis, of the austere and serious girding of the loins in youth.

> But it is in Italy, in the fifteenth century, that interest of the Renaissance mainly lies, —in that solemn fifteenth century which can hardly be studied too much, not merely for its positive results in the things of the intellect and the imagination, its concrete works of art, its special and prominent personalities, with their profound aesthetic charm, but for its general spirit and character, for the ethical qualities of which it is a consummate type.

> Source: *The Renaissance: Studies in Art and Poetry* by Walter Horatio Pater

So the first paragraph seems to be saying nice things about the Renaissance in France, even if the author is not writing his opinion very succinctly. But when you get to the second paragraph, the fact that it begins with a "But" should alert you to the fact that the author is going to modify his previous statements in some way. In this case, France may have been great, but Italy is where it's at in terms of the Renaissance.

Within a paragraph, transitions can also be useful. Consider the following paragraph:

> The fact that in modern times drama as well as epic and romantic fiction is usually composed in prose has made some critics dissatisfied with what to them seems to be an unsatisfactory criterion. On the one hand, Wackernagel, who believes that the function of poetry is to convey ideas in concrete and sensuous images and the function of prose to inform the intellect, asserts that prose drama and didactic poetry are inartistic. He thus advocates that present practise be abandoned in favor of the custom of the Greeks. On the other hand Newman, while granting that a metrical garb has in all languages been appropriated to poetry, still urges that the essence of poetry is fiction.
>
> Source: *Rhetoric and Poetry in the Renaissance* by Donald Lemen Clark, Ph.D.

The "on the one hand" and "on the other hand" help the reader elucidate that the intention of the author is to set up a dichotomy between two ways of classifying prose and poetry. Even if the distinction is somewhat cloudy to the reader, the student can nonetheless gather that there is one.

Definitions

If the author defines anything for you, even if it is a familiar concept, highlight it. The MCAT likes to ask questions about how the author defines particular concepts. Take note especially if the definition is somehow different from yours or the typical dictionary definition. Let's look at a quick example:

> Not much more than a quarter of a century ago the word "animism" began to be used to describe that particular phase of the psychological condition of primitive peoples by which they believe that a spirit (*anima*) resides in everything, material and immaterial. The spirit is generally associated with the thing itself, sometimes actually identified with it. When it is thought of as distinct from the thing, it is supposed to have the form of the thing, to be in a word its "double".
>
> Source: *The Religion of Numa* by Jesse Benedict Carter

It is likely that with a passage like this, the MCAT will either ask what the term "animism" means or ask you to apply the concept to a new situation.

Annotation

There is no "Notes" feature on the real MCAT, so don't get used to the one in the AAMC's online practice tests. They can't take the power of annotation away from you, however. You can still carry out this important step, because as noted earlier in the book, the test center will provide you with either scratch paper or a dry erase board.

The primary purpose behind annotation is to create a map of the passage. With only a few minutes of reading time, you cannot capture the complexities within a passage. What you can do within a few minutes is get a sense of where things are so that when the MCAT asks a question on a particular topic, you can quickly locate the relevant information. The best way to approach annotation is to jot down one to three words immediately after each paragraph you read. One to three words is sufficient to capture the main topic of each paragraph. Remember that your job is not to write a dissertation on the passage, so don't get carried away. If you consistently write more than three words per paragraph, you are writing too much.

When deciding what to write down for each paragraph, think of your job as labeling or titling the paragraph. Again, you just want to put things in place, not pin down their deeper meaning. Aside from creating a map of the passage, annotation has another advantage. A common complaint about the Verbal section is that the mind tends to wander; you may find that you've let your eyes pass over (as opposed to reading) three paragraphs worth of information without absorbing anything. If you stop and sum up at the end of each paragraph, this "zoning out" phenomenon is much less likely to happen or is at least unlikely to go on for too long. Consider the following paragraphs and suggested annotations below them:

> The red man peoples air, earth, and the waters with countless creatures of his fancy; his expressions are figurative and metaphorical; he is quick to seize analogies; and when he cannot explain he is ever ready to invent. This is shown in his inappeasable love of story telling. As a *raconteur* he is untiring. He has, in the highest degree, Goethe's *Lust zu fabuliren*. In no Oriental city does the teller of strange tales find a more willing audience than in the Indian wigwam. The folk lore of every tribe which has been properly investigated has turned out to be most ample. Tales of talking animals, of mythical warriors, of giants, dwarfs, subtle women, potent magicians, impossible adventures, abound to an extent that defies collection.

> Nor are these narratives repeated in a slip-shod, negligent style. The hearers permit no such carelessness. They are sticklers for nicety of expression; for clear and well turned periods; for vivid and accurate description; for flowing and sonorous sentences. As a rule, their languages lend themselves readily to these demands. It is a singular error, due wholly to ignorance of the subject, to maintain that the American tongues are cramped in their vocabularies, or that their syntax does not permit them to define the more delicate relationship of ideas. Nor is it less a mistake to assert, as has been done repeatedly, and even by authorities of eminence in our own day, that they are not capable of supplying the expressions of

abstract reasonings. Although pure abstractions were rarely objects of interest to these children of nature, many, if not most, of their tongues favor the formation of expressions which are as thoroughly transcendental as any to be found in the *Kritik der Reinen Vernunft*.

Their literary faculty is further demonstrated in the copiousness of their vocabularies, their rare facility of expression, and their natural aptitude for the acquisition of other languages. Théophilie Gautier used to say that the most profitable book for a professional writer to read is the dictionary; that is, that a mastery of words is his most valuable acquirement. The extraordinarily rich synonomy of some American tongues, notably the Algonkin, the Aztec, and the Qquichua, attests how sedulously their resources have been cultivated. Father Olmos, in his grammar of the Aztec, gives many examples of twenty and thirty synonymous expressions, all in current use in his day. A dictionary, in my possession, of the Maya, one of the least plastic of American tongues, gives over thirty thousand words, and scarcely a hundred of them of foreign extraction.

Source: *Aboriginal American Authors* by Daniel Garrison Brinton

Although this is a rather long excerpt, all a student would really need to write down is the following.

Paragraph 1: fanciful creatures

Paragraph 2: nice expressions

Paragraph 3: large vocabularies

This is just enough to pin down the topic of each paragraph without overdoing it.

After you have finished annotating each of the paragraphs, jot down the main idea of the whole passage. What do those paragraph labels add up to when you put them all together? Concretely acknowledging the main idea will make it a lot easier to identify it when you see its echoes in the answer choices and can also serve as a quick reference against which to check answer choices.

One final note on annotation: Many students write down annotations but do not reference them all that often. The question of whether or not annotation is worth the time sometimes arises. We would argue that the benefits of annotation are worth a few extra seconds. Even if you don't often look at your notes, just the act of expressing and jotting down the main idea of the paragraph helps the passage to gel in your mind.

Bringing It All Together

Highlighting and annotation will definitely slow you down, especially at first. Expect this, and don't get frustrated if your first few attempts take you five to six minutes to read, highlight, and annotate a passage. Pare down your timing a little bit at a time. It could take about a month to develop a system that works for you in a reasonable amount of time. Your primary concern is developing a methodology that you can employ systematically, regardless of how unfamiliar or difficult the passage material may be.

HANDLING THE QUESTIONS

The MCAT people can ask you any question they like, as long as it pertains to the passage. However, these people are test writers, not poets, so they aren't necessarily the most creative people on the planet. Consequently, there are really only about six kinds of questions they ask over and over again, just on different subject matter. This is very fortunate for you, the test taker, because if you can learn the various question types and the tricks and traps commonly associated with each one, then you can gain quite a bit of control over the test. Integrating the question types into a systematic way of handling the test is one of the hardest things to do in Verbal Reasoning, but the potential increase in accuracy is well worth the effort. Before we get into particulars, let's examine the various formats in which a question can be framed.

Question Formats

There are three formats in which MCAT questions appear. They can show up in any of the sections, not just Verbal Reasoning, so you can use these techniques in the science sections as well.

Standard Multiple Choice

Old-fashioned multiple choice represents the majority of questions by far. POE reigns supreme. Enough said.

Negation

The negation format usually entails the word EXCEPT or NOT in capital letters, but some variations involve words like *inconsistent* or *unlikely* in italics. These questions are specifically written with the intent to make you mess up. They often put the negation words in capital or italic letters so that they have the appearance of being helpful, but trust us, it's simply a token gesture that only works some of the time.

Peripheral Questions
These are questions that bear only a tenuous relationship to the passage and are usually answerable with little or no reference to the text.
Source: *Cracking the MCAT*, 2006

Consider what happens when you are not 100 percent on top of your game: You read the question fully intending to remember the negation, you consider the first few answer choices, and somewhere around the third answer choice you forget the question, at which point you confidently choose an answer choice you know reflects the author's arguments, never realizing your mistake. These are needlessly lost points that can do serious damage to your score over the course of an entire section.

You need to fundamentally change the way you handle negation questions precisely because they are so ripe for errors. First, for negation questions, use your scratch paper for POE. Write down EXCEPT, NOT, or whatever the negation word happens to be. Then, treat the question like a true/false question. When you find an answer that you know to be true, put a "T" next to it, or an "F" if you know it is incorrect. Lastly, pick the one that is not like the others. You can modify your approach for variants. For example, if the negation word is "inconsistent," label the answer choices "I" for inconsistent or "C" for consistent. A little extra effort can help cut down silly mistakes on the test.

Roman Numerals

This question format obviously contains statements with Roman numerals before the answer choices. One or more of the Roman numeral statements may be correct. What is not so obvious is that these questions are designed to test your ability to use POE. The test writers would like you to spend a lot of time deciding whether each individual Roman numeral statement is correct or not. What they hope you won't realize is that in many cases, POE will resolve whether a Roman numeral is right or wrong. For example, imagine that you have arrived at the following evaluation of the three Roman numeral statements:

    I.   definitely right
   II.   no clue
  III.   definitely wrong

    A.   I only
    B.   I and III
    C.   II and III
    D.   III only

They often include a Roman numeral statement that is very ambiguous. Considering II on its own merit could suck up a lot of time, but if you are confident III is wrong and eliminate any choice that contains III, then it turns out you don't have to worry about II at all. Seek out the statements of which you are sure, and if one is clearly correct, eliminate any answer that does not contain it. If a Roman numeral statement is clearly incorrect, eliminate any answer that contains it. Play the absolutes.

Finally, any question type can be asked in any of the formats. When you run into a negation or Roman numeral question, it is your cue to slow down a bit so that you can keep more balls in the air. Now that we've got the three question formats down, let's move on to the question types.

Question Types

Different question types require different strategies. For instance, let's compare asking someone out with asking your boss for a promotion. There are definite, successful strategies for each endeavor, but they have almost nothing in common. To your boss, you might enumerate your strengths and recap your accomplishments. If you try that with someone you fancy, you may come off as arrogant. Similarly, if you bat your eyelashes at your boss, she probably won't be impressed. The bottom line is that the approach to a question is everything, and strategies mustn't be confused. For each of the question types, we'll teach you how to identify it, discuss what skill it was designed to test, and examine the particular traps the MCAT is likely to include in the answer choices.

Retrieval Questions

Identify: Retrieval questions usually include phrasing such as "according to the passage," "according to the author," "the passage indicates," or "the author indicates." You can also consider retrieval questions as a sort of default question. If you're not sure of the question type and the question is specific to a part of the passage, then treat it as a retrieval question.

Skill: Find the right info in the passage to answer the question. For retrieval questions, you should go back to the passage to find that piece of information. It sounds easy, but generally speaking, the hard part is finding the right location. Two things will help you identify the correct part of the passage—your annotations and key words in the passage. The one to three words you jot down for each paragraph is like a label that will help you find which paragraph contains the information for which you are looking. Also, keep an eye out for key words or proper names in the question for which it's easy to skim the passage. Lastly, if you see a word of emphasis in the question, look for a similar word of emphasis in the passage which should be aided by your highlighting.

Trap: Incorrect answer choices for retrieval questions often contain true statements from the passage, but they come from the wrong location. Correct answers to retrieval questions typically don't stray too far from where the authors write about them. Also, watch out for what we call deceptive language, which means answer choices that seem to be taken word for word from the passage, but the actual meaning of the answer choice doesn't follow from the context of the passage or doesn't answer the question actually being asked.

Inference Questions

Identify: Inference questions contains phrasings such as "infer," "suggest," "imply," "most likely," and "reasonable to conclude."

Skill: Point to the evidence in the passage. Inference questions can be tricky because there is a disconnect between what normal people think of as an inference and what MCAT test writers think of as an inference. Most people think of an inference as a logical assumption. For instance, if a woman walks into a room with wet hair, you would probably infer that it was raining or she had just taken a shower. Sounds reasonable, right? To the MCAT people, however, there's no way you could possibly know that for sure. Therefore, the best strategy for an inference question is to think about it as if you aren't making an inference at all. look for an answer that is directly supported by the passage. If none of the four have direct support, pick the choice that takes the smallest, safest step away from the passage. A good guideline is that you should be able to point to the words on the screen that support that answer choice.

Trap: Extreme wording is a big no-no on inference questions. If you see words such as "never," "always," "none," "all," or "most," or the answer makes too strong of a claim, then it's probably wrong. Also be careful of answer choices that bring up information not presented in the passage. If the author doesn't write about it, then it's probably not the answer. Lastly, be suspicious of answer choices that make a value judgment about passage information, such as claiming that something is inappropriate.

Main Idea Questions

Identify: Main idea questions usually involve words such as "main idea," "primary purpose," "central theme," or "central thrust." Sometimes there are hidden main idea questions that ask about the author and are very open ended. For example: "The author believes that…" These may be main idea questions, and the scope of the answer choices will help elucidate whether they are going for a main idea or something more specific.

Skill: Look at the big picture rather than details from the passage. The correct answer should reflect the two to four words that you jotted down at the end of the passage.

Trap: Usually at least a couple of the trap answers are details from the passage, so if the answer seems too specific to only a portion of the passage, you should probably eliminate it. Occasionally, the MCAT will include an answer that is overly broad. For example, if the passage is about neo-behaviorist theory and the answer references psychology in general, you should be wary.

Application Questions

Identify: Application questions sometimes employ phrases such as "suppose," "imagine," or "this information, if true." Generally, these questions are quite long, which makes them easy to spot, but fundamentally, the question brings up some situation that was not discussed in the passage. Note that the new situation could be in the question itself or the four answer choices could be new situations.

Skill: Lock onto the main idea of the passage. The question may bring up some new scenario, but it is still directly relevant to the same old main idea of a paragraph or of the passage as a whole. Hints in the question will signal whether the question is dealing with the main idea or something more specific. Think of it as the main idea dressed up in different clothes.

When Answering a Peripheral Question
Do not let an answer choice send you back to the passage on a wasteful, wild goose chase.
Focus on the stem of the question, think logically, answer the question, and move on.

Source: *Cracking the MCAT*, 2006

The Tendency to Paraphrase

When a Verbal Reasoning question asks for the characterization of an author's belief or position, the correct answer will not reproduce, precisely, the author's own words. It will paraphrase them. Therefore, you should search for an answer that convey's the author's meaning in different words than those used in the passage.

Source: *Cracking the MCAT,* 2006

Trap: Avoid details or coincidences that are drawn directly from the passage. The question may reference passage information, but correct answers are usually a twist on a concept from the passage.

Strengthen/Weaken Questions

Identify: These questions usually use either the word "strengthen" or "weaken," but some alternatives include "most support," "challenge," or "undermine."

Skill: For strengthen questions, you want to prove the author's claim; you need an answer choice that makes his argument true. For weaken questions, you want to break the author's argument; you need an answer choice that proves him wrong. For both types, the kind of answer choice you want to see is the exception to the rule for MCAT questions; you actually want an answer with strong wording. This makes sense in this particular case because an answer with wishy-washy safe wording, including words like "occasionally," "may," and "some," cannot do the job of proving or disproving the author.

Trap: Silly mistakes are often a problem on strengthen/weaken questions. It's easy to accidentally pick an answer that strengthens the argument on a weaken question and vice versa. You may want to put letters next to the answer choices on your scratch paper. For example, put an "S" for an answer that strengthens, a "W" for one that weakens, and an "I" for any answer that is irrelevant to the argument. Also, be suspicious of any answer that has wording that isn't strong enough and strengthens or weakens too little.

Support Questions

Identify: These questions generally directly cite a word or phrase from the passage signified by quotes or italics in the question. Also, the question may have the word "support" in it. The question may ask for the purpose of a particular reference in the passage, or it may ask if, how, or how well a part of the author's argument is supported.

Skill: Locate the support in the passage. On support questions, you should go back to the passage and read five lines before and after the cited part of the passage. When the MCAT asks about a specific sentence, it is usually because that part of the passage is difficult to understand, so look to the sentences around it to help make sense of it. Also, the sentences near the citation are the best place to look for supportive material. In fact, the correct answer to many support questions is a paraphrase of a nearby sentence.

Trap: When the question asks about a difficult line of text, a bad answer choice is often an interpretation of the line that is far too literal.

Last Word on Question Types

There are also hybrid questions that involve a combination of skills. Some of the most common include retrieval/inference questions. If you spot one of these, it is a cue to slow down and pick safe answers with strong textual support.

Another common hybrid is the strengthen/weaken question with an application twist. To recognize them, look for a question that provides new information and then asks if that information would strengthen or weaken the author's claims.. Weaken/strengthen questions are already rather difficult, so these tend to be absolute monsters. Even the most skilled readers are hit and miss with these, so it may not be worth your time and energy to spend three minutes on a question and still end up with equally likely chances for success and failure. You may choose to attempt them if you feel you have a strong, nuanced understanding of the passage, but be prepared to cut your losses and move on if you get lost in the answer choices.

QUESTION-TYPE DRILL

Identify the question type, the skill you need, and the common traps.

1. Which of the following findings would most weaken the author's argument about the extent to which classification of women into a single category blurred class distinctions among women?

   Question Type: _____

   Skills Needed: _____

   Common Traps: _____

2. The author suggests that the relationship between the personal economic interests of the Founding Fathers and the writing of the Constitution was one of:

   Question Type: _____

   Skills Needed: _____

   Common Traps: _____

3. The author's assertion that the small farmers "acted as a buffer between the rich and the dispossessed" is supported by which of the following?

   Question Type: _____

   Skills Needed: _____

   Common Traps: _____

4. The passage suggests that the author believes pamphleteering was the primary motivation to action because it:

   Question Type: _____

   Skills Needed: _____

   Common Traps: _____

5. Given the information in the passage, one would expect the nature of the reaction of the Democratic Party following the Gulf War to be one of:

   Question Type: _____

   Skills Needed: _____

   Common Traps: _____

6. In stating that the Panama operation was on "too small a scale" to accomplish the administration's goals, the author apparently intends to counter the views of:

   Question Type: _____

   Skills Needed: _____

   Common Traps: _____

7. Assume that a local Communist party leader organized a large scale campaign to attain rent relief for needy people. The reaction of the city government would most likely be:

   Question Type: _____

   Skills Needed: _____

   Common Traps: _____

8. The central thesis of the passage is that:

   Question Type: _____

   Skills Needed: _____

   Common Traps: _____

9. Which of the following inferences regarding the role of the Justice Department is justified by information in the passage?

   Question Type: _____

   Skills Needed: _____

   Common Traps: _____

10. Which of the following, if true, would reinforce the author's claims about the effect of the Stamp Act?

    Question Type: _____

    Skills Needed: _____

    Common Traps: _____

11. According to the passage, private foreign investment in the United States:

    Question Type: _____

    Skills Needed: _____

    Common Traps: _____

12. The author asserts that Progressive reforms helped stabilize the capitalist system. This claim would be most strengthened by evidence that:

    Question Type: _____

    Skills Needed: _____

    Common Traps: _____

13. The passage indicates that the ultimate reasons for the declaration of war were:

    Question Type: _____

    Skills Needed: _____

    Common Traps: _____

14. The passage indicates that the merchant class and the aristocratic monopoly had which of the following goals in common?

    Question Type: _____

    Skills Needed: _____

    Common Traps: _____

ANSWERS TO QUESTION-TYPE DRILL

1. Weaken/Application hybrid. Look for a strong answer that disproves the author's argument. Eliminate answers that strengthen or weaken too little.

2. Inference. Look for a safe answer with strong textual support. Avoid extreme answers and answers that are beyond the information given.

3. Support. Go back and read five lines before and after. Beware of answers that are too literal.

4. Inference. Look for a safe answer with strong textual support. Avoid extreme answers and answers that are beyond the information given.

5. Retrieval. Go back and find the relevant information. Eliminate answers that cite text from the wrong location in the passage and be wary of deceptive language.

6. Support. Go back and read five lines before and after. Beware of answers that are too literal.

7. Application. Look for answers that reinforce a concept that is either the main idea or the main idea of a paragraph. Avoid answers that are coincidences from the passage.

8. Main Idea. Reference the two to four words you wrote down after reading the passage, and look for an answer that sounds like them. Eliminate details from the passage.

9. Inference. Look for a safe answer with strong textual support. Avoid extreme answers and answers that are beyond the information given.

10. Strengthen. Look for a strong answer that helps prove the author's argument. Eliminate answers that weaken or that strengthen too little.

11. Retrieval. Go back and find the relevant information. Eliminate answers that cite text from the wrong location in the passage and be wary of deceptive language.

12. Strengthen. Look for a strong answer that helps prove the author's argument. Eliminate answers that weaken or that strengthen too little.

13. Retrieval. Go back and find the relevant information. Eliminate answers that cite text from the wrong location in the passage and be wary of deceptive language.

14. Retrieval. Go back and find the relevant information. Eliminate answers that cite text from the wrong location in the passage and be wary of deceptive language.

Chapter 11
Mastering Verbal Reasoning: Distracter Answer Choices

We've examined the question types and the commonly used trap answers associated with each. However, this cursory glance at the answer choices has barely skimmed the surface. The more detailed exploration of bad answer choices that follows will go a long way in enhancing your approach to POE.

HANDLING THE ANSWER CHOICES

The MCAT is notorious for its difficult answer choices. Even adept readers who are comfortable with arcane, dense material and feel they have a strong understanding of a passage get frustrated when they can't pin down a reasonable answer choice. This is par for the course in MCAT land. The aim in this chapter is to help you to identify the seductive answer choices that the MCAT employs to trip you up. Up to this point, you have probably tentatively eliminated answer choices because they just seemed weird or wrong. The goal is to be able to put a name to exactly what is weird or wrong so that you can more confidently eliminate answer choices.

We would like to emphasize that the rules for bad answer choices are more guidelines than ironclad laws; they work the majority of the time, but occasionally an answer that looks like a trap turns out to actually be correct. Thus, getting a really fantastic score may require a little flexibility. The following is a list of the most common distracter answer choices. The types presented differ in name from those discussed in The Princeton Review's *Cracking the MCAT CBT* but nonetheless reflect the same ideas. We've also included a couple of additional distracters not mentioned in *Cracking the MCAT* in order to represent trap answers on the most recent MCATs. So as to alleviate any confusion for those using this book in tandem with *Cracking the MCAT*, the name of each answer choice as it appears in the *Cracking* book is provided in parentheses.

Extremes (The Absolute)

Extreme answers contain language that is too strong for the safe answers the MCAT likes. Answer choices that contain words like "never," "always," "all," "only," and "none" are usually incorrect. Other words are harder to pin down but nonetheless reflect too strong an opinion. Those include words such as "unacceptable," "complete," "total," "utter," and "inevitable." The tone of an answer choice may also be off. For example, an answer choice may say something along the lines of "vulgar" when the passage merely says "colloquial". Keep in mind that MCAT authors tend not to get too impassioned, so answer choices that are immoderate are probably wrong. Let's examine the following Roman numeral question:

1. Which of the following claims is/are explicitly supported by a specific example in the passage?

   I.   Scientific concepts are universal.
   II. Descriptive definitions state or explain meaning.
   III. Scientific purists demand that all terms be defined.

   A. I only
   B. II only
   C. II and III only
   D. I, II, and II

We don't have the passage here, but with attention to extreme wording and a little common sense, we should be able to pick out the answer. The question pretty much is asking which of the three Roman numerals can be proven by the passage. The first statement contains the extreme word *universal* and is saying that there is proof in a five-paragraph MCAT reading comprehension passage that scientific concepts are true everywhere in the universe. This is unlikely. If you dismiss I, then you can get rid of all answers that contain I. In this case, A and D are gone, leaving you with a 50/50 chance at picking the correct answer. But wait, we still have two more statements to consider. Do you see any more extreme language up there? Statement III has a little word that means a lot—the word "all." So those scientific purists really want *all* terms defined, like "scientific," "purist," "the," "word," "is," etc? Not likely.

When an answer choice has an extreme word within it, take it literally. Based on the question, if a situation or other detail from the passage is contradicted by the phrasing in an answer choice, or if something you know to be outside the scope of the passage is included, then the answer must be eliminated.

The Danger With Extremes
The reason extreme answer choices are usually incorrect is that they lend themselves rather easily to dispute.

Beyond the Information Given (The Seducer)

Bad answer choices often bring up information that was never discussed in the passage. This sounds like an easy thing to avoid, but the test writers are rather tricky; they tend to present statements that are commonly associated with information in the passage or that appeal to popular public sentiment. Beware of answer choices, especially on inference questions, that bring in common-sense notions related to but not directly supported by passage information. As a general rule, if the author doesn't discuss it, then you should probably eliminate it. Consider the following paragraphs and related question:

> When parents innocently follow traditions considered acceptable in their cultures, they may face prosecution because their conduct is misinterpreted by the dominant culture as child abuse. Their children may be taken out of the home because the courts regard this as being in the child's best interest. A classic example of this phenomenon is coining, or *cao gio*, a form of folk medicine commonly practiced among Southeast Asians believed to cure individuals of influenza and other physical ailments. The technique required applying mentholated oil to the body and then rubbing the skin with a coin with a serrated edge hard enough to break blood vessels. The pattern of bruising caused by the coin massage looks to the untrained eye like child abuse. Despite its gruesome appearance, coining involves only mild discomfort, and the bruises disappear in a few days. In many communities, those who work with children mistake this innocuous folk remedy for child abuse.
>
> Source: "In Defense of Culture in the Courtroom" by Alison Dundes Renteln from *Engaging Cultural Differences: The Multicultural Challenge in Liberal Democracies*

2. The author most likely cites the Southeast Asian practice of coining in order to support which of the following conclusions?

Now let's look at just one answer choice that illustrates this seductive distracter:

A. Diligent efforts should be made to ensure that parents are legitimately guilty of child abuse before removing children from the home and breaking apart the family unit.

Don't Be Seduced!
MCAT answer choices will often make statements that seem very sensible and are related to passage information, but if the author doesn't actually say what's in an answer choice, you should eliminate it.

This answer choice is a totally appropriate response to the issue of child abuse in general, and it probably reflects the values of many people. However, this is a seductive answer choice because it is difficult to disagree with it outright, yet it manages to completely ignore the issue of the consequences that can stem from miscommunication between the majority and minority cultures with which the author is concerned. The right answer will most likely address the phenomenon of a cultural practice that does not match up with mainstream practices. Let's look at another attractive answer choice:

C. Social workers and judges must err on the side of caution when it comes to the welfare of children; the right of the child to be protected from abuse overrides the prerogatives of parents.

Again, the sentiment within the answer choice is difficult to refute and mirrors conventional wisdom. However, the author does not directly compare the rights of children to those of parents and thus goes off topic.

A related but not exactly identical problem is using outside knowledge. The tendency to pick an answer choice that is absolutely true in real life but not actually presented in the passage is especially common when a passage relates to the sciences or typical topics in the premed curriculum such as introductory psychology and sociology. These answers are often seductive because you've studied the material and know that they are, in fact, totally correct; they wouldn't work as attractors if they weren't. It is difficult to disassociate yourself from the entirely appropriate skills you use in the Physical and Biological Sciences sections, but this is exactly what you must do. The MCAT does not expect you to use your outside knowledge in the Verbal Reasoning section, so avoid answers that may be true in the real world but are not discussed in the passage.

Deceptive Language (The Mangler)

Deceptive language is the use of words in an answer choice that are directly drawn from the passage, but the meaning of the words has diverged from the question's original intent. The MCAT folks tend to prefer answers that are paraphrases of passage information. However, they realize that people tend to be drawn to familiar words and phrases and exploit this by concocting answers that sound exactly like the passage and may even quote from the passage directly. These answers might seem good at first glance, but they are actually erroneous when you take into account what it is that the question is actually asking. If you see answers that seem to be verbatim from the passage, carefully inspect them to ensure that the meaning has not been mangled. Consider the following paragraph and question:

> The most sophisticated analysis of cultural rights under international law is found in the work of Sebastian Poulter. His theoretical position is as follows: If a cultural tradition violates human rights, it should not be permitted; if disallowing a cultural tradition violates human rights, it should be permitted. Poulter's analysis highlights the hierarchy problem—the reality that the right to culture must necessarily be limited. If one can show that cultural traditions deserve legal protection, then the question is, what are the limiting principles? Even if the right to culture is a human right, that does not deny that other competing rights must also receive protection. As no analytic framework exists that is capable of solving all rights conflicts, a case-by-case approach is desirable.

> Source: "In Defense of Culture in the Courtroom" by Alison Dundes Renteln from *Engaging Cultural Differences: The Multicultural Challenge in Liberal Democracies*

3. The author's discussion of human rights and cultural tradition assumes which of the following?

    B. Theoretical positions are subjected to limiting principles in order to establish the legitimacy of their legal protections.

While the author of the paragraph does employ such terms as "theoretical positions," "limiting principles," and "legal protection," the usage of these terms in the answer choice is out of context. For example, the "limiting principles" apply to the legal protection of cultural traditions, not to Poulter's theoretical positions. A correct answer would most likely paraphrase these terms and remain true to the context. For example, the test writers could change the term "legal protection" to "legal safeguard," "limiting principles" to "qualifying rules," and "theoretical position" to "speculative conception." Let's analyze another troublesome answer choice:

    C. A case-by-case approach to the adjudication of cultural rights cases is undesirable because a hierarchical framework for such cases has not yet been formulated.

If you look carefully at this answer choice, it actually refutes the advice of the author of the paragraph who would prefer a case-by-case approach. However, this choice is initially attractive because it so closely mirrors the language of the paragraph, employing such terms (or variations of terms in the paragraph) as "case-by-

Don't Be Fooled By Familiar Words and Phrases
Be wary of answer choices that use words directly drawn from the passage. Examine them carefully to ensure that the meaning of the words has not been altered from what it was in the passage.

case approach," "undesirable," "hierarchical," and "framework." A better answer choice might exchange terms such as "case-by-case approach" for, say, "model based on the individual merits of a case" or switch "hierarchical framework" to "a system that weighs the importance of human rights against that of cultural rights."

Fancy Language

Answer choices that contain 50-cent words can be really seductive. The test writers hope that you will select fancy-sounding answer choices because you want to prove your intellectual prowess by opting for answers that sound smart. What the unaware test taker doesn't realize is that the MCAT folks actually prefer simpler, safer wording rather than phrasing that is overly convoluted and ornate. Answer choices that utilize big words and florid language are designed to attract your attention but are generally incorrect. Consider the following passage and accompanying question:

> Through mapping human genes, detailed information may be obtained about biologically determined features of individuals. The biosurveillance made possible by this relates to the likely course of physical and psychological development of individuals. Such scientific foreknowledge of potential life courses is thus of great interest, especially to employers and insurance companies, who wish to use such data as a means of discrimination between candidates or clients, based on genetic testing and screening. As we shall see, the combination of rising employer health insurance costs and the increasing reliability of genetic testing is likely to encourage the development of such biosurveillance on the large scale.
>
> Source: "Under My Skin: From Identification Papers to Body Surveillance" by David Lyon from *Documenting Individual Identity: The Development of State Practices in the Modern World*

4. The author would most likely agree with which of the following assumptions about the future of biosurveillance?

A. Genetic determinism may contribute to the obfuscation of the capitalist system in which the remuneration of employees is a function of their productivity and market forces.

This answer choice certainly sounds authoritative, but in reality it has little to do with information from the passage, which does not directly discuss capitalist systems or market forces. The overwrought vocabulary is simply an attention-getting device; a simpler, clearer answer choice is preferred. A little tough vocabulary is not unheard of, however, so just be on the lookout for answers that seem to be deliberately confusing.

True Statement but not the Answer to the Question (The Irrelevant Truth)

MCAT test writers often include answer choices that are completely true statements from the passage; the only problem is that they are not answers to the question being asked. This is generally a location issue and occurs most frequently with questions that ask about a specific detail. The answer to these questions usually doesn't stray far from its source, so make sure that the answer you select is coming from the section of the passage that the question is referencing and not some other paragraph. We find that these errors are most common when a test taker is tired or rushing. One way to check yourself to ensure you don't make this mistake is to read the answer choice you have selected along with the question to make sure your answer makes sense and truly answers the question being asked. Let's look at the following portion of a passage:

> Whether one is prepared to entertain a cultural defense often depends on which of the three main theories of punishment—retribution, deterrence, and rehabilitation—one favors. The notion that a person who commits a culturally motivated act is less blameworthy is based on retribution and the corollary principle of proportionality—that is, that a person should be punished only as much as he or she deserves.
>
> Those who think punishment is principally for deterring other crimes may fear allowing cultural traditions because the ethnic minority community might interpret the court's judgment lessening the punishment as giving license to continue a practice. If the law is supposed to promote assimilation of the newly arrived, then it should not permit cultural factors to influence legal proceedings. But the law is often a poor vehicle for altering cultural identity.
>
> A similar problem may exist for rehabilitation. It is unclear what it would mean to rehabilitate a person who follows tradition. If the purpose of the law is to force assimilation, then rehabilitation would require rejecting the cultural defense. If, however, the point is that the culturally motivated act is not one that requires condemnation, then it does not make sense to "rehabilitate" a person who is simply acting in accordance with his or her culture.
>
> Source: "In Defense of Culture in the Courtroom" by Alison Dundes Renteln from *Engaging Cultural Differences: The Multicultural Challenge in Liberal Democracies*

Consider the following question:

5. The author cites the possible role of the courts in the promotion of assimilation in order to:

   D. Point out that one of the aims of the courts is to mete out punishment in proportion to the severity of the crime.

Remember!
One way to avoid selecting an irrelevant truth as the answer is by reviewing the question. Make sure the answer you select comes from the section of the passage referenced by the question.

Notice that the author does indeed discuss this aspect of the courts in the first paragraph, so, in that respect, (D) seems to be an appropriate answer choice on its own merit. However, when you consider the answer choice within the context of the question, you realize the test writers are actually referencing the second, or possibly the third, paragraph. Thus, a good answer should reflect the author's notion that the courts are often not successful in changing cultural attitudes. Let's look at another question:

6. The author apparently believes that the consideration of cultural factors in relation to the process of rehabilitation is:

   B. Possibly problematic in that consideration of tradition may perpetuate the practice of traditions that the court finds objectionable.

Again, the author does discuss the problems associated with cultural considerations in the second paragraph in relation to the issue of deterrence of further crimes. However, the question is specifically concerned with rehabilitation, so test takers should probably refer back to the third paragraph. An answer that concedes that consideration of cultural factors depends on the perceived role of the courts in assimilation is probably more on track.

A similarly related issue is that of scope. MCAT test writers often include answer choices that are either too broad or too narrow but nonetheless in line with passage information. We previously discussed that incorrect answers on main idea questions are often details from the passage. The same is true of specific questions. Bad answers are sometimes too broad for the question being asked or for the passage information. For example, let's say a passage discusses methods of organizing scientific research. An answer that references scientific progress in general is probably too broad. Conversely, an answer that references strictly drug study data is probably too narrow. The scope of the answer choice should fit the scope of the question and the passage: Specific questions get specific answers; general questions get general answers.

Relationship Issues (The Flip)

There are two primary ways these answers can go wrong. The first is that the answer choice invents a relationship where none existed before. For example, the passage may discuss two concepts, maybe even in the same paragraph, but the answer choice says that one concept caused the other. Unless the author expressly says there is a causal relationship, you can't actually infer one, although it is tempting to do so.

The second is that the answer choice reverses a relationship in the passage. For example, the author writes that one event caused a second event, and the answer choice says the second event caused the first. When an answer choice proposes a relationship between two ideas, double check that the two are in fact tied together and in the right order. Let's examine a paragraph and a related question:

Employers, wishing to minimize risk, may use genetic screening to determine susceptibility to disease, such as breast, ovarian, colon, thyroid, eye, kidney, and skin cancers, or Huntington's Disease, among employees, or to check levels of damage from exposure to hazardous materials at work. But genetic discrimination could result on the basis of such tests. At the same time, fear of such discrimination could discourage some people from undergoing tests from which they might benefit. This points up, once more, the all-too-frequently forgotten fact that surveillance has two faces.

Source: "Under My Skin: From Identification Papers to Body Surveillance" by David Lyon from *Documenting Individual Identity: The Development of State Practices in the Modern World*

7. The author's discussion of genetic discrimination implies that:

    D. The refusal of employees to undergo genetic testing may lead to reluctance on behalf of employers to hire or promote such employees.

The author does in fact set up a relationship between genetic testing and discrimination. However, the author asserts that an employee's fear of discrimination may lead an employee not to undergo testing. The answer choice, on the other hand, contends the opposite, that an employee's refusal to undergo testing will lead to discrimination. Though related, the answer choice does not mirror the passage.

Let's look at another:

One report found that local health departments' 'normal daily workload suffered when staff were diverted from their usual responsibilities to work on bioterrorism response planning.' Another noted that 'the process of realignment to emphasize biodefense skill sets damaged morale in departments where preexisting programs and positions were trimmed to make way for what many perceived to be yet another "silo" of special interests.' More than half of local health officials surveyed in one study said that the smallpox vaccination program had forced them to defer, delay, or cancel other public health programs.

Source: "Under My Skin: From Identification Papers to Body Surveillance" by David Lyon from *Documenting Individual Identity: The Development of State Practices in the Modern World*

8. It is reasonable to conclude which of the following about the possible effects of biodefense planning?

    C. Re-routing the responsibilities of health department employees leads to a drop in morale within the department.

Potential Problems With Relationships
There are two primary ways these answer choices can go wrong:

1) A relationship is created where none existed before.

2) A relationship discussed in the passage is reversed.

This is extremely subtle, because all of the paragraph's details support the contention that biodefense programs are not universally successful. However, this answer choice draws a relationship between re-channeling the duties of employees and morale, whereas the passage draws a relationship between re-channeling the duties of employees and the way the employees' workload suffered. Within the passage, the phenomenon of a damaged morale is associated with trimming preexisting programs. Watch out for answer choices that create relationships between two independent concepts.

Half Right Equals All Wrong

Answer choices that are at least partially correct are popular traps. An answer that supports the author but then also includes something that refutes the author can be rather seductive. Test takers will often try to justify the incorrect part of the answer in order to legitimize the whole answer, especially when the other answers seem unattractive as well. However, if any part of an answer disputes passage information or falls under other distracter answer categories, you should eliminate it, even if the rest of the answer seems to fit. Let's look at an example:

> The distinction between "defensive" and "offensive" research is increasingly difficult to maintain, and biodefense research in particular is by nature "dual use." Development of vaccines, therapeutics, and diagnostic and surveillance technology requires knowledge of the ways in which biological agents can be manipulated, weaponized, and disseminated. This presents researchers and institutions with difficult decisions about whether biodefense research can be ethically justified as truly "defensive" in nature. Increasingly, researchers in and outside of biodefense programs are faced with the question of whether their research constitutes "forbidden knowledge" whose potential harms outweigh its benefits to society.
>
> Source: "Under My Skin: From Identification Papers to Body Surveillance" by David Lyon from *Documenting Individual Identity: The Development of State Practices in the Modern World*

9. The author indicates which of the following to be true about biodefense research?

   A. Intimate knowledge about the application of bioterrorism weapons presents ethical dilemmas to scientists who research the defensive aspects of biodefense; however, such concerns should not hamper the efforts of such researchers.

The first half of this answer choice is absolutely in agreement with the author of the paragraph and thus seems appropriate at first glance. However, the second half of the answer is contrary to the author's concerns about the "dual use" problem, which destroys its credibility as a good answer choice. This answer choice should also reinforce the point that careful reading of the answer choices may indeed be more important than careful reading of the passage. Skipping or skimming the remainder of an answer choice once you've found a part you like can lead to unnecessary mistakes. Let's analyze another potentially bad answer:

> **C.** Research that produces information about the uses of biodefense weapons could be potentially dangerous to communities, and thus, institutions take precautions to ensure that such information cannot be leaked to the wrong people.

Again, the passage information affirms the portion of the answer choice that deals with the potential harms of biodefense research. However, there is nothing in the passage that deals with the security of such research. Though it is logical to conclude that such research is protected, this is actually beyond the information given and therefore a highly unlikely correct answer.

Remember!
If *any* part of an answer choice contradicts passage information, get rid of it.

Narrowing down the answer choices

When you approach passage questions, practice naming what exactly irritates you about each particular answer and identify distracter answers. This should give you more confidence when using POE. However, test takers often run into situations in which they have eliminated all but two answers and spend way too much time deciding which one to choose. Re-reading paragraphs multiple times and debating the merits of two answer choices can do a lot of damage to your timing and keep you from getting to more questions if you're not careful. You need a systematic way to deal with a question when you have whittled it down to two answer choices that seem equally good (or equally problematic). Here are four steps to work through when you get down to two answer choices and have difficulty deciding which one to choose.

What to Do When Down to Two

Reread the question   When you are down to two answer choices, the temptation is to overanalyze the answer choices and the passage. Actually, the first thing you should analyze closely is the question itself. Reread the question looking not only for the type of question it is, but also for any hints you may have missed the first time such as words of emphasis. Often, this alone will clear up the confusion between the two choices. For example, if you realize the question is an inference question, you might lean toward the answer with safer wording, or if you catch a key word, you may be able to figure out which part of the passage is appropriate.

Simplify the remaining answer choices   Choosing between choices is often difficult because they seem so similar to one another. Instead of harping on the differences, simplify the remaining answer choices looking for the differences between the two. The deciding factor may come down to a tiny detail one choice has and the other lacks.

Trust your intuition   If you initially feel an answer choice is correct, you should probably trust your instincts; they are accurate a majority of the time, and you want to avoid over thinking and talking yourself into a bad answer. But aside from your gut reaction, there are a couple of qualities you are looking for in an answer choice. When in doubt, choose the answer with safe wording that reflects the main idea of the passage.

Go back to the passage...BRIEFLY   After settling on a choice, go back quickly to the passage to confirm your choice. This is only to make you feel more confident in your selection, not to suck up more time. Nothing should change your mind at this point except a huge mistake, such as realizing that you misread or misunderstood something in the passage.

After these four steps, you must click on an answer choice and move on. No question of the MCAT requires more consideration than this; it simply isn't worth the time.

Chapter 12
Mastery Applied:
Verbal Reasoning Practice

That's right—it's time to apply your skills once again! As with the previous Mastery Applied chapters, this one provides several passages and questions for your practicing pleasure. Work through all of them following the guidance we've provided and see how well you do. Detect any pattern in the types of questions you're missing, and be sure to give those question types extra special care when you take the two online practice tests. There are more passages here than you will encounter on the actual MCAT in order to give you comprehensive practice.

Passage I (Questions 1–6)

A great deal of postmodernist theory depends on the maintenance of a skeptical attitude, and here the philosopher Jean-Françoise Lyotard's contribution is essential. He argued that we now live in an era in which legitimizing "master narratives" are in crisis and in decline. These narratives are contained in or implied by major philosophies, such as Kantianism, Hegelianism, and Marxism, which argue that history is progressive, that knowledge can liberate us, and that all knowledge has a secret unity. The two main narratives Lyotard is attacking are those of the progressive emancipation of humanity—from Christian redemption to Marxist Utopia—and that of the triumph of science. Lyotard considers that such doctrines have "lost their credibility" since the Second World War.

Metanarratives traditionally serve to give cultural practices some form of legitimation or authority. The basic attitude of postmodernists was a skepticism about the claims of any kind of overall, totalizing explanation. Lyotard was not alone in seeing the intellectual's task as one of "resistance," even to "consensus," which "has become an outmoded and suspect value." Postmodernists responded to this view, partly for the good reason that by doing so they could side with those who didn't "fit" into the larger stories—the subordinated and the marginalized—against those with the power to disseminate the master narrative. However, although there are good liberal reasons for being against such "grand narratives" (on the grounds that they do not allow for disputes about value, and often lead to totalitarian persecution), the general sociological claim made by postmodernists that such narratives are in decline in our period looks pretty thin…because allegiances to large-scale, totalizing religious, and national beliefs are currently responsible for so much repression, violence, and war. (Postmodernists tend not to be well informed about current practices in science and religion.)

The confidence with which [postmodernist] claims were made was influenced to a huge degree by a reading of the philosophy of Jacques Derrida, in whose voluminous writings the most elaborate version of this "deconstructive" attitude was to be found. The central argument for deconstruction depends on relativism, by which I mean the view that truth itself is always relative to the differing standpoints and predisposing intellectual frameworks of the judging subject. It is difficult to say, then, that deconstructors are committed to anything as definite as a philosophical thesis. Indeed, to attempt to define deconstruction is to defy another of its main principles—which is to deny that final or true definitions are possible. Literary people in particular were accused by Derrideans of a naïve trust in what was ironically dubbed the "classic realist text." Such persons simply fail to appreciate the nature of the language from which they derive their false confidence. In reading George Eliot's *Middlemarch* (1882), for example, we may have the illusion (not actually shared by George Eliot) that she simply opens a window upon reality, and that her discourse is fully adequate to a description of the real. Our reliance upon Eliot's narrative voice and language puts us in a dominating, even God-like position, especially if we rely on the generalizations that she makes. So we think we know the truth about Dorothea Brooke, when all we really know is Eliot's descriptions of her.

Deconstruction (particularly as practiced by literary critics) was culturally most influential when it refused to allow an intellectual activity, or a literary text, or its interpretation, to be organized by any customary hierarchy of concepts. The text, as really constructed by the reader, was thereby liberated and democratized for the free play of the imagination. Meanings became the property of the interpreter, who was free to play, deconstructively, with them. It was thought to be both philosophically wrong and politically retrogressive to attempt to determine the meaning of a text…to particular ends. The pursuit of verbal certainties in interpretation was thought to be as reactionary in its implications as was the manufactured consensus of the established political order.

Adapted from: Christopher Butler, *Postmodernism: A Very Short Introduction.* ©2002 by Oxford University Press.

1. Which of the following statements best expresses the main point of the passage?

   A. The sociological claims of postmodernists, while attractive in theory, do not accurately describe current reality.
   B. While Lyotard and other postmodernist thinkers claim to offer an alternative to destructive political and literary "master narratives," they are vulnerable to the criticism that deconstruction is simply an alternative metanarrative or unifying story.
   C. Postmodernism and deconstruction offer an intriguing intellectual critique of political and literary master narratives, although they are less useful as depictions of sociological practice in modern society.
   D. Postmodernist literary deconstruction is based on the claim that there is no one single "correct" interpretation of the meaning of a work of literature.

2. The passage suggests that Lyotard attributes the decline of legitimizing "master narratives" in part to:

   A. skepticism about the legitimacy of authority, arising from the experience of war.
   B. new literary interpretations of the meaning of traditional novels such as Eliot's *Middlemarch*.
   C. a growing recognition of the inconsistencies between major philosophies such as Kantianism and Hegelianism.
   D. sociological studies showing the decline in widespread allegiance to totalizing religious and national beliefs.

3. Which of the following is LEAST consistent with the author's depiction in the passage of metanarratives?

   A. A college curriculum based on identifying and teaching the "great books" of Western civilization
   B. A theory of history that claims that nations naturally evolve into more democratic forms
   C. An anthropological study that describes differing perceptions of the meaning of the word "freedom" within a particular culture
   D. A Marxist belief in the inevitable triumph of the proletariat and the "withering away" of the state

4. According to the passage, Derrida influenced postmodernism by:

   I. critiquing the master narratives contained in the philosophies of Kant and Hegel.
   II. suggesting that there is no one true interpretation of a work of literature.
   III. arguing for a more politically informed interpretation of the influence on society of literary works.

   A. I and II only
   B. II only
   C. II and III only
   D. III only

5. The passage suggests that the author appreciates postmodernism because it:

   A. offers an intellectual framework that validates the defense of marginalized and subordinated peoples.
   B. brings to light the post-WWII evolution away from repressive religious and political regimes.
   C. critiques George Eliot's claim to open a window on the reality of her time.
   D. expresses a critical attitude toward grand narratives that enforce a particular value system.

6. Based on the passage, relativism is to consensus as:

   A. interpreter is to text.
   B. philosophy is to politics.
   C. narrative is to meaning.
   D. deconstruction is to metanarrative.

_____

It is sometimes useful to remind ourselves of the simpler aspects of things normally regarded as complicated. Take, for instance, the writing of a poem. It consists of three stages. The first is when a man becomes obsessed with an emotional concept to such a degree that he is compelled to do something about it. What he does in the second stage, namely, is construct a verbal device that will reproduce this emotional concept in anyone who cares to read it, anywhere, any time. The third stage is the recurrent situation of people in different times and places, setting off the device and re-creating in themselves what the poet felt when he wrote it. The stages are interdependent and all necessary. If there has been no preliminary feeling, the device has nothing to reproduce and the reader will experience nothing. If the second stage has not been well done, the device will not deliver the goods, or will deliver only a few goods to a few people, or will stop delivering them after an absurdly short while. And if there is no third stage, no successful reading, the poem can hardly be said to exist in a practical sense at all.

What a description of this basic tripartite structure shows is that poetry is emotional in nature and theatrical in operation, a skilled recreation of emotion in other people, and that, conversely, a bad poem is one that never succeeds in doing this. All modes of critical derogation are no more than different ways of saying this, whatever literary, philosophical or moral terminology they employ, and it would not be necessary to point out anything so obvious if present-day poetry did not suggest that it had been forgotten. We seem to be producing a new kind of bad poetry, not the old kind that tries to move the reader and fails, but one that does not even try. Repeatedly he is confronted with pieces that cannot be understood without reference beyond their own limits or whose contented insipidity argues that their authors are merely reminding themselves of what they know already, rather than re-creating it for a third party. The reader, in fact, seems no longer present in the poet's mind as he used to be, as someone who must understand and enjoy the finished product if it is to be a success at all; the assumption now is that no one will read it, and wouldn't understand or enjoy it if he or she did. Why should this be so? It is not sufficient to say that poetry has lost its audience, and so we need no longer consider it. Lots of people still read and even buy poetry. More accurately, poetry has lost its old audience, and gained a new one. This has been caused by the consequences of a cunning merger between poet, literary critic and academic critic (three classes now notoriously indistinguishable). It is hardly an exaggeration to say that the poet has gained the happy position wherein he can praise his own poetry in the press and explain it in the class-room, and the reader has been bullied into giving up the consumer's power to say 'I don't like this, bring me something different.' Let him now so much as breathe a word about not liking a poem, and he is in the dock before he can say Edwin Arlington Robinson. And the charge is a grave one: flabby sensibility, insufficient or inadequate critical tools' and inability to meet new verbal and emotional situations. Verdict: guilty, plus a few riders on the prisoner's mental upbringing, addiction to mass amusements, and enfeebled responses. It is time some of you playboys realized, says the judge, that reading a poem is hard work. Fourteen days in stir. Next case.

The cash customers of poetry, therefore, who used to put down their money in the sure and certain hope of enjoyment as if at a theatre or concert hall, were quick to move elsewhere. Poetry was no longer a pleasure. They have been replaced by a humbler squad, whose aim is not pleasure but self- improvement, and who have uncritically accepted the contention that they cannot appreciate poetry without preliminary investment in the intellectual equipment which, by the merest chance, their tutor happens to have about him. In short, the modem poetic audience, when it is not taking in its own washing, is a student audience, pure and simple. At first sight this may not seem a bad thing. The poet has at last a moral ascendancy, and his new clientele not only pay for the poetry but pay to have it explained afterwards. Again, if the poet has only himself to please, he is no longer handicapped by the limitations of his audience. And in any case nobody nowadays believes that a worthwhile artist can rely on anything but his own judgement: public taste is always twenty-five years behind, and picks up a style only when it is exploited by the second-rate. All this is true enough. But at bottom poetry, like all art, is inextricably bound up with giving pleasure, and if a poet loses his pleasure-seeking audience he has lost the only audience worth having, for which the dutiful mob that signs on every September is no substitute. And the effect will be felt throughout his work. He will forget that even if he finds what he has to say interesting, others may not. He will concentrate on moral worth, or semantic intricacy. Worst of all, his poems will no longer be born of the tension between what he non-verbally feels and what can be got over in common word-usage to someone who hasn't had his experience or education or travel grant, and once the other end of the rope is dropped what results will not be so much obscure or piffling (though it may be both) as an unrealized, 'undramatized' slackness, because he will have lost the habit of testing what he writes by this particular standard. Hence, no pleasure. Hence, no poetry.

What can be done about this? Who wants anything done about it? Certainly not the poet, who is in the unprecedented position of peddling both his work and the standard by which it is judged. Certainly not the new reader, who, like a partner of some unconsummated marriage, has no idea of anything better. Certainly not the old reader, who has simply replaced one pleasure with another. Only the romantic loiterer who recalls the days when poetry was condemned as sinful might wish things different. But if the medium is in fact to be in fact rescued from among our duties and restored to our pleasures, I can only think that a large-scale revulsion has got to set in against present notions, and that it will have to start with poetry readers asking themselves more frequently whether they do in fact enjoy what they read, and if not, what the point is of carrying on. And I use 'enjoy' in the commonest of senses, the sense in which we leave a radio on or off. Those interested might like to read David

Daiches's essay 'The New Criticism: Some Qualifications' (in *Literary Essays*, 1956); in the meantime, the following note by Samuel Butler may reawaken a furtive itch for freedom: 'I should like to like Schumann's music better than I do; I dare say I could make myself like it better if I tried; but I do not like having to try to make myself like things; I like things that make me like them at once and no trying at all'

Philip Larkin, "The Pleasure Principle" from *Required Writing: Miscellaneous Pieces, 1955-82.* ©1983 by Faber and Faber.

7. The author suggests that present-day poetry differs from older poetry in that:

   A. present-day poetry is written by professionals, while poetry in the past was more likely written by amateurs.

   B. present-day poetry is written to entertain students, while older poetry was written to entertain the average reader.

   C. present-day poetry is more likely than older poetry to try and yet fail to communicate emotional concepts to the reader.

   D. present-day poetry is written to instruct, whereas older poetry was written for the enjoyment of the reader.

8. The author most likely quoted Samuel Butler in paragraph 4 in order to:

   A. suggest that music, like poetry, is often now less enjoyable than it used to be.

   B. introduce the argument that writing music, like writing poetry, is a simple process.

   C. encourage people to read poetry they actually enjoy rather than try to better appreciate poetry that they think they should like.

   D. illustrate an emotional reaction to a particular composer's music that is analogous to how people emotionally react to the new kind of poetry.

9. Suppose it were to be demonstrated that modern technology like the Internet has had the effect of fundamentally changing what kinds of experiences we find to be enjoyable. What would be the relevance of this new information to the author's argument in the passage?

   A. It would undermine the author's argument that the audience for poetry has changed because poetry itself has changed.

   B. It would strengthen the author's argument that poetry in the past sought to recreate certain emotions in the reader.

   C. It would weaken the author's analogy between music and poetry.

   D. It would have no effect on the author's argument because the passage does not discuss modern technology.

10. Which of the following would best exemplify "the old kind" of bad poetry, as described by the author?

    A. A poem written as an intellectual exercise that does not try to emotionally move the reader

    B. A poem inspired by the poet's emotions that, because of the poet's lack of skill, fails to emotionally affect the reader

    C. A poem that students of literature find enjoyable

    D. A poem that is read only by a small audience

11. Which of the following would be most similar to the author's recommendation in the last paragraph?

    A. A student of fashion, unable to find clothing that she likes, decides to sew her own garments.

    B. Shoppers decide to boycott a store because it does not carry the products they want.

    C. A businessperson employs a new marketing scheme in order to attract new customers.

    D. A musician decides to perform popular instead of classical music because she finds classical music to be too technically challenging.

12. The author most likely uses the phrase "happy position" (paragraph 2) in order to suggest that:

    A. modern readers of poetry would be happier if they learned to enjoy poetry as it is now written.

    B. it is easier for poets to act as poet and critic at once than to try to appeal to the existing preferences of their audience.

    C. poets who can bully readers into buying their work will make a greater profit than those who have to cater to people who lack the necessary intellectual tools to appreciate good poetry.

    D. it is possible to rescue poetry by encouraging poets to go back to writing for the enjoyment of the reader.

———————

Passage III (Questions 13–18)

The spirit of criticism and the measures of reform designed to meet it, which characterized the opening years of the twentieth century in the United States, were merely the signs of a new age. The nation had definitely passed into industrialism. The number of city dwellers employed for wages as contrasted with the farmers working their own land was steadily mounting. The free land, once the refuge of restless workingmen of the East and the immigrants from Europe, was a thing of the past. As President Roosevelt said, "In earlier days, a man who began with a pick and shovel might come to own a mine. That outlet was now closed as regards the immense majority. The majority of men who earned wages in the coal industry, if they wished to progress at all, were compelled to progress not by ceasing to be wage earners but by improving the conditions under which all the wage earners of the country lived and worked."

The disappearance of the free land, President Roosevelt went on to say, also produced "a crass inequality in the bargaining relation of the employer and the individual employee standing alone. The great coal-mining and coal-carrying companies which employed their tens of thousands could easily dispense with the service of any particular miner. The miner, on the other hand, could not dispense with the companies. Individually, the miners were impotent when they sought to enter a wage contract with the great companies; they could make fair terms only by uniting into trade unions to bargain collectively."

This changed economic life was acknowledged by several great companies and business concerns. All over the country, decided efforts were made to bridge the gulf which industry and the corporation had created. Among the devices adopted was that of the "company union." The employees were given a voice in all decisions affecting their work and welfare; rights and grievances were treated as matters of mutual interest rather than individual concern. Representatives of trade unions from outside, however, were rigidly excluded from all negotiations between employers and the employees. Another proposal for drawing capital and labor together was to supplement the wage system by other ties. For example, sometimes employees were allowed to buy stock on easy terms and thus became part owners in the concern. Though opposed by regular trade unions, profit sharing was undoubtedly growing in popularity in the late nineteenth century. Employers were seeking to develop a spirit of cooperation to take the place of competition and enmity; and to increase the production of commodities by promoting the efficiency and happiness of the producers.

Meanwhile, between 1830 and 1890, several aggressive steps were taken in the American labor movement. In 1886, the "National Labor Union" was formed. The purpose of the National Labor Union was not merely to secure labor's standard demands touching hours, wages, and conditions of work. Above all, it sought to eliminate the conflict between capital and labor by making workingmen the owners of shops through the formation of cooperative industries. At the same time, there grew up in the industrial world a more radical organization known as the "Noble Order of the Knights of Labor." In philosophy, the Knights of Labor were socialistic, for they advocated public ownership of the railways and other utilities and the formation of cooperative societies to own and manage stores and factories. As the Knights were radical in their spirit and their strikes were often accompanied by violence, the organization alarmed employers and the general public, raising up against itself a vigorous opposition. Weaknesses within, as well as foes from without, eventually started the Knights on the path to dissolution.

Adapted from Charles Beard and Mary Beard, *History of the United States.* ©1921 by The Macmillan Company.

13. The authors state in the last paragraph that internal weaknesses contributed to the dissolution of the Knights of Labor. Is this claim directly supported by evidence provided in the passage?

    A. Yes: The fact that they carried out violent strikes is described as a reason why employees would abandon the union.
    B. Yes: The claim is supported by the description of the fear raised in the minds of the public by the activities of the union.
    C. No: The fact that the union formed cooperative societies is logically inconsistent with this claim.
    D. No: No direct evidence is provided in the passage.

14. The authors most likely refer in the first paragraph to the spirit of criticism and reform in the early twentieth century in order to:

    A. suggest that these were characteristics that led to the beginnings of the labor movement.
    B. contrast the oppositional nature of the labor movement in the twentieth century with the largely cooperative spirit that characterized business-labor relations in the nineteenth century.
    C. indicate that the twentieth-century critical and reformist spirit had its roots in an economic transformation begun in the previous century.
    D. argue that twentieth century reforms were merely a continuation of a process that had come to maturity in the previous century.

15. The authors' description of the National Labor Movement indicates that:

   A. The National Labor Movement, like company unions, encouraged cooperation between employees and business owners.
   B. The National Labor Movement, unlike the Knights of Labor, supported socialism.
   C. The National Labor Movement had the goal of turning workers into business owners.
   D. The National Labor Movement, unlike the Knights of Labor, did not carry out strikes.

16. With which of the following statements made by President Roosevelt, as he is quoted in the passage, would the authors of the passage be most likely to disagree?

   A. Coal miners were more dependent on the mining company than the mining company was dependent on any individual miner.
   B. In the past, it was possible for a laborer to become a business owner.
   C. Miners could get fair treatment from the company only through collective bargaining within a trade union.
   D. Coal miners were more in need of union protection than were other kinds of laborers.

17. The authors' discussion of profit sharing best supports which of the following inferences?

   A. Owners of companies that offered profit sharing expected to gain more in increased productivity than they expected to lose by distributing stock to employees.
   B. Stock options were offered only to discourage employees from joining regular trade unions.
   C. Employees who represented regular trade unions were excluded from profit-sharing plans.
   D. Coal mining companies were among the businesses that sought to foster a spirit of cooperation among employees by giving them a stake in the business.

18. The passage argues that a significant difference between agricultural and industrial economies is that:

   A. independent farmers in an agrarian society generally have a higher standard of living than do workers in an industrialized society.
   B. cooperation is not necessary to farmers, while it is essential to industrial workers.
   C. the gap between rich and poor is higher in agrarian than in industrialized societies.
   D. industrial workers are less able than are farmers working their own land to improve their own lives without also contributing to the improvement of the lives of others.

Passage IV (Questions 19–23)

Calling it a cover-up would be far too dramatic. But for more than half a century…physicists have been quietly aware of a dark cloud looming on a distant horizon. The problem is this: There are two foundational pillars upon which modern physics rests. One is Albert Einstein's general relativity, which provides a theoretical framework for understanding the universe on the largest of scales—stars, galaxies, clusters of galaxies, and beyond— to the immense expanse of the universe itself. The other is quantum mechanics, which provides a theoretical framework for understanding the universe on the smallest of scales— molecules, atoms, and all the way down to subatomic particles like electrons and quarks. Through years of research, physicists have experimentally confirmed, to an almost unimaginable degree of accuracy, virtually all predictions made by each of these theories. But these same theoretical tools inexorably lead to another disturbing conclusion: As they are currently formulated, general relativity and quantum mechanics cannot both be right.

If you have not heard previously about this ferocious antagonism, you may be wondering why. The answer is not hard to come by. In all but the most extreme situations, physicists study things that are either small and light…or things that are huge and heavy, but not both. This means that they need use only quantum mechanics or general relativity and can, with a furtive glance, shrug off the barking admonition of the other.

But the universe can be extreme. In the central depths of a black hole, an enormous mass is crushed to minuscule size. These are realms that are tiny and yet incredibly massive, therefore requiring that both quantum mechanics and general relativity be brought to bear. The equations of general relativity and quantum mechanics, when combined, begin to shake, rattle, and gush with steam like a red-lined automobile. Put less figuratively, well-posed physical questions elicit nonsensical answers from the unhappy amalgam of these two theories. Can it really be that the universe at its most fundamental level is divided, requiring one set of laws when things are large and a different, incompatible set when things are small?

Superstring theory answers with a resounding no. Intense research over the past decade by physicists and mathematicians around the world has revealed that this new approach to describing matter at its most fundamental level resolves the tension between general relativity and quantum mechanics. In fact, within this new framework, general relativity and quantum mechanics require one another for the theory to make sense. But superstring theory takes this union one giant step further. For three decades, Einstein sought a unified theory of physics, one which would interweave all of nature's forces and material constituents within a single unified theoretical tapestry. He failed. More than half a century later, his dream of a unified theory has become the Holy Grail of modern physics. And a sizable part of the physics and mathematics community is becoming increasingly convinced that string theory may provide the answer. According to string theory, if we could examine subatomic particles with a precision that is many orders of magnitude beyond our present technological capacity, we would find that each is not point-like but instead consists of a tiny, one-dimensional loop. From one principle— that everything at its most microscopic level consists of vibrating strands—string theory provides a single explanatory framework capable of encompassing all forces and all matter.

Adapted from Brian Greene, *The Elegant Universe: Superstrings, Hidden Dimensions, and the Quest for the Ultimate Theory.* ©1999 by B. Greene

19. Which of the following best expresses the main point of the passage?

   A. Quantum mechanics and general relativity each provide insight into different aspects of the universe, but the two theoretical approaches are inconsistent with each other.
   B. String theory may resolve a long-standing paradox in physics while at the same time providing a unified theoretical framework that has never before been achieved.
   C. String theory solves a longstanding problem in physics by providing accurate observational data where none was before available.
   D. While Einstein was not successful in his time at creating a unified theory of physics, string theory has succeeded where he failed.

20. The author states that the mutual exclusivity of quantum mechanics and general relativity has not been widely discussed because:

   A. physicists in each field, due to the different nature of the phenomena they study, were unaware of the conflict until the discovery of black holes.
   B. inaccuracies in experimental observations obscured the fact that the two theories are incompatible.
   C. while physicists were aware of the conflict, they believed that a resolution would never be necessary.
   D. physicists tend to be separated into two areas, each of which relies on only one of the two theories.

21. Which of the following statements best expresses the relevance of black holes to the author's argument in the passage?

   A. Only with recent technological advances have we been able to observe that matter and forces within and around a black hole cannot be explained by any existing theoretical framework.
   B. Black holes are huge and tiny at the same time, and therefore neither of the two foundational theories of physics can explain them.
   C. They illustrate how the universe in certain rare extreme cases is divided into phenomena that are only explicable using two different sets of laws.
   D. They cannot be explained by any currently existing theoretical framework, and so the author argues that we must search for some alternative way of understanding the relationship between matter and force in the universe.

22. Elsewhere, the author writes that "particle properties in string theory are the manifestation of one and the same physical feature: the resonant patterns of vibration. The same idea applies to the forces of nature as well; force particles are also associated with particular patterns of string vibration." This description would most strengthen which of the following claims made in the passage?

   A. String theory is capable of providing a unified theory of physics.
   B. A combination of quantum mechanics and general relativity provides nonsensical answers to questions about extreme phenomena in the universe.
   C. Neither quantum mechanics nor general relativity provides accurate predictions about the behavior of quarks.
   D. The conflict between quantum mechanics has been recognized yet ignored for the last fifty years.

23. According to the passage, string theory reconciles the conflict between quantum mechanics and general relativity in part by:

   A. showing that the conflict is only empirical, not theoretical, and so need not be resolved.
   B. illustrating how each in its current formulation can be subsumed within a new theoretical model.
   C. positing a radically new formulation of the nature of matter, within which the two theories are interdependent rather than mutually exclusive.
   D. ignoring both in favor of an entirely new scientific paradigm.

_____

The genius of archaeology lies in its uncanny ability to recreate entire civilizations out of the most meager shards and dusty fragments of ancient lives. Inspiration for this imaginative act comes from many sources, including the insights and self-discoveries brought about by archaeological role-playing. This novel technique penetrates centuries of oblivion by manufacturing replicas of artifacts found in communities buried long ago and figuring out what crucial purpose they served in the daily needs and routines of those antecessor societies.

Archaeologists such as the University of Miami's Professor Knecht revive the artifacts of Cro-Magnon tribes by re-creating the actual manufacturing process likely employed in antiquity to create spearpoints out of deer antlers or animal bone. To be certain that the re-created spearpoints are as identical as possible to the originals recovered at sites, archaeologists test the aerodynamics, hardness, and power of their reproductions. Because Cro-Magnon hunters often used an "atlatl" to hurl spears, role-players must take into account the increased velocity and improved aim achieved with that ancient device. The atlatl is a hooked stick which plugs into a hollowed-out pocket at the bottom of a spear, and seems to have operated on a principle similar to that of the slingshot, adding heft and accuracy to the natural ability of a skilled hunter. Cro-Magnon ruins dating from 22,000 years ago have left evidence of functional atlatls. As they test the conformity of their replicated spearpoints, archaeologists can approximate the additional force and velocity contributed by the atlatl by using an adjustable crossbow.

Archaeologists estimate that the Cro-Magnon, one of the first *Homo sapiens*, populated Western Europe as early as 40,000 years ago, at the start of the Aurignacian period. Remnants of Cro-Magnon civilization have been traced from sites dating as recently as the Gravettian period, which began 12,000 years later. Over the course of those 120 centuries, Cro-Magnon artisanry was not standing still; on the contrary, spearpoints recovered and replicated from later colonies are distinguished from earlier models by a relatively repair-friendly design and ready adaptability to different spears.

Their observations of reindeer and red deer jousts must have led the earliest Cro-Magnon hunters to imagine the advantages they might enjoy with weapons of the kind deer came by naturally. In the more immature artisanry, spearmaking pioneers split antlers lengthwise in two and shaped them with wedges to fashion spearpoints with a split base. To fasten the finished point to a spear pole, artisans cut a cleft in the shape of a "U" into the shaft's end, and bound the point into the cleft with fibers from plants or animals. Then they jammed a small wedge into the point's split base, forcing each side of the base into the wood of the shaft. The mechanical pressures acting on the shaft, point, and wedge, reinforced by the fibrous ligature, kept the weapon in one piece even through the accumulated trauma of multiple hurls and successive hits. These weapons nevertheless were subject to damage and dulling, and the surviving examples found at sites indicate that repairs were, at best, improvisational and awkward.

Despite the difficulty of repairing these weapons, the split-based spearpoints must have proven fairly effective because they enjoyed eight thousand years of popularity with Cro-Magnon hunters. But 320 centuries ago, points shaped like lozenges displaced the earlier forms. The new designs enabled hunters to resharpen their points efficiently, a feature that represented an economic and practical advance over the earlier split-based points, and one which in all likelihood was the cause of the eventual predominance of new round-based or lozenge points.

24. The passage suggests that by re-creating the working techniques that reproduce ancient artifacts, archaeologists:

    A. inspire fanciful reconstructions of the archaeological past.
    B. establish the truth or falsity of ancient histories.
    C. gain insight into the needs and desires of past cultures.
    D. reinvent antiquity from contemporary perspectives.

25. Suppose several split-based spearpoints dating from the late Gravettian period were discovered in a perfect state of repair. How would this information affect the author's claims about the development of spearpoint design?

    A. It would support the claim that round-based points replaced split-based points.
    B. It would not significantly weaken the claim that Cro-Magnon weapons technology improved over time.
    C. It would weaken the claim that split-based points were developed in the Aurignacian period.
    D. It would weaken the claim that Gravettian Cro-Magnon weaponry was more advanced than that of Aurignacian Cro-Magnon.

26. Based on information in the passage, it is reasonable to conclude that during the Aurignacian period:

    A. deer caused serious injuries with their antlers.
    B. red deer were threatened with extinction.
    C. reindeer were considered a prize game.
    D. deer were regularly dehorned while still alive.

27. In describing the techniques by which Cro-Magnon artisans fastened points to their spears, the author cites all of the following factors EXCEPT:

    A. fiber binding.
    B. wedge pressure.
    C. mechanical friction.
    D. shaft cleft.

28. The passage suggests that before the development of the atlatl, hunters:

    A. did not rely on spears as primary weaponry.
    B. did not possess much natural ability.
    C. had spearpoints which were difficult to sharpen.
    D. were at a greater disadvantage with swiftly moving prey.

29. Which of the following findings, if true, would most support the value of the tests described in the second paragraph?

    A. The replicated spearpoints are strong enough to withstand being trampled on, yet light enough to not cause the spear to wobble in flight.
    B. The re-created spears fly smoothly with minimum deviation and maximum penetration of the target.
    C. Climatic conditions in Gravettian Europe were similar to those in Western Europe today.
    D. The re-created spearpoints, when thrown at animal carcasses, leave holes and splits in the bones similar to those found in bones unearthed from Cro-Magnon ruins.

30. According to the author, the difficulty in repairing some spearpoints:

    A. initiated rapid development of better designs.
    B. was an economic advantage because the spearpoints would eventually become obsolete.
    C. decreased the efficacy of Cro-Magnon hunts.
    D. was an inconvenient but not disabling defect.

_____

Passage VI (Questions 31–35)

For Marc Chagall, art served less as a mirror of reality than as the tangible construct of the artist's "chemistry": the combination of artistic craftsmanship, spirituality, and life experience. The dynamic synthesis of these elements transformed previously blank canvas to vibrant artifact, giving birth to a dramatic testament of faith, morality, and beauty.

Forged in the brutal poverty and religious persecution of late nineteenth-century rural Russia, and hardened by the hellish horrors of twentieth-century warfare, Chagall's artistic visions manifest both the supremacy of the human spirit and the possibility of salvation through divine guidance. Acknowledging the mortal truth that "all life inevitably moves towards its end," Chagall believed that he therefore "should illumine his life with the colors of love and hope"; love, according to the painter, constitutes the core principle of all religions. Given his formation and creed, it is not surprising that themes of suffering and loss interweave inextricably with those of hope and redemption throughout Chagall's work.

Captivated since childhood by the Bible's epic sweep and moral depth, Chagall assimilated the grand, heroic histories his parents and grandparents read to him from the Old Testament. Surrounded by the by-products of poverty—hunger, infirmity, disease, and despair—the artist's developing consciousness seized on those ancient mystic teachings as on a lifeboat in a raging storm. Powerless to overcome his community's oppressors and vulnerable to the uncontrollable natural elements, the young painter sought refuge in an artistic vision in which myth and imagery transmuted to waking dream so vividly it bore the force of psychic visitation.

The intimate link between spiritual truth and the vision and mission of the artist is starkly rendered in Chagall's 1917 painting *The Apparition*, in which the painter depicts himself at his easel, mesmerized and dumbfounded at the appearance of a heavenly angel before him. The French critic Fernand Hazere observes that "the picture is a key that helps us to better understand Chagall's spiritual world and mission." In *The Apparition* the brightly glowing angel by its presence bestows on the artist (both on the canvas and in reality) the privileges and responsibilities of spiritual ministry. Through his craft, then, the painter brings love and salvation to humankind.

This theme is reiterated in the painting *Jacob's Dream*. Here, Chagall shows Jacob in luminescent red at the center of the canvas. Jacob's head is tilted slightly upwards and to the right, inclined away from a swirling maelstrom of purple, black, and plaintive yellow that darkens the left side of the painting. That maelstrom, populated by vaguely human figures, reveals a hectic state of perilous imbalance and futility.

Jacob, glowing in his dream, seems impervious to all that sound and fury around him, charmed and strangely appeased by the cool blues and pure white that define the large, winged, celestial angel dominating the right half of the picture. Thus split between the fierce frenzy of the bodily world and the tranquil reassurance of the spiritual, the canvas would seem a schizophrenic nightmare were it not for Jacob's confident, central presence as mediator. Refracted through the dreaming figure, Chagall's colors penetrate the schism, surprising the dark, turbulent world with brave reverberations of grace and light.

31. The main idea of the passage is that:

 A. an artist's spiritual beliefs provide the most powerful influence on his or her artistic themes.
 B. Chagall could not have made great art without his early education in the Bible.
 C. Chagall saw himself as a spiritual mediator who could bring hope and love to the world through his art.
 D. genius emerges only through a life of genuine suffering.

32. According to the passage, how did Chagall's life experience affect his artistic vision?

 A. It led him to believe that the artist is powerless in the face of the suffering caused by war and disease.
 B. It prevented him from seeing reality and moving forward artistically.
 C. It led him to protest against the oppressive policies of the Russian state and to call for political reform.
 D. It inspired images of the artist guiding humanity through the turmoil of worldly existence toward redemption through love.

33. The passage suggests that Chagall's use of color in *Jacob's Dream* is related to his artistic themes in that:

 A. color instills a dynamic interaction among related parts of his composition.
 B. the theme of redemption in this work is subordinate to the emotional effect of the colors themselves.
 C. each artistic idea is color-coded throughout his work.
 D. primary colors like red and yellow usually symbolize hope, while dark colors represent chaos and fear.

34. The author quotes the French critic Fernand Hazere in the fourth paragraph primarily for the purpose of:

A. supporting his own interpretation of other scholarly works.

B. relating modern French criticism to other critical approaches.

C. further describing Chagall's artistic inspiration and purpose.

D. calling into question the sincerity of Chagall's self-appointed missionary role.

35. In another essay, the author of the passage posits that for Chagall, the reality of art lies in its impact on the "eyes, hearts, and minds of those who view it." Which of the following interpretations of *Jacob's Dream* best exemplifies both this claim and the mission of the artist, as that mission is described in the passage?

A. The central human figure represents a sinner torn between the temptations of bodily pleasures and the joy of spiritual redemption.

B. Jacob represents the antithesis of the painter, as Jacob is mired in a maelstrom depicting hell while the painter wishes to deliver himself and others from suffering.

C. The contrast between light and dark represents the eternal and irresolvable struggle between good and evil that defines human existence.

D. Jacob represents the painter, who acts as an intercessor for humanity by bringing a message of hope to the world.

Passage VII (Questions 36–42)

As the largest land animal on the planet, the elephant is a potent symbol of the animal kingdom, distinguished by its size, prehensile trunk, ivory tusks, and enormous ears. In the West, where the elephant is an exotic creature known only from books, movies, circuses, and zoos, its image suffers distortion and even exploitation. Whether romanticized or trivialized, the elephant is rarely presented in its complex reality. But in Africa, where humans and elephants—or their respective ancestors—have coexisted for a million years or more, the elephant is known in fuller dimensions. It has been a source of food, material, and riches; a fearsome rival for resources; and a highly visible, provocative neighbor. Inevitably it has had an impact on artistic imagination. Even in areas where the elephant has now vanished, it persists as a symbol in expressive culture. As interpreted in African sculpture, masquerade, dance, and song, its image undergoes a startling range of transformations. But no matter how it is represented, its size and power are the features most likely to be dramatized, for they not only inspire respect, but also stand, for better or worse, as emblems for human values.

The elephant is, of course, only one creature within the vast drama of intricate relationships that link the animal world with the human one. It should not be isolated from the hierarchy of fauna that give it context not just in actuality but also in its symbolic life. In its symbolic functions, it is at times interchangeable with other creatures, depending on culture and circumstance: Qualities ascribed to the elephant in one instance may be given to the leopard or duiker in another. Even within a single culture, the meanings ascribed to it can shift. Or it may be just one of an array of animals treated more or less equally, much like those of the biblical Noah's ark—a theme that has been explored in glass paintings from Senegal, thorn carvings from Nigeria, and popular paintings from Ethiopia.

The elephant may be considered as a microcosm—a large one, to be sure. By virtue of its sheer size and prominence, the roles it plays in art and historical processes are magnified. In the broader terms of the macrocosm, one might ask how humans relate to their environment and the fauna they share it with, and above all, how they interpret that relationship. In Africa as elsewhere, people represent their relationship to animals in multiple ways, and their complex experience of it can be read in the symbolic language of their respective cultures. Although elephant imagery may have its origins in actual observation, it is just as often a product of the imagination, and African depictions of the elephant have as much to say about human society as about the animal itself. Ultimately, historical events, social responsibilities, religious beliefs, and political relationships are the primary subjects of elephant imagery.

For some, this may appear problematic. Within the scientific community, finding *human* traits in *animals* is often seen as sentimental anthropomorphizing, even though it is, according to Levi-Strauss, a fundamental activity of the human mind. On the other hand, finding *animal* traits in *humans* tends to be seen outside the scientific community as pernicious and degrading. Mary Midgley puts it quite succinctly:

> Unquestionably there does remain a nonscientific but powerful tendency to resent and fear all close comparison between our own species and any other. Unquestionably we often tend to feel—at times extremely strongly—that the gap between our own species and all others is enormous.

Yet in African cultures, the perception of this "enormous gap" provokes much thoughtful and creative response. Of all creatures, the elephant—so huge, so remote, and yet so apparently human—most dramatizes the gap between the species. Donal Cosentino, surveying the elephant in oral traditions, sees it as the Gray Planet, whose sightings are full of mystery and portent. But the phenomenon is by no means confined to oral literature; indeed, many visual representations are driven by the impulse to mediate the breach between worlds.

36. The passage suggests that Africans' long-standing coexistence with elephants has caused them to regard elephants primarily with:

   A. appreciation.
   B. contempt.
   C. fear.
   D. reverence.

37. Suppose that the elephants in a particular region of Africa were to disappear. How would this new information affect the author's claims about the animal's impact on the artistic product of humans living in the area?

   A. Owing to their scarcity, talismanic objects carved from elephant tusks would acquire considerable value as magical totems.
   B. Communities would barter their local products for cultural works and artisan crafts from communities that remained physically close to elephants.
   C. The dance and song of the local inhabitants would gradually lose all traces of elephant imagery.
   D. Elephant imagery would continue to play an important role in the local culture.

38. Suppose it is discovered that muralists in a number of African communities portrayed jaguars as provisioners of food, material, and wealth; as dangerous competitors for resources; and as dramatically inspirational cohabitants. How would this information affect the author's claims about the interchangeability of symbolic function?

   A. It would support the claim that culture and circumstance help determine which qualities are ascribed to which animals.
   B. It would support the claim that some people believe the gap between animals and humans to be enormous.
   C. It would weaken the claim that Senegalese glass paintings are comparable in their imagery to Noah's ark.
   D. It would weaken the claim that the elephant may be viewed as a microcosm.

39. The claim that elephant imagery in African culture reveals information about Africans' social lives is based mainly on:

   A. western European cultural analysis.
   B. African representations of the microcosm and macrocosm.
   C. Nigerian thorn carvings.
   D. Ethiopian popular art.

40. Levi-Strauss and Mary Midgley are cited in the passage in order to support the point that:

   A. African cultures tend to anthropomorphize to a much greater degree than European cultures.
   B. science scholars have systematically identified a number of human qualities in animals.
   C. the human capacity to liken human characteristics to animal traits is a complex and contradictory phenomenon.
   D. anthropological scholars have achieved a general consensus of opinion with regard to anthropomorphism.

41. According to the passage, a gap exists between all of the following EXCEPT:

   A. African and Western versions of elephant imagery.
   B. the size of an elephant and its symbolic import.
   C. actual elephants and elephant imagery.
   D. the perspective of the elephant as a microcosm and as a macrocosm.

42. It can be inferred from the passage that humans view their relationship to animals:

   A. in nearly universal symbols across different cultures.
   B. in varied ways that depend on each culture's symbolic forms.
   C. in superficial and simplistic terms.
   D. in more practical than symbolic terms.

Passage VIII (Questions 43–48)

Just as an embryo retraces much of the human evolutionary past, the budding artist reinvents the first stages of art. Soon, however, he or she completes that process and begins to respond to the culture around him or her. Even children's art is subject to the taste and outlook of the society that shapes his or her personality. In fact, we tend to judge children's art according to the same criteria as adult art—only in appropriately simpler terms—and with good reason, for if we examine its successive stages, we find that the youngster must develop all the skills that go into adult art: coordination, intellect, personality, imagination, creativity, and aesthetic judgment. Seen this way, the making of a youthful artist is a process as fragile as growing up itself, and one that can be stunted at any step by the vicissitudes of life. No wonder that so few continue their creative aspirations into adulthood.

Given the many factors that feed into it, art must play a very special role in the artist's personality. Sigmund Freud, the founder of modern psychiatry, conceived of art primarily in terms of sublimation outside of consciousness. Such a view hardly does justice to artistic creativity, since art is not simply a negative force at the mercy of our neuroses, but a positive expression that integrates diverse aspects of personality. Indeed, when we look at the art of the mentally ill, we may be struck by its vividness; but we instinctively sense that something is wrong because the expression is incomplete.

Artists sometimes may be tortured by the burden of their genius, but they can never be truly creative under the thrall of psychosis. The imagination is one of our most mysterious facets. It can be regarded as the connector between the conscious and the subconscious, where most of our brain activity takes place. It is the very glue that holds together our personality, intellect, and spirituality. Because the imagination responds to all three, it acts in lawful, if unpredictable, ways that are determined by the psyche and the mind. Thus, even the most private artistic statements can be understood on some level, even if only an intuitive one.

The imagination is important, as it allows us to conceive of all kinds of possibilities in the future and to understand the past in a way that has real survival value. It is a fundamental part of our makeup. The ability to make art, in contrast, must have been acquired relatively recently in the course of human evolution. The record of the earliest art is lost to us. Human beings have been walking the earth for some two million years, but the oldest prehistoric art that we know of was made only about 35,000 years ago, though it was undoubtedly the culmination of a long development no longer traceable. Even the most "primitive" ethnographic art represents a late stage of development within a stable society.

Who were the first artists? In all likelihood, they were shamans. Like the legendary Orpheus, they were believed to have divine powers of inspiration and to be able to enter the underworld of the subconscious in a deathlike trance. But, unlike ordinary mortals, they were then able to return to the realm of the living. Even today, the artist remains a magician whose work can mystify and move us—an embarrassing fact to civilized people, who do not readily relinquish their veneer of rational control.

In a larger sense, art, like science and religion, fulfills our innate urge to comprehend ourselves and the universe. This function makes art especially significant and, hence, worthy of our attention. Art has the power to penetrate to the core of our being, which recognizes itself in the creative act. For that reason, art represents its creator's deepest understanding and highest aspirations; at the same time, the artist often plays an important role as the articulator of our shared beliefs and values.

43. The main idea of the passage is that:

   A. artists serve as mediators between our daily reality and the world of the unconscious.
   B. as human society has evolved and become more sophisticated, so has human artistic expression.
   C. artistic expression reflects the psychological processes and makeup of its creator.
   D. the essential appeal of art is its power to mystify.

44. In the context of the passage, the word "genius" at the beginning of the third paragraph refers primarily to:

   A. the recognition and appreciation of an artist's ability by critics and the public at large.
   B. the psychological sensitivity to reality that an artist develops.
   C. the intellectual attainments of individual artists.
   D. the neurotic and psychotic manifestations of artistic perception.

45. The passage implies that art relates to its audience:

   A. by delivering both a personal and a universal communication from artist to audience.
   B. less intensely today because, no longer associated with magic, its power to mystify and to move has dwindled.
   C. by providing insight into another's creativity only, while science and religion allow us to comprehend ourselves and the universe.
   D. irrespective of an audience's emotional and spiritual needs.

46. The passage suggests that the ability to create art:

   A. evolved before the imagination evolved.
   B. evolved primarily as a survival skill.
   C. has been documented to exist as early as two million years ago, when humans first inhabited the Earth.
   D. was the result of a long developmental process that occurred within stable societies.

47. According to the passage, why is art embarrassing to some people who pride themselves on their civilized rationality?

   A. Art's essential mystery frustrates those who like to appear cultivated.
   B. Art makes many social sophisticates feel ignorant.
   C. Art's simultaneous universality and individual relevance seems paradoxical to some who pride themselves on their logical powers.
   D. Art is able to access the most fundamental and private essence of the self.

48. The author's discussion of Sigmund Freud's view of art and artists most supports the claim that:

   A. art represents an integrative psychological function rather than an uncontrolled psychic expression.
   B. art, which sublimates psychological ambiguity, is superior to that which generates mystery.
   C. successful psychotherapy would enable an artist to sublimate the need for artistic expression.
   D. development of individual artistic consciousness retraces much of humans' evolutionary past.

In his book *The Expression of Emotions in Man and Animals*, Charles Darwin had dared to imagine a dog's conscious life: "But can we feel sure that an old dog with excellent memory and some power of imagination, as shown by his dreams, never reflects on his past pleasures in the chase and this would be a form of self-consciousness?" Even more evocatively, he asked: "Who can say what cows feel, when they surround and stare intently on a dead or dying companion?" He was unafraid to speculate about areas that seemed to require further investigation.

A pivotal book in my thinking about animal emotions was Donald Griffin's *The Question of Animal Awareness*. Attacked in many quarters upon its publication in 1976, it discussed the possible intellectual lives of animals and asked whether science was examining issues of their cognition and consciousness fairly. While Griffin did not explore emotion, he pointed to it as an area that needed investigation. Convincing and intellectually exciting, it made me want to read a comparable work on animal emotions, but I learned that there was almost no investigation of the emotional lives of animals in the modern scientific literature.

Why should this be so? One reason is that scientists, animal behaviorists, zoologists, and ethologists are fearful of being accused of anthropomorphism, a form of scientific blasphemy. Not only are the emotions of animals not a respectable field of study, but the words associated with emotions are not supposed to be applied to them. Among the first people I asked about the emotional lives of animals were researchers working with dolphins. Dolphins show such delight in performing, even in creating new performances of their own, that an elaborate emotional component seems obvious. Thinking that experts who work with and study animals might offer observations in person that they would be reluctant to put into a scientific article, I asked renowned scholars of dolphin behavior about their experiences with the emotions their dolphins expressed. They were unwilling to speculate or even offer observations. One said, "I don't know what emotion means." [However], what this scholar said was undermined by what he did; he hugged his dolphin in a clearly emotional moment, at least for the researcher. It is hard to believe that scientists would express intense feelings toward creatures they genuinely felt were emotionally insensate.

Comparative psychology to this day discusses observable behavior and physical states of animals and evolutionary explanations for their existence but shies away from the mental states that are inextricably involved in that behavior. When such states are examined, the focus is on cognition, not emotion. The more recent discipline of ethology, the science of animal behavior, also seeks functional and causal, rather than emotive, explanations for behavior. The causal explanations center on theories of "ultimate causation"—the animal pairs because this increases reproductive success—as distinguished from "proximate causation"—the animal pairs because it has fallen in love. Although the two explanations are not necessarily mutually exclusive, the field as a whole has continued to treat emotions as unworthy of scientific attention.

With the advent of laboratory studies of animals, the distance maintained from the world of animal feelings became even greater. This distance supported scientists who do painful studies on animals in believing that animals feel no pain of suffering, or that at least the pain animals feel is removed enough from the pain humans feel that one not need take it into account. The professional and financial interests in continuing animal experimentation help to explain at least some resistance to the notion that animals have a complex emotional life.

Adapted from Jeffrey Moussaieff Masson and Susan McCarthy, *When Elephants Weep: The Emotional Lives of Animals*. ©1995 by Jeffrey Moussaieff Masson and Susan McCarthy.

49. Based on information in the passage, it is most reasonable to infer that Griffin's book was attacked upon publication for which of the following reasons?

   A. Its discussion of the emotional lives of animals was seen by scientists as scientific blasphemy.
   B. It focused on emotive causes for animal behavior rather than functional, ultimate causes.
   C. It raised issues of animal cognition in a way that some scientists perceived to be unscientific.
   D. Experts in animal behavior felt that his expression of personal feeling about animals was inappropriate.

50. The discussion in the passage about interpreting the meaning of animal behaviors is in part based on which of the following assumptions?

   A. The same emotions will produce the same behaviors in different species of animals.
   B. When animals exhibit behavior that is similar to human behavior, it is likely true that they are experiencing similar emotions as well.
   C. Cows and other animals mourn their dead.
   D. Animals are able to sense and to some degree understand emotions felt by their human caretakers.

51. Rabbits often freeze when confronted by a potential predator, remaining immobile for long periods of time. Which of the following best represents an explanation of this behavior based on a theory of "ultimate causation"?

A. The animal freezes because this behavior maximizes the probability that it will survive.
B. The animal freezes because it is afraid.
C. The animal freezes because external stimuli have overwhelmed the capacity of its nervous system to respond appropriately.
D. The animal freezes because it believes that if it remains still, the predator may lose interest and leave.

52. The author describes the behavior of a well-known expert in dolphin behavior (paragraph 3) in order to:

A. provide evidence of animal behavior that suggests that they do in fact feel emotion.
B. introduce the argument that proximate causes and ultimate causes are in many cases mutually exclusive.
C. criticize scientists who inflict discomfort on their animal subjects.
D. develop the argument that scientists are uncomfortable expressing agreement with the idea that animals may have feelings.

53. The author suggests which of the following as possible motivations for scientists' resistance to the idea that animals have emotions?

I. Scientists may be personally embarrassed to admit in front of colleagues the belief in the existence of animal emotions.
II. Scientists may profit financially from the suffering of animals.
III. Scientists may suffer harm to their professional reputation if accused of anthropomorphism.

A. I only
B. II only
C. II and III only
D. I, II and III

54. It is reasonable to conclude that Darwin raised questions about a dog's consciousness and a cow's emotions because he believed:

A. that the possibility of animal thought and emotion had not yet been sufficiently considered.
B. that the theory of evolution could explain the existence of animal emotive states.
C. that his professional reputation would allow him to survive the inevitable criticism from other scientists.
D. that cognition is more likely than emotion to appear in animal species.

_____

Passage X (Questions 55–59)

The human sciences have long grappled with profound methodological and ideological crises, crises that began as colonial expansion drew Europe into global cultural, economic, and political structures, as popular urban cultures challenged the monopoly of academic elites, and as natural science demanded to be recognized as a comprehensive world view. The humanist project of interpreting the textual monuments of European history had for centuries served Europeans as a privileged mode of understanding what it meant to be human and as a hegemonic ideology and civic identity. By the late nineteenth century, critics of humanism pointed to its narrow focus on Europe, its elitism, and its disregard of the natural sciences. Defenders of humanism emphasized the utopian potential of hermeneutic interpretation, in which the humanity of both interpreter and subject of interpretation is recognized and elevated. The outlines of the major positions in contemporary debates about humanism originated in nineteenth- and twentieth-century Germany.

While the discipline of anthropology emerged all over Europe in the nineteenth century, it was above all in Germany that it functioned as a new antihumanist worldview, and it was in Germany that this anthropological antihumanism had some of its most important and far-reaching effects… The new global situation allowed anthropologists to challenge humanism and the academic humanities. Anthropologists proposed a new basis for working out the European self through human scientific scholarship: Rather than excluding the colonized other, anthropology would focus explicitly on societies that, all agreed, were radically separate from narratives of Western civilization. Instead of studying European "cultural peoples," societies defined by their history and civilization, anthropologists studied the colonized "natural peoples," societies supposedly lacking history and culture. Anthropologists proposed that that their study of so-called natural peoples would reveal human nature directly, unobscured by the masks of culture and the complications of historical development. For the empathetic interpretation characteristic of humanism, anthropologists substituted what they regarded as objective, natural scientific knowledge of a non-European other. Anthropology focused not on canonical texts of celebrated cultural peoples but on the bodies and everyday lives of the colonized natural peoples. The European self should no longer… work itself out through a solipsistic repression of the rest of the world. Anthropology offered Europeans a modern identity as a cultural people whose status depended less on a humanistic *Bildung*, or self-cultivation, than on the development of the natural sciences, including anthropology as the study of natural peoples.

Notions of biological evolution were conspicuously absent from most anthropologists' understanding of the natural sciences throughout the nineteenth century. Nature functioned in German anthropology as an unchanging realm of eternal truth, which contrasted with the ephemeral developments of history. This understanding of nature was diametrically opposed to that embodied in the theory of evolution… Applying a static concept of nature to living humans, however, presented insurmountable theoretical and practical difficulties. From the beginning, anthropologists complained that the people they encountered were corrupted by contact with Europeans and thus were poor examples of natural peoples. By the early twentieth century, presenting the customs and artifacts of particular societies as instances of a timeless nature would come to seem arbitrary and artificial to anthropologists. In a single conceptual shift just after the turn of the twentieth century, anthropologists would embrace the idea of a changeable nature, thus abandoning their search for ahistoric natural peoples and accepting theories of biological evolution. However, throughout the last third of the nineteenth century, nature functioned as a timeless opposite to culture and history and provided the conceptual grounding for anthropology's challenge to the Eurocentric humanism of the German academy.

Adapted from Andrew Zimmerman, *Anthropology and Humanism in Imperial Germany.* ©2001 by The University of Chicago Press.

55. The passage suggests that colonialist expansion:

   A. at once contributed to and frustrated the goals of nineteenth-century German anthropologists.
   B. was criticized by German humanists for disregarding the true humanity of colonized peoples.
   C. contributed to the rise of a belief in biological evolution by exposing German scientists to a variety of formerly unknown animal species in colonial territories.
   D. made it impossible to carry out useful anthropological studies, by tainting formerly pure "natural peoples" with European cultural influences.

56. The passage suggests that German anthropologists distinguished "cultural peoples" from "natural peoples" on the basis that:

   A. the culture and history of "cultural peoples" was more highly evolved than the history and culture of "natural peoples."
   B. "cultural peoples" seek to control nature, while the culture of "natural peoples" is primarily influenced by appreciation and respect for the forces of nature.
   C. "cultural peoples" are fundamentally constituted by their social and historical context, while "natural peoples" have no history or culture.
   D. the domination of "natural peoples" by "cultural peoples" was inevitable, given the superiority of Western civilization.

57. It is reasonable to infer that the anthropological belief in nature as "an unchanging realm of eternal truth" (paragraph 3) is most similar to which of the following beliefs, also attributed by the author to German anthropologists?

A. The belief in natural evolution
B. The belief in cultural evolution
C. The belief in "natural peoples"
D. The belief in a humanist Bildung

58. The defenders of humanism mentioned in the first paragraph most likely believed that humanists could raise the humanity of both interpreter and the subject of interpretation because:

A. the study of more "primitive" societies would reveal a pure core of human nature.
B. European intellectual achievements gave them special insight into the true nature of humanity.
C. the observations of European humanists trained in the natural sciences would give them special insight into human nature.
D. their belief in utopianism included the basic tenet that all peoples are essentially created equal.

59. A German book contains photographs of a variety of simple cooking implements used in a particular African village. This book was most likely written by:

A. an early nineteenth-century humanist.
B. a late twentieth-century anthropologist.
C. a twentieth-century humanist.
D. a nineteenth-century anthropologist.

Passage XI (Questions 60–64)

To understand the politics of the Voting Rights Act of 1965, one must understand the issues at stake in the struggle for meaningful political membership. Questions of political identity are always at the heart of debates over representation; this is so because claims about how representational institutions ought to be designed always hinge on prior conceptions of who is to be represented in the first place. Representational debates thus draw on competing notions of who "the people" are and turn on questions of how self-government ought to be achieved. The politics of minority representation, no less than other representational conflicts, engenders contests over fundamental political identities and basic governmental aims. Engaged in the politics of minority representation, the Supreme Court helps ascertain what the basic structure of the political community ought to be.

The constitutive role of the Court extends even further. Involvement in the politics of minority representation confronts the Court with the challenge of articulating the foundations of its own political authority. Since the earliest days of the republic, claims of judicial power have derived from the Court's capacity to speak on behalf of the people as a whole. As a result, when the Court responds to questions of minority representation, it not only selects a notion of "the people" around which representational institutions may be organized, but also chooses a conception of "the people" on which its own actions may be premised.

If our government is to remain democratic, if it is to engender rule by the sovereign people rather than to foster rule by an unaccountable judiciary, then the Court must not rely on conceptions of "the people" that prevent the citizenry from finally speaking for themselves. I use this standard to gauge the debate over the Voting Rights Act as it has developed on the bench. During the 1960s and 1970s, members of the Court adopted a diversity of approaches to minority representation, organizing their views around conceptions of popular vigilance, abstract individualism, legislative learning, and interest group competition. I argue that each of these approaches is problematic, for each sustains an understanding of judicial authority that ultimately fails to preserve the capacity of the people to speak for themselves.

In the last twenty years, the Court has abandoned its original diversity of views, settling on a dichotomous treatment of minority representation polarized around "individualist" and "group" notions of political identity. The individualist and group views have fractured the Court, just as conflicting views of political identity have splintered the broader ideological debate. Although the two camps each offer some valuable insights, I argue that both finally stumble over a mistaken account of political identity. In particular, both views have an important feature in common: Each takes political identity to be something formed prior to and

apart from politics itself. The shared belief that political identity is "prepolitical" has hardened the line of opposition, creating a zero-sum debate that has foreclosed valuable democratic options. In short, by predicating judicial authority on essentialized conceptions of identity, the Court has truncated the range of political possibilities, ultimately leaving the people unable to control the grounds on which political community is constructed.

Given these circumstances, I suggest that the emphasis on fixed, prepolitical notions of political identity should be left behind for a more flexible, politically informed rendering of "the people." The Court should develop its earlier views of legislative learning, focusing on how understandings of political identity are forged within the process of political deliberation. Rather than policing claims about immobile identities, the Court should work to preserve the conditions that allow elected representatives to learn, ultimately permitting the people to speak for themselves even as the Court speaks on their behalf.

Adapted from Keith Bybee, *Mistaken Identity: The Supreme Court and the Politics of Minority Representation*. ©1998 by Princeton University Press

60. The primary purpose of the passage is to:

   A. describe the provisions of the Voting Rights Act and explain how they worked to increase minority political representation.
   B. argue that the Supreme Court should reassert its earlier views of legislative learning as a way of more fully representing the voice of "the people."
   C. recommend that the Supreme Court adopt a view of political identity and judicial authority that better allows the voice of the people to be expressed and heard.
   D. argue that the power of the Court to impose and enforce an essentialist view of Constitutional rights has often been abused in the past.

61. By "essentialized conceptions of identity" (paragraph 4), the author most likely means:

   A. the view that political identities exist independently of the political process.
   B. the view that the Court should rely on conceptions of "the people" that allow important political beliefs and desires to be expressed.
   C. fundamental concepts of rights enshrined in the U.S. Constitution.
   D. the political identities of minority populations.

62. Which of the following best captures the role the author believes should be played by the Supreme Court?

- **A.** teacher
- **B.** parent
- **C.** bodyguard
- **D.** facilitator

63. With which of the following statements would the author be most likely to agree?

- **A.** Citizens often have incomplete or inaccurate conceptions of their own political power and must learn through greater political participation to play a more effective role in the political system.
- **B.** By adjudicating the Voting Rights Act, the Supreme Court played an active part not only in forming new political identities but also in reconstituting its own role in politics and society.
- **C.** The Supreme Court should not overstep the boundaries of its constitutionally defined role by making policy rather than simply evaluating the constitutionality of policies promulgated by the legislature.
- **D.** "Individualist" and "group" definitions of identity have divided both the Court and society; both notions should be rejected in favor of a more abstract and therefore less controversial view.

64. The author's discussion of the "constitutive role of the Court" (paragraph 2) implies that:

- **A.** the most important function of the Court is to protect those who cannot protect themselves.
- **B.** the core function of the Court is to mediate between groups who represent different interests in society.
- **C.** the Court has a special capacity to both represent and define the nation as a whole.
- **D.** the Court has a special duty to define and represent individual interests in a way that is not affected by changing social conditions or political ideologies.

———————————

Passage XII (Questions 65–69)

During some years of study of Greek and Indian mythologies, I have become more and more impressed with a sense of the inadequacy of the prevalent method of comparative mythology. That method is based on the belief that myths are the result of a disease of language, as the pearl is the result of a disease of the oyster. It is argued that men at some period spoke in a singular style of coloured and concrete language, and that their children retained the phrases of this language after losing hold of the original meaning. The consequence was the growth of myths about supposed persons, whose names had originally been mere "appellations." In conformity with this hypothesis, the method of comparative mythology examines the proper names which occur in myths. The notion is that these names contain a key to the meaning of the story, and that, in fact, of the story the names are the germs and the oldest surviving part.

To desert the path opened by the most eminent scholars is in itself presumptuous; the least an innovator can do is to give his reasons for advancing in a novel direction. If this were a question of scholarship merely, it would be simply foolhardy to differ from men like Max Müller, Adalbert Kuhn, and many others. But a revolutionary mythologist is encouraged by finding that these scholars usually differ from each other. Why, then, do distinguished scholars and mythologists reach such different goals? Clearly because their method is so precarious. They all analyze the names in myths, but where one scholar decides that the name is originally Sanskrit, another holds that it is partly Greek, and a third, perhaps, is all for an Acadian etymology. Again, even when scholars agree as to the original root from which a name springs, they differ as much as ever as to the meaning of the name in its present place. The inference is that the analysis of names, on which the whole edifice of philological "comparative mythology" rests, is a foundation of shifting sand. The method is called "orthodox," but among those who practice it, there is none of the beautiful unanimity of orthodoxy.

These objections are not made by the unscholarly anthropologist alone. Curtius has especially remarked on the difficulties which beset the "etymological operation" in the case of proper names. "Are we to seek the sources of the divine names in aspects of nature, or in moral conceptions: in special Greek geographical conditions, or in natural circumstances which are everywhere the same?" Every name has, if we can discover or conjecture it, a meaning. That meaning is always capable of being explained, for example, as an epithet of the sun, or of a cloud, or of both. Whatever then a name may signify, some scholars will find that it originally denoted the cloud, if they belong to one school, or the sun or dawn, if they belong to another faction. This logic would be admitted in no other science.

The method of philological mythology is thus discredited by the disputes of its adherents. The system may be called orthodox, but it is an orthodoxy which alters with every new scholar who enters the sacred enclosure. Even if there were more harmony, the analysis of names could throw little light on myths. In stories the names may well be, and often demonstrably are, the latest not the original feature. Tales, at first told of "Somebody," get new names attached to them, and obtain a new local habitation, wherever they wander. One of the leading personages to be met in the traditions of the world is really no more than—Somebody. There is nothing this wondrous creature cannot achieve; only one restriction binds him at all—that the name he assumes shall have some sort of congruity with the office he undertakes, and even from this he often times breaks loose. We may be pretty sure that the adventures of Jason, Perseus, Oedipus, were originally told only of "Somebody." The names are later additions, and vary in various lands.

Adapted from Andrew Lang, *Custom and Myth*. ©1884 by Longmans, Green and Co.

65. The author uses the analogy between a myth and a pearl in order to:

   A. criticize the emphasis placed on names in the study of comparative mythology.
   B. argue that myth expresses the view that society is diseased.
   C. suggest that names can be defined in many different and inconsistent ways.
   D. suggest that names contain a key meaning expressed in the story told by a myth.

66. By referring to "the beautiful orthodoxy of unanimity" (paragraph 2), the author is suggesting that:

   A. scholars should not disagree with each other in public.
   B. a particular set of scholars has imposed an unfairly rigid set of interpretations onto the academic field of the study of myth.
   C. a valid method of scientific study will engender widespread agreement among experts in that field.
   D. all myths are generated by a set of archetypal themes common to all cultures.

67. The author's argument against the etymological approach to mythology would be most *weakened* by which of the following?

   A. the discovery of errors in data collection made by Kuhn and Müller
   B. the claim that the story of Jason appears in many different cultures with different names ascribed to the main character
   C. a general acceptance in the field of comparative mythology that Kuhn and Müller's work was methodologically flawed
   D. the discovery of common themes uniting both Indian and Greek mythology

68. All of the following are illustrated in the passage by an example EXCEPT:

   A. specific names attributed to an anonymous "Somebody"
   B. a logically valid approach to the study of mythology
   C. scholars who agree with the author's critique
   D. languages that have generated names found in myths

69. With which of the following statements would the author be most likely to agree?

   A. The adherents to the method of philological mythology themselves dispute the legitimacy of the methodology.
   B. In order to criticize the dominant methodology in an academic field, the dissenter must first present a coherent alternative method of study.
   C. Names, while they may have many different possible interpretations, are the oldest surviving part of a myth.
   D. The analysis of names has little if nothing of value to tell us about a myth.

Chapter 13
Verbal Reasoning Practice:
Answers and Explanations

Passage I (Questions 1–6)

1.　**C**　The author discusses both the political and literary manifestations of postmodernism and (as part of postmodernism) deconstruction, suggesting that they offer interesting and at times valuable insights (see paragraph 2 where the author uses the phrases "good reason" and "good liberal reasons"). The author also criticizes postmodernism's sociological analysis (paragraph 2) by suggesting that in the real world, master narratives are not really in decline and that "postmodernists are not well informed about current practices in science and religion." Choice A is too narrow to be the main point of the passage; this is only one of the arguments made by the author. Choice B is incorrect because the author never suggests that deconstruction is itself a unified or totalizing "metanarrative." In fact, the author states that the "deconstructors" are not "committed to anything as definite as a philosophical thesis" (paragraph 3). Choice D, like choice A, is too narrow. In particular, it mentions only the literary aspect of postmodernism, ignoring its sociological and political aspects.

2.　**A**　Choice A is supported by the end of the first paragraph, where the author states that Lyotard argues that the master narratives of "the progressive emancipation of humanity" and "the triumph of science" have lost credibility since WWII. This suggests that the experience of the war played a role in undermining the power of master narratives. The author also describes master narratives (or metanarratives) as serving to "give cultural practices some form of legitimation or authority" (paragraph 2). Choice B is incorrect, because while the author does discuss new literary interpretations of novels such as *Middlemarch* (paragraph 3), these literary interpretations are not described as playing a causal role (in Lyotard's view or in the view of other postmodernists) in the actual decline of master narratives. Choice C brings up an issue which is never discussed in the passage. Major philosophies such as Kantianism and Hegelianism are similar (paragraph 1) in that they express master narratives; no differences or inconsistencies are discussed in the passage. As for choice D, the author does not mention any sociological studies that support Lyotard's views or that themselves have played a role in the decline in master narratives. If anything, the author suggests that sociological studies would show that master narratives are in fact not in crisis and decline (paragraph 2).

3.　**C**　The correct answer to this question will be a choice that expresses relativity rather than consensus or some "totalizing" and unified view (see the first half of paragraph 2). Choice C describes a study that looks at different perspectives on the same thing: There is no single consensus or unified narrative. Choice A describes a curriculum based on a single, identifiable set of 'great books,' with the implication that there can be some consensus on what books should be included in this list. Choice B is similar to the master narrative of "the progressive emancipation of humanity" mentioned in paragraph 1. It involves the idea that there is some single identifiable course that nations take through history. Choice D describes a different belief but with the same theme; there is some unified, identifiable process that guides human history.

4. **B** Item II is the only statement supported by the passage. The author states that Derrida's main influence was through his argument for relativism and that the Derrideans claimed that works of literature do not "[open] a window on reality" (paragraph 3) but instead are open to the interpretation of each reader (paragraph 4). Item I raises an issue that is not connected in the passage to Derrida and his influence. We know that Lyotard critiqued these particular master narratives (paragraph 1), but the passage does not state or suggest that Derrida did so. As for Item III, while the passage suggests that Derrida saw a connection between literature and politics (see the last two sentences of the passage), the author doesn't imply that Derrida was concerned specifically with the influence of literature on society.

5. **D** Choice D is supported by paragraph 2 where the author states that "there are good liberal reasons for being against such 'grand narratives' (on the grounds that they do not allow for disputes about value and often lead to totalitarian persecution)." Choice A is incorrect; while the author does suggest that he agrees with the postmodernists' defense of marginalized and subordinated people (paragraph 2), the first part of this choice contradicts the passage. The passage argues that postmodernism does not in fact constitute an "intellectual framework." Rather, postmodernists argue that "truth itself is always relative to the differing standpoints and predisposing intellectual frameworks of the judging subject" (paragraph 3). Choice B also contradicts the author's argument in the passage. He states that Lyotard and the postmodernists are incorrect to argue that we have evolved away from repressive regimes and that "totalizing religious and national beliefs are currently responsible for so much repression, violence, and war" (paragraph 2). Choice C incorrectly suggests that George Eliot herself claimed that her work "opens a window on reality." The author states that this illusion was "not actually shared by George Eliot" (paragraph 3).

6. **D** The correct choice will be analogous to the relationship between relativism, the idea that there is no single truth or reality (see paragraph 3), and consensus, which is the opposite (see paragraph 2). Choice D matches this relationship. Deconstruction was founded on the idea of relativism, the view that "truth itself is always relative to the differing standpoints and predisposing intellectual frameworks of the judging subject." Postmodernism, which includes deconstruction, rejected consensus (agreement on a master narrative or unified story) as "an outmoded and suspect value" (paragraph 2). Choice A does not represent two opposing ideas. The last paragraph describes the deconstructionist view that the text is "really constructed by the reader." Thus, text and interpreter may even be the same. Choice B has a similar problem; it doesn't represent an opposition or contradiction. The postmodernists saw politics and philosophy as connected, not as inherently at odds with each other. Choice C fails to present an opposition as well. For example, master narratives find specific meanings in texts.

Passage II (Questions 7–12)

7.   **D**   Choice D corresponds to the contrast between old and new forms of poetry. The author states that current poetry is largely written for the edification, not the enjoyment, of the reader, and that the goal of those who read poetry today is "not pleasure but self-improvement" (paragraph 3). The author goes on to state that "the modern poetic audience is a student audience, pure and simple." In contrast, older poetry was written with the idea of a reader who "must understand and enjoy the finished product" (paragraph 2), the "cash customers of poetry…who used to put down their money in the sure and certain hope of enjoyment" (paragraph 3). Choice A is incorrect; the author does not suggest that different kinds of people are writing poetry, just that the kind of poetry they write has changed, and that this has led to a change in their readership. Amateurs and professionals are never mentioned in the passage. Choice B misrepresents present-day poetry, which is written to instruct, not to entertain students. Choice C also misrepresents present-day poetry. The author states that poets today do not even try to entertain readers by giving them poetry that they will enjoy (paragraph 2).

8.   **C**   In the last paragraph, the author begins by discussing what we would need to do in order to restore pleasure to the reading of poetry, calling for a "large-scale revulsion…against our present notions." This involves "poetry readers asking themselves more frequently whether they do in fact enjoy what they read." The author then introduces the Butler quote by saying that it may "awaken a furtive itch for freedom," meaning freedom from the dutiful task of reading poetry that we do not enjoy. The quote, then, is meant to encourage us to follow Butler's lead in reading (or listening to, in Butler's case) material that we like rather than trying to make ourselves like something that is unlikable. Choice A is incorrect because the author is not making a general claim about music. The analogy is between a specific composer who Butler does not enjoy and un-enjoyable poetry, not between modern poetry and modern music in general. Choice B refers to an issue that the author raises in the beginning of the passage (taking a less complicated view of poetry) that is not relevant to the quote at the end of the passage. Choice D reads too much into the quote. We have no evidence that Butler is experiencing or expressing emotion. If anything, the analogy suggests the opposite: We do not have an emotional reaction to present-day poetry because it is not written to evoke an emotional response, and this is one of the reasons why we do not enjoy it.

9.   **A**   The new information in the question would undermine the author's causal argument in the passage. The author claims that poetry changed, no longer taking into account the enjoyment of the reader. Then, according to the passage, the people who used to read poetry "were quick to move elsewhere" (paragraph 3), abandoning poetry for other, more enjoyable activities. If people had in fact changed what they found enjoyable, as suggested by the new information, it would suggest that perhaps poetry changed because its audience changed, rather than the other way around. Choice B, while accurately representing part of the author's argument, does not accurately describe the impact of the new information. The new information is about what people today feel or enjoy, not what poetry sought to do in the past. For choice C, there is

nothing in the new information that is relevant to the author's analogy between poetry and music. As for choice D, although the author does not discuss modern technology, information about the impact of technology on what people do or do not find enjoyable is directly relevant to the causal logic of the author's argument.

10. **B** Choice B corresponds to the author's description of the old kind of bad poetry as poetry that "tries to move the reader and fails" (paragraph 2), perhaps because the poet is not skilled enough to accomplish the second stage of writing poetry (paragraph 1). Choice A describes the new, not the old kind of bad poetry—poetry that "does not even try" to move the reader (paragraph 2). In the case of choice C, the author doesn't suggest that the old kind of poetry should not be enjoyable to students; good "old" poetry would be enjoyable to everyone. Finally, the author doesn't equate the size of a poet's readership with the quality of the poem. The standard of quality is the impact the poem has on those who do read it.

11. **B** Choice B is most similar to the author's recommendation in the last paragraph that people refuse to read poetry that they do not like. In choice B, shoppers are refusing to patronize a store that does not serve their needs. Choice A describes someone deciding to do it him- or herself; the author doesn't suggest that we should write our own poetry. Choice C is about the producer, not the consumer. Furthermore, the author does not suggest that poets should try to find more readers—"lots of people still read and even buy poetry" (paragraph 2). Choice D is also about the producer of art, whereas the recommendation in the passage is intended for the consumer of poetry. Also, the author does not say that enjoyable poetry is not technically challenging to write.

12. **B** The author suggests in the second paragraph that poets may be perfectly happy with their new audience; it is we the former readers of poetry who are unhappy with the new poetry. The author states that it is through a "cunning merger [suggesting intentionality on the part of the poet] between poet, literary critic, and academic critic" that the poet is in the "happy position" where he or she can not only write the poem but praise and promote it, bullying or forcing the consumer or reader into accepting it. This implies that it is easier for a poet to impose a work on the public than to appeal to the public's tastes. Choice A contradicts the tone of the passage and goes against the recommendation in the last paragraph that we reject (rather than force ourselves to accept) the new poetry. Choice C sounds a lot like choice B, but it brings in the issue of greater profit, an issue that the author never raises. Furthermore, the author does not agree that we need certain "intellectual tools" to appreciate good poetry. Choice D is consistent with the passage but is not relevant to the phrase quoted in the question.

Passage III (Questions 13–18)

13.   **D**   Choice D best answers the question while also being supported by the passage text. The authors assert that internal weaknesses contributed to the downfall of the union but give no supporting evidence. Choice A incorrectly states that direct evidence is provided. The fact that the union carried out strikes that became violent, while supported by the passage, does not support the cited claim. Nothing in the passage suggests that violence would turn union members against the union. Choice B has a similar problem. While this relates to lack of public support for the union, it gives no evidence of why those inside the organization would turn against it. While the first part of choice C is correct, the second part of the choice is not supported by the passage. The authors do not indicate that the existence of cooperative societies ("to own and manage stores and factories") would guarantee loyalty to the union.

14.   **C**   The authors state in the beginning of the passage that "the spirit of criticism and the measures of reform to meet it" were "merely the signs of a new age." The next sentence states that "The nation had definitely passed into industrialism." The rest of the first paragraph discusses how industrialism (the "new age") affected workers. Therefore, we can infer that this first sentence is intended to connect these aspects of the twentieth century to their beginnings in the years that came before. The rest of the passage describes the beginnings of the labor movement in the 1800s. Therefore, A, which describes the twentieth century as leading to the beginnings of the labor movement, is incorrect. Choice B is incorrect because the passage never specifically describes the labor movement in the twentieth century (as conflict-ridden or otherwise). Furthermore, while the authors describe efforts toward business-labor cooperation in the 1800s, they do not characterize that era as "largely cooperative." Choice D is too strong; while twentieth century reforms, or at least the economic factors that drove them, may have begun in the 1800s, the authors do not suggest that this is a process that matured in the previous century.

15.   **C**   Choice C is supported by the fourth paragraph, where the authors state that the National Labor Movement "sought to eliminate the conflict between capital and labor by making workingmen the owners of shops through the formation of cooperative industries." Choice A is incorrect; the passage suggests that the union sought to turn workers into capitalists or employers, not that they tried to encourage cooperation between employees and business owners. Choice B incorrectly connects the National Labor Movement to socialism; the authors make no such connection. As for choice D, the authors suggest that the strikes carried out by the Knights of Labor were more violent than those carried out by other unions (paragraph 4), but they do not indicate that other unions, including the National Labor Movement, carried out no strikes at all.

16.   **C**   In paragraph 3, the authors describe efforts made by businesses to increase cooperation and good feelings between employees and the company. These efforts did not involve labor unions. These efforts are described in a positive tone; nothing in the passage suggests that they did not in fact benefit the workers. Thus, the authors would most likely disagree with Roosevelt's statement that miners could get fair treatment only through collective bargaining and within a trade union. Nothing in the passage conflicts with either choice A or choice B. Choice D is incorrect in part because Roosevelt, based only on the quotes provided in the statement, did not make this claim. There is also nothing in the passage to suggest that the authors would disagree (or agree) with this statement; it is an issue that is never raised in the passage.

17.   **A**   Choice A is the best supported of the four choices. At the end of paragraph 3, the passage states that one motive held by employers was to "increase the production of commodities by promoting the efficiency and happiness of the producers." This suggests that profit was a goal. Therefore, we can infer that the employers did not believe that they would lose money through profit sharing. Rather, happy employees would be productive employees, which would profit the company itself. Note the word "only" in choice B. While it is reasonable to infer that this was one goal, we can't go so far as to conclude that it was their only goal. Choice C is incorrect as well. While the passage states that representatives from trade unions were excluded from negotiations within company unions, the passage gives no evidence that union employees were excluded from profit-sharing plans. Choice D is too specific to a particular type of company. We know from the passage that some businesses offered profit sharing (paragraph 3), but we don't know that coal mining companies were among them.

18.   **D**   Choice D is supported by the first paragraph of the passage. The authors state that with the coming of industrialization, increases in urban population, and the end to easy availability of land, people were now forced to remain as laborers. As individual workers, they had little power to negotiate with their employer (paragraph 2). Thus, they were forced to cooperate with other workers to improve wages and/or conditions for the body of workers as a whole. Choice A is not supported by the passage; while farmers may have been more independent, we don't know that they had a higher income or better lifestyle than industrial workers. Choice B is too extreme. While cooperation was essential to workers in the face of corporate power, we have no evidence that cooperation in any form was entirely unnecessary to farmers. Finally, there is no discussion of a lessening (or widening) gap between rich and poor to support C; this issue is out of the scope of the passage.

Passage IV (Questions 19–23)

19. **B** Choice B includes the two major themes in the passage—that quantum mechanics and general relativity are inconsistent with each other (the long-standing paradox resolved by string theory) and that string theory may go even further by providing a unified theory of physics. Choice A is too narrow. This is only one of the two major themes in the passage. Choice C is inaccurate based on passage information. The author states that to observe string theory in action, we would need to "examine subatomic particles with a precision that is many orders of magnitude beyond our present technological capacity" (paragraph 4). While choice D is supported by the last paragraph, it leaves out the author's discussion of the inconsistency between quantum mechanics and general relativity that inspired string theory in the first place.

20. **D** Choice D is supported by the second paragraph, where the author states that in most cases, physicists study only small- or large-scale phenomena using only quantum mechanics or relativity theory, and that therefore, they were able to overlook the fact that the two theories were mutually exclusive. Choice A contradicts the passage; the author states that physicists have been "quietly aware of a dark cloud looming on a distant horizon" for more than 50 years (paragraph 1). He also states that they were able to "shrug off" the conflict with "a furtive glance" (paragraph 2), indicating that they were in fact aware that the conflict existed. Choice B is incorrect in part for the same reason. Furthermore, the passage describes the experimental observations and predictions made by both sets of scientists as highly accurate (paragraph 1). The language used by the author in the first paragraph ("dark cloud looming") and in the second paragraph ("furtive glance") indicates that C is incorrect; they had some awareness that the conflict was a problem that would at some point need to be addressed.

21. **B** The author states that black holes constitute areas of the universe where quantum mechanics (small scale) and general relativity (large scale) would both need to be used at once, and yet, this is impossible (paragraph 3). This sets the stage for the author's discussion of how string theory may have solved this dilemma. Choice A is incorrect; the author does not discuss recent technological advances or new observations; the issue in the passage is purely theoretical. Choice C directly contradicts the author's argument. At the end of paragraph 3, the author poses the question of whether or not the universe can really function according to two sets of laws, and then states at the beginning of the next paragraph that "superstring theory answers" this question "with a resounding no." As for choice D, the author suggests that we have already found the alternative—string theory.

22. **A** The new information in the question stem describes how the behavior of all matter and all forces may be caused by the same phenomenon—vibration of strings. This is most directly relevant to the author's discussion in the passage of how "string theory provides a single explanatory framework capable of encompassing all forces and all matter" (paragraph 4). While choice B is supported by the passage, it is not directly supported by the new information in the question stem. Choice C contradicts the passage. The author states in paragraph 1 that both

theories have in fact provided highly accurate predictions. Choice D, like choice B, is consistent with the passage but has no direct connection to the question.

23.   **C**   The passage states that string theory describes subatomic particles as "not point-like but instead a tiny one-dimensional loop" (paragraph 4). Earlier in that same paragraph, the author states that "within this new framework, general relativity and quantum mechanics require one another for the theory to make sense." Choice A is inconsistent with both the content and tone of the passage. The author argues that string theory recognizes and resolves the theoretical conflict and suggests that this resolution is quite necessary. While choice B is attractive, it conflicts with the author's statement at the end of the first paragraph that "As they are currently formulated, general relativity and quantum mechanics cannot both be right." However, on the other hand, string theory does encompass or include the two within its new theoretical framework (paragraph 4), which eliminates choice D.

Passage V (Questions 24–30)

24.   **C**   Choice C is supported by the discussion in paragraph 1, in which the author refers to firsthand experience gained by "role-playing" as the basis for discovering "the daily needs and routines" of ancient societies. Choice D is inconsistent with the passage. Archaeologists, as described in this passage, attempt to experience and understand aspects of life as it was lived at the time, not view it from their own contemporary perspective (see paragraphs 1 and 2). In paragraph 1, the author says that the inspiration for archaeological insights comes from re-creating ancient artifacts "and figuring out what crucial purpose they served." Therefore, the reconstructions are not described as "fanciful" (choice A), nor are they created to test the accuracy of ancient histories that have already been written (choice B).

25.   **B**   The discovery of some split-based points would not significantly undermine the author's claim that the manufacture of lozenge-shaped points "displaced the earlier forms" (middle of last paragraph). A hunter from the later period may still have used a point from the old model, or the points that were found may have been discarded, used or unused, when the new points became available. While this finding does not strengthen the author's claim, it does not give enough information to weaken it either. Choice D is the opposite of the correct choice, B. The existence of early-model spearpoints in the Gravettian (later) period does not significantly undermine the claim that a different technology existed in that time. Alternatively, just because a point may have been made in a later period does not show that the model was not developed in an earlier period (choice C). The discovery of a split-based spearpoint from a later time period gives no support for the claim that split-based points were replaced by round or lozenge-shaped points (choice A).

26.   A   At the beginning of the fourth paragraph, the author writes that "observations of...deer jousts must have led Cro-Magnon hunters to imagine the advantages they might enjoy with weapons of the kind deer came by naturally." The author then describes how the Cro-Magnon fashioned deer antlers into weapons of their own. This implies that they saw and appreciated the kinds of wounds antlers can inflict. Choice B is too extreme. Although Cro-Magnon use of antlers for spearpoints suggests that they may have hunted deer for their antlers, nothing in the passage implies the threat of extinction. In fact, for all we know from the passage, the Cro-Magnon may have used antlers from deer that died of natural causes. Choice C is incorrect. The author gives no indication that reindeer were valued more than red deer or that usefulness for weapons making was the most valuable or prized characteristic of potential game or prey. Nothing in the passage suggests whether or not deer were killed before their horns were taken (choice D).

27.   C   This is an EXCEPT question; the correct answer will NOT be cited in the passage. Choices A, B, and D are mentioned in the passage. In the middle of the fourth paragraph, the author writes that Cro-Magnon artisans fastened a "finished point to a spear pole...and bound the point into the cleft with fibers from plants or animals," represented by choice A; the artisans "jammed a small wedge into the point's split base.... The mechanical pressures...kept the weapon in one piece...." (second half of the fourth paragraph, represented by choice B); and that "artisans cut a cleft in the shape of a 'U' into the shaft's end, and bound the point into the cleft...." (represented by choice D). In that same paragraph, the author mentions mechanical pressures but never talks about "mechanical friction" (choice C) as a way of fastening spearpoints to a shaft. Thus, choice C is the only choice not cited in the passage and is, therefore, correct.

28.   D   If the atlatl improved speed and aim, hunters before its invention would have been at a disadvantage compared to those hunting after, so choice D is correct.

The passage states that atlatls have been found dating from 22,000 years ago. The author implies that Cro-Magnon spear-making dates from the early Aurignacian period, which began 40,000 years ago (paragraph 3). Therefore, spears were used long before the earliest indication of the use of the atlatl. Given that no other weapons are mentioned in the passage, we have no reason to conclude that spears were not a primary weapon in the earlier period and therefore, we can eliminate choice A. In paragraph 2, the passage states that the atlatl added "heft and accuracy to the natural ability of a skilled hunter," and nowhere indicates that Cro-Magnon hunters lacked natural ability (choice B). Choice C is also incorrect. The passage states that "points shaped like lozenges with rounded bases" came into use "three hundred twenty centuries [32,000 years] ago," and represented "new designs" that "enabled hunters to resharpen their points efficiently" (paragraph 5). Because the earliest found atlatls date from 22,000 years ago (paragraph 2), the best available evidence indicates that the spearpoints that were easier to sharpen predated the atlatls by some 10,000 years.

29. **D**   Remember: The purpose of the tests is "to be certain that the re-created spearpoints are as identical as possible to the originals recovered at sites" (beginning of the second paragraph). We do not know from the passage that the findings noted in choice A or choice B are true of the original spearpoints. These findings do not support the value or usefulness of the tests and are therefore incorrect. Nothing in the passage tells us that climatic conditions are relevant to the accuracy of these tests, so we can eliminate choice C. Choice D indicates that the re-created spears have an effect on bone that is similar to damage done to bones in the time of Cro-Magnon hunters. It gives further evidence that the re-creation was reasonably accurate and therefore, it is the correct answer.

30. **D**   We can eliminate choice B because we know nothing from the passage about the Cro-Magnon economy, nor do we know that spearpoints were sold or bartered or that anyone would benefit from their obsolescence. At the beginning of the fifth paragraph, the author writes, "Despite the difficulty of repairing these weapons, the split-based spearpoints must have proven fairly effective, because they enjoyed eight thousand years of popularity with Cro-Magnon hunters." Eight thousand years of popularity hardly indicates "rapid development of better designs," so choice A is incorrect. We can eliminate choice C, because the passage states that the new points were easier to resharpen, not that they were more effective in hunting than the older model. This leaves choice D. The fact that the spearpoints were difficult to repair did not mean that they were not useful. Choice D is correct.

Passage VI (Questions 31–35)

31. **C**   The theme in choice C is reiterated throughout the passage. In particular, the second and third paragraphs describe how Chagall, faced with the suffering he experienced and saw around him, came to believe in the primacy of hope and love. Paragraphs 4–6 describe his vision of the "spiritual ministry" of the artist. At the end of paragraph 4, the author states, "Through his craft, then, the painter brings love and salvation to humankind." Choice C is correct.

Choice A is too broad to be the main idea of this passage. While this may be true of Chagall, the author does not suggest that it is true of all artists. Choice D is also too broad to be the main point and is not supported by the passage. While Chagall's genius was formed in part through his suffering (paragraphs 2 and 3), the author does not argue that this is the only way his genius could have emerged. In addition, the passage is specifically about Chagall, not all artists or individuals. Choice B is too extreme to be supported by the passage (the author describes the influence of the Bible on Chagall but does not indicate that he could not have been a great artist without it). Furthermore, even if it were supported, it would be too narrow to be the main idea.

32. **D** In paragraphs 2 and 3, the author describes how Chagall's experience of turmoil and suffering inspired him to turn to themes of love, hope, and redemption. The author states that for Chagall, "the painter brings love and salvation to humankind" through his work (in the last sentence of paragraph 4). The image of the painter as a guide appears in *The Apparition* (described in the fourth paragraph).

Choice A contradicts the passage. Far from powerless, the artist in Chagall's artistic vision "brings love and salvation to humankind" (last sentence of paragraph 4). We can eliminate choice B, because although the author states that Chagall's work was not "a mirror of reality" (first sentence of the passage), Chagall's life certainly did not prevent him from seeing reality. Rather, his life experience inspired him to create an artistic vision and philosophy that sought to provide hope to a suffering world (paragraphs 2, 4, and 6). Furthermore, there is no negative tone or criticism in the passage to indicate that the author believes Chagall failed to progress artistically. Finally, the passage never mentions political protest or calls for reform (choice C). Chagall's idea of salvation, as described, was spiritual, not political.

33. **A** Support for choice A is found in paragraphs 5 and 6. The author describes the "swirling maelstrom of purple and black and plaintive yellow" on the left of the painting and the "cool blues and pure white that define...the right half of the picture." Split between these two halves defined by a contrast in color, Chagall's canvas achieves a dynamic interaction between these separate parts, as "through the dreaming figure, Chagall's colors penetrate the schism, surprising the dark, turbulent world with brave reverberations of grace and light."

Choice B mistakes the relationship described in the passage; Chagall's use of color facilitated his expression of the themes of suffering and redemption (see paragraphs 5 and 6). The word "subordinate" in particular makes choice B wrong. While the author interprets the meaning of the colors in the canvases described in the passage (see paragraphs 5 and 6), she does not argue that every idea is always coded to the same color in all of Chagall's works (choice C). Choice D is inconsistent with the author's description of *Jacob's Dream*, in which yellow is used in the dark and chaotic side of the painting (paragraph 5). Furthermore, the author does not generalize about Chagall's use of colors in other paintings.

34. **C** In paragraph 4, the author uses Hazere's comment transitionally to emphasize the point that Chagall's spiritual understanding led him to recognize his "privileges and responsibilities" as an artist.

The author of the passage presents no interpretations of other scholarly works (choice A), nor does she criticize Chagall in any way in the passage or call into question his sincerity (choice D). In addition, the author of the passage does not discuss French criticism generally or compare it to other approaches (choice B). The fact that Hazere is French is not a significant issue in the passage.

35.   D   Choice D is consistent with the information in the question as well as with the author's interpretation of the painting and the main idea of the passage as a whole. The author writes, "through his craft, the painter brings love and salvation to humanity" (last sentence of paragraph 4). This theme which characterizes *The Apparition* is "reiterated in the painting *Jacob's Dream*" (beginning of paragraph 5), where Jacob acts as "mediator" between "the fierce frenzy of the bodily world and the tranquil reassurance of the spiritual" (paragraph 6). The meaning or reality of Chagall's art, then, lies in its redemptive and inspirational effect on those who view it.

In paragraphs 5 and 6, the central figure represents a mediator or redeemer who looks toward the light, not a sinner, and the "bodily world" is described as "plaintive," chaotic, dark, and full of "fierce frenzy," not as pleasurable. Therefore, choice A is incorrect. Choice B is inconsistent with the passage. In paragraphs 4–6, the author suggests that Jacob represents the painter who is moving himself and his viewers away from darkness and chaos, not the "antithesis of the painter." Choice C is not supported in the passage. According to the author, Chagall saw his painting as a way to redeem (bring communion to) humanity. In paragraph 4, the author writes, "Through his craft, then, the author brings love and salvation to humankind." At the end of the passage, she writes, "Refracted through the dreaming figure [of Jacob as mediator], Chagall's colors penetrate the schism, surprising the dark, turbulent world with brave reverberations of grace and light." It follows that the author would not accept an interpretation based on an irresolvable conflict.

Passage VII (Questions 36–42)

36.   A   According to the middle of the first paragraph, to Africans, "the elephant is known in fuller dimensions. It has been a source of food, materials, and riches; a fearsome rival for resources; and a highly visible, provocative neighbor." The choice that best characterizes the full range of an elephants' impact on Africans is A.

Although "fearsome" is mentioned in the description of the elephant's role in African people's lives, choice C can be ruled out because fear is, according to the passage, by no means the defining attitude of Africans toward elephants. Choices B and D are not supported by the passage because neither hate nor worship characterizes Africans' relationship to the elephant.

37.   D   The second half of paragraph 1 furnishes the justification: "Even in areas where the elephant has now vanished, it persists as a symbol in expressive culture."

Neither choice A nor choice B is supported by the passage. Choice C is excluded because it directly contradicts the substance of the second half of paragraph 1.

38.   A   The middle of the first paragraph explains that in African culture, the elephant is known as "a source of food, material, and riches; a fearsome rival for resources; and a highly visible, provocative neighbor." The question represents these same characteristics in different words and ascribes them to the jaguar, in effect making the elephant interchangeable with the jaguar in a different cultural milieu (see the first half of the second paragraph for the author's observation of interchangeability). None of the statements presented by the other options would be affected by the new information.

39.   B   The final two sentences of paragraph 3 contain the relevant information: "...African depictions of the elephant have as much to say about human society as about the animal itself...[and] historical events, social responsibilities, religious beliefs, and political relationships are the primary subjects of elephant imagery." The author makes this statement in the context of a discussion of the elephant as both microcosm and macrocosm.

Choice A might tempt you, but you don't know if the author writes from a European, African, Asian, Latin, or other perspective. Nigerian carvings (choice C) and Ethiopian art (choice D) show animals treated equally; this does not give us information specifically about the relevance of elephant imagery to Africans' social lives.

40.   C   Paragraph 4 presents the contradictory points of view. On the one hand, "finding *human* traits in *animals* is...a fundamental activity of the human mind." At the same time, among nonscientists, "finding *animal* traits in *humans* tends to be seen...as pernicious and degrading." Nothing in the passage supports any of the other options; in fact, the paragraph just cited tends to contradict them.

41.   B   Remember that you are looking for a statement that is *not* correct. The passage begins with the phrase, "As the largest land animal on the planet, the elephant is a potent symbol..." In addition, early in paragraph 3 it is stated, "By virtue of its sheer size and prominence, the roles [the elephant] plays in art and historical processes are magnified." Therefore, the size and symbolic import of the elephant are both large and there is no gap.

The remainder of paragraph 1 emphasizes the discrepancy between the African and Western modes of elephant imagery, thus negating choice A. Choice C is ruled out by the first paragraph with "its image undergoes a startling range of transformations" and the third with "elephant imagery...is just as often a product of the imagination" which deal with the differences between the actuality of elephants and images of them. Choice D can be ruled out based on the beginning of the third paragraph where the author indicates a difference between the elephant as microcosm and as macrocosm.

42.   B   The middle of the third paragraph states the case unambiguously: "In Africa as elsewhere, people represent their relationship to animals in multiple ways, and their complex experience of it can be read in the symbolic language of their respective cultures."

Choices A and C contradict the above citation and run counter to the general sense of the passage. Paragraphs 4 and 5 make choice D incorrect.

Passage VIII (Questions 43–48)

43.   C   In the first paragraph, the author lists "the skills that go into adult art: coordination, intellect, personality, imagination, creativity, and aesthetic judgment." According to that paragraph, the making of an artist is "a process as fragile as growing up itself." The second paragraph states that art is "a positive expression that integrates diverse aspects of personality." Furthermore, in the third paragraph, the author observes that "the imagination...acts in lawful, if unpredictable, ways that are determined by the psyche and the mind."

Although the third paragraph says that the imagination is "the connector between the conscious and the subconscious"; and the fifth paragraph adds that artists were believed "able to enter the underworld of the subconscious...but, unlike ordinary mortals, they were then able to return to the realm of the living," this motif represents a subordinate theme and not the main idea of the passage; choice A is wrong. Paragraphs 1, 2, and 5 contain information that may lead you to choose B, but this idea is more implied than directly addressed in the passage. The end of the fifth paragraph claims that "the artist remains a magician whose work can mystify and move us," but this notion, expressed in choice D, is too narrow to be the main idea of the passage.

44.   B   In the first paragraph, the passage states that the artist's imagination "is subject to the taste and outlook of the society that shapes his or her personality," that forms, that is, his or her sensibility. The word "genius" appears in the opening sentence of paragraph 3, in which the author asserts that a psychotic sensibility cannot make truly great art. Later in the same paragraph, imagination appears as "the very glue that holds our personality, intellect, and spirituality together." A phrase in the middle of the last paragraph adds that "art has the power to penetrate to the core of our being," and "represents its creator's deepest understanding and highest aspirations...our shared beliefs and values," the outside reality an artist creates from, about, and to.

While the author does discuss the response of others to an artist's work (in the first paragraph "we tend to judge children's art..." and in the last paragraph "worthy of our attention. Art has the power to penetrate to the core of our being,..."), the passage does not use the response of critics or others as a criterion for evaluating genius. Therefore, choice A is not the best answer in relation to this question. The word "genius" may refer, generally, to one's intellectual capability and/or achievements, but it is not used in that sense in this passage. Choice C is incorrect. Paragraphs 2 and 3 directly contradict choice D, as explained above.

45. A The end of the third paragraph notes that "even the most private artistic statements can be understood on some level, even if only an intuitive one," implying a relationship between the intensely personal and the universal. Later, the last paragraph emphasizes that "art represents its creator's deepest understanding and highest aspirations; at the same time, the artist often plays an important role as the articulator of our shared beliefs and values."

Choice B is clearly contradicted by the fifth paragraph: "Even today, the artist remains a magician whose work can mystify and move us." Choice C claims that we can find no universal truth in art, a statement contradicted by the citations above. Choice D is ruled out by statements in the fifth and sixth paragraphs.

46. D The end of the fourth paragraph points the way: "[Prehistoric art]...was the culmination of a long development"; and "even the most 'primitive' ethnographic art represents a late stage of development within a stable society." The beginning of the fourth paragraph states that "the imagination is important...in a way that has real survival value... The ability to make art, in contrast, must have been acquired relatively recently in the course of human evolution." Choices A and B contradict that text. The middle of the fourth paragraph establishes that the oldest known prehistoric art is dated only 35,000 years ago, which excludes choice C.

47. D The end of the fourth paragraph refers to "civilized people, who do not readily relinquish their veneer of rational control," and in the fifth paragraph, the author observes that "art has the power to penetrate to the core of our being." Taken together, these two assertions make D the best choice.

Choices A, B, and C may all reflect some element of truth, but they are truths not touched on in the passage.

48. A The middle of the second paragraph states that "art is not simply a negative force at the mercy of our neuroses but a positive expression that integrates diverse aspects of personality." This assertion immediately follows the allusion to Freud and serves generally to negate Freud's hypothesis as presented.

Choice C does not follow logically from the passage; nowhere is it supported by the text. Choice B seeks to confuse you with a hodgepodge of tempting terminology. Paragraph 2 actually does reflect the assertion offered in option D, but it is not directly related to the discussion of Freud.

Passage IX Solutions (Questions 49–54)

49.   **C**   Choice C is consistent with the author's tone and argument in the passage as a whole and is consistent as well with the paragraph in which the author describes Griffin's book (paragraph 2). The author uses this discussion to introduce the argument that there is "almost no investigation of the emotional lives of animals in the modern scientific literature" (paragraph 2) and that this is partly due to a widely held belief that "the emotions of animals [are] not a respectable field of study" for scientists (paragraph 3). Note that the author states that Griffin "did not explore emotion" but rather discussed the "possible intellectual lives of animals" and issues of "cognition and consciousness." Choice A incorrectly describes Griffin's book as dealing with emotions rather than cognition. B is incorrect for the same reason. Choice D is incorrect because the author of the passage does not indicate that Griffin disclosed personal feelings or emotions in his book.

50.   **B**   In the third paragraph, the author writes, "Dolphins show such delight in performing, even in creating new performances of their own, that an elaborate emotional component seems obvious." In the fourth paragraph, the author suggests that animals who pair up may do so because they are in love. These statements involve the assumption that human-like behavior suggests human-like emotion. In choice A, although the author suggests an emotional analogy between animals and humans, he does not describe a similar comparison between the behaviors of different species of animals. The passage never describes the same behavior (or emotions) among different animals. Choice C appears to refer to the first paragraph. However, neither Darwin nor the author is assuming that cows do in fact mourn, just that we need to consider the possibility. Furthermore, mournful behavior among other species is not described. Choice D appears to refer to the third paragraph. However, it reverses the relationship between dolphin and scientist; the author suggests that it is the scientist reacting emotionally to the dolphin's feelings, not that the dolphin is reacting to the emotions of the scientist.

51.   **A**   The question asks for an explanation based on ultimate causes. Based on the passage, ultimate causes involve "functional" explanations for behavior based on evolution (which plays a theoretical role in both comparative psychology and ethology, according to paragraph four) and factors like maximization of reproductive success. Choice A comes closest to matching that causal idea. Choice B suggests a proximate, not ultimate cause—the emotion of fear. Choice C suggests that the behavior is not related to evolutionary success; this is the opposite of the correct choice. Choice D suggests cognition (the bunny freezes because it thinks that this will help it survive), which would qualify as a proximate, not an ultimate cause.

52.   **D**   In the third paragraph, the author indicates that the scientist really must believe that the dolphin has feelings (despite the scientist's protestations to the contrary); otherwise, the scientist would not have hugged it with such emotion. This develops the argument the author has already begun, that even those scientists who may accept the possibility of animal emotion are unwilling to admit it in public. The example is of human behavior that suggests that animals

have emotions, not of animal behavior. Thus, A is incorrect. Choice B contradicts the author's statement at the end of paragraph 4 that the two are not mutually exclusive. Choice C focuses on the issue of the last paragraph, which is not directly related to the story referred to in this question. There is no suggestion in the passage that the scientist is mistreating the dolphin.

53. D All three items are supported by the passage. For item I, the author states in paragraph 3 that he thought that "experts who work with and study animals might offer observations in person that they would be reluctant to put into a scientific article." This part of the passage also supports item III, as does the reference in the final paragraph to scientists' "professional and financial interests." The first two sentences of the third paragraph also support item II.

54. A The author ends the first paragraph (in which he quotes Darwin) with "He was unafraid to speculate about areas that seemed to require further investigation." In evaluating choice B, be careful not to use outside knowledge. The only mention of evolution in the passage is in the context of theories that reject the existence of emotions in animals (paragraph 4). For choice C, there is no indication of the strength or relevance of Darwin's reputation. The author suggests in fact that the scientific disdain for the discussion of animal emotions is a modern phenomenon (see the end of paragraph 2) that may or may not have existed in Darwin's time. Choice D is out of the scope of the relevant part of the passage; there is nothing in paragraph 1 to suggest that Darwin was comparing the likelihoods of cognition and emotion.

Passage X (Questions 55–59)

55. A Choice A is supported by the passage. The author argues that colonial expansion challenged the hegemony of humanism by exposing Germans to other, quite different peoples in the world (paragraphs 1 and 2). However, now that Europeans were more frequently traveling to these other areas, "anthropologists complained that the people they encountered were corrupted by contact with Europeans and thus were poor examples of natural peoples" (paragraph 3). Choice B is incorrect; the colonial experience challenged the humanist "monopoly," but the author does not suggest that the humanists challenged or critiqued colonialism. The second half of choice C is not supported by the passage. Be careful not to use outside knowledge; the passage does not discuss study of, or experience with, animals. Choice D is too extreme and does not represent the author's own opinion. While European anthropologists may at some point have made this claim (paragraph 3), the author does not suggest that anthropological study was impossible or that there was in fact such a thing as "formerly pure 'natural peoples.'"

56.   C   Choice C corresponds with the author's description in paragraph 2. The passage states "Instead of studying European 'cultural peoples,' societies defined by their history and civilization, anthropologists studied the colonized 'natural peoples,' societies supposedly lacking history and culture." Choice A is incorrect because the passage states that these German anthropologists believed that "natural peoples" have no history or culture, not that their history and culture existed in a less evolved form. The passage never discusses European attempts to control nature or colonized peoples' attitudes toward nature, and so choice B is incorrect. Finally, on choice D, the passage never describes any European belief that *domination* of inferior people is inevitable. Be careful not to use outside knowledge or opinion when answering questions.

57.   C   The author draws an implicit parallel between the belief cited in the question and the 19th century anthropologists' belief that "natural peoples" lacked "history and culture" and so revealed "human nature directly, unobscured by the masks of culture and the complications of historical development." That is, just as nature itself was supposedly unchanging over time, so were these "natural peoples." Choice A is the opposite of the correct answer. While German anthropologists eventually came to accept "notions of biological evolution" (paragraph 3), this represents an opposing, not a similar view. Choice B has the same problem (change instead of no change). Choice D mentions a humanist view that was rejected by German anthropologists (paragraph 2).

58.   B   Choice B corresponds to the author's depiction in paragraph 1 of humanist ideas. Humanists believed that "interpreting the textual monuments [i.e., books] of European history had for centuries served Europeans as a privileged mode of understanding what it meant to be human." Choice A describes an anthropological rather than a humanist idea, and the two are directly contrasted in the passage. On choice C, while the author suggests that the humanists believed they had special insight, the passage links anthropology, not humanism, to the natural sciences. Choice D is a misinterpretation or over-interpretation of the author's reference to the "utopian potential of hermeneutic interpretation" in paragraph 1. The author suggests in fact that humanists believed in European superiority rather than in equality.

59.   D   The passage states that nineteenth-century anthropologists studied the "bodies and everyday lives of 'natural peoples'" (paragraph 2). Furthermore, when the author states in paragraph 3 that by "the early twentieth century, presenting the customs and artifacts of particular societies as instances of timeless nature would come to seem arbitrary and artificial to anthropologists," he is suggesting that this was in fact a practice of the nineteenth-century anthropologists. Therefore, this book was most likely written by a nineteenth-century anthropologist. As for choice A, anthropologists, not humanists, were interested in the practices and artifacts of colonized peoples. For choice B, the twentieth-century anthropologists were no longer interested in displaying such artifacts (see paragraph 3). Choice C has the same problem as choice A; it refers to humanists rather than anthropologists.

Passage XI (Questions 60–64)

60.   **C**   Choice C best captures the purpose and the content of the passage as a whole. The author is not simply describing the role and actions of the Court (paragraphs 1–4) but is also identifying problems within that history and recommending that it "develop its earlier views of legislative learning" to better allow "the people to speak for themselves even as the Court speaks on their behalf" (paragraph 5). The passage does not describe the specific provisions of the Act (choice A); furthermore, the author mentions the Act in order to talk about broader issues involving the Court's role. Choice B suggests that the author argues that the Court should return to this earlier view. However, the author argues that it should further "develop" this view (paragraph 5), not simply reassert it. The author argues in paragraph 3 that this view, as held in the 1960s and 1970s, was "problematic." Choice D is too extreme. The author never suggests that the Court has abused its power.

61.   **A**   Choice A best captures the author's description of "essentialized conceptions of identity" as a "prepolitical" identity that is "formed prior to and apart from politics itself" (paragraph 4). Choice B is the opposite of the correct answer. This is what the author thinks the Court should do rather than what it has done in certain periods by taking political identity to be something apart from the political process. Choice C raises an issue that is never specifically discussed in the passage or in this context. Choice D is too limited: The phrase refers to a concept of political identity that applies to everyone, not just to minority populations.

62.   **D**   "Facilitator" best captures the role described by the author in the passage as a whole and specifically in the last sentence—"permitting the people to speak for themselves even as the Court speaks on their behalf." That is, facilitating the expression of public will and the formation of political identities. Choice A suggests that the Court has special knowledge to be imparted to the public, whereas the passage suggests that the Court's opinion should be informed by the views and desires of the public. Choice B has the same incorrect connotation of paternalism. Choice C is too limited; while the Court may in fact protect the public, the image of a bodyguard does not capture the issues of representation and facilitation of self-expression that are so important to the author.

63.   **B**   Choice B is most specifically supported by the author's references to the Voting Rights Act in paragraphs 1 and 3. On choice A, the author never argues or suggests that people have inaccurate or mistaken political identities. The reference to "legislative learning" in the last paragraph relates to "elected representatives," not the people. For choice C, the author does not critique the Court for taking on more than its appropriate role, and the passage does not support the argument that this role should be limited in this way. The first half of choice D is supported by paragraph 4. However, the second part of the choice misrepresents the author's opinion. In fact, the author argues that notions of identity should be constituted through political practice rather than defined in the abstract.

64.   C   In the second paragraph, the author states that the "constitutive role of the Court" confronts the Court with "the challenge of articulating the foundations of its own political authority" and that "since the earliest days of the republic, claims of judicial power have derived from the Court's capacity to speak on behalf of the people as a whole." The author goes on to say that when the Court acts, "it selects a notion of "the people" around which representational institutions may be organized." For choice A, while this may be one function of the Court, it is not described in this paragraph or elsewhere in the passage as its most important function. Choice B is inconsistent with the author's reference in paragraph 3 to the problems with seeing the Court as essentially involved in "interest group competition." Choice D is inconsistent with the author's argument at various places in the passage (see, for example, paragraph 5) that defining group identities is an ongoing, active process.

Passage XII (Questions 65–69)

65.   A   Choice A accurately expresses the intent of the analogy, which is introduced with a sentence that says in part that the author has "become more and more impressed with a sense of the inadequacy of the prevalent method of comparative mythology." Choice B is incorrect; the author does not argue that myth expresses this idea. While the author suggests that the statement in choice C is true, he does not use the analogy in the context of the analogy. Choice D contradicts the author's argument in the passage.

66.   C   In paragraph 2, the author develops his critique of comparative mythology by describing how scholars disagree amongst themselves. He then states that "among those who practice [this method], there is none of the beautiful unanimity of orthodoxy." At the end of paragraph 3, the author suggests that the level of disagreement among scholars of myth would not be accepted in any other scientific field. A is incorrect: The author himself is disagreeing "in public" with other scholars. Choice B is contradicted by the passage. The field is too flexible rather than too rigid. Choice D (themes common to all cultures) is never discussed in the passage.

67.   A   Choice A would weaken the author's argument by suggesting that perhaps specific flaws in the scholarship of these men (mentioned in paragraph 2), rather than a fundamentally flawed methodology, account for the wide variety of claims about the origin of names. The author himself suggests that the statement in choice B may be true (paragraph 4). Thus, it would not weaken the author's argument. Choice C would strengthen the author's argument; he himself makes this claim in paragraph 2. The author never claims that myths in different cultures do not display any common themes, and so choice D has no effect on the author's argument.

68. **B** The author never gives us an alternative to philological mythology. Nor does he describe an alternative offered by another scholar. For choice A, see paragraph 4. For choice C, see paragraph 3 and the reference to Curtius. For choice D, see paragraph 2.

69. **D** The author makes the claim stated in choice D in paragraph 4. Choice A misrepresents the first sentence of paragraph 4. The author criticizes the dominant methodology and yet does not offer an alternative. Therefore, he would not agree with choice B. The author refutes the statement in choice C in paragraph 1 of the passage.

Part IV:
The MCAT
Writing Sample

Chapter 14
Overview of
the Writing Sample

HOW IMPORTANT IS THE WRITING SAMPLE IN THE ADMISSIONS PROCESS?

Truthfully, it's not all that important. It is the least important section on the MCAT, and it is way down on the list of relevant factors for the medical colleges. However, the essays do play a role, and you should not entirely neglect preparation for them, especially since the essay format is unfamiliar to the vast majority of students. In short, just having decent essay writing abilities probably won't carry you through the essay, so a little practice is in order. The primary reason you can't just shrug off the essay is that the medical schools use it for two important things—a tiebreaker and to verify the authenticity of your personal statements, which is the real writing sample that they care about.

Given two students with the same scores and all else being equal, medical schools may opt for the student with the higher essay score. Most schools pay more attention to your personal statement to get a better picture of you and to see your writing abilities under real world circumstances rather than under time constraints. However, if there is a large disconnect between your personal essay and your MCAT essay score, they may assume you didn't write your personal statement yourself. Overall, an excellent writing sample score won't guarantee your acceptance into medical school, but a very poor score can definitely hurt your admissions prospects.

Students often want to know how much of their study time they should devote to the essay. The answer to this is as much time as it takes to do a decent job; more than that may be too much unless a top score is a point of pride for you.

SCORING OF THE WRITING SAMPLE

The scoring system for the writing sample is a little bizarre and requires some explanation. Each essay is scored by two graders who use a "holistic" scoring rubric, meaning that they consider everything about the essay and they don't, say, take off a specific number of points for each error. By the way, each grader only spends about two minutes on an essay, so it is to your advantage to make your arguments as clear and concise as possible.

Each grader assigns a number score from 1 to 6 in half point increments (for example, you could get a 4.0 or a 4.5 but not a 4.25 from a grader) with 6 being the highest. The two scores are averaged if they are within a point apart; if not, the scores are thrown out and the essay is scored by a third, supervisory reader. Then, the two separate essay scores are added together (stay with me here) yielding one final average score. The MCAT takes that final average and translates it into a letter score of J through T that corresponds to the 1 through 6 scale (1.0 is a J, 1.5 is a K, etc.). So what shows up on your final score report is a letter and does not factor into any of the other scores or your composite score.

QUALITY OF ESSAYS

Here we would like to distinguish between qualities of an essay that are prerequisites for a decent score and those qualities that earn an essay an impressive score. Prerequisites for a good score include fundamental writing skills such as good grammar, style, structure, and few errors in spelling and punctuation. Common impediments to a good score include not finishing the essay and not adequately addressing all three tasks of thesis, antithesis, and synthesis (discussed in detail below). This goes part and parcel with the issue of length. While length is not necessarily an indicator of a strong essay, a short essay is definitely an indicator of an essay that does not fully accomplish each task. Similarly, without the fundamentals of style, grammar, structure, and punctuation, an essay is unlikely to get more than an average score.

These qualities alone will not warrant fantastic scores. High-scoring essays also have well explained, detailed examples and particularly fitting conditions. So, if you are attempting to get a score beyond a P, you will have to expend more effort researching current events and practicing developing conditions, especially with difficult prompts.

Basic Advice

For most of the prompts, current events serve as useful examples to shore up arguments (current events are anything in the last, say, fifty years). So you may want to stay abreast of the news. Reading major newspapers or news magazines is a good way to do this. Local news and headline news aren't as useful unless they happen to go into depth, because the graders are looking for detail and background. Think depth, not breadth.

APPROACHING THE PROMPT

Good essays rarely come from students who simply begin writing anything that comes to mind. You should spend some time analyzing the prompt and brainstorming. The prompts are intentionally vague and require you to define ambiguous terms or elaborate on the underlying issues involved in the statement. For instance, consider the prompt:

> A democracy consisting of different subpopulations lacks unified policy.

Exactly What Is The Prompt?

It's a quasi-philosophical statement concerning some aspect of human thought or activity.

Source: *Cracking the MCAT,* 2006

Analyzing the Prompt

Let's examine the vague terms beginning with the most obvious. There is no definitive understanding of the term "unified policy." Lack of unified policy could include differences in law between states or areas or simply disagreement on behalf of lawmakers or constituents on a particular law. The word "policy" in itself is problematic, because it does not necessarily mean enacted legislation. However, it would probably be easier for a student to define it as such in order to narrow the discussion or at least to acknowledge that this entails a variety of concepts.

The term "subpopulations" is less vague, but this should probably be defined more precisely as segments of society divided, if not regionally, then ideologically, by class, gender, religion, ethnicity, etc.

Lastly, the term "democracy," while not really vague, could use some elaboration. It might be useful to ask, "Why is the prompt specifying a democracy?" Students should discuss within the essay the fact that societies in which the constituents vote on policy may have trouble agreeing on policy when different subpopulations have different interests. Thinking about these ambiguities and either more narrowly defining them or else acknowledging their causes will help you write a more coherent essay. Also, before beginning to write, you want to do some brainstorming.

When the Writing Sample Can Make a Difference

In the case of a disconnected application—a beautifully written personal statement with low Verbal Reasoning and/or low Writing Sample scores.

Source: *Best 168 Medical Schools,* 2008

Brainstorming

Start brainstorming by setting up two columns labeled true and false respectively. The true column is for examples that support the prompt, and the false column is for examples that disprove the prompt. Don't worry yet about how well the examples would work within an essay. The goal is to think of four to five examples for each so that you can find a pattern. This will ultimately be useful for articulating the condition that determines when the prompt is true and when it is false.

You should probably start with the true column, because it's generally easier to agree with the prompts. The true column might include examples like gun ownership laws, gay marriage, abortion laws, the death penalty, health care, international trade laws, etc.

The false column may be a bit harder and require more generalization; it may contain examples such as freedom of speech, freedom of press, freedom of religion, right to a jury of one's peers, right to vote, right to a speedy trial, right to education, equal opportunity employment laws, etc.

Lastly, compare the two columns looking for both commonalities within a column and differences between columns. You may notice that examples within the true column affect or distress certain subpopulations more than others or that examples in the true column seem geared toward the protection of the rights of people. So you may conclude that democracies lack unified policy when those policies disproportionately affect certain subpopulations, or you may decide that democracies achieve unified policy when those policies equally protect everybody.

There is no exact condition for which the essay graders are looking. Regardless, brainstorming both helps develop some sort of condition and aides in developing a condition that is general enough to fit several situations and is not too specific to the examples in your essay. In any case, you now have a condition, or synthesis, which is by far the most difficult task of the three you are given.

THE THREE TASKS OF THE WRITING SAMPLE

Each thirty-minute essay presents the student with a statement that relates to anything from government, politics, laws, and rights to business, education, technology, and advertising. Though the variety of topics is vast, the tasks for each prompt will always be the same. The directions will ask you to write a unified essay in which you perform the following tasks:

1) Explain what you think the statement means
2) Describe a specific situation in which the prompt is not true
3) Discuss what you think determines whether the prompt is true or false.

This doesn't mean you should ignore the directions. The directions are tailored to the prompt and occasionally are more specific than you might initially think. Although the first task doesn't change from one prompt to another, the second and third tasks may be different.

The first task is called the thesis, the second the antithesis, and the third the synthesis. The thesis, antithesis, synthesis set-up is a very specific, structured essay format. It has nothing to do with the typical introduction, body paragraphs, and conclusion about which you probably learned in school, so you can throw all that out the window.

To make it clear to the grader that you understand the structure of the essay at hand, you should write your essay in three paragraphs, which will in turn reflect the three tasks.

The First Task: The Thesis

There are four primary objectives that you should accomplish in your thesis:

> 1) Start off with an introductory sentence
> 2) Paraphrase the prompt
> 3) Address vague terms and underlying causes of the prompt
> 4) Give an example that supports the prompt

Introductory Sentences

It is a little abrupt to begin the essay with "The statement means...," so begin the essay with a general statement that reflects the sentiments of the prompt but not the prompt directly. A sentence such as "America is unique in that its citizens represent a wide variety of cultures whose values don't always mesh, circumstances not often encountered in other nations," can act as an effective springboard into the rest of the essay. Other material may urge you to begin the essay more directly by starting with the prompt. This will produce an essay that is satisfactory, but to receive the highest score, try to exhibit some finesse. You don't need more than one sentence to accomplish this, so be careful not to ramble.

Paraphrase the Prompt

Next, you want to tackle the prompt. You need to express the prompt in your own terms. There are two ways to do this. You can either write: "The statement asserts that ...," or you can restate the prompt in its entirety: "The statement that 'A democracy consisting of different subpopulations lacks unified policy' asserts that..." You can follow either phrase with a restatement of the prompt in different language. Consider the following sentence: "The statement that 'A democracy consisting of different subpopulations lacks unified policy' suggests that in nations in which the constituency has a hand in forming legislation and whose constituency is also diverse, coming to agreement on legislation is typically problematic." This basically paraphrases the prompt but also begins to explain it. This alone, however, is not enough.

Address Vague Terms and Underlying Issues

Third, you want to further define any vague terms or underlying issues in the prompt. The easiest way to do this is to simply articulate your thoughts during your initial analysis of the prompt. This will act as the bulk of your explanation or clarification.

Support the Prompt with Examples

Lastly, you want to include a specific example, preferably from current events. We know that the directions do not explicitly ask for an example, but an example does two things: It helps make your argument more concrete by solidifying what would otherwise be general analysis, and it will act as a nice contrast to your counterexample later in the essay. Generally speaking, you should choose the topic about which you know most from your true column. Be careful to not get carried away with your example; limit the example to two or three sentences in the essay. Remember that your primary job is to explain the statement; an example is just an aide to this task.

The Second Task: The Antithesis

You have two primary goals in this paragraph:

> 1) Provide a transition sentence
> 2) Present a counterexample

Provide a Transition Sentence

A transitional sentence is critical for writing a coherent essay. This essay is strange in that in the first paragraph, you must argue for the prompt, and in the second paragraph, you must turn around and argue against the prompt. You cannot simply present a counterexample and still make sense; you have to alert the reader to what you are doing by using a transition sentence. Consider the following sentence: "Conversely, there are some situations in which a democracy consisting of diverse populations can achieve unified policy." Sentences like this are simple and clearly alert the reader that you are about to provide a contrast to your previous arguments.

Present a Counterexample

After a transition, you want to present your counterexample. Unlike your first example in the thesis, which you want to keep somewhat limited, the counterexample is your time to shine. From your false column examples, choose the topic you feel you can best explain with the most detail. The ideal situation is that you wow the graders with your knowledge, background information, and analysis of a current event. You want to show them that you are thoughtful, well rounded, and interested in the world around you. This, admittedly, is the ideal. If you cannot think of an example about which you know a lot of details, make the example as specific and concrete as you can; avoid hypothetical situations, if possible. Under no circumstances should you make something up; the graders will probably know when you do this and will not look favorably upon it.

The Third Task: The Synthesis

You have four primary aims in this paragraph:

1) Provide a conclusion sentence
2) Present the condition
3) Support with examples
4) Get out gracefully

Provide a Conclusion Sentence

First, you want to provide a conclusion sentence that shows the grader you are bringing the essay to a close. However, this is a very different conclusion sentence than that in typical essays where the aim is to present a final argument or position. A common mistake of rookie MCAT test takers is that they attempt to either agree or disagree with the prompt or reconcile the discrepancies. In this essay format, the conclusion sentence should acknowledge that the prompt is neither right nor wrong but rather that the prompt is sometimes right and sometimes wrong. Demonstrate to the grader that you recognize the dichotomy. Consider the following sentence: "In conclusion, it is clear that diverse democracies often lack unified policies but that some policies can inspire agreement among the citizens." This clearly demonstrates that the writer understands the task at hand.

Present the Condition

Next, you want to present the condition under which the prompt is true or false. As discussed previously, you should have decided on the condition during the brainstorming process, as it is difficult to come up with a condition on the fly. Again, this is definitely the most troublesome task, but when done well, it can really boost an essay score. Once you have settled on a condition, the goal is to articulate it as succinctly and clearly as possible. Consider the following sentence: "Nations with diverse subpopulations lack unified policy when those policies disproportionately affect subsets of the populace." Conversely, you could state the condition in the positive: "Democracies with diverse populations can establish unified policy when those policies seek to protect everyone, regardless of their differences." Both nicely articulate a condition that applies to many situations without resorting to multiple explanatory sentences or multiple conditions.

Support with Examples

Third, you want to bolster your condition with your thesis and antithesis examples. The point here (since it may seem a bit redundant to reiterate your examples) is to demonstrate that you not only have a condition but that it is genuinely applicable. You should not bring in new examples at this point; it is not only distracting but also wastes time. Supporting the condition with examples need not take up a lot of time and energy; you only need one sentence for each example. Consider the following two sentences: "The discrepancies from state to state in gun ownership laws illustrates that policies that disproportionately affect urban and rural constituents will necessarily be contentious. However, the rights that protect the freedom of the press to conceal its sources in turn protect constituents from abusive practices and thus are generally agreed on by citizens." Two quick statements go a long way in showcasing the efficacy of your condition.

Get Out Gracefully

Finally, you want to end the essay gracefully, meaning that you want to conclude the essay neither too abruptly nor too verbosely. There are many ways to do this, but the easiest is to return to whatever statement you used as an introduction at the opening of the essay, which also provides some nice symmetry within the essay as a whole. Another tactic some students like is to use famous quotes, which is absolutely fine as long as they are relevant to the prompt, accurately quoted, and correctly attributed. Also, fluff, while not a good idea in the rest of the essay, is perfectly acceptable in the last sentence. Ending on a feel good thought such as, "No matter the differences among America's subpopulations, beneficial legislation is a universal concern that unites us all," is a reasonable way to conclude an essay.

In the next chapter, we analyze some prompts and essays that are effective to varying degrees in order to illustrate what works, what gets by, and what doesn't fly.

Chapter 15
Practice Essays for the
MCAT Writing Sample

Consider this statement:

Citizens in a democracy must always obey the law.

Write a unified essay in which you perform the following tasks. Explain what you think the above statement means. Describe a specific situation in which a citizen in a democracy might not obey the law. Discuss what you think determines when a citizen in a democracy should or should not obey the law.

Sample Response 1 (low-scoring)

In a democracy, citizens should never break the law. Widespread law-breaking would lead to mass chaos, with everyone doing whatever they felt like. People would speed on the highways, steal whatever they liked, and kill whoever they didn't like. The law is necessary for a well-ordered society. I think that the statement means that law is important and we must obey it even if we don't want to. Unless a totalitarian country like the former Soviet Union, or a non-democratic country like China today. In those cases, people should break the law to try to change things, like in the Student Democracy Movement in China, when people camped out in Tiananmen square to try to encourage the government to allow more democratic freedoms. In this case, law breaking was not only OK but necessary for the cause of freedom.

So, what I think determines whether or not people should break the law is whether or not the country is a democratic country or a non-democratic nation. People in an oppressive system have human rights, and those human rights include protest unfair rules and laws. But, if the system is a fair one, like in a democracy, then they should obey the law. Except, if they need to break the law in self-defense, which would be allowed. Or, if breaking the law wouldn't cause great harm to others (like speeding a little bit on the highway), it is OK because no one is really hurt by that.

Analysis of Sample Response 1

The essay begins with the statement that in a democracy, citizens should never break the law. In the second paragraph, however, the essay mentions cases in which citizens in a democracy may in fact be allowed to break the law (in self-defense or if no great harm comes to others). Thus, the essay argues for two mutually exclusive positions rather than discussing some situations in which the prompt statement would be true and other, different situations in which it would be false.

The most serious weakness of the essay, however, is that it strays from the question. Rather than discussing (at any length) when citizens in a democracy would be justified in breaking the law (as required by the second task in the question), the essay for the most part explains when citizens of *non*-democratic nations would be justified in doing so. Finally, the essay contains several errors in grammar and sentence structure that undermine its clarity and coherence.

Sample Response 2 (medium-scoring)

Law is essential to a well-ordered society. Therefore, in most cases, citizens in a democracy should obey the law. Laws in a democracy are decided upon by a legislature elected by the people, and therefore law represents the will of the people. Furthermore, law is passed in the best interests of the majority. Even if an individual feels that a law is unfairly constraining on them as an individual, that is not enough justification to break it. People in a democracy must sacrifice, in some cases, their own well-being or best interest for the good of the whole. However, there are some exceptions to this rule.

When a law is unfair, citizens are allowed to break that law. For example, during the Vietnam War, people marched in the streets and performed acts of civil disobedience in protest of the war. These marches were sometimes illegal, but in these cases freedom of speech took precedence. When people feel that a law is unjust or unfair, they have the constitutional right to do whatever is necessary to protest and to try to change that law. This is a fundamental right in a democratic state; without free speech, we wouldn't be democracy anymore. The same was true in the Civil Rights Movement and in the movement for women's suffrage.

Therefore, what determines whether or not citizens in a democracy must obey the law is the fairness of the law itself. When a law is just, and has been agreed upon by a majority of citizens through their elected representatives, that law must be obeyed to preserve social stability and peace. However, when a majority of people decide that a law is unjust, they have an obligation as citizens to protest and try to change that law, and this may require breaking the law itself.

Analysis of Sample Response 2

The writer begins with a thoughtful discussion of why obeying the law is important in a democracy. This part of the essay would be even stronger if the writer gave a more concrete example of how breaking the law in the service of individual self-interest might compromise the best interests of the majority of society. In the second paragraph, the writer raises a relevant exception to the duty to obey the law—when the law itself is unjust. However, the example given in that paragraph is not logically coherent; the laws being broken through civil disobedience were not the laws (or policies, more precisely) that the protestors believed to be unjust (the war). In fact, there is no example given of an unjust law, even though this is the supposed focus of that part of the essay.

The writer lists two additional examples at the end of the second paragraph but doesn't go on to explain their relevance to the terms of the question. In the final paragraph, the writer again raises a thoughtful point (when it may be legitimate to break the law as a form of protest) but does not fully develop the argument by giving clear criteria that would justify breaking the law in the interests of justice.

Sample Response 3 (high-scoring)

Democratic nations are founded on the idea of a social contract. As expressed by thinkers such as Hobbes, Locke, and Rousseau, the formation of a state requires that citizens give up some of their individual liberties for the good of the society as a whole. Moving from a state-less "state of nature" (which Hobbes described as a "war of all against all") to a peaceful and ordered society imposes upon each individual the duty not to act out of pure individual self-interest, but to instead conform to the "sovereign will." This sovereign will, in a democracy, is embodied in our three branches of government, and that government has the duty to pass and enforce laws that are for the good of all people. Thus, it is the duty of citizens in a democracy to obey the law in most cases. This applies even to instances when breaking the law would benefit ourselves at apparently little cost to others. No one likes to pay taxes, for example, and it seems that for most people, breaking the law by using illegal loopholes would have little impact on society as a whole. However, each citizen has a moral as well as legal duty to play his or her part in the social contract and make the sacrifice. Part of living in a society is acting as you would like others to act; if no one paid his or her taxes, then a lot of the public infrastructure we depend upon would be in big trouble.

This duty to obey the law is especially important for powerful or famous figures in society. When well-known people break the law, even in seemingly trivial ways, it undermines faith in the strength of the social contract, and encourages others to do the same. For example, when Michael Milkin was convicted of insider trading and securities fraud in the 1980's, some argued that his transgressions, while technically illegal, represented common practice and that he should not be punished for it. However, this and other insider trading scandals had the impact of undermining people's faith in the fairness of the financial system and gave the impression that the laws that apply to the average person do not apply to the rich and powerful. This weakens the economy as a whole, as people either are afraid to invest because they feel powerless or come to believe that they too can break the law with impunity.

However, there are times in which breaking the law is in fact not only allowable, but imperative. These are times when the laws themselves are inconsistent with the founding ideas of the social contract. During the Civil Rights Movement in the 1950's and 1960's, people protested against Jim Crow laws that enforced racial segregation and that limited African Americans' voting rights. Segregationist laws were even validated by the Supreme Court in decisions such as Plessy v. Ferguson, which accepted "separate but equal" as a legitimate notion. While largely non-violent, civil rights demonstrations such as sit-ins at segregated restaurants often broke the law, and protesters, including Martin Luther King Jr. himself, were often arrested and jailed. And yet, we now see these protests as not only valid, but heroic as well. The Civil Rights Movement led to a change in the law, with legislation such as the Civil Rights Act of 1968 and the Voting Rights Act of 1964. These are laws that continue to be used to protect people's civil rights today.

The question then becomes, how do we decide when it is and is not legitimate to break the law in a democratic system? It cannot simply be an issue of individual conscience; if each individual did what he or she "thought was right" in every circumstance, we would have chaos, given that most peoples' perceptions of right and wrong tend to be influenced by selfishness and self interest. A better determining factor is the nature of the law itself, and if it is consistent or inconsistent with the basic principles embodied in the social contract governing our society. In the United States, the ideal enshrined in the Constitution, including equality for all citizens, should be embodied in all of our laws. If a law violates this principle, then citizens may break that law with the goal of creating a more fair law that is consistent with Constitutional ideals. The Constitution itself has been used in the past to justify practices that we now see as unethical, including slavery, the denial of suffrage to women, and the treatment of Native Americans. And yet the ideals embodied in that document have been used to change those practices over time. To maintain a stable society, in most cases we must abide by the law, even if our selfish impulses tell us otherwise. But if we are to evolve as a society, we must accept that in some cases, citizens must break laws and write better ones, in order to create a better society for all.

Analysis of Sample Response 3

The writer of this essay has an insightful, sophisticated central point: Citizens of a democratic state have a duty to uphold the social contract, which also entails remaining true to core constitutional ideals. The essay consistently and coherently develops that central point while also directly responding to the three tasks set out by the question.

The writer also uses relevant concrete examples to illustrate abstract ideas. The final paragraph gives clear criteria by which to determine when citizens should and should not obey the law, based on the nature and value of the social contract. These criteria are consistent with the ideas and examples described in the previous paragraphs and serve to further develop and explain those ideas. Finally, the writer displays a facility with language and is able to express complex concepts while maintaining at all times a focus on the precise terms of the question.

Consider this statement:

Modern technology, while making our individual lives easier, weakens the social fabric.

Write a unified essay in which you perform the following tasks. Explain what you think the above statement means. Describe a specific situation in which modern technology might enhance the fabric of society. Discuss what you think determines whether modern technology will weaken or enhance the social fabric.

Sample Response 1 (low-scoring)

Computers are an example of how technology undermines the quality of our social life. Instead of people talking to each other face to face, now people communicate through email. Where people used to have actual face to face conversations, or send letters, now they communicate through short messages that are often not even well written. This makes it more difficult to communicate things like emotions, when you can't see the expression on someone's face. Also, people spend a lot of time on the internet and playing computer games.

However, computers can also be used to unite people and make social life better. Through email, we can communicate with people who are far away. While in the past, we would have to travel for days and long distances to talk to friends and relatives, now we can communicate at the touch of a button. This way we can maintain relationships that in the past we would have lost over time.

Therefore, what determines whether technology undermines or enhances social fabric is how it is used. If we use technology to isolate ourselves, like by playing computer games all day, then social life is undermined. But if we use it to communicate with others, like through email, it can keep us connected.

Analysis of Sample Response 1

This essay begins with an implied definition of "social fabric" (quality of our social life). However, it does not fully explain or develop that definition. The writer mentions two types of technology that may undermine social interaction but does not explain those examples; this is especially true of the example of computer gaming.

In the second paragraph, the writer repeats the e-mail example but now uses it to illustrate the opposite point—i.e., how e-mail strengthens rather than weakens social life. Thus, the writer argues that e-mail both weakens and strengthens social life but gives no clear criteria we can use to determine when it will in fact do one or the other. It is suggested that one distinction may be whether or not the people with whom we are communicating are close by or far away, but this distinction is not made sufficiently explicit.

In the final paragraph, the writer relies on circular reasoning (communication with others connects us with others). Overall, the essay raises some promising ideas and examples but does not develop them into a coherent and unified argument that directly addresses the three tasks set out in the question.

Sample Response 2 (medium-scoring)

This is the Age of Technology, or, as some have called it, the Information Age. Much of modern technology helps us to carry out our everyday tasks more quickly and easily. This comes at a cost, however, as often we lose the human factor in the process. People used to have to go to the library to do research, but now they can do it on their own at home using the internet. Whereas people used to write letters, now they use email. Even air conditioning has reduced social interaction. People used to sit on the porch to catch cool breezes, but now they sit inside and turn on the air conditioner, and people often don't even know the names of their neighbors. When people do not regularly interact with neighbors and even strangers, they become isolated within the limited spheres of family, work and friends.

But, some forms of technology have made society better. Advances in medical technology have clearly improved our quality of life. People used to commonly die from diseases for which we now have a cure, or that we can prevent in the first place. The discovery of penicillin and other antibiotics made it possible to cure diseases that most people used to die from. In the past, people used to keep their children indoors for fear that they would contract polio, but now the polio vaccine has eradicated the disease and with it the "social fear" of catching it by interacting with others. In times of plague, people would barricade themselves indoors for weeks and months, but now plague is rarely seen in industrialized nations.

What determines whether or not modern technology reduces the quality of our social lives is the type of technology. Technology that is used by individuals all by themselves cuts those people off from society and reduces or eliminates social interaction. However, medical technology improves people's lives on both an individual and societal level. By allowing us to interact with each other without fear of disease transmission, it allows people to go out into society instead of barricading themselves behind closed doors in fear. We can't live without technology, so we must work to make sure that the costs never outweigh the benefits.

Analysis of Sample Response 2

This essay begins well with a discussion of how certain forms of modern technology have reduced our social interactions. The writer's definition of "social fabric" is implied but reasonably clear.

The second paragraph focuses largely on how medical technology has improved our quality of life. A connection to social interaction is asserted but is somewhat strained; the writer does not make a compelling case that fear of disease has had a widespread impact on social interactions in the past, and so it is not clear why modern technology has substantively changed the quality of social life today.

The final paragraph gives a criterion by which we can determine whether or not technology weakens the social fabric (if it is used by individuals in isolation). However, that criterion is not developed in further detail; the final paragraph largely repeats points that have already been made earlier in the essay. Overall, the essay is clearly written and coherent, but it does not directly address the topic of the impact of technology on the social fabric with great depth or complexity.

Sample Response 3 (high-scoring)

We live in an era that is fundamentally defined and shaped by technology. That technology is often created and used with the intent of making our everyday tasks easier and faster to complete. However, that ease sometimes comes with a price; we gain convenience at the cost of the basic human interactions that used to define our existence in a social network or fabric, a network that was built and strengthened through everyday interactions with a variety of people. One area of social life in which the negative impact of technology has been especially egregious is the family. There used to be a clear line between work and home; when you left the workplace, the assumption used to be that you had in fact left the workplace and you were now in the arena of your "private life." In the past, it was common for parents and children to eat dinner and spend the evening together. Yes, the adults often took work home with them, and children had their homework to complete, but this was all done in the realm of the home, with the assumption that this was a communal sphere that could be separated from the actual workplace. When the family left the home for an evening out or a vacation, this was truly "family time," since employers could not easily communicate with their employees. Now, however, with the ease of communicating through email, cell phones, and Blackberries, workers are often expected to be reachable at any moment, and available to complete any task that arises. Technology that makes it possible for an employee to access his or her workplace computer from home has also contributed to this degrading of the quality of "family time" by further blurring the line between work and home. Even telecommuting has not solved this problem. While an employee may in fact work from home and be physically present with his or her family, the worker is not mentally or emotionally present, and the complete lack of a distinction between work and home pushes the worker to always be working to keep up with higher and higher expectations of productivity. This in fact may be the true hidden cost of technology; as it becomes easier and faster to complete tasks from any location, employers' expectations of how much can and should be done also keep rising, with the result that workers have less and less free time to spend with family and friends. Statistics show that U.S. workers work more hours per week than almost any other country, and this can in large part be attributed to technological advances.

However, the impact of technology on social life is not entirely destructive. Some forms of communication technology have made it possible to communicate with friends and family in ways that were not possible in the past. Technology has even made it possible to communicate with people we would not even have been able to communicate with before, creating new communities or "societies" where none previously existed. Email and other forms of computer-aided communication make it possible to easily speak with people in other parts of the world. Internet communities have grown where groups of people, whether through direct communication or through participation in a joint enterprise, form ongoing networks defined around specific issues or undertakings. Wikipedia is one such case. This on-line encyclopedia is not simply a service provided to the public. It sees itself as a community or a "wikiworld," formed around the basic idea that everyone, not just the experts, has useful knowledge to contribute. Through the ongoing submission and editing process, a sort of society is formed, with common goals, governed by commonly accepted rules of behavior. This is essentially the definition of a society, after all.

Even computer gaming has evolved in this same direction, with players taking on defined identities and participating in an on-going and constantly evolving set of interactions. These gaming societies have many of the characteristics of what we think of as a real society: people cooperate, fight, become alienated or accepted, and even sell goods to each other within the game's "economy." Thus, computer technology has gone beyond simply facilitating communication between people within an existing social network (e.g. by allowing friends and family to communicate over long distances). It has even led to the creation of new kinds of societies.

Therefore, what determines whether technology will undermine or improve the quality of our social lives is whether it allows what we have always done to be done faster, or instead opens new lines of communication that have not previously existed. Gore Vidal once said, "Thanks to modern technology, history now comes with a fast-forward button." The need for speed has become one of the hallmarks of modern society, and technology has both created and fed this desire to get everything done faster. In some ways, this speed has degraded the quality of our social interactions, because by allowing us to be more productive in our working lives, the value of productivity has been raised to take precedence over all other aspects of life. By placing productivity on such a high pedestal, we have in some ways created a culture that downgrades the value of the lives we live, or should live, outside of work with family and friends. However, technology has also given us ways not only to maintain existing connections but to create new ones, even to create a new kind of society or community that reproduces and recreates social networks. That is, some technologies create and maintain an entirely new social fabric. In a sense, technology has brought us closer to the "other" by making it possible to bond in a new arena with those with whom we would have had no real connection in the past. In the end, the long-term impact of technology on the character and strength of our society will depend on whether we allow it to eat away at existing social bonds and create a new culture of isolation, or whether we instead incorporate it within our existing social culture to strengthen those bonds and create new ones.

Analysis of Sample Response 3

This essay directly addresses the trade-off between convenience and social interaction that is at the heart of the question, using concrete examples to illustrate more abstract ideas. It clearly explains what kinds of technology will either weaken or strengthen the social fabric and why. The final paragraph sets out criteria that determine the effects of different forms of technology on social interactions and further develops the concepts raised earlier in the essay without simply repeating the specific points that have already been made. The author also displays a clear control of language. Overall, the writer makes a complex, sophisticated, and well-organized argument that directly and coherently addresses all parts of the question.

Essay Prompt 3

Consider this statement:

The primary goal of a business should be to maintain a competitive edge over other businesses.

Write a unified essay in which you perform the following tasks. Explain what you think the above statement means. Describe a specific situation in which a business's primary goal might not be to maintain a competitive edge over other businesses. Discuss what you think determines when the primary goal of a business should be to maintain a competitive edge over other businesses.

Sample Response 1 (low-scoring)

Sink or swim. A business must compete to stay alive. Therefore, a business must have as its first goal competing with other businesses in its field. If a business doesn't always try to produce better products and gain a larger share of the market, it might go bankrupt. This would not be good for the business itself, or for the workers it employs. Competition is also good for the economy, as it makes businesses more efficient and productive, and helps keep unemployment rates low. The only situation in which a business might not be better off by competing would be if it can form a cartel with other businesses. One example of a successful cartel would be OPEC, the Organization of Oil Producing Countries, which was formed in 1960. By cooperating with each other and agreeing on production levels and prices, OPEC is able to protect the economies of all of its member nations. This also helps OPEC nations compete with non-OPEC oil companies. OPEC controls almost half of the world's oil production, and about 60 % of the world's oil reserves. OPEC includes nations such as the UAE, Saudi Arabia, Venezuela, Nigeria, and Indonesia, and has its headquarters in Vienna. It was responsible for the 1973 oil crisis when it embargoed sales of oil to certain countries for political reasons. If the oil companies in each of these nations were to try to compete with the companies in all the other nations, they would have to lower prices and none of them would have as much profit as they do now.

Therefore, a business should do whatever it needs to do in order to maximize profit, and this may mean either competing or cooperating. Cooperation often increases stability, which may also be of benefit.

Analysis of Sample Response 1

This essay has a catchy beginning. However, it goes on to argue in the first half of the first paragraph that businesses should *always* compete, and then argues in the second half of the first paragraph that in some cases cooperation is better than competition. Therefore, rather than offering a unified essay, this writer presents two mutually exclusive positions on the prompt statement.

The statement that cooperation within a cartel helps OPEC nations compete with non-OPEC businesses further confuses the issue; it is unclear if the writer intends to argue that cooperation is a method of competition, or rather if it is a true alternative to competition.

The essay provides many details about OPEC (listing, for example, the member nations and mentioning the oil embargo). However, the writer doesn't explain the relevance of those details (e.g., how the embargo illustrates the power of a cartel and therefore the success of a cooperative strategy).

The essay ends abruptly, without giving criteria that would determine when and why a business should either compete or cooperate. In the same way, the writer raises the issue of stability in the final sentence, with no explanation of what stability means in this context (stability of the business? of the nation?) or how stability should factor into a business's strategy.

Overall, while the essay is written in clear language and raises a promising example (OPEC), it does not adequately develop its major ideas and it fails to fully address all three parts of the question.

Sample Response 2 (medium-scoring)

In a free market economy, businesses succeed or fail largely on the basis of market share. Those that can sell the most, while minimizing their production costs, will survive while those that do not offer products that people want to buy will tend to fail. Thus, in many ways one could argue that the primary goal of a business should be to maintain its competitive edge. Businesses compete in two ways. First, they try to maximize sales. Second, they try to minimize production costs. The first goal is often reached by offering new products that are, or are perceived by consumers as, new and innovative. Thus we see soft drink companies constantly coming out with new versions of their product, or shoe manufacturers like Nike always coming out with new models. The new versions may not be all that different from the old ones, but by offering something new, companies try to fool consumers into buying yet another pair of shoes, or trying a new soft drink. By creating fads, clothing companies try to do the same, keeping consumers coming back for more, even if they really don't need any new clothes. Businesses that produce consumer products are like sharks; they have to keep moving forward, or they will sink and die, when consumers flock to another brand that appears to have a newer and therefore supposedly better product.

However, there are limitations to this. There are some areas in which competition cannot be the first priority. For example, a business cannot sacrifice the well being of its workers in the pursuit of profit. Nike, for example, has been accused of using sweatshop labor in its search for lowering production costs. A classic example of the potentially tragic consequences of taking this route is the Triangle Shirtwaist Fire in 1911. The sweatshop had locked its doors in order to keep the workers from leaving the building and lowering production. A fire broke out and many of the workers were trapped inside, and many died.

Therefore, what determines whether or not a business's primary goal should be maintaining a competitive edge is whether or not they are putting their workers at risk by doing so. A business should and must do everything it can to compete, but not at the cost of worker's lives.

Analysis of Sample Response 2

This writer does a nice job of setting out two ways in which businesses compete: maximizing sales and minimizing production costs. The essay then goes on to discuss the first in detail, in the context of explaining when competition is in fact essential. Thus, the first paragraph explains in both abstract and concrete terms when and why competition should be a priority. The first paragraph also suggests the point of contrast that will be further developed in the second paragraph (when minimizing production costs should not take precedence over other concerns), which provides a unifying framework for the essay as a whole.

In the second paragraph, the writer gives a relevant example and suggests why competition may not always be the primary goal. This paragraph, however, is underdeveloped, and it relies too much on the reader to make the connection back to the terms of the question. This is even more of a problem in the final paragraph.

The writer states the point of contrast (profit vs. workers' lives) but does not go on to explain how we should weigh risk to workers against profit in deciding what the primary concern of a business must be. Is any risk to workers illegitimate in the service of profit and competition? Is it only risk of death that should be factored in?

Overall, the essay is clearly written, it provides relevant examples, and it progresses logically from one paragraph to the next. However, its core ideas are not fully developed in the second and third sections.

Sample Response 3 (high-scoring)

Free market economies are ruled by the principle of economic Darwinism. Businesses that adapt to changing market conditions survive, and those who do not die, and their market niche is filled by some other, better adapted, company. To continue to evolve and survive, businesses must constantly be aware of their competitors and continually strive to produce products that will attract the consumer. Thus, maintaining a competitive edge is crucial for any business and, within certain limitations, should be a top priority.

Businesses can remain competitive in a variety of ways; they can capture and maintain a majority of the market, or they can eke out a stable niche for themselves by creating strong consumer loyalty to their brand. Apple is a prime example of the latter strategy. While Apple computers represent, and likely will continue to represent, a minority of the computer market, Apple has devised a competitive strategy based on distinguishing itself from Microsoft, as the "creative" alternative. With its slogan "Think different," Apple sets itself up as the "anti-Microsoft" alternative, appealing to people who think to think of themselves as unique and different. The fact that it does not define the market becomes a selling point rather than a disadvantage. Apple's television commercials illustrate this competitive strategy, as the young, hip, and cool Apple guy who is into music and other creative past-times is in clear contrast with the stodgy, white-shirted, and bloated PC representative. The message is clear: Apple is created for your individualistic, creative needs, while a PC is fine for the anonymous and repressed office worker. Interestingly, Apple was able to capture a majority market share with a similar marketing strategy for its iPod. Because it was able to capture the market at its birth, with the creation of MP3 players, Apple was able to use the same antiestablishment image to become the establishment. While most would agree that the iPod is not inherently better than other players, Apple has been able to hold onto its competitive edge by maintaining its image and adapting to the market with updated variations on the same theme, like the iPod shuffle. If Apple did not actively maintain this edge by constantly promoting its image and offering new products, it would soon be overwhelmed by the Microsoft behemoth.

However, businesses do not exist in a vacuum, and sometimes other factors must take precedence over maintaining that constant competitive edge. Companies that do not take a long term view of the effects of their actions, and who act illegally or unethically in order to stay on top, will eventually fail as well. The story of Enron has become a cautionary tale of what can happen when greed and pursuit of immediate profit take over. For years Enron was praised as an innovative company that not only maintained high profit margins with its efficient management style, but also provided its workers with good benefits and a strong pension program. In 2001, however, it became public knowledge that its manager, in particular Kenneth Lay and Jeffrey Skilling, had been "cooking the books" to maintain an appearance of efficiency and profitability, when in fact the opposite was true. Enron was failing, but its founder and CEO and others were committing fraud, hiding debts and losses, to maintain a good public image and maintain competitiveness in the energy market. This was a case of managers doing everything they could to remain competitive in the short run, but their scheme inevitably failed and Enron went bankrupt, putting thousands of employees out of work with no pension, and bankrupting as well many investors who had put their faith in the false financial reports. This raises as well the issue of social responsibility. By their actions, Skilling and Lay not only hurt themselves and their employees, but as well many others in society, even the economy as a whole. The scandal raised doubt in the minds of investors in general who now felt as if they could not trust a company's financial statements or the fairness of the investment arena. One could say that this was the "Watergate" of the financial world.

Therefore, we can say that a company should always strive to maintain a competitive edge in the long term, but that this long-term view may require prioritizing other things in the short term. Without a long term perspective, a business cannot build and maintain brand loyalty. This strategy often involves creating an image that will continue to attract consumers to the product, even as tastes and the market change. Older consumers will continue to buy the product that they feel represents their self-image and their needs, while updating the product both keeps the original buyers coming back for more and as well attract new, younger consumers. By creating a specific, identifiable image, businesses like Apple distinguish themselves from their competitors and gives people a reason to remain loyal. However, that image must be at least in part based on reality. When corporate practices are in fact at odds with the image, inevitably this will become public and the company will decline, even if the decline is not as dramatic as Enron's public humiliation and bankruptcy. Consumers care not only about the product but the image of the company, as can be seen in the uproar when it was known that Kathy Lee Gifford's clothing line employed child labor. Sales and the stock price declined, as people decided that they did not want, through their purchases, to be identified with these practices. Maintaining good business practices and displaying at least a modicum of social responsibility in a long term view, along with having a keen competitive edge in the short term and adapting to a changing market, will do the most to keep a business alive and healthy.

Analysis of Sample Response 3

This writer does an excellent job of using examples to illustrate more abstract ideas. While a large part of the essay is taken up by description of two examples (Apple and Enron), the examples are used to illustrate the writer's core argument (when and why competition should be the primary goal of a business) and are made directly relevant to the three parts of the question.

The essay gives clear criteria to determine when the prompt statement would and would not be true (short vs. long term). The essay also raises a thoughtful point about social responsibility—i.e., that a business may have duties to employees, investors, and to society as a whole that go beyond and may even conflict with making a profit.

The essay is not perfect. There are two grammatical errors (subject-verb agreement) and the wording is at times repetitive (the phrase "as well" is used over and over). However, these errors do not take away from the coherence and logic of the writer's argument and therefore would not affect the score.

Overall, the essay shows depth and complexity of thought, is well organized, and fully addresses the question on both a concrete and a philosophical level.

Consider this statement:

The first priority of politicians must be to serve the needs of their constituents.

Write a unified essay in which you perform the following tasks. Explain what you think the above statement means. Describe a specific situation in which the first priority of a politician might not be to serve constituents' needs. Discuss what you think determines when the first priority of a politician should be to serve the needs of constituents and when it should not.

Sample Response 1 (low-scoring)

Politicians are elected to do what is best for their constituents, that is, the people who elected them. Therefore, in most cases, the politician should put the needs of the people first. This means that when they are performing their public duties, they should do what is best for the nation. When they are deciding whether or not to go to war, they should do so if it will benefit the public in some way. If going to war with or invading another country, for example, would help the economy, then it would be justified because one's own people always come first. This is the duty of a politician at any level, from local to national. They shouldn't however, make decisions based on their own personal beliefs or do things just because it would make them better of financially. Politicians should not be corrupt, that is they should not take bribes in order to create policies that powerful and wealthy people in society want, if those policies won't serve the interests of the public.

Politicians are people too, and sometimes their personal needs take precedence even when they shouldn't. The headlines are full of cases when politicians took bribes or did other unethical things. This happens a lot in totalitarian countries too. Leaders increase their own power even when this means oppressing their people. Also, you can't expect a politician to always be working; sometimes they need time off, just like anyone else. A politician shouldn't take a vacation in the middle of a crisis, but when things are calm, a politician should be able to take a few days off to rest, so that they can do their job better when they come back.

A politician should make serving the needs of their constituents a first priority when they are performing their job; that is what they are elected to do in a democracy. Of course, politician in a non-democratic country might not put the people's needs first, since they are not elected. This kind of politician might act to preserve their own power in ways that are not good for the people as a whole. However, even a democratically elected politician sometimes put himself first and take care of himself and his family. Politicians are people too, and we can't expect them to work every moment. This wouldn't be fair, and it isn't practical either.

Analysis of Sample Response 1

This essay makes a good point in the first paragraph; politicians have a duty to serve the needs of their constituents. As part of that discussion, the writer makes a fairly controversial claim (it is valid to invade other countries for purely economic motives) that requires more explanation and defense to be considered part of a reasonable argument. Overall, however, the first paragraph is adequate. Significant problems arise, however, in the second paragraph.

The last sentence in the prompt statement asks in part when the first priority of a politician should not be serving the needs of their constituents. Therefore, the writer must discuss not just when constituents' needs might be the first priority, but also when they should *not* be the first priority. The second paragraph largely discusses hypothetical cases when leaders *illegitimately* put their own desires first. The second part of the first paragraph comes closer to addressing the terms of the question, but there is no transition between the discussion of invalid and potentially valid motivations, and the paragraph as a whole is not logically coherent.

This problem continues in the final paragraph, where there is no clear distinction between ethically defensible and indefensible cases of putting other considerations above constituents' needs. There are a few grammatical and/or typographical errors in the essay (e.g., "better of" instead of "better off" in the first paragraph, "politician" instead of "politicians," and "put" instead of "puts" in the final paragraph). However, these mistakes are not serious enough to significantly affect the score. The central problems in this essay are that it does not consistently address the terms of the question, and it does not make a logically coherent argument.

Sample Response 2 (medium-scoring)

A leader in any political system has a duty to do just that—to lead. A politician in a democratic nation has a special duty—to do what is best for the nation, state or community that elected him or her. This is the nature of a representative democracy. A politician is elected with the assumption that he or she will put the needs of the public first, ahead of all other interests. Therefore, politicians must make decisions based on what is good for the whole, not just what will serve the interests of that politician, his or her family, or powerful people that have donated to the politician's campaign. We expect politicians to sacrifice themselves for the good of the nation, to some extent. Therefore, it is especially bad when politicians make decisions based on their own personal financial interests; this is why politicians are sometimes required to put their investments in to "blind trust" so that they are less likely to take their own financial interests into account when making policy. A case in which a politician failed to fulfill his duties was the case of Randy "Duke" Cunningham, a senator who took bribes from defense contractors to help them get lucrative contracts. This was especially bad because he may have put national security at risk in his own self interest, which is antithetical to the duty of a public representative.

However, politicians at a national level do not just represent their constituents' needs; they also play a role on the world stage. They also represent the nation in the world, and this sometimes requires that they place the needs of people in other countries ahead of their own constituent's immediate needs. Democratic nations have a duty to intervene and save the lives of citizens of other nations. This was the case in Eastern Europe, when the U.S. and other nations intervened to protect the Bosnians from the Serbs. It should also have been the case in the situation in Rwanda and today in the Sudan with Darfur. Other nations should sacrifice their own money and even their own soldiers to help people who cannot save themselves.

Therefore, we can say that in most cases, politicians should serve the needs of their constituents, since that is why they were elected in the first place. However, sometimes they have the duty to instead help people elsewhere in the world. This may mean spending money that could have been spent at home to make people's lives better. It may even mean sacrificing our own soldiers when they are sent into violent situations. Politicians at a high level play more than one role. They must represent their people, but they also represent powerful nations who have a role to play on the international stage.

Analysis of Sample Response 2

This essay has at its core a sophisticated idea—i.e., national-level politicians may have conflicting ethical duties, and sometimes a choice between two conflicting responsibilities must be made. The first paragraph does a good job of explaining why a politician has a duty to serve the needs of his or her constituency and gives a solid example of a politician who failed to do so. The relevance of this example is also clearly (if somewhat briefly) explained (national security was put in danger). There is a factual error in this section (Cunningham was a member of the House of Representatives, not the Senate), but this error isn't serious enough to affect the coherence or clarity of the argument, and therefore doesn't affect the score.

The second paragraph lists a series of examples but does not explain any one of them in detail. Thus, it isn't entirely clear at that point in the essay when, or under what circumstances, the needs of people elsewhere in the world should take precedence.

The final paragraph essentially repeats points that have already been made rather than developing criteria that would determine when constituents' needs or the needs of others should take precedence.

Overall, this essay is clearly written, well organized, and thoughtful, but it would need to further develop its core idea in order to receive a higher score.

Sample Response 3 (high-scoring)

"The happiness of society is the end of government." By this statement, John Adams meant that a primary function of government, and therefore of politicians, is to work for the betterment of society as a whole—that is, to serve the needs of the constituents. When we think of our "needs" or our "happiness" in this context, what comes first to mind is our standard of living and way of life. One of the primary functions of a politician, then, is to enact and carry out policies that improve our lives. Economic policy has, in most situations, the biggest impact on how we live, and it is well known that people most often vote for the leader who they believe will have the most positive impact on things like taxes, wages, investments, and employment. As President Clinton once said, "It's the economy, stupid." National level politicians have special knowledge and resources, and we expect them to use those resources to do what is best for us in a material sense, looking at both the short and the long term. This is especially true in situations of economic crisis. President Hoover was widely condemned during the Great Depression as a "do nothing" president, for not taking strong, proactive measures to pull the nation out of crisis. President Roosevelt, however, is and was widely praised for his "New Deal" policies that dealt both with short term needs of the populace and the long term needs of the nation. To deal with the immediate problem of unemployment, he enacted measures like the public works projects, in which work was created in order to give people some kind of wages to sustain them. Many of the trails in our public parks in fact were constructed by men employed by these projects. He also created programs like Social Security to deal with the problem of older people in poverty. At the time, a high percentage of impoverished people were elderly; now, a relatively small percentage of the poor are elderly. This program was forward looking in that it not only addressed an immediate problem, but sought to prevent the same problem from recurring in the future. While Roosevelt is known now for many things, his greatest legacy was in instituting an economic program that has at its core the goal of serving his constituents' need to be able to make a living through honest work.

However, politicians at a national level play other roles as well. One of those roles is to represent not only our material needs and desires, but our ideals. What people want is not always consistent with those ideals, and another role played by politicians is to see what is best in us and to make policy based on high ethics and morals, not just on our economic needs and desires. There are many cases in our history of widespread support for what we now view as unconscionable beliefs and policies such as slavery, racial discrimination, or the denial of the vote to women. Politicians have the special duty to make policy based not just on what people believe to be right, but what is in fact right and in accordance with basic constitutional principles. In the case of segregation, President Eisenhower is well known as a leader who fought discrimination and segregation in a variety of arenas. In 1957, he sent troops into Little Rock Arkansas to enforce the desegregation of Little Rock High School. This was done in opposition to the governor of the state, and at the cost of disruption of the peace (which had economic consequences as well), but it was the right thing to do. In contrast, Governor George Wallace did not represent high ideals in his "stand at the schoolhouse door" in Alabama when he vowed to protect and enforce segregation now and forever. In cases when constitutional rights and ideals are being violated, the primary concern of a politician must be to protect those rights, not to simply ensure material well-being.

Therefore, we can see that the job of a politician is a complicated one. We expect a leader to serve our material, economic interests by enacting policies that are good for the economy in both the short and the long term. No one is served by shortsighted or wrong headed economic policy; everyone suffers when the economy suffers. And in the normal course of things, we expect this to be the main focus of a national, or local, leader. In times of economic crisis, this duty becomes especially important, as a destabilized economy can destabilize the political system as well. However, we also expect a politician to have a larger view of the nation than we might have, with our own self-interests and immediate concerns. For the good and long-term stability of the nation, a politician must sometimes make it a priority to enact change, even radical disruptive change, when our core principles are being violated. When the two are at odds with each other, principle must come first. Many totalitarian countries have had healthy economies; after all, Mussolini made the trains run on time. That is, a totalitarian system can be efficient and well-functioning. However, our country is founded on the idea that basic principles like equality and freedom cannot be sacrificed for economic well-being.

Analysis of Sample Response 3

This writer begins by defining "needs" of constituents, which lends clarity and depth to the discussion that follows. This definition leads smoothly into a discussion of politicians' duty to enact policies that improve our lives, and the writer gives a detailed example of when and why this would apply.

In the second paragraph, the writer raises a sophisticated point of contrast. Here, the essay explains when politicians may have an even greater duty to represent and protect our fundamental ideals. Again, an appropriately detailed and thoughtful example is given, and the relevance of the example to the terms of the question is clearly explained.

In the final paragraph, the author provides criteria by which we can determine whether standard of living or other concerns should take precedence. The final paragraph does not simply repeat points that have been made earlier, but instead extends the discussion of core issues involved in the question (for example, how prioritizing economic stability can have a long-term detrimental effect on the nation).

Overall, the essay is well-written and well-organized and displays a firm command of language. It not only directly addresses all parts of the question but also shows that the author has thought about the deeper issues involved.

Essay Prompt 5

Consider this statement:

History always repeats itself.

Write a unified essay in which you perform the following tasks. Explain what you think the above statement means. Describe a specific situation in which history might not repeat itself. Discuss what you think determines when history repeats itself and when it does not.

Sample Response 1 (low-scoring)

It is difficult to say whether or not history really repeats itself. One argument would be that "there is nothing new under the sun." People are always people, and people do similar things. We always have had and will have wars, for example. Although the tecnology is changing and becomes more destructive, the basic nature of war is the same: people are trying to kill each other based with greed or ideology. Economic really doesn't change either. There are always upturns and downturns, and people have always trade one thing like money for another, or bartering goods. Therefore, there is really nothing new in human history, if you look beyond the superficial changes.

However, one argues the opposite. Although, for example, we have always had war, the improvements in arms in modern times makes war very different. When you can kill a lot of people at once, that is very different from arrows or spears or even rifles, as they did in wars in the past like the Revolutionary War. It is the same for economics. When you have trading on a large scale, even a global scale, things work differently than when people are trading good or service or money face to face.

Therefore, it depends on your perspectives whether or not you believe that history repeats itself. You could say that always it is the same kind of human activity, just on a larger or smaller scale. Or, you could argue that scale matters, and that warfare or economics large scale is really quite different from the same activities on a smaller scale.

Analysis of Sample Response 1

This essay illustrates a common mistake. Rather than discussing certain conditions under which the prompt statement would be true and other, different conditions under which the prompt statement would be false, this writer presents two opposing, mutually exclusive interpretations of the statement. The essay argues that in war and economics history always repeats itself and then goes on to argue that in economics and war, history does not repeat itself.

The final paragraph then essentially argues that "it depends on how you look at it," rather than giving criteria by which we can determine whether or not, in different cases, history does in fact repeat itself. There is a promising idea buried in the last paragraph: scale matters. This writer could have drawn a distinction based on whether or not the scale of a particular activity has changed significantly in modern times, but that point of contrast is not brought out clearly in the essay.

Finally, the essay contains so many errors in grammar, spelling, and syntax that it is difficult to follow and understand what the writer is trying to say. These mistakes, therefore, would negatively affect this student's score.

Sample Response 2 (medium-scoring)

A true historian does not simply write a list of events and dates and famous people. The deep study of history involves looking for patterns in those events, and teasing out commonalities between seemingly different times and places. In many ways, then, it can be said that history repeats itself. The same kinds of events occur over and over, just with different faces and places. This is why knowledge of history is so important to policy makers. It is said that those who do not learn from their mistakes are doomed to repeat them. If there were no repeating patterns in history, it wouldn't be important to understand our failures (and successes) of the past. For example, we can learn a lot about economic cycles from past events. There have always been economic depressions, or times of monetary inflation. By looking back to the inflationary period of the 1970's for example, we can tweak current economic policy to avoid a recurrence. This is why the Fed increases or decreases interest rates; to avoid having the same kind of damaging inflation today. Computer trading on the stock market now shuts down if the market falls fast and far enough, to avoid the kind of stock market crash that we experienced in the 1980's. Looking further back, we now have federal insurance of bank accounts to avoid the runs on banks that happened in the Great Depression. Therefore, we can say that in areas like the economy, history does in fact repeat itself, and we can learn from studying those patterns.

However, there are some rare exceptions to this statement. In modern society, there are some things that occur that have never happened before. For example, Y2K. At the turn of the century, it was feared that computer systems would crash world wide because programmers had not thought ahead to the need to deal with what would happen when the year changed to 2000. Programmers had always used the last two digits of the year, not realizing that "00" could mean 2000, or 1900. Because we didn't have computers in the year 1900, this problem had in fact never arisen before in history. Rather than looking to historical patterns, then, to solve the problem, we had to come up with entirely new solutions.

Therefore, we can say that in most areas of life, history repeats itself because human beings have not changed significantly since the beginnings of human society. Therefore, in the realm of things like economic behavior, there really is nothing new under the sun. However, in the world of computers, there is no real history, as the technology is entirely new, taken from a historical perspective.

Analysis of Sample Response 2

The essay begins well with an explanation of what it means to say that "history repeats itself." It then goes on to connect this idea to a larger issue: what we can learn from the study of history. The first paragraph also gives a relevant example of a certain type of historical pattern and how we have learned from past experiences and mistakes. Thus, the first paragraph does a good job of addressing the question on both a specific and a general, more abstract, level.

The second paragraph introduces a clearly contrasting example (Y2K). However, the relevance of the example is not sufficiently explained. The writer states that we could not learn from history in this case, but that claim is stated rather than fully argued.

The final paragraph suggests a good point of contrast by implying that human nature doesn't change, but technology does. As in the second paragraph, however, this point of contrast is not substantially developed.

Overall, this essay is clearly written and coherent, but the ideas become less and less well developed as the essay progresses.

Sample Response 3 (high-scoring)

When we speak of "human nature," we mean something that is an essence of humanity. There are certain qualities that are shared by all people in all times and in all cultures. It is difficult to find an aspect of human experience today that does not in some form correspond to the human experience even of thousands of years ago. Thus, we can say that in many ways, history truly repeats itself. People have always formed communities, small and large, defining themselves against "the other"; that is, people not like "us." Those communities, in the form of tribes or of nations, have always fought at some times and cooperated at others. Human history is essentially defined by this tension between warfare and cooperation. This is why we study the past—to understand and learn from it. We take exemplars from that past and compare them against ongoing events. This is why, for example, you hear the phrase "another Vietnam" when our military involvement in other nations is discussed. While many still debate the issue, the Vietnam War is seen as an instance when we became entangled in a conflict overseas without truly understanding the nature of the conflict or of the people involved. This is applied to the current war in Iraq, as people debate whether or not the Iraq war is in fact "another Vietnam." However, the issue of invasion and/or conquest of other nations is not a new issue. The Roman Empire was created as Rome invaded and took over a vast array of different peoples. Nations or other political entities have always tried to conquer and control others, for economic or ideological reasons. Therefore, we can say that in the realm of warfare and violence, history repeats itself.

However, there are some aspects of modern life that are in fact "new," in the sense that they have never occurred before. Human society is evolving, even though human beings have not (noticeably, at least, for the last few thousand years). Part of that evolution is globalization. Whereas travel between different countries used to take weeks or months, now we can be on the other side of the world in a few hours. Globalization is not limited to people, however. Pollutants travel too, and this has created a problem that is really something new in human history. With the high levels of industrialization occurring around the world, and the high levels of and great variety of pollutants being pumped into the atmosphere, we have the capacity to affect the global climate like never before. Thus, we have the problem of global warming not purely by natural cycles but due in part to human activity. This new problem has also created the need for a new kind of solution. While countries and peoples have always felt the need to cooperate in the past for economic and military goals, we now discover the need to cooperate on environmental issues. In the past, what one country did to its air, land or sea was largely limited in its effect to that country or at the most to its neighbors. Modern pollution, however, travels, and the problem of global warming cannot be addressed without some kind of global cooperation, like the Kyoto Protocols, on an environmental basis.

Therefore, what determines whether or not history repeats itself is whether or not the events in question arise from basic human nature, or from the new nature of human society and technology. War and treaties and alliances have basic commonalities, often being driven by fear or "the other," by greed, or by a feeling of fellowship with other nations or peoples. However, although people have always used technology, the nature of modern industrial technology causes it to have an effect on us and on our world that is unprecedented. People have always formed societies, but the size and industrial output of those societies is qualitatively different from the past in its global impact. These qualitative changes will require us to find new solutions to our problems that require not simply looking to our failures and success of the past, but innovation and creativity.

Analysis of Sample Response 3

This essay begins on an abstract level, discussing "human nature," and then ties that abstract concept directly to the terms of the question. It goes on to detail ways in which we can say history does repeat, still in the context of that initial discussion of the essence of human nature. Thus, the writer does an excellent job in this first paragraph of tying together a philosophical idea with a concrete example, all in service of addressing the first task set out by the question.

The essay then continues in this same mode. The writer returns to the idea of unchanging human nature in order to introduce a point of contrast: aspects of society that have in fact substantively changed. Again, the author illustrates his or her more general point with a relevant, concrete example.

Finally, the third paragraph introduces clear criteria that determine whether or not we can determine patterns in history. These criteria tie back to the author's discussion of human nature in the beginning of the essay.

There are some imperfections in this essay. There are instances of awkward wording and several misuses of a semicolon. The final paragraph could be further developed with an even clearer distinction drawn between aspects of modern society that are or are not fundamentally determined by the unchanging aspects of human nature. However, this writer does show an overall facility with language, and each paragraph further develops a core idea while always remaining directly responsive to the terms of the question. Finally, the writer expresses sophisticated abstract ideas and skillfully illustrates those ideas with concrete examples. The content of the essay is on a high enough level to receive a top score.

Essay Prompt 6

Consider this statement:

Great art must be enjoyable, not instructive.

Write a unified essay in which you perform the following tasks. Explain what you think the above statement means. Describe a specific situation in which great art may be instructive. Discuss what you think determines whether or not great art should be instructive.

Sample Response 1 (low-scoring)

By its very nature, art should be enjoyed. Art is meant to show us beauty in the world, not to teach us about that world. All of the great art in the world is enjoyable to view. This is why people go to art museums. They go to be entertained, in their leisure time, not to have an educational experience.

Now, people in an art class may be instructed about art. It is important, in order to fully enjoy a work of art, to understand what the artist was thinking when he or she painted or sculpted, and what kind of society or culture that artist was working in. For example, it heightens our enjoyment of the painting The Raft of the Medusa by Gericault to know the story being depicted of a shipwreck and the tragic consequences that ensued. It also increases our enjoyment to learn of the ways in which the painter used perspective and form to communicate the despair of the sailors on the raft.

Therefore, we can say that art itself should never seek to educate or instruct us. That is the role of a teacher, not of an artist. However, to truly enjoy art we must be instructed about it, to learn how and why the painter and culture produced the images that we see in our museums.

Analysis of Sample Response 1

The first paragraph begins with a reasonably thoughtful point about our enjoyment of art. However, this paragraph stays on a very general level and does not significantly engage with the terms or issue of the question. A more serious problem emerges in the second paragraph, however.

Here, the writer goes off on a tangent. The question asks when great art may be itself instructive, not when we may be instructed about great art. Although the writer's knowledge of Gericault's painting is impressive, examples only add to the value of an essay if they directly respond to the question at hand.

The final paragraph denies the validity of half of the question by stating that great art should never be instructive. Although the essay as a whole is clear and well written (although overly brief and superficial), an off-topic response cannot get a high or even an average score.

Sample Response 2 (medium-scoring)

Art has many functions, and one of those functions is to provide enjoyment to the viewer or listener. Art that has been labeled "great" always has this quality. Enjoyment may mean pure entertainment; we enjoy a work of art that is pleasing to the eye. Or, our enjoyment may come from a deeper place; enjoyable art may challenge us by making us view reality in a different way. One example of great art is the work of the Impressionists like Monet. Monet's Waterlilies is a beautiful depiction of a moment of peace and solitude in nature. People spend hours gazing at it in the museum. The painting inspires no deep thought and presents no great challenges to our eye. We enjoy it just as we enjoy looking at flowers in nature, for its own sake.

However, enjoyable art works can also instruct us. Monet painted in a "pointillist" style. This means that he broke down the hard surface of reality into thousands of points of light and color. Thus his paintings challenge us to look at reality and our own perceptions in a different way. His series of paintings of the Rouen cathedral show us how the same object looks quite different at different times of day, thus challenging us to see everything around us in a different light.

Therefore great art really always does both. It provides enjoyment, and instructs or educates us to see and perceive reality in a different way.

Analysis of Sample Response 2

The writer begins by discussing a variety of ways in which great art may be enjoyable and provides an example that illustrates this point.

In the second paragraph, the writer raises a relevant contrasting point; art may also instruct us to see reality in a new light. The force of this argument is undermined, however, by the fact that the writer uses the same example to illustrate a contrasting idea. To make this work, the writer would need to show a clearer distinction between different aspects of Monet's work. There is also a factual inaccuracy in the example. Monet did not paint in a "pointillist" style (although others around the same time did so). However, the inaccuracy is not enough to significantly undermine the force of the writer's argument. The larger problem is the lack of a clear contrast between the first and second examples. However, the writer's overall argument in this section is serious and thoughtful.

The final paragraph, while making a valid and logically consistent point, does not provide clear criteria by which we can determine whether or not great art will entertain or instruct. To get a high score, the essay would need to more directly address the third task in the question, based on a clear contrast.

Sample Response 3 (high-scoring)

Artists serve a special function in our lives. They show us the objects and images that surround us, but through the lens of the artist's own eye. In many cases, art simply presents us with a beautiful picture, or a pleasing sound. Great art pleases the senses, and often does no more than that. Some great painters and sculptors achieve greatness simply because they are able to capture a line or a color or a scene in such a way that entrances us. Unlike the fleeting nature of these things in life, we can stare at a painting or a sculpture for hours. Great artists often capture a particular moment in time. For example, the photographer Ansel Adams shows us a mountain peak in Yosemite captured at one particular angle, at one special time of day. We could go there ourselves and stare at that same peak for hours, and never see the beauty that Adams captures with his camera. Therefore, great art may reflect reality with the goal of heightening it, or of focusing our eye on one special aspect of it. While these artists show us something we may not have been able to see or appreciate without the intervention of the artistic eye, they often do so in the service of our enjoyment, not in order to teach us or instruct us about the world around us.

However, sometimes artists feel a special calling to do more than provide enjoyment, and instead to instruct or educate us about some aspect of society or politics. This often happens in times of crisis or conflict, when artists feel compelled to show us a different reality better than our own, or at least to show us the true nature of human experience. Picasso, in his painting Guernica, showed the horror and carnage of the Spanish Civil War. In the images he used, he criticized the dictator Franco and the violence he carried out against his own people. While many find the disjointed images and tortured shapes enjoyable to look at (because of the skill of the artist, not because the scene is in any way pleasant), Picasso's fundamental goal was to show us both the horror of war in general and the tragedy of the Spanish Civil War in particular. Similarly, the Dadaists in Europe after WWI, by presenting absurdist stage plays, attempted to show the absurdity of a world that could create such a war. While the audience may have enjoyed the silliness of these ridiculous scenes, the goal of the artists was not at heart to entertain or divert the audience, but to open their eyes to the true ridiculousness of a world that could find some meaning and purpose in mass slaughter. The Dada movement evolved into surrealism, which had a similar pedagogical goal. Surrealist painters like Max Ernst and Hans Arp, by painting strange and twisted visions of reality, attempted to teach the viewer that what we think of as real is only an illusion, and that a deeper and truer "reality" lies behind and beyond our normal perceptions of the world. Interestingly, many of the surrealists at least temporarily joined the Communist Party. These artists believed that art and politics were inextricably intertwined, and that art could be a tool in the service of social and political transformation.

Great art is always enjoyable in some way. Sometimes our enjoyment comes from the beauty of the image. At other times we enjoy art not because what it portrays is inherently beautiful, but because we get pleasure from the skill of the artist. However, at times of social upheaval, art is often created with the intent to instruct us, by showing us the true nature of our surroundings and at times a path to what the artist sees as a better reality. Artists are often engaged with political and social issues, and when change is seen as necessary in these arenas, art is often used as a tool in the service of some kind of transformation that goes beyond aesthetics. It is important to recognize that enjoyment and instruction are not mutually exclusive. We can find great beauty, for example, in the murals of Diego Rivera, while also understanding his socialist, political message. Rivera painted in the 1930's, when industrialization was radically transforming society and when many artists were caught up in communist or socialist movements that promised, they believed, to make a better, more egalitarian world. While art with a purpose of instructing the people in the service of social change can be created at any time, it is most likely to appear in times like the 30's, when reality appears to be in the process of reconstitution, and artists feel as if they can play a role in that process.

Analysis of Sample Response 3

The writer begins with some thoughtful points about the function of art and then directly connects those issues to the terms of the first part of the question. A specific example is given, and the example clarifies and extends the writer's more general claims.

The second paragraph begins by introducing a point of contrast, a contrast that logically leads us into the writer's response to the third part of the question in the final paragraph. Again, specific examples are given and explained in a way that adds to the force of the writer's analysis.

Finally, in the third paragraph, the author provides clear criteria (times of crisis or upheaval) that determine whether great art should be merely enjoyable or instructive. These criteria are consistent with the discussion in the first two paragraphs but do not simply repeat points that have already been made.

Overall, each paragraph builds on the previous text, and the writer presents a thoughtful and complex response to the question on both a very specific and an abstract level.

Part V:
Biological Sciences
on the MCAT

Chapter 16
Overview of
Biological Sciences

INTRODUCTION

If you're reading this text carefully from cover to cover, you may be wondering "Hey, why am I getting an 'Introduction' for this chapter and not the other ones?" That's an excellent question! If you didn't ask it, don't feel badly. We just want to be clear for those who've read everything up to this point. Those that have will notice that many of the points made in this chapter are similar to or the same as ones made in Chapter 2, Overview of Physical Sciences. This repetition is present for several reasons: 1) It reinforces important strategies that bear repeating; 2) some strategies for Biological Sciences, although very similar to some for Physical Sciences, have subtle but important differences; 3) those of you who are using this book to hone your skills in one particular area of the test may not have read the Physical Sciences material; and 4) some people may be skipping around, not following the chapters in the order presented. Whatever the case, know that there is some repetition here and be comfortable with it. Trust us—you'll be a lot more uncomfortable during the actual MCAT!

BIOLOGICAL SCIENCES STRUCTURE AND SCORING

The Biological Sciences section is the last section you take before completing the ordeal known as the MCAT. It consists of 52 multiple choice questions covering the major subjects of Biology and Organic Chemistry. The AAMC says that the section includes 7–9 passages and about 10 freestanding questions. Recent test administrations at press time included 7 passages and 13 freestanding questions. Of these, approximately 75–80% are Biology and the remainder are Organic Chemistry. You will have 70 minutes to complete this section, providing approximately 80 seconds to answer each question. This time allotment includes the time required to read the passage for those questions that are passage-based.

The Biological Sciences section is scored on a scale of 1–15, similar to that of the Physical Sciences and Verbal sections. As with those sections, there is no guessing penalty, so you should answer every question. There may be experimental questions in the section that will not count toward your score; however, you should treat every question as if it counts. Because this section is last on the MCAT, test takers generally feel some fatigue at this point; taking full-length practice tests and building up stamina for the exam is especially important for success on the Biological Sciences section.

Atlthough the AAMC boldly states that the MCAT does "not test your ability to memorize scientific facts," the exam asks fact-based questions that are not related to a specific passage. The list of general themes of material that may be covered on the MCAT is provided on the next page. The Biological Sciences material on the MCAT is typically covered in a better than average Introductory Biology course and in an Organic Chemistry course, both at the college level; however, even if you have only rudimentary Biology and Organic Chemistry knowledge, you can succeed on this section of the exam.

BIOLOGICAL SCIENCES IN A CBT

Your ability to answer questions in the Biology portion of this section depends heavily on how well you can harvest information from the passages, so the challenges you face on the Verbal portion of the exam and the tools you use to overcome them will also be relevant to this section. Using the CBT tools such as the Highlighting feature to emphasize important information in the passages is helpful for time efficiency because it allows you to get back to the information quickly if a question requires. The Organic Chemistry passage-based questions are generally less often based in reading comprehension and usually require you to analyze a given reaction or set of data. Remember to use the CBT strikeout function for POE. Ruling out answer choices will aid in increasing the likelihood that you answer questions correctly. Also available for use in this section is a pop-up window with the periodic table that will probably be more useful for the Organic Chemistry questions than for the Biology questions. The scratch paper given at the testing center can also be useful if structures need to be re-drawn and you need to interact with them, such as when you assign absolute configuration to a chiral center.

BIOLOGY AND ORGANIC CHEMISTRY THEMES

The major themes of Biology that are covered on the MCAT include the following:

- Cellular Biology
- Microbiology
- Molecular Biology
- Physiology
- Comparison of Hypotheses
- Experimental Data Analysis
- Prokaryotes vs. Eukaryotes

Although the information in the Biology questions can span a number of college courses, it is really focused on basic principles of Biology and does not require one to have taken advanced Biology courses to perform well on this section.

Thankfully, there are fewer Organic Chemistry topics than Biology topics covered on the MCAT. They can be broadly classified into five categories:

- Biologically-Relevant Macromolecules
- Laboratory Techniques
- Molecular Structure
- Predicting the Products of Reactions
- Stability of Intermediates and/or Products

Popular Test Topics
Although no premed student is expected to come to the MCAT with an understanding of diseases and conditions that will be studied while in med school, MCAT passages frequently concern medical syndromes and diseases.

Source: *Cracking the MCAT*, 2006

As with the Biology questions, a fundamental understanding of basic Organic Chemistry principles is the key to increasing the number of questions one gets correct on the MCAT. For a complete list of Biological Science topics covered on the exam, visit **www.aamc.org** and block out a little time—the list is 17 pages long!

New Information

The MCAT writers like to introduce new information that can initially seem daunting to a test taker. It is important to remember that within this information, you will find just the basic principles of Biology and Organic Chemistry. In the Biology section, this is often in the form of new experimental data or a schematic representation of a hypothesized mechanism, while in Organic Chemistry, this is often in the form of a large molecule or familiar reaction type with complex structures. It is important to not get overwhelmed by the new terms or complex structures and to instead identify the familiar themes that are underlying the passage. For the Biology passages, it is sometimes helpful to draw a flowchart on your scratch paper to simplify how things are related to each other. For the Organic Chemistry section, it is helpful to focus on the functional groups involved in the reactions and not the structure as a whole.

Experiment-Based Questions

Ability to interpret experimental data and read tables and graphs is imperative for the Biological Sciences section. Questions can require you to read data off a graph or table, or to make a conclusion from the data given. It is always important to identify what the control or comparator is in the data (if pertinent) and to pay attention to what the axes or units are in a graph. In this section, sometimes minor calculations need to be performed with data given, so it is important to know what units are being used to express the data (e.g., exponential or linear; mm or cm). It is also important to be able to assess what variables are actually being tested in the experiment. When interpreting the data, look for what variable is being altered in each step or trial and how that is affecting the outcome of the experiment.

Hypothesis-Based Questions

You will find that most MCATs have at least one hypothesis-based passage. This type of passage gets its apt name for the 2–4 hypotheses that are being compared and contrasted with one another. It is important to understand what the particular hypothesis is suggesting about a particular mechanism and to identify the important players resulting in cause and effect of the process—e.g., if it is proposed that A → B, make sure that relationship has been identified and is clear. Common questions involve identifying answer choices that support or refute particular hypotheses, so it is important to understand what the suggested relationships are in order to recognize information that will support or negate a hypothesis. It is also important to remember that lack of support for a hypothesis does not necessarily refute it. If the question is asking to refute a hypothesis, the correct answer will have information directly contradicting the proposed mechanism in the hypothesis. Understanding the type of answer choice you are looking for in the repeating theme questions on the MCAT can also make it more likely you get those questions correct.

Biological Sciences Content

The content of the Biological Sciences section is heavily skewed towards Biology. It is possible for Biology and Organic Chemistry to overlap in passages, but in most cases, the division is clear and a passage can easily be identified as Biology or Organic Chemistry. Some topics you may encounter, such as Biologically Relevant Macromolecules, Enzyme Kinetics, or Lab Techniques (gel electrophoresis, for example), draw from the realms of both Biology and Organic Chemistry. For Biology, the questions are often presented in the context of the mammalian system, but other systems that behave similarly have been addressed on the MCAT.

Something to be aware of is that there is often extraneous information given in the Biological Sciences passages, so you must balance your time carefully when reading over the passage and not get hung up on details that may not matter for answering the questions. The extra information is sometimes helpful to jog your memory about something if you have forgotten it, but again, do not spend too much time focusing on something in the passage since it may not be necessary for the questions. Also, the less you need to rely on the passages to remind yourself of basic information, the more time you can devote to focusing on the other information and answering the questions.

The questions that accompany Biology-based passages have a large reading comprehension component to them, so an ability to apply the information given in the passage to the questions is almost as important as understanding the breadth of Biology required for the MCAT. If you have learned all of the facts but cannot apply them or do not have a strong grasp of logical reasoning skills, your final score will suffer. Thus, in many ways, studying for the Verbal section will also help improve your score on the Biology section. The Organic Chemistry passage questions are less dependent on reading comprehension and generally involve answering questions about a given reaction or data.

BIOLOGICAL SCIENCES TEST-TAKING SKILLS

Preparing for the MCAT should include a combination of improving content knowledge and improving test-taking techniques. For example, if completing timed exams is difficult for you, then working on this issue should be built into your study regime. Going too slow or too fast through the test can be detrimental. Timing yourself on passages and/or sections and taking practice exams is one way to tackle this issue. There are a number of techniques to improve timing, efficiency, and accuracy on the MCAT. It is important during your preparation process that you figure out what works best for you. Taking full-length practice MCATs under conditions as similar as possible to the actual MCAT will be beneficial in monitoring your progress.

Attack the Section in Your Order

As we said in the Overview of Physical Sciences, there are a number of possible benefits to adjusting the order in which you attack the questions:

1) If you have problems finishing the section on time, it is better to run out of time for the subject matter you know the least. For example, if you are better in Biology, then it is better to do all the Biology-based questions first and the Organic Chemistry-based questions on a second pass, so that if you run out of time, it is on the subject of which you are less sure. You may even want to prioritize the passages within each discipline so that you do the passages on subjects with which you are most comfortable first, in either Biology or Organic Chemistry. You can take this a step further and first address the easiest questions, then the more difficult ones within a freestanding set or the questions for a particular passage.

2) Completing the questions on material with which you are most comfortable first can help to build confidence. The CBT makes it easy to switch between passages, and it is possible to mark questions for review so that you can go back to the ones you left blank or marked for review very easily. A good way to assess what works best for you is to take a practice test answering the questions in the order they are presented and to take another practice test attacking the passages in a particular order with which you feel most comfortable.

Whether you are skipping around in the passages or not, always be mindful of the time. You do not want to leave any questions blank because there is no guessing penalty. Also, if time is getting short and you still have freestanding questions left, you may want to bypass a passage to complete the freestanding questions since single questions tend to take less time. Also, Organic Chemistry passage-based questions are often faster to answer than Biology passage-based questions because they generally require less reading comprehension. The bottom line is—if you are running out of time, pick the questions that are easiest and take the least time to complete.

Attack the Questions in Your Order

Within a group of questions for a passage or series of freestanding questions, there may be questions that appear easier to you than others. Doing the ones with which you are most comfortable first can help you for some of the same reasons as taking the passages in a particular order. Also, doing the passage questions with which you are most comfortable first helps acquaint you with the passage more thoroughly before you take on the harder questions. If you can complete some of the questions for a passage quickly, you will feel more comfortable spending a little more time on the harder questions or the ones that require more interaction with the passage. Even if you know you can afford a little more time on a question, do not ever get hung up too long. As the clock runs down, you may panic and perform poorly on later questions that you would usually answer correctly. If you are not sure about an answer, the best thing to do is eliminate as many answers choices as possible, pick an answer from the remaining choices, and Mark the question for review so you can come back to it if there is time.

Process of Elimination (POE)

With a multiple-choice test, this technique can help you save time, choose the correct answer more accurately, and improve your chances when guessing. It is generally easier to eliminate wrong answers than to be immediately sure of picking the right answer. The MCAT also likes to word things in ways that make it easy to choose an incorrect answer despite knowing the concept or fact required for the question.

When scanning answer choices, it is important to immediately rule out answers that are factually wrong in part or in sum. If you are not sure about an answer, be sure to hold onto the answer during the first pass. If you are confident an answer is wrong, eliminate it by using the strikeout feature on the CBT. Unless you are running out of time, try to scan all the answer choices, even if you are confident you have already identified the correct answer choice. This allows you to double-check yourself by making sure the other choices are indeed wrong and can help prevent silly mistakes. If you have eliminated three wrong answer choices, but you're still not sure if the last remaining answer choice is right, choose it anyway. There are a number of ways to get to a correct answer, and you do not always have to be sure it is correct if you are fairly confident the *others* are wrong. This is one of the advantages of multiple-choice tests. Specific techniques for Biology and Organic Chemistry questions are addressed further in the Mastering Biology and Mastering Organic Chemistry chapters.

Foreign Medical Schools
Make sure you research the prospective school's USMLE pass rate and residency placement rate. Although foreign medical schools are much easier to get into, they will put you in just as much debt as U.S. schools, without the same assurance of a career after graduation that will enable you to pay off the debt.

Source: *Best 168 Medical Schools*, 2008

Reading Comprehension

As mentioned previously, improving your reading comprehension skills should improve your performance on the Biological Sciences section, because so many questions in this section are Biology passage-based questions. When dealing with questions based on the passage, don't get sidetracked by information you may have learned in one of your advanced Biology courses and don't start counter-reasoning what is in the passage. Most of the time, the Biology passage-based questions will require you to use the information *in the passage* to answer the question. For this reason, it is important to go back to the passage and read what was mentioned about the subject matter in a particular question before answering it. In many cases, you will be able to rule out/in answer choices based on what was said in the passage. Also, new information may be introduced that you must now refer back to the passage to obtain.

The questions that accompany an Organic Chemistry passage tend to rely less on the passage, but sometimes there is information in the text that is necessary or useful in answering a question. Again, if a question warrants it, go back to the passage and see what was mentioned about the question's subject matter.

Use the Highlighting function as you skim through the passage to flag significant terms and information you will want to refer back to while answering the questions. While relying on the passage is important, you do not want to waste too much time reading through it repeatedly. It is best to get a general map in your mind of what information is present where, and then go back and focus on it more specifically when the questions require it. In most cases, you are given a lot of details that you will never remember, so do not even try to memorize them. What is most important during your initial scan is that you recognize the basic concepts being addressed in the passage, not that you take note of all the specific details discussed.

Chapter 17
Mastering Biological Sciences: Organic Chemistry

ORGANIC CHEMISTRY CONTENT

The first thing to remember is that Organic Chemistry occupies only 20–25% of the Biological Sciences section. There are usually 1 or 2 Organic Chemistry passages on the computerized exam. There may be anywhere from 4–7 questions per passage, but typically no more than 2 passages will concern Organic Chemistry. Of all the freestanding questions, typically only 3–5 cover Organic Chemistry.

Nearly all of Organic Chemistry is related to the behavior of electrons. If you understand how electrons behave, you will have a better comprehension of the chemical reactions and reaction mechanisms. This way, no matter what series of reactions the MCAT throws at you (and they may well show you the synthesis of a molecule that you have never seen before), you won't get tripped up because you will understand how the electrons should behave.

As a result, one of the primary strategies you will utilize in this section is *focusing on the electrons*. First off, electrons are negatively-charged; consequently, they like positively-charged things, like nuclei or carbocations. Compounds are most stable when the electrons reside on the more electronegative atom. So, a basic knowledge of General Chemistry is necessary to fully understand electron behavior.

Another strategy you will employ is *counting*. It sounds odd, but it can prove quite beneficial. Take the example on the next page:

Which of the following represents an adequate resonance structure for the sulfite ion, SO_3^{2-}?

A.

B.

C.

D.

First off, we know that the overall molecule needs to have a 2⁻ charge. Counting up the overall charge on each molecule represented in the answers indicates that answer choice A is incorrect since it is neutral with an overall charge of 0. Remember that the negative charge resides on the more electronegative atom. This allows us to eliminate answer choice B, since oxygen is more electronegative than sulfur, and thus, the negative charge should be borne by the oxygen. The positively charged oxygen also does not have an octet of electrons—another reason to eliminate this answer. Finally, answer choice D is incorrect because there is much more separation of charge in the molecule. Try to minimize formal charge whenever possible. C is the best answer—sulfur can have an expanded octet because it has empty *d* orbitals that can hold the extra electrons.

ORGANIC CHEMISTRY TOPICS

Thankfully, there are fewer Organic Chemistry topics than Biology topics covered on the MCAT. They can be broadly classified into five categories:

> 1) Molecular structure
> 2) Predicting the products of reactions
> 3) Stability of intermediates and/or products
> 4) Laboratory techniques
> 5) Biologically-relevant macromolecules

General Concepts

You will be asked to classify compounds according to their functional groups and then name them. You will be expected to know the products of certain reactions, the missing reagents, and even the starting compounds to form those products.

Molecular Structure

This topic is very broad and includes IUPAC nomenclature and the ability to recognize functional groups, Lewis dot structures and formal charge, hybridization and shape of molecules as predicted by VSEPR (valence shell electron pair repulsion) theory, and isomerism and stereochemistry of molecules. The MCAT may ask a relatively straightforward question about one of these topics, or it may ask you to combine your knowledge of structure with another of the ideas listed below. The purpose here is to have you predict the product of a reaction based on the functional groups that are present, predict the stereochemical outcome of a reaction, or use the different physical properties of two or more molecules to experimentally distinguish between them.

Reaction Types and Predicting Products

Long Hours Ahead

The average doctor works 60 hours per week, and it's not unusal for some doctors to work as many as 80 hours in a week. Residents may work up to 100 hours per week.

Source: *Best 168 Medical Schools*, 2008

Often on the MCAT, you will only need to recognize, in very broad terms, what type of reaction has taken place in a passage. While you may be given a complicated mechanism or synthetic sequence, you will likely only have to pay attention to one small part of it. These questions can often be answered by noting the change in the number of sigma bonds versus pi bonds from reactants to products. Typically, you are asked to identify one of five classes of reactions (or some minor variation of them): substitutions, additions, eliminations, oxidations, or reductions. Alternatively, if given two reactants instead of a reactant and a product, you may need to recall how the functional groups that are present in the starting materials are likely to react with each other. A solid grounding in the next topic, stability, will go a long way toward making those predictions easier.

Stability of Intermediates and Products

Many times, the MCAT focuses not on predicting the product of a reaction but on why a reaction proceeds via a specific mechanism, or why one intermediate is more likely to be formed than another. There are several ways a molecule may become more or less stable; because stability is closely tied to reactivity, understanding how a molecule may be stabilized or destabilized will go a long way toward predicting the outcome of a reaction. Induction and resonance tend to be the main methods of maintaining stability in an intermediate. Major products of reactions are often those that incorporate the least steric strain or ring strain into the structure of the molecule.

Laboratory Techniques

Just when you thought your days of organic laboratory experiments were over, the MCAT decided that you should know some of these procedures that can be used to separate and/or identify compounds. *Extraction* can be used to separate a mixture of compounds based on their relative solubilities in two immiscible solvents while taking advantage of the acid/base properties of functional groups on the molecules. *Chromatography* is used to separate compounds based on their relative polarities and may show up as thin-layer, column, or gas chromatography. *Distillation* and *recrystallization* are also techniques to be familiar with. Identification techniques that are often seen on the MCAT include infrared (IR) spectroscopy and both ^{1}H and ^{13}C NMR spectroscopy.

Biologically-Relevant Macromolecules

Carbohydrates, amino acids, proteins, and lipids are the highest yielding macromolecules on the MCAT and are usually used to provide context for many passages. Although they may seem to be complex compounds with more complex reactions, most organic chemistry questions about these macromolecules test the straightforward, fundamental concepts already described above—*structure, stability,* and *separation.*

PASSAGE-BASED STRATEGIES

The MCAT presents the Organic Chemistry passages in a variety of ways. You may see a synthesis passage, which contains a series of several reactions. Another passage option is a separation of a solution containing three different compounds. The MCAT also likes to give application-based passages, i.e., those passages that require you to apply Organic Chemistry to Biology, as in pharmacology of therapeutic agents.

Reaction Scheme Passage

There are several types of questions that can be asked about a synthesis passage. You may be asked about some chemical property of the product based on its structure. The MCAT can ask you to identify the number of chiral carbons in the product formed from the series of reactions or any intermediate along the way. This requires you to be able to recognize the carbons that contain bonds to four distinctly different substituents.

You may be asked to predict the changes in the infrared spectra between the starting compound and the product, indicating how you would be able to determine if the reaction went to completion. You will therefore need to remember some of the more common infrared spectroscopy bands. For example, if the mechanism illustrates an aldehyde being reduced to an alcohol, you would want to look for the appearance of an –OH band, typically located at the 3200–3600 cm^{-1} location. You could also potentially be asked to predict the result of the synthesized product undergoing a different type of reaction.

You may also encounter questions that ask you to predict the product if a new reagent were subjected to the reaction conditions in the passage. This type of question requires you to be able to follow the series of reactions in the pathway to determine what new product would be formed. The main strategy used here is to find the exact changes that occurred to the first compound and then apply them to the new reactant. If, as in the previous example, the reaction demonstrates a conversion of an aldehyde to an alcohol, the MCAT might ask you to predict the product if you started with benzaldehyde. You would need to follow the series of reactions as if you were using benzaldehyde, and you would likely end up with benzyl alcohol.

Separation Passage

This type of passage tends to be quite common since it allows the MCAT to test several different Organic Chemistry principles all in one fell swoop. The passage will describe a student wanting to separate a mixture of several different compounds which tend to have acidic and/or basic functional groups of various strengths. These molecules are often mixed with a non-acidic, non-basic compound. The passage will then provide a separation mechanism as shown on the next page:

Patient Care

Ninety percent of doctors spend their time seeing patients. The average doctor sees 20–25 patients every day.

Source: *Best 168 Medical Schools*, 2008

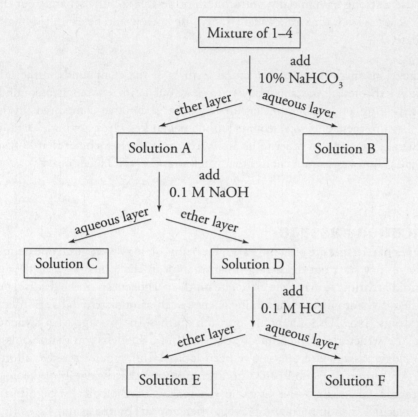

Extraction Scheme to Separate Compounds 1–4

The key to this passage is following each separation in a step-by-step fashion. You need to recall that relatively strong organic acids, such as carboxylic acids, can be extracted into an aqueous layer using a weak base, such as sodium bicarbonate. A strong base, such as sodium hydroxide, would be able to extract both carboxylic acids as well as weaker acids such as phenols. Weak bases, like amines, can be extracted by strong acids, such as hydrochloric acid. Any compound that is non-acidic and non-basic will not be extracted, and therefore it will remain in the organic layer.

In the example provided [phenol (1), carboxylic acid (2), and amine (4)], you need to realize that the first step of the extraction process is the addition of a weak base in order to remove the stronger acid (2). If you were to start off with a strong base, you would remove both acids (1 & 2). You would not have a complete separation. The next step is to use a strong base to remove the weaker acid (1) and then finally a strong acid to remove the weak base (4) from the non-acidic, non-basic compound (3).

There are several questions related to this passage that could appear on the MCAT. One type is predicting what compound would be present in the aqueous layer of the first step of the separation. Again, you will need to follow the scheme, step-by-step, to see what is being used to extract the compound into the aqueous layer. If a weak base is being used, you will extract the stronger acid, or compound 2. Another type of question could ask you to explain why the order of extraction is important. This is based on the principle, previously mentioned, that if you were to use a strong base initially, you would not be able to fully separate out the stronger acid (2) from the weaker acid (1), because both would be extracted by the strong base.

Other questions might focus on structural features of the compounds in the mixture, ask in a theoretical way about how to separate out a different set of compounds in a new mixture, or ask about major differences between other compounds in the mixture. Again, these questions require a fundamental knowledge of both Organic and General Chemistry in order to be answered correctly. Remember that POE is your friend. Eliminate answer choices that you know CANNOT be correct.

Application Passage

These types of passages are often mistaken for being Biology passages. For example, the passage may start out discussing inflammation in the joints of patients with rheumatoid arthritis. It may even elaborate on the pathogenesis of the disease, but it will then dive into disease-modifying agents, such as non-steroidal anti-inflammatory drugs (NSAIDs), auranofin, or azathioprine. The passage then switches focus to the structures of these medications. All of a sudden, you realize this is not a Biology passage after all; you've been fooled! This type of passage affords the MCAT writers the opportunity to ask questions that bridge both Biology and Organic Chemistry. The Organic Chemistry of Biologically Significant Macromolecules is an important topic that often appears on the exam.

The approach to follow for this type of passage includes reading the questions carefully. If the question asks you for the number of chiral carbons found in aza-thioprine, then you go directly to the structure and count them. If the question asks you what chemical property of auranofin makes it a good candidate for oral administration, you find the structure and realize that it remains unionized in the gastrointestinal tract and can therefore be absorbed readily. All you are doing is applying your Biology knowledge to Organic Chemistry.

Another question type that tends to appear in these passages is a "new info" question. In this question, the MCAT provides you with some new information and then asks you to apply information from the passage to the new situation. Continuing the example of the passage described above, the MCAT may provide you with the information that a new compound has been discovered to modify rheumatoid arthritis, but it needs to be administered intravenously. The structure of the drug is provided, and then you are asked to decide why it needs to be administered intravenously. Look carefully at the structure. What stands out? Well, if it contains an amine in the compound, then you know it is a weak base. A weak base, when ingested, gets ionized in the stomach, where the pH is 1.5 from the hydrochloric acid present. This prevents the drug from being absorbed into the bloodstream.

Ethical Issues
Some of your ethical dilemmas as a doctor in the twenty-first century are likely to involve the following:

- Saving time vs. money
- End-of-life care
- Rule of doctor-patient confidentiality

Source: *Best 168 Medical Schools*, 2008

FREESTANDING QUESTION STRATEGIES

There are usually 3–5 freestanding questions for Organic Chemistry throughout the entire Biological Sciences section. Remember, these are straightforward questions that provide you with a little information, and then they expect you to be able to utilize your profound knowledge of Organic Chemistry to answer the questions easily. Because these questions are not associated with a passage, you are required to know what is going on.

These questions can be simple in the sense that they are very direct, like "Predict the major product of the following reaction." This requires you to recall the major products that are formed given the reagents used. A Grignard reagent would add an alkyl group to an existing compound. Adding H_2 over palladium (Pd) allows you to reduce a double bond. Nitric acid added to aniline will result in p-aminonitrobenzene (due to steric hindrance of the amino group, the nitro group will add para more than ortho).

Other questions could be in a multi-step format. This forces you to answer the first part, perhaps predicting the product of a reaction, and then answer a separate question regarding that compound. So if you can't predict the product in the first question, you won't be able to answer the question of what the ^1H–NMR would look like for the second question. Even if you can't predict the product, though, you *may* be able to make an educated guess at the right answer. Look at your answers and determine to what structures they refer. A triplet that integrates for three hydrogens indicates a CH_3 group with two neighbors (likely CH_2). One hydrogen split into a septet indicates a CH sandwiched between two methyl groups, otherwise known as an isopropyl group. Once you figure out these features, do any of them seem possible as a product of the reaction? If any are <u>impossible</u>, then you eliminate them. If possible, you keep them. Then, you make an educated guess from the remaining answer choices.

FREESTANDING EXAMPLES

Now, let's go through some examples to see how we can apply what we know to answer some freestanding questions.

1. Which of the following represents the intermediate of the reaction of benzene with CH_3Cl and $AlCl_3$?

    A. $H_3C\cdot$

    B. $H_3C:^{\ominus}$

    C. $H_3C^{\oplus}$

    D.

The first thing to do for this question is look at the answer choices. Answer A is a radical. Answer B is a carbanion. Answer C is a carbocation. Answer D represents a dehydrogenated benzene. So we need to remember that a radical will form only in the presence of ultraviolet light or extreme energy conditions. This is rather unlikely given the reaction in the question; therefore, eliminate A. A carbanion is unlikely to form in this case since Cl is more electronegative than C. Therefore, when the bond between these atoms breaks, Cl is much more likely to take both electrons with it. B is not the best answer. $AlCl_3$ is a Lewis acid, since Al has only three bonds to Cl and therefore requires a lone pair of electrons to make a complete octet. The Cl from CH_3Cl will complex with the Lewis acid, leaving a fairly large, partial, positive charge on the carbon, resulting in CH_3^+ and Cl^- for all intents and purposes. This carbocation is now susceptible to attack by a double bond that is rich in electrons, so C looks really good. The benzene ring very rarely will lose a hydrogen, resulting in a carbocation on an sp^2 hybridized carbon in a sea of delocalized electrons. Therefore, answer D is eliminated, leaving C as the correct answer.

2. Which of the following sets of reagents are needed to make the following reaction occur?

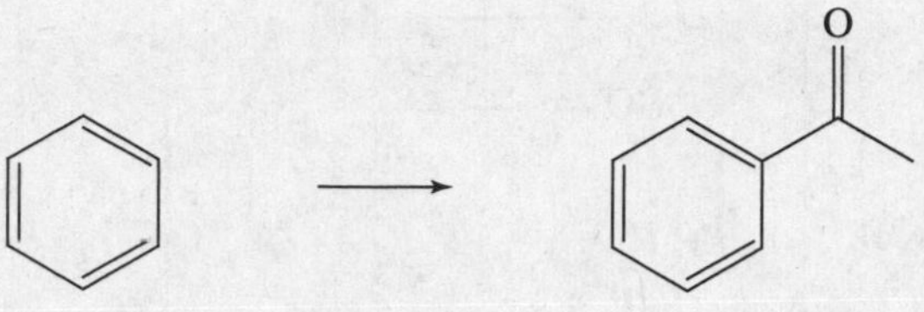

A. CH_3CH_2Cl with $AlCl_3$

B.

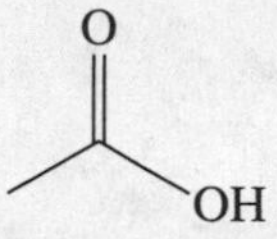

OH with $NaOH_3$

C.

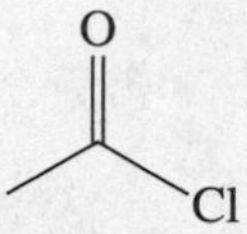

Cl with $AlCl_3$

D.

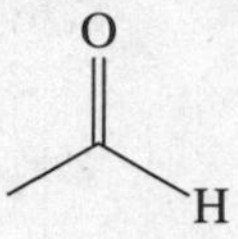

H with $AlCl_3$

The first thing we need to do to answer this question is figure out exactly what transpired. We started with benzene and we ended up with methylphenylketone. We should look for an answer that has at least a carbonyl as part of the reagent. This eliminates A. The next answer to be eliminated should be B. Why? Well, it's a relatively strong acid compound (carboxylic acid) in the presence of a strong base (NaOH). Nothing will happen to benzene because an acid-base reaction will occur between the reagents. Now we are left with an acid chloride and an aldehyde. The aldehyde is quite unlikely to react because, as we remember from the above example, the $AlCl_3$ is a Lewis acid. It needs a lone pair of electrons. The –H in the aldehyde does not have a spare pair of electrons. Therefore, the aldehyde will not likely react and we eliminate D. Even if we were not sure about C, by POE, it must be the correct answer (which it is). As described above, the Cl of the acid chloride can interact with the Lewis acid to leave behind a good electrophile (partial positive charge on the carbonyl carbon) that the benzene ring can attack.

3. Which of the following compounds has optical activity?

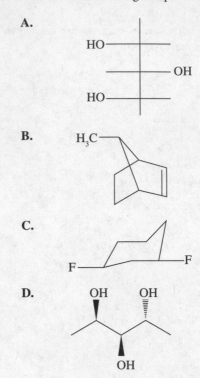

A.

B.

C.

D.

For this type of question, we need to determine what exactly is being asked. In order for a compound to have overall optical activity, it must contain a chiral carbon, but it canNOT contain an internal plane of symmetry. Which of those compounds does NOT contain an internal plane of symmetry? Answer choice A certainly does: It is sitting through the third (middle) carbon. Molecule A also incidentally contains no chiral carbons. Answer B also has an internal plane of symmetry. If you divide directly down through the methylated carbon and the double bond, you will see an exact mirror image of the compound front to back. Answer choice C also contains a plane of symmetry, though it may be harder to see: It bisects the ring through carbons 2 and 5 (carbon 2 is the one between the fluorines). Imagine this cyclohexane chair drawn in a flat representation. Both fluorine atoms would be represented on the same face of the ring (both pointing up, for example), and the axial hydrogens on carbons 1 and 3 (not shown in the structure) would be on the opposite face, pointing down. We are now left with only answer D, which by POE must be the correct answer. Answer D certainly does NOT contain an internal plane of symmetry. The only place the symmetry plane might be is through carbon 3 and the middle OH group. However, the OH group on the left shown with a wedge doesn't reflect into the OH group shown as a dash. Because these hydroxyl groups are on the opposite sides of the molecule, there is no mirror plane. Therefore, D is our answer.

4. Which of the following is the major product formed by the following reaction?

$$\text{NaBH}_4 \atop \overline{\text{CH}_3\text{OH}}$$

A. *S*-2-butanol
B. *R*-2-butanol
C. Racemic mixture of 2-butanol
D. The hemiacetal 2-hydroxy-2-methoxybutane

The key feature here is to recognize that NaBH_4 is a strong reducing agent given its significant amount of hydrogens (actually hydrides). Therefore, the ketone will be fully reduced to a secondary alcohol. This occurs via a nucleophilic addition reaction. As such, the hydride will come in and attack the carbonyl carbon. Because there is a methyl group on one side and an ethyl group on the other side of the carbonyl carbon, the approach of the hydride can cause either an *R* or an *S* configuration of the resultant alcohol. Because the carbonyl is planar, the hydride can attack from both sides of the double bond, thereby resulting in the formation of a pair of enantiomers. There is no favoritism of one configuration versus the other, and so a racemic mixture results (answer C). Answer choice D should be eliminated quickly, as hemiacetals are formed from aldehydes and/or ketones reacting with alcohols in the presence of an acid catalyst.

Chapter 18
Mastery Applied:
Organic Chemistry Practice

Passage I (Questions 1–5)

Ethanol can be formed by refluxing ethyl ethanoate with a dilute acid and heat. The ester reacts with the water in the dilute acid to produce ethanoic acid and ethanol by the equation below.

$$CH_3C(O)OCH_2CH_3 + H_2O \rightleftarrows CH_3COOH + CH_3CH_2OH$$

Equation 1 (occurs in a dilute acid)

Because the reaction is reversible, an equilibrium mixture is produced containing all four substances. In order to obtain a great degree of hydrolysis, a large excess of water must be used. The mechanism series is outlined below.

Step 1. In the first step, the ester takes a proton from the hydronium ion. The proton becomes attached to one of the lone pairs of oxygen.

Step 2. The positive charge on the carbon atom is attacked by one of the lone pairs on the oxygen of a water molecule.

Step 3. A proton is then transferred from the bottom oxygen atom to the ethoxy group.

Step 4. Ethanol is then removed from the compound.

Step 5. Water abstracts a proton from one of the remaining hydroxyl groups, resulting in the formation of ethanoic acid.

Reaction 1 Multi-step synthesis of ethanol

1. Which of the following serves as the catalyst in the reaction mechanism above?

    A. Sulfuric acid
    B. Ammonia
    C. Hydronium ion
    D. Water

2. Which of the following products would be expected if methyl ethanoate were used as the starting agent?

    A. Methanol and ethanol
    B. Methanol and ethanoic acid
    C. Ethanol and formaldehyde
    D. Ethanol and methanoic acid

3. Which of the following represent accurate resonance structures for the product formed in Step 1?

    A.

    B.

    C.

    D.

4. Which of the following ^{1}H-NMR findings would be expected for ethanol?

A. $\delta = 4$ ppm (q, 2H), $\delta = 2$ ppm (s, 1H), $\delta = 1$ ppm (t, 3H)

B. $\delta = 4$ ppm (s, 1H), $\delta = 2$ ppm (t, 3H), $\delta = 1$ ppm (q, 2H)

C. $\delta = 4$ ppm (t, 3H), $\delta = 2$ ppm (s, 1H), $\delta = 1$ ppm (q, 2H)

D. $\delta = 4$ ppm (s, 1H), $\delta = 2$ ppm (q, 2H), $\delta = 1$ ppm (t, 3H)

5. Which of the following explains why a proton transfer to the ethoxy group instead of to the upper hydroxyl group occurs in Step 3?

A. The ethoxy oxygen has greater electron-withdrawing character than the upper hydroxyl oxygen.

B. The upper hydroxyl oxygen has greater electron-donating character than the ethoxy oxygen.

C. The ethoxy oxygen has greater electron-donating character than the upper hydroxyl oxygen.

D. They both occur equally; however, the same starting product results if the proton transfers to the upper hydroxyl group.

Polypropylene is a versatile synthetic polymer used in the production of bottles, upholstery, carpet fibers, sewing thread, and rope. It is an example of a chain growth or addition polymer, which is produced by a successive lengthening of a reactive intermediate. The addition of an initiator to the double bond of propylene forms a free radical, which subsequently reacts in a propagation step with another propylene molecule, as shown in Figure 1. Each new radical reacts successively with another propylene molecule to lengthen the chain.

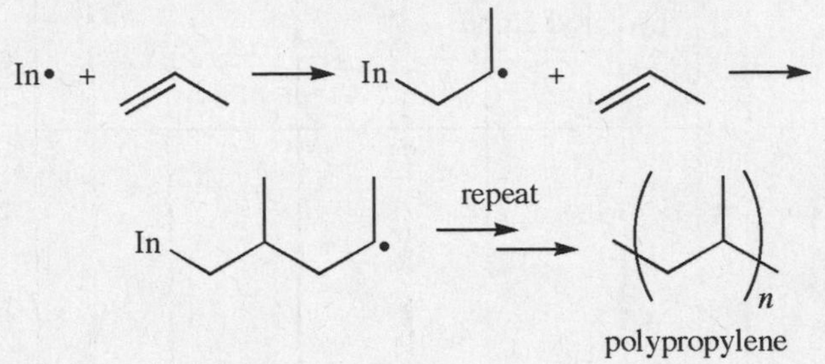

Figure 1 Radical polymerization

Polypropylene can also be produced by a cationic mechanism using a Lewis acid initiator, and monomers such as acrylonitrile, also known as cyanoethene, can be used to produce polymers via an anionic intermediate. The type of intermediate is dependent upon the electronic properties of the substituents present on the monomer units.

Polymerization of substituted alkenes leads to structures with numerous stereocenters on the backbone of the polymer. Unless special measures are taken, the configuration of each stereocenter will be random, producing an *atactic* polymer. Through use of the Ziegler–Natta catalyst, polypropylene and other polymers can be produced in both the *isotactic* form in which all substituents are on the same side of the chain, or in the *syndiotactic* form, in which the positions of the substituents alternate sides.

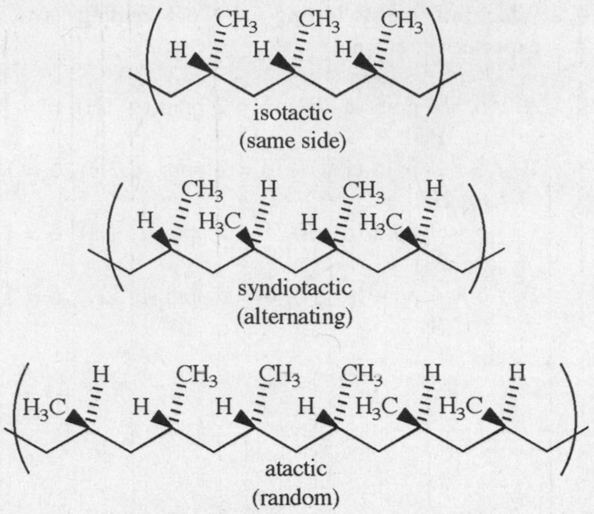

Figure 2 Polypropylene isomers

These isomeric forms have somewhat different properties, and therefore different uses. Isotactic and syndiotactic polymers tend to have higher melting points and are more resilient than their atactic forms.

Natural rubber and gutta-percha are natural polymers formed by the polymerization of 2-methyl-1,3-butadiene. These molecules differ only by the E/Z geometry of their double bonds. While natural rubber is soft and tacky, gutta-percha is harder and more brittle. Rubber can be made more durable by introducing sulfur, which will cross link the backbone chains through disulfide bonds in a process called vulcanization.

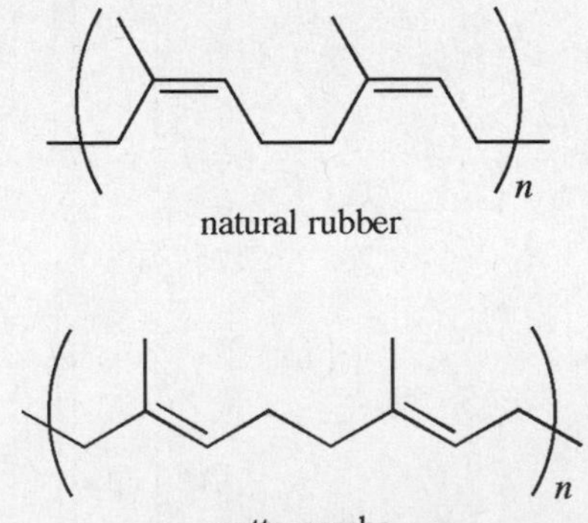

Figure 3 Natural polymers formed by polymerization of 2-methyl-1, 3-butadiene

6. Which of the following compounds should one expect to find in the largest quantity upon treatment of 1,4-dimethyl-1-cyclohexene with bromine and ultraviolet light?

A.

C.

B.

D.

7. Which of the following reagents would most likely be used as the radical initiator in the polymerization of polypropylene?

A. Sodium borohydride
B. Potassium hydroxide
C. Benzoyl peroxide
D. Phosphorus trichloride

8. Radial tires have sidewalls made of natural rubber and tend to crack and weather rapidly near cities with high levels of industrial pollutants. What is the best explanation for this observation?

A. The sulfuric acid from acid rain catalyzes the addition of water across the double bonds of the rubber, making the rubber more hydrophilic.
B. Ozone cleaves the double bonds in the rubber, reducing the structural integrity of the tire.
C. The UV light–induced decomposition of chloro-fluorocarbons facilitates radical halogenation of the double bonds, allowing for some isomerization to the E isomer.
D. Ozone reduces the disulfide cross-links of the rubber, allowing the polymer chains to slide past each other.

9. The reactive intermediate most likely involved in the polymerization of methylpropenoate is a:

A. carbanion, because the electron donating group will destabilize the negative charge on the intermediate.
B. carbocation, because the electron donating group will stabilize the positive charge on the intermediate.
C. carbocation, because the electron withdrawing group will stabilize the positive charge on the intermediate.
D. carbanion, because the electron withdrawing group will stabilize the negative charge on the intermediate.

10. Compared to their stereoisomers, gutta-percha and isotactic polypropylene have higher melting points because they:

A. have larger dipole–dipole interactions because of the orientation of their substituents.
B. have stronger London dispersion forces since each strand can overlap with the next more easily due to the orientation of their substituents.
C. have stronger London dispersion forces due to their greater molecular weights.
D. can hydrogen bond, whereas their isomers cannot.

11. Which of the following could NOT be a possible compound with the formula $C_6H_{12}O_2$?

    A. hexanoic acid
    B. 1-hydroxy-3-hexone
    C. 1,3-cyclohexanediol
    D. hydroxypropyl propyl ether

12. Which of the following would NOT be a reasonable nucleophile in a S_N2 reaction?

    A. NH_3
    B. CN^-
    C. H_2O
    D. OH^-

13. The major reason that phenol is a better Bronsted-Lowry acid than cyclohexanol is:

    A. it is a better proton donor.
    B. the cyclohexyl group is an electon-withdrawing group by induction, which destabilizes the anion formed in the reaction.
    C. phenol is able to stabilize the anion formed in the reaction by resonance.
    D. the phenyl group is an electron-donating group by induction, which stabilizes the anion formed in the reaction.

14. Which of the following is the most likely product of the Diels-Alder addition of 2-methoxy-1,3-butadiene and cis-1,2-dichloroethene?

    A. 1-methoxy-4R,5S-dichlorocyclohexene
    B. 1-methoxy-4S,5S-dichlorocyclohexene
    C. 1-methoxy-4R,5R-dichlorocyclohexene
    D. 2-methoxy-4R,5R-dichlorocyclohexene

15. The addition of Br_2 to E-2-butene gives which major product(s)?

    A. 2S,3R-dibromobutane
    B. 2R,3R-dibromobutane
    C. 2S,3S-dibromobutane
    D. racemic mixture of B and C

Passage III (Questions 16–20)

Isopropyl alcohol is a colorless liquid with an odor characteristic of alcohols. It melts at –89.5°C and boils at 82.5°C. The compound is soluble in water, ethanol, and ether. It is often used as a disinfectant and as a skin-cooling agent, called "rubbing alcohol." Many alcohols are made commercially by the hydration of alkenes. Isopropyl alcohol is prepared by reacting propylene ($CH_3CH=CH_2$) with a strong acid such as sulfuric acid, followed by treatment with water.

The initial step is shown below:

$$CH_3-CH=CH_2 + H^+ + HSO_4^- \longrightarrow \text{Intermediate} + HSO_4^-$$

The reaction of the intermediate with water then yields isopropyl alcohol.

$$\text{Intermediate} + H_2O \longrightarrow CH_3-\overset{\overset{\textstyle OH}{|}}{\underset{\underset{\textstyle H}{|}}{C}}-CH_3 + H^+$$

16. In the preparation of isopropyl alcohol, what is the role of sulfuric acid?

    A. It acts as a catalyst.
    B. It increases the pH of the solution.
    C. It ionizes the alkene.
    D. It causes a reduction of the alkene.

17. How many chiral centers are featured within the isopropyl alcohol molecule?

    A. 0
    B. 1
    C. 2
    D. 3

18. What property of isopropyl alcohol makes it most useful as a skin-cooling agent?

    A. It forms hydrogen bonds.
    B. It is weakly acidic.
    C. It is relatively volatile.
    D. It acts as a proton acceptor.

19. Between isopropyl alcohol and *n*-propanol, which compound likely has the higher boiling point?

    A. *N*-propanol, because it has the higher molecular weight
    B. *N*-propanol, because it is a straight chain alcohol
    C. Isopropyl alcohol, because its density is higher than that of *n*-propanol
    D. Isopropyl alcohol, because its carbon chain branches

20. All of the following are isomers of isobutyl alcohol EXCEPT:

    A. $(CH_3)_3COH$.
    B. $CH_3CH_2COCH_3$.
    C. $CH_3CH_2CH_2CH_2OH$.
    D. $CH_3CHOHCH_2CH_3$.

Passage IV (Questions 21–26)

Cholesterol is a steroid widely found in animal tissues. It is a major component of human gallstones and egg yolks. Cholesterol is an important intermediate in the biosynthesis of steroid hormones such as testosterone and estradiol. It has received much popular attention because of its association with atherosclerosis or "hardening of the arteries."

Cholesterol

21. How many chiral centers does the above cholesterol molecule feature?

- **A.** 7
- **B.** 6
- **C.** 5
- **D.** 4

22. What is the product of the reaction shown below?

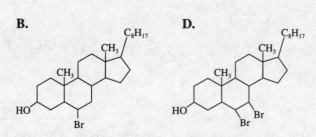

A.

C.

B.

D.

23. When cholesterol reacts with CH_3COOH, it forms:

- **A.** a carboxylic acid and water.
- **B.** a carboxylic acid and an alcohol.
- **C.** an ester and water.
- **D.** an ester and an alcohol.

24. A student believes that cholesterol will readily undergo electrophilic addition when reacted with hydrogen (H_2). Is the belief reasonable?

- **A.** Yes, because cholesterol is a conjugated diene.
- **B.** Yes, because cholesterol may undergo a hydrogenation reaction.
- **C.** No, because cholesterol is not aromatic.
- **D.** No, because electrophilic addition of H_2 requires catalysis.

25. Which of the following is the most probable product when cholesterol undergoes ozonolysis?

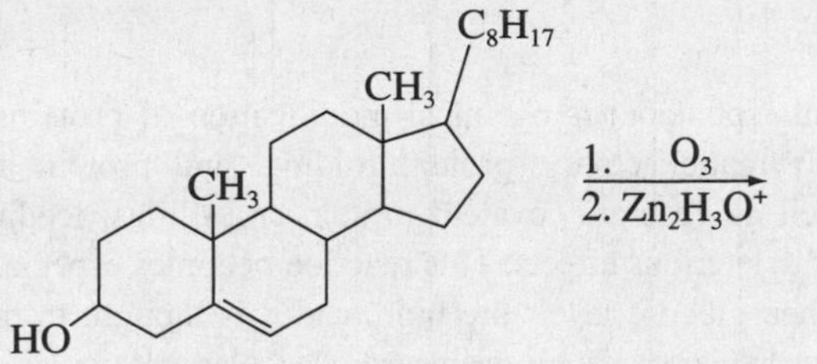

$$\frac{1. \quad O_3}{2. \; Zn_2H_3O^+}$$

A.

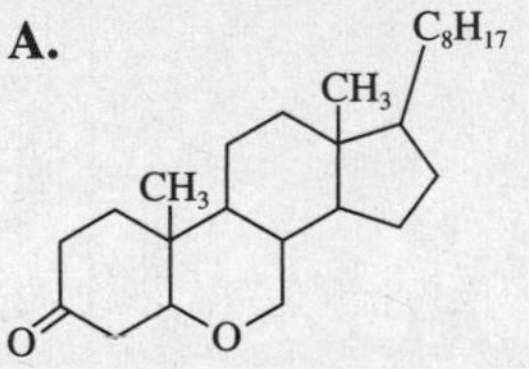

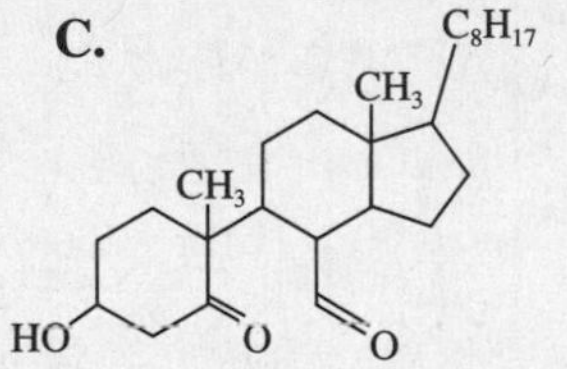

B.

C.

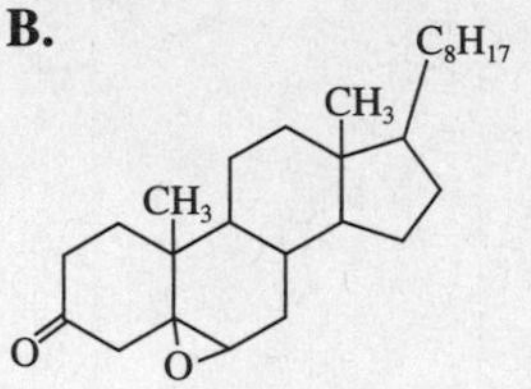

D.

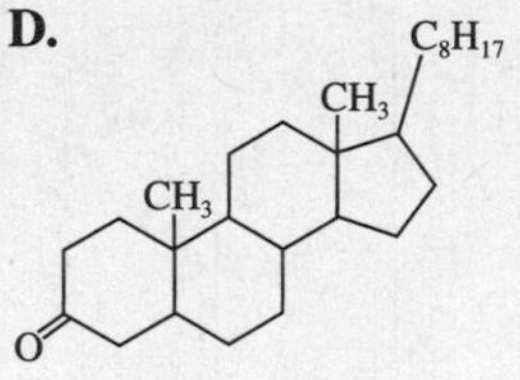

26. Suppose an investigator attempts to produce 5-cholestene-3-one from cholesterol. Which of the following infrared spectroscopic findings would inform the investigator that the reaction has occurred?

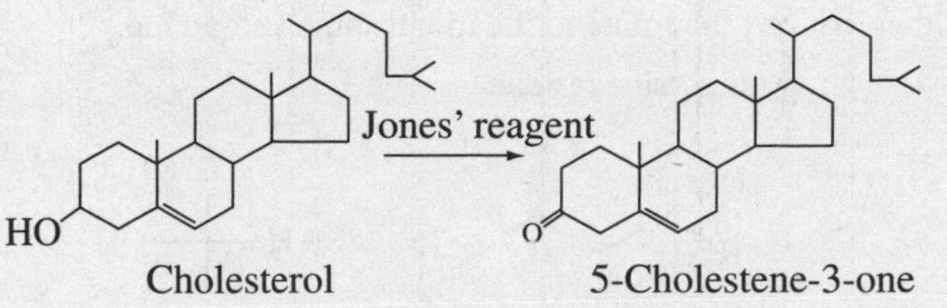

Cholesterol   5-Cholestene-3-one

A. The disappearance of OH absorption from the reactant

B. The disappearance of the carbonyl group in the product

C. The disappearance of a double bond from the reactant

D. The disappearance of a methyl group from the reactant

Passage V (Questions 27–31)

Carbonyl groups in the linear form of carbohydrates can react with primary amines to form imines (Schiff bases). A spontaneous two-step isomerization known as the *Amadori rearrangement* can then convert the imine to the more stable ketoamine.

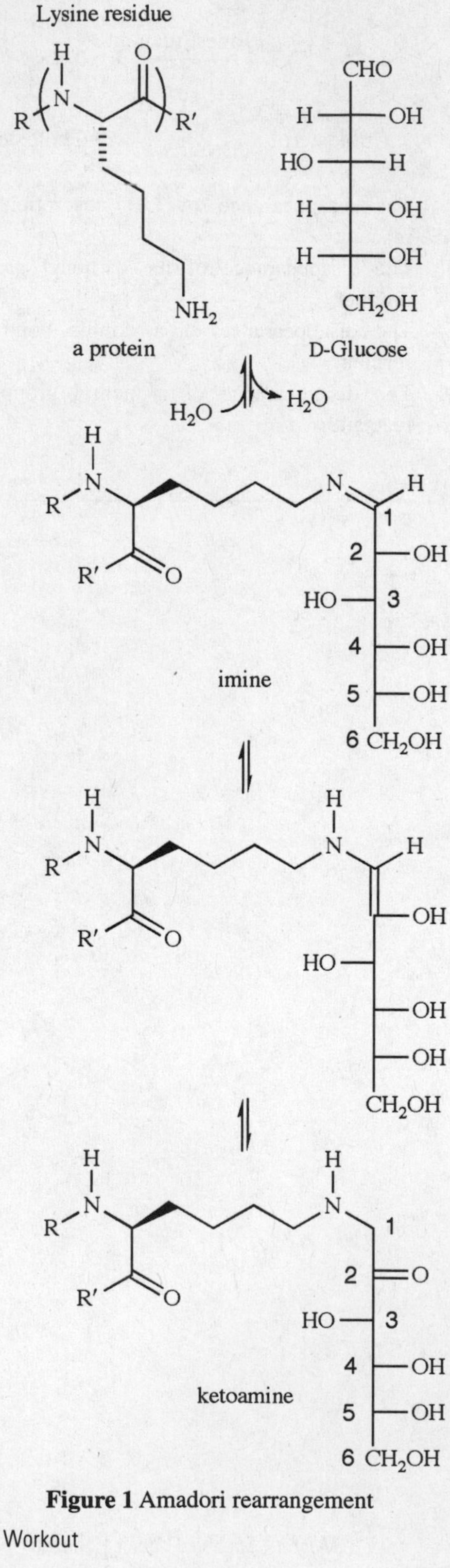

Figure 1 Amadori rearrangement

This reaction occurs within the human body between natural carbohydrates (such as glucose) and primary amines in proteins (such as the lysine side chain).

This spontaneous chemical modification of proteins can inhibit enzymatic activity, protein folding, and protein assembly, as well as generate covalent protein cross-links, leading to a host of deleterious effects. This reaction becomes especially prevalent when glucose levels are high, and it is thought to be one of the mechanisms of long-term cardiovascular and ocular degeneration in diabetic patients.

27. Which of the following is the most likely intermediate in the conversion of glucose to the imine in Figure 1?

A.

B.

C.

D.

28. The imine and ketoamine shown in Figure 1 are best described as:

A. resonance forms.
B. tautomers.
C. conformational isomers.
D. diastereomers.

29. Following formation of the ketoamine in Figure 1, which carbon stereocenter is most likely to undergo racemization?

A. C-3
B. C-4
C. C-5
D. C-6

30. What other nucleophiles present in proteins might form Schiff bases with glucose?

A. Any cysteine side chain
B. Any glycine side chain
C. The C-terminal amino acid
D. The N-terminal amino acid

31. When treated with Benedict's reagent, the ketoamine formed after lysine reacts with glucose will show:

A. a positive Benedict's test, because the product is a reducing sugar.
B. a negative Benedict's test, because the product is not a reducing sugar.
C. a positive Benedict's test, because the product is not a reducing sugar.
D. a negative Benedict's test, because the product is a reducing sugar.

Chapter 19
Organic Chemistry Practice:
Answers and Explanations

Passage I (Questions 1–5)

Here is a passage dealing with a multi-step reaction and questions about a product. It requires you to have an understanding of nomenclature and knowledge of NMR spectroscopy. The MCAT often asks questions on a reaction mechanism provided to you on the exam. Those questions tend to be regarding the actual process itself or predicting the product with a different starting substrate using the same process.

1.   **C**   The catalyst of the reaction must be the compound that is regenerated, such that there is no net loss or gain of the compound in the overall reaction scheme. The reaction mechanism shows that the hydronium ion, H_3O^+, is utilized in the first step and reformed in the last step. Therefore, it is the catalyst for the reaction. Water is formed in the first step, but then it is used in the second step. The sulfuric acid would be too strong an acid to even be present, let alone reformed at the end of the reaction series. Ammonia is a weak base, and the passage states that the reaction series occurs in the presence of a dilute acid, not a base.

2.   **B**   Methyl ethanoate would consist of a methyl group attached to the ester oxygen. Since the ester oxygen becomes the alcohol, one product would be methanol (eliminate C and D). What remains of the molecule becomes the carboxylic acid. Since it began as an ethanoate, it will become ethanoic acid (eliminate A).

3.   **A**   An accurate resonance series needs to maintain the same charge and electrons throughout each resonance structure. The molecule begins with one positive charge, so it must maintain one positive charge (eliminate B). The positive charge represents an absence of an electron, so the carbon should only make 3 bonds because it is missing its fourth electron (eliminate C and D). Answer C can also be eliminated based on the fact that a resonance structure cannot change the ethoxy group into two methoxy groups.

4.   **A**   Ethanol contains 3 different types of hydrogens: 3 hydrogens from the CH_3 group, 2 hydrogens from the CH_2, and 1 hydrogen from the OH. The 3 hydrogens have 2 neighbors each; this corresponds to a triplet. The 2 hydrogens have 3 neighbors each; this corresponds to a quartet. The 1 hydrogen has 0 neighbors that contribute to its splitting pattern since it's attached to an oxygen; this is a singlet. However, understanding the splitting patterns alone is not enough to eliminate any answer choices, and some knowledge of chemical shift is necessary. By recognizing that the CH_2 hydrogens should be farthest downfield (the greatest chemical shift) because of their close proximity to the oxygen, choices B, C, and D can all be eliminated. The 3 hydrogens would have the smallest chemical shift (1 ppm) since they are farthest from the oxygen. OH groups can have a wide range of possible chemical shifts, from roughly 2–5 ppm.

5.   **D**   They both should occur equally given the resonance structures; however, if the upper is attacked, the same original molecule is reformed. The reaction series would not continue. Electron-donating or electron-withdrawing character does not affect proton transfers.

Passage II (Questions 6–10)

6.   **A**   The major product arises from the most stable radical intermediate. The vinyl radical that gives rise to the molecule in choice C cannot be stabilized effectively by either induction or resonance. The tertiary radical that leads to the molecule in choice B is stabilized by induction, but the resonance stabilization of the allylic radicals in both A and D is stronger. In D, there will be primary and secondary allylic resonance structures, whereas in A there are two secondary allylic structures, making it the most stable of all.

7.   **C**   Peroxides are often used to initiate radical reactions because the O–O bond is so weak and cleaves homolytically.

8.   **B**   Ozonolysis cleaves carbon–carbon double bonds, leaving either aldehydes or ketones as products. Breaking the chain of the polymer will make the material weaker. Addition of a reagent across the double bond as in A will have no effect because the chain will remain intact. The isomerization suggested in choice C does not break the chain or significantly alter the structure. Since ozone is an oxidizing agent, it cannot reduce disulfide bonds.

9.   **D**   The passage states that the substituent on the alkene affects the identity of the preferred intermediate in the polymerization reaction. Since an ester group is electron withdrawing, it can stabilize a negative charge on the alpha carbon, making a carbanion the best suited intermediate.

10.   **B**   Since both polypropylene and gutta-percha are hydrocarbons, they are nonpolar molecules and can neither hydrogen bond nor participate in dipole–dipole interactions. Since the passage makes no mention of molecular weights of the polymers, and since the major difference between the isomers in question is stereochemistry and orientation of substituents, choice B is better than choice C.

Freestanding Questions 11–15

11.   **D**   The compound has one degree of unsaturation based on the formula. That one degree of unsaturation can be in the form of a double bond or a ring structure. Hexanoic acid has one double bond, and the formula fits (eliminate A). B has a double bond, and its formula also fits (eliminate B). C is a cyclic compound, and it does not contain any other degrees of unsaturation, so its formula works as well. D, however, does not work. There is no double bond or ring structure. Therefore, it should have no degrees of unsaturation.

12.   **C**   Strong nucleophiles are necessary for S_N2 reactions because the nucleophile attacks at the same time the leaving group leaves. Since both CN^- and OH^- have negative charges, they are much better nucleophiles than the remaining choices. Eliminate B and D. While both ammonia and water have a lone pair of electrons, making them nucleophilic, ammonia is the better nucleophile since nitrogen is less electronegative than oxygen and is therefore more likely to donate its electrons to an electrophile.

13. **C**   A Bronsted-Lowry acid is a molecule that readily donates a proton, and the more stable an acid's conjugate base is, the stronger the acid. Answer choice A simply restates the question but does not explain why phenol is the better acid. Eliminate A. The cyclohexyl group is electron-donating, not electron-withdrawing (B is incorrect). While the phenyl group is also electron donating, pushing more electron density toward a negative charge will *destabilize* it, not stabilize it (D is incorrect). Because the phenolate ion has a conjugated pi electron system, it has several resonance structures that stabilize it relative to the cyclohexoxide ion that has none. C is therefore the best answer.

14. **A**   Before even considering the reaction, you can eliminate choice D based on IUPAC nomenclature, since the methoxy group will always be located on the first carbon of a ring system. In a Diels-Alder reaction, a dienophile reacts with a diene in a cycloaddition reaction to form a cyclohexene product with the double bond located in between the original diene double bonds. The stereoselectivity of the reaction forces the two chlorine atoms that are *cis* on the dienophile to end up *cis* on the product ring. The attached chlorines will therefore be on the same face of the ring.

diene   dienophile

However, the reaction will form a mixture of enantiomers instead of just one product, so by using good test-taking tricks, you can eliminate choices B and C, as these molecules are also enantiomers of each other with opposite configurations at C_4 and C_5. They must therefore both be wrong (they are the products if *trans*-1,2-dichloroethene were to react). With regards to R and S configuration of the true product, the C_4 chlorine will be R and the C_5 chlorine will be S for one enantiomer and vice versa for its mirror image.

15. **A** When adding Br_2 across a double bond, one bromine will add to each of the two carbons of the double bond in an *anti* fashion, meaning to opposite faces of the double bond. In this case, since the starting double bond is in the *E* configuration, one bromine adds to form an R configuration while the other adds to make an S configuration. There is no racemic mixture, however, since after the *anti* addition, an internal plane of symmetry exists in the molecule, so the 2S,3R-dibromobutane is the same as the 2R,3S-dibromobutane.

Passage III (Questions 16–20)

16. **A** Examine the two steps set forth in the passage and note that sulfuric acid is present at the beginning of the first (in dissociated form, as H^+ and HSO_4^-) and at the end of the reaction as well. That a substance should be necessary to a reaction and regenerated at its conclusion is strong evidence that it serves as a catalyst. Choice B is wrong because sulfuric acid is a strong acid and decreases ambient pH. Choice C is a true statement, but A is a more complete answer for the role of the acid. Choice D is wrong because there is no basis to conclude that sulfuric acid reduces the alkene.

17. **A** A chiral center is a carbon atom bonded to four substituents, none of which is identical to any other. The isopropyl alcohol molecule features three carbons. The central carbon is bound to two CH_3 moieties and cannot be chiral. The other two carbons are those of the CH_3 moieties themselves, and each, quite obviously, is bound to three hydrogen atoms. None of the carbon atoms can "boast" four dissimilar substituents.

18. **C** "Rubbing alcohol" is designed to cool the skin. A volatile liquid—one that tends to vaporize rapidly—will cool the skin by drawing heat away from it as it moves from the liquid to the gaseous phase. Choices A, B, and D all represent isopropyl alcohol's properties, but they do not explain the cooling of skin.

19. **B** Recognize that because *n*-propanol is a straight-chain alcohol, its molecules experience increased van der Waals attractions. Choices A and C are true but have no bearing on the question; they're irrelevant. Choice D is wrong because branching tends to *reduce* boiling point.

20. **B** The term "isomer" refers to two compounds whose molecular formulas are identical but differ in the arrangement of their composite atoms. The isobutyl alcohol molecule is composed of four carbon atoms, one oxygen atom, and ten hydrogen atoms. Examine the four molecules shown in the answer choices. Note that all have four carbon atoms, all have one oxygen atom, and all *except* choice B have ten hydrogen atoms. The molecule shown in choice B has only eight hydrogen atoms.

Passage IV (Questions 21–26)

21. **A** The definition of chirality requires that a tetrahedral central atom be connected to four different atoms. Thus, any atom that is involved in a double bond or is bonded to less than four different atoms or groups cannot be considered chiral. A careful examination of the structure of cholesterol, as it is depicted in Figure 1, will reveal that it has seven chiral carbon atoms.

22. **C** Halogen molecules undergo electrophilic addition reactions with alkenes. In this case, the bromine molecule adds to the carbon-carbon double bond. As Br_2 approaches the double bond, the Br–Br bond is polarized and ultimately breaks. Choice A is wrong because it shows not two but one bromine atom bonded to the product. Choice B is wrong for the same reason. Choice D is wrong as well. It shows the bromine atoms incorrectly positioned; they should be positioned on either side of the preexisting double bond.

23. **C** An ester (RCOOR) is a carboxylic acid derivative. It may be synthesized from a carboxylic acid and an alcohol. Cholesterol *is* an alcohol. (It is also a steroid.) When it reacts with a carboxylic acid, it forms an ester and water, as shown in this illustration:

24. **D** Recall that in the presence of H_2 and a metal catalyst such as nickel, palladium, or platinum, an alkene will undergo electrophilic addition of hydrogen across the alkene double bond. As is seen in the figure of cholesterol above, one of the functional groups within the cholesterol molecule is a double bond, enabling cholesterol to undergo hydrogenation via an electrophilic addition reaction but only in the presence of a metal catalyst, which the question does *not* mention. Choice A is wrong because a conjugated diene features single and double bonds in alternating series. Cholesterol does not. Choice B is true but not under the conditions provided in the question. Choice C has no bearing on the issue raised in the question.

25. **C** Ozonolysis represents the cleavage of a molecule by ozone. When ozone is added to a carbon–carbon double bond in the pictured reaction, two carbonyl entities result, as shown in choice C.

26. **A** Infrared spectroscopy identifies a molecule's functional groups. Examine the illustration that depicts the reaction. The reactant features a hydroxyl group. The product shows a carbonyl group but no OH group. The investigator will know the reaction has occurred if IR spectroscopy shows the disappearance of an OH group. Choice B refers to the disappearance of a carbonyl group in the product. Since the product features a carbonyl group, such a finding is incorrect. Choice C refers to the disappearance of an alkene group from the reactant. Again, both reactant and product feature alkene groups; the alkene group does not disappear. Choice D refers to the disappearance of the methyl group in the reactant, an event that does not arise with this reaction.

Passage V (Questions 27–31)

27. **C** The passage states that imines are formed from primary amine nucleophiles and aldehyde or ketone electrophiles. The first step involves formation of a new C–N bond between the nitrogen and the carbonyl carbon. After proton transfer from nitrogen to the alkoxide oxygen, the structure in choice C is formed. Choice A, an amide, can be formed only from an amine and a carboxylic acid derivative, while B is an amide analog of the keto–enol tautomerism that occurs in ketones and aldehydes. Choice D shows reaction at the alpha carbon of the aldehyde, which is not electrophilic.

28. **B** The imine and ketoamine are structural isomers in a rapid equilibrium and are therefor tautomers. Resonance forms involve the movement of only electrons, not atoms, eliminating A. Choice C is false because conformational isomers have all the same connectivities of atoms. These molecules are not diastereomers because they do not differ at any stereocenters.

29. **A** Choice D can be eliminated since C-6 is not a stereocenter. Racemization involves the inversion of configuration of a stereocenter. C-3 will be easily racemized since the alpha proton is acidic. When the enolate of the ketone is formed, it can be reprotonated from either side of the double bond, forming both R and S configurations at that carbon.

30. **D** The passage states that primary amines are needed to form imines. The N-terminal amino acid of a protein will have a primary amino group. The C-terminal amino acid has a free carboxylic acid group, eliminating choice C. Cysteine has a sulfur in its side chain and glycine has no side chain.

31. **A** Benedict's test is a test for the presence of aldehydes and ketones, and a positive test indicates that the carbonyl functional group has reduced the copper reagent. Because the ketoamine still has a free carbonyl group, the reagent will show a positive test.

Chapter 20
Mastering Biological Sciences: Biology

This chapter is a more in-depth look at the content and techniques specific to the Biology section of the MCAT. Many of the techniques will look familiar, as they can be applied universally to other sections of the MCAT. The content outline presented is based on the topic list for Biology provided on the AAMC website.

BIOLOGY CONTENT

The outline of all potential Biology topics on the AAMC site covers information from a number of college Biology courses but only at a basic level. This makes understanding the fundamental concepts of these topics more important for the MCAT than knowing all of the minute details. Getting too focused on small details at the expense of solidifying fundamental knowledge can be counterproductive.

There is often a wealth of information in the passage that helps you recall your prior knowledge of a topic. The less you need to acquire these fundamental facts from the passage the better, although it is nice to know some information will be there. One key to success with the Biology questions is being comfortable reading tables and graphs and interpreting and processing data. This section tests your knowledge of Biology as well as your knowledge of experimental design and reasoning skills. Sometimes minor calculations are required with data given in the Biology section, but this is infrequent and at most encompasses a few questions in the section.

The MCAT Biology section contains consistent formats for asking questions, so acquainting yourself with the structure of the MCAT and Biology section can help you prepare. The ability to recognize types of questions and be aware of the types of answers that generally go with those questions is often beneficial. Also, realizing the mistakes commonly made with certain types of questions can help prevent you from making those mistakes as well. It can be very frustrating to miss a question due to a trap answer or a common mistake even though you know the content required to answer the question. Overall, succeeding on the Biology section and MCAT in general requires adequate review and mastery of the content as well as good test-taking and reading comprehension skills.

BIOLOGY TOPICS OUTLINE

Molecular Biology

The topics covered within Molecular Biology include the following:

- DNA
- enzymes
- control of eukaryotic gene expression
- metabolism
- protein synthesis

Enzyme structure, the function in catalyzing biological reactions, and specificity of enzymes for substrates are all fundamental to understanding the enzyme portion of Molecular Biology. When normal enzymatic activity is understood, then an understanding of inhibitory effects will come naturally. These will provide a framework to organize the various cellular biochemical processes that occur, such as glycolysis, the Krebs cycle, and the electron transport chain.

The structure and function of DNA and RNA are important for understanding replication, transcription, and translation. These processes are integral to the normal life cycle of the cell and therefore are very important to know for the MCAT.

There are fundamental differences between prokaryotic and eukaryotic gene expression and the control of that expression; these differences provide a rich source of potential questions that may be asked on the MCAT.

Underlying all the topics listed above is a thorough understanding of the biologically relevant macromolecules (proteins, lipids, carbohydrates, nucleic acids) that are involved in the structure and function of all cells.

Genetics

In the natural progression of Biology and physiological development, the subject of Genetics will be encountered after DNA, RNA, and protein synthesis. An understanding of genetics allows you to apply your knowledge of what happens at a cellular level to the overall phenotypic expression of the individual or organism. Mitosis and meiosis sound alike, sort of look alike, but in reality are quite different. Being able to distinguish between the two is important for the MCAT.

Reviewing Mendelian principles will allow a deeper understanding of topics such as co-dominance and linked genes, both of which have appeared on the MCAT. Computing relative probabilities of phenotypes or genotypes in the progeny will require a facility with Punnett Squares and the Hardy-Weinberg equation. Performing basic pedigree analysis to determine patterns of inheritance, such as autosomal vs. sex-linked and dominant vs. recessive has also been required previously on the MCAT.

Microbiology

Non-mammalian organisms, such as bacteria, viruses, and fungi, comprise the basis of Microbiology. You should be familiar with the general characteristics of fungi, including their life cycles. Knowledge of basic viral structure and the viral life cycle will help you identify the pathogenesis of some viruses as well as their ability to transfer genetic material from one organism to another (or potentially from a test tube to an enzyme-deficient organism).

Since there are so many differences between prokaryotes and eukaryotes, bacteria comprise a majority of the Microbiology that is covered on the exam. This includes an understanding of their structure, shape, accoutrements on the cell membrane, growth, and physiology. Bacteria are also a great source for gene expression questions because they are heavily used in the laboratory for recombinant DNA techniques. Advanced, passage-based topics that have appeared in the past include creating genomic libraries, transposons, and mechanisms of bacterial resistance to antibiotics.

Generalized Eukaryotic Cell

We swiftly move out of the prokaryotic world into our own eukaryotic world next. Having a basic understanding of the organelles and structure and functions of the cell will enable you to apply these concepts to a passage that may discuss medical pathology, such as I-cell Disease. The components of the cell membrane and their function will provide a foundation for future study of physiology. It is important to understand the transport mechanisms that are utilized to move hydrophilic and hydrophobic substances across the cell membrane. The cell cycle, its stages, and specifically what occurs during those stages provides a background for mitosis and cancer. Not all eukaryotic cells look alike; there are specialized cells, such as neurons, that are distinct from other cell types.

Physiology

On a larger scale, we see the interactions of all these cells in the form of human physiology. The neuroendocrine systems are important because they provide the backbone to movement, sensation, and reflex responses of the body. The main differences in peptide versus steroid hormones are important distinctions that the MCAT likes to test. The action potential and synaptic transmission are crucial to the understanding of the coordination of the nervous and musculoskeletal systems. A recurrent topic on the MCAT has been the peripheral nervous system and understanding differences in structure and function between the somatic and autonomic (sympathetic and parasympathetic) nervous system.

The circulatory and lymphatic systems are similar in their travels throughout the body, but they differ in their structure and function. Tracing the course of blood from exercising tissue to the heart to the lungs back to the heart and then back to the tissue will give you a better appreciation of how hard your heart works (even when you are not stressed!). The heart pumps blood not just to transport oxygen to the tissues that need them but also to circulate the immune system's cells, your primary defense against foreign invaders like viruses. The unique and quite diverse immune system is impressive and has been a source of several questions on the MCAT.

The heart circulates the oxygenated blood to the tissues that require it, but how did the blood get oxygenated? This is the main function of the respiratory system. It also serves to regulate temperature and acid-base status of the blood. Your lungs possess an inherent mechanism to prevent you from breathing in large particles of dust or other harmful substances. The surfactant made by specialized lung cells helps prevent the collapse of the alveoli; without the surfactant, the surface tension of the hydrated air would cause massive alveolar collapse and an impairment in gas exchange.

To gain a better understanding of the digestive and excretory systems, trace a piece of your favorite food from that first delicious bite you take to the last itty bitty particle it becomes. Appreciate the delicate yet intricate mechanism by which your body has adapted the ability to extract as much possible nutrition from any morsel of food that enters the digestive cavity. Although often taboo in conversation, the very necessary bodily functions of excretion and urination do appear on the MCAT. The complex inner-workings of the kidneys coordinate a metabolic homeostasis that keeps a tight control on the acid-base status of the body, maintaining a blood pH of 7.35–7.45. Firm knowledge of the functional unit of the kidney, the nephron, will help answer questions related to these issues.

Most physiologic systems cannot function without some reliance on the musculoskeletal system. Whether it is the smooth muscle that allows peristalsis to occur in the digestive tract or the cardiac muscle that allows your heart to go on, muscles play a critical role in mammalian physiology. The skeletal system not only serves as, literally, the backbone for the human body, but also a rich source of calcium and a means of protection for the vital organs.

One of the principles of evolution is fitness and natural selection. Fitness is determined by one's ability to procreate and pass viable genes on to one's progeny and other generations to come. This relies on the actions of the reproductive systems of both men and women. Fertilization of a spermatozoon and an oocyte is only the beginning of a long nine-month journey for the fetus. For the MCAT, you will need to understand the coordinated concert of the various stages of gametogenesis and development (blastulation, gastrulation, etc…) as well as knowing the functions of the key hormones (progesterone, testosterone, estrogen, etc…) involved in reproduction.

GENERAL STRATEGIES

One of the hardest parts of tackling the Biology questions is remembering that the MCAT is not out to get you. The AAMC is not purposefully trying to trick you when it writes questions for the MCAT. The questions that appear on the exam are rooted in the basic principles that are taught during the first year of Biology. If you happen to be (or have been) a Biology major, you have more than enough familiarity with the material and potentially some detrimental knowledge. Knowing too much can harm you on the MCAT if it leads you to switch to a higher gear than a question requires. Again, these questions target everyone who has completed one year of introductory Biology. There will not be questions asking you to identify the structure of argininosuccinate. If you took Biochemistry, you may have needed to know that concept for an exam in class, but you will NOT need to know that for the MCAT.

RECOGNIZE THE FUNDAMENTAL CONCEPTS

That being said, the MCAT does like to "dress up" its questions. A fundamental principle may be hidden in the midst of superfluous information or even buried within a new topic with which you are not familiar. When you come across a question where you have no idea what the answer is, you should Mark the question for review, choose an answer, and then return to it. There is no need to forge a crusade on one question. Your time is valuable on this exam; why waste ten minutes on one question, that you may not get correct anyway, when you can answer six questions to which you *do* know the answers?

If you have the extra time at the end of the section to review your marked answers, you should ask yourself, "What are they trying to ask me?" Look at the answers. Do they give you a hint as to what principle is being addressed? Are they trying to ask you to differentiate prokaryotes from eukaryotes, the parasympathetic nervous system from the sympathetic? This can often help you with making an educated guess at the answer.

USE THE STRIKEOUT FUNCTION TO ASSIST WITH POE

Always remember that the Process of Elimination (POE) is your friend. The computerized exam gives you the ability to strike out answer choices that you know CANNOT be correct. So, strike it out, just like you would have crossed it out if it were a paper and pencil exam. This increases your chances of choosing the correct answer. Also, remember to read the question carefully. When you are rushed, you can easily miss the word "not" or "except" and consequently choose the incorrect answer, or you can misread "thymus" for "thyroid."

COMMON QUESTION TYPES

There are several types of questions that may be asked of you. We can generally divide them into the "know something" and "know nothing" types of questions. The "know something" questions often ask you to cull a tidbit from your knowledge base to answer a question directly or to apply that datum to new information to answer the question. The "know nothing" types of questions tend to be reading comprehension questions, which means the answer is sitting somewhere in the passage.

You will come across "I/II/III" questions. These Roman numeral questions ask you to identify more than one possible correct answer within a question. Your approach here would be to first look at your answers. If one Roman numeral is in all the answer choices, then you know it is correct. Once you have established that one of the Roman numerals is *in*correct, then eliminate all the answer choices that contain that Roman numeral. Remember, POE is your friend.

As illustrated before, if you are not reading the question carefully, you may well miss the negatively-phrased questions. The MCAT *should* capitalize these trigger words; however, you should be aware of them when you come across them: EXCEPT, LEAST, NOT.

Try this example of an EXCEPT/LEAST/NOT question.

1. All of the following are characteristic of X-linked disorders EXCEPT:

    A. More males are affected than females.
    B. They can be dominant or recessive.
    C. Fathers cannot pass the disorder to their sons.
    D. Affected females always pass the disorder to their sons.

This type of question generally requires you to review each answer choice carefully and rule out the answer choices that you know are true while looking for the answer choice that you know is false and thereby meets the "EXCEPT" criteria. Be careful on these types of questions; it is a bit of a mental shift to mark false information as the correct answer to a question.

In this question, we want to rule out any answer choices that are true. Answer choice A says that more males are affected than females, and in X-linked recessive disorders that is true because males are hemizygous and only have one X chromosome. Males do not have a second X to cancel out the disorder as females do, so A is eliminated. Answer choice B says the X-linked disorders can be dominant or recessive, which is true as well. Dominant X-linked disorders are rarer than recessive ones but can happen, so B is eliminated. Answer choice C says that fathers cannot pass the disorder to their sons; that is true because fathers must pass the Y chromosome to their sons, so C is eliminated. Answer choice D says that affected females always pass the disorder to their son, which is only true for X-linked *recessive* disorders because both of a woman's X chromosomes are affected. However, in an X-linked *dominant* disorder, the female could be homozygous or heterozygous for the disorder, so if she only has one affected X chromosome, then it would be expected that she would only pass it along 50% of the time. D is false, so that is the correct answer to the question.

TIMING IS IMPORTANT

Managing your time throughout the Biology section is important. In the Biological Sciences section there are 52 questions to be completed in 70 minutes. That gives you roughly 80 seconds per question. If you have eliminated as many answer choices as possible on a question and still are not sure which to choose, it is important that you pick an answer and move on. You can use the CBT Mark for Review function so that you can come back to the question at the end and review it if you have time. If timing is a problem, you should work on this skill while preparing for the MCAT. Never let the time run out without marking an answer for each question. There is no guessing penalty, so you must NEVER leave a question blank. If it is difficult to complete the questions on this section in the given amount of time, then practice doing passages at a slightly uncomfortable pace to get used to speeding up. If you tend to finish the section with a considerable amount of time left over, you may want to consider slowing yourself down a little to prevent picking trap answers and making silly mistakes.

PASSAGE-BASED STRATEGIES

As discussed in Overview of Biological Sciences, when approaching a passage, you can first decide if you want to complete it or skip to another passage that seems easier or covers a subject more familiar to you. Completing passages you find easier can build your confidence and increase the number of questions you get correct as well as help you with timing in the later stages of the section.

When you approach a passage, there are two ways to attack it: (1) read the passage or (2) don't read the passage. If you decide to read the passage, you then have to decide if you are going to peruse the questions first to get a sense of what will be asked of you or just dive right into the passage. One way is not necessarily better than the other; it depends on what works for you. If you read quickly and can get a good idea of what is happening in the passage, then reading first may suit you best. If you have difficulty reading long and/or scientific passages, you may benefit from the "search and destroy" method of going to the questions first and then trying to find the answer in the passage. The computer format of the MCAT may make the "search and destroy" option more difficult because you may have to scroll through the passage on the screen, whereas if you practice with a paper exam, the entire passage is staring at you on the page.

One efficient technique is to do a general quick read of the passage, aiming for an understanding of where the important items are located. Use your scratch paper to map out where in the passage topics appear. This could take the form of a couple words that describe the main idea of a paragraph, an illustration, or a chart or graph. The key is to get just enough information from the passage to center your mind on the general topics that the questions will address.

Within a passage, you should ALWAYS pay attention to **boldface** type, *italicized* words, phrases or words in parentheses, diagrams, graphs, and tables. These tend to be a source of at least one question for the passage. It could be a question asking you to interpret the graph or the data in the table. For graphs, make sure that you look at the units. Occasionally, the units in the question may be different than on the graph. The diagrams are important; they may be used to refamiliarize you with the anatomy of an organ system or to illustrate a technique, such as hemodialysis, with which you may not be familiar. If you are reading or scanning the passage, it is useful to use the CBT Highlight tool and highlight the terms, some of which are mentioned above, that seem important or key points of the passage. Generally speaking, it's important to highlight the names of enzymes, hormones, types of mutations, and hypotheses or theories. For the figures, tables, and graphs, it is important to note what information is contained in those items. There is no need to look at the information in detail until a question requires you to do so.

You should not feel intimidated if you come across a passage discussing a topic you've never heard of before taking the MCAT. Keep in mind that the MCAT is testing *fundamental* Biology principles, and this passage may be a way for the test writers to try to obfuscate those principles (such as ion movement down its gradient across a membrane). You may choose to Mark each question and skip the passage, and then hopefully return to it if time permits. This way you may have a fresh look at the passage. If you plan on skipping a passage, don't forget to select an answer for each question.

Here is a sample passage and question that shows how the MCAT might test a hypothesis-based question. Give it a try.

Treatment for the seizure disorder Infantile Spasms in children often includes administering either corticosteroids or adrenocorticotropic hormone (ACTH) which can act on the adrenal gland to release corticosteroids. In some cases, giving high doses of ACTH has been shown to be more effective than giving corticosteroids. Two general hypotheses have emerged for the mechanism of action of these treatments:

Hypothesis 1: Corticosteroids provide feedback onto receptors in the brain which suppress neuronal excitability and thus decrease the seizures. Therefore, ACTH is actually working through corticosteroids and not directly to suppress seizures.

Hypothesis 2: ACTH provides feedback directly onto receptors in the brain for ACTH which can suppress neuronal excitability and thus decrease seizures.

2. Which of the following best supports hypothesis 2?

A. Giving ACTH to convulsing rats in an experiment does not stop their seizures.
B. Giving corticosteroids to convulsing rats does reduce their seizure activity.
C. When high doses of radiolabeled ACTH are given to rats, they are shown to cross the blood brain barrier.
D. Giving corticosteroids to many children with Infantile Spasms does not suppress their seizures.

When the MCAT asks these types of questions, they generally give you two to four theories/hypotheses to compare and then ask you to pick an answer choice that supports or negates one of the hypotheses. There are some common wrong answer choices for which you should always be on the lookout while you search for the correct answer.

Med School Interviews, Part II
The golden rule for interviews is "Be yourself". What interviewers are trying to determine is what kind of person you are and how you relate to others. Questions are often open-ended, giving you the chance to direct the conversation toward your strengths and away from your weaknesses.

Source: *Best 168 Medical Schools*, 2008

For this question we are looking for a piece of information to support hypothesis 2, which states that ACTH acts directly on the brain to suppress seizures and does not work through a corticosteroid intermediate. Answer choice A says ACTH was given in an animal experiment and did not stop seizures. This answer choice is negating hypothesis 2, so it should be eliminated. Answer choice B says giving steroids to rats did reduce their seizures; this would actually support hypothesis 1, so it should be eliminated. Answer choice C says when high doses of ACTH are given, they are shown to cross the blood brain barrier, which would suggest that ACTH is able to get to the brain and act directly. This indeed is the answer and does support a mechanism with a direct action of ACTH on the brain.

It is always good to check every answer choice, as these types of questions are tricky and it is easy to be misled by an answer. Answer choice D says that giving corticosteroids to many children that have this disorder does not work to suppress their seizures, so this would actually fail to support hypothesis 1.

The common answer choices on questions like these are the following:

A. Supports the other hypothesis

B. Negates the other hypothesis

C. Does the reverse of what you are looking for (i.e., negates hypothesis in question if the question is asking for support)

D. Does nothing, so does not directly support or negate a particular hypothesis. Remember that if you are looking to disprove something, then an answer choice that is just a lack of support is not necessarily going to be the best answer.

QUESTION TYPES WITHIN THE PASSAGE

Within the passages there will be certain types of questions. If you find some of these question types easier than others, then it might help to complete the easier questions first in order to better acquaint yourself with the passage before tackling the hard questions. The first question types to look for are questions that only require memory and not content from the passage. These are the least common within the passage-based questions but do sometimes occur on the MCAT. Because they do not require reading the passage, they are often faster to complete.

The second easiest questions are often the ones that are shorter and/or have shorter answer choices. They tend to be more straightforward and take less time. Also, data analysis or reading graph questions can be less time consuming if you are proficient in those analytical skills.

The question types that seem to be the hardest and require the most time are: 1) long questions with long answer choices, 2) Roman numeral questions that are essentially three true/false questions in one, 3) LEAST/NOT/ EXCEPT questions, and 4) questions that introduce new information. While these tougher questions can be a challenge, they also represent an opportunity to separate yourself from the pack on the MCAT. Getting these questions correct can help propel you to the higher percentile scores. Also, if you recognize a question as a more difficult type, it can alert you to be wary of trap answers and pitfalls.

FREESTANDING QUESTION STRATEGIES

The freestanding questions are scattered throughout the section in clumps of two to five questions. These questions have absolutely nothing to do with any of the passages in the rest of the section. That is not to say that they cannot be on the same topic, such as a passage based on kidney function and a freestanding question asking you about tubular secretion of potassium. But they will require you to use knowledge you already have. Some test takers think of these freestanding questions as a relief from the tedium of passage-based questions. They certainly provide a nice break between long passages!

The general approach to these questions is fairly direct. POE is a very valuable tool for answering them. Often, there is one answer that is clearly wrong. Eliminating it increases your chances of getting the question right from 25% to 33%, and every little bit of advantage to you is valuable. The worrysome flip side to these freestanding questions is that a few may be "know something" questions for some test takers, but to you, they're "I know nothing" type questions. Because they tend to be fact-based questions, if you do not recall the fact, then answering the question correctly will prove to be difficult, especially if you cannot eliminate any answer choices. If this occurs, you should mark the question, select an answer, and move to the next question. Do not risk losing future points on the uncertain chance of getting one point.

EXAMPLES

Here are a few examples to help illustrate how to use some of the techniques discussed above.

1. Which of the following is a clear distinction between oogenesis and spermatogenesis?

   A. At the end, 4 ova and 1 spermatozoon are made.
   B. During the first meiotic division, the sister chromatids separate in oognesis, but the centromeres separate in spermatogenesis.
   C. In spermatogenesis, there is equal division of cytoplasm during cytokineses, whereas in oogenesis there is an unequal division.
   D. In spermatogenesis, 4 identical spermatozoa are made while only 1 viable oocyte is formed in oogenesis.

This is a "know something" type of question. You need to know the processes of gametogenesis and the differences between spermatogenesis and oogenesis. We'll go answer by answer and see if we can eliminate any answer choices.

Answer choice A: At the end, there are actually 4 spermatids and 1 ootid formed. The answer choice has it reversed, so we eliminate it. Answer choice B states that there is a difference in anaphase I in spermatogenesis and oogenesis. Since both are meiotic divisions, they should have identical anaphase I stages because that is the segregation of chromosomes. Therefore, we shall eliminate B. Answer choice C sounds really good. We remember that in oogenesis, we get 1 ootid and 3 polar bodies. A polar body is another daughter cell from the meiotic division; however, there is unequal cytokinesis resulting in the polar body getting the short end of the stick, that is, cytoplasm. During spermatogenesis, on the other hand, there is equal cytokinesis and therefore all the spermatids will have the same amount of cytoplasm. We'll hold onto answer choice C until we glance at D. Answer choice D looks good also. We remembered that spermatogenesis generates 4 spermatids and oogenesis only 1 ootid, but the answer specifies "identical spermatozoa." We should also remember that the purpose of meiosis is to generate genetic diversity in the gametocytes; therefore, the spermatozoa should NOT be identical. As a result, answer D is incorrect and we eliminate it, leaving us with C as the correct answer.

Ready for another example? Here we go:

2. In the disease celiac sprue, most of the brush border of the small intestines is destroyed. Which of the following would be impaired?

   I. Conversion of trypsinogen into trypsin
   II. Secretion of cholecystokinin
   III. Digestion of lactose

   A. III only
   B. I and III only
   C. II and III only
   D. I, II, and III

Well, this is one of those I/II/III types of questions. So, the first thing we do is glance at our answer choices to see if there is one particular roman numeral present in all of the answers. Lo and behold, there is! Roman numeral III is found in each answer choice; therefore, it HAS to be right. We don't even need to think about it, because we know it is true.

So, now we have to figure out I and II. Let's look at I: "Conversion of trypsinogen into trypsin." We need to remember that the enzyme that catalyzes this reaction is enterokinase. Enterokinase is located in the brush border of the duodenum. If celiac sprue destroys the brush border, then anything that is normally located there will not be present. Therefore, enterokinase will not be present and cannot convert trypsinogen into trypsin. So, statement I is true. As a result, we eliminate A and C (since neither contain I).

Statement II states "Secretion of cholecystokinin." CCK, as it is fondly known, is an intestinal hormone that causes the gallbladder to contract and release its secretions into the duodenum. Because it is a hormone, it needs to travel through the blood from its origin (duodenal cell) to its target cells (gallbladder). If it travels through the blood, then it does not originate in the brush border. Therefore, statement II is false and consequently, we eliminate D, leaving us with B as the correct answer.

Okay, one last question and then you should try some on your own.

3. Zifturon is a drug that blocks the release of calcium from the sarcoplasmic reticulum in skeletal muscle cells. Which of the following would you expect to see after administration of zifturon?

   A. Increased rate of contraction of the skeletal muscle resulting in tetany
   B. Impaired release of myosin heads from the actin chain
   C. Increased strength of contraction of the skeletal muscle
   D. Impaired attachment of the myosin heads to the actin chain

This is a difficult question. It requires us to incorporate and analyze new information in the construct of muscle contraction. We need to remember the purpose of calcium and the sarcoplasmic reticulum in skeletal muscle cells. Calcium is necessary for binding to the troponin portion of actin. This binding causes a conformational change in the troponin-tropomyosin complex, allowing the myosin binding sites on actin to become exposed. Once exposed, these myosin binding sites are quickly filled by the myosin heads and muscle contraction ensues.

If zifturon inhibits the release of calcium, then it is, in effect, inhibiting muscle contraction. Answer choice A states that there will be more contraction. We know that cannot be correct because the drug essentially blocks muscle contraction. Therefore, we eliminate A. Answer choice B states impaired release of myosin. We need to remember that this step depends on the presence of ATP, not calcium. We eliminate B. Answer choice C states increased strength of contraction. In order to increase the strength of skeletal muscle contraction, we need to have more muscle cells contracting. Because we know that there is impaired muscle contraction, this cannot be the correct answer and C is eliminated. Hopefully, D is correct. Answer choice D states exactly what we remembered regarding the action of calcium and troponin. D is correct.

So You've Been Accepted!

Here are some some factors to consider:
- How much the school values teaching versus research
- Quality of student life
- Quality of the residents (they'll often be the ones teaching you)
- Availability of research opportunities
- Teaching methodology used

Source: *Best 168 Medical Schools,* 2008

ACHIEVE A GOOD BALANCE OF STUDY AND PRACTICE

Preparing for the Biology portion of the MCAT requires a substantial review of material and learning how to apply your knowledge to the reasoning-based questions that appear on the test. The MCAT is not about regurgitation, so just memorizing a bunch of facts is not enough to do well on it. It is important that after studying a particular Biology topic you practice applying the information to MCAT practice questions and passages to assess your ability to retain and apply the information. It is also important to practice completing the passages and questions on the computer using the CBT tools such as Highlighting, Strikeout, and Mark for review functions.

In general, while taking a practice test or timed Biology section, you should not do anything you will not be able to do on the actual MCAT in order to gauge appropriately where you are at score-wise. That means skip the Notes function on the practice MCAT and get used to annotating on scratch paper instead. Likewise, avoid the Search function and practice scanning a passage with your eyes for the information you seek.

Chapter 21
Mastery Applied:
Biology Practice

Ah, your last set of practice questions in *MCAT Workout*! All good things must come to an end, right? As with previous Mastery Applied chapters, this one gives you several passages and freestanding questions on which to try out the strategies discussed in the book and determine those concepts on which you need to spend additional time studying. The number of passages and freestanding questions presented here for biology exceeds that which you will encounter on the actual MCAT in order to give you comprehensive practice. Enjoy your final workout!

Passage I (Questions 1–7)

Proteins are separated primarily due to differences in charge. The net charge depends on the number of acidic and basic amino acids in the protein and on the pH of the solution. For each protein, there is some unique pH at which the net charge on the molecule is zero. If electrophoresis is carried out at this pH, known as the isoelectric point, the protein remains stationary. If the electrophoresis buffer has a pH above the pI of the protein, that protein will be negatively charged and migrate toward the anode. An example of gel electrophoresis using two different pH media is shown in Figure 1.

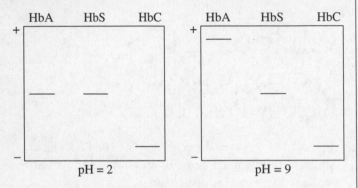

Figure 1 Gel electrophoresis of different hemoglobins at pH of 2 and pH of 9

Hemoglobin, the erythrocytic protein which transports oxygen in the human body, exists in five distinct forms: Hemoglobin A, A_2, F, S, and C. Hemoglobin A (Hb A) is the normal adult hemoglobin and accounts for 97–98% of the hemoglobin in the adult. Hb A contains two identical α-globin chains, each with 141 amino acids, and two identical β-globin chains, each with 146 residues. Thus, the formula for the Hb A tetramer can be written as $\alpha_2\beta_2$. Each globin chain is associated with an iron-containing heme group, a nonprotein component that is the site of oxygen binding. Hemoglobin A_2 (Hb A_2), accounting for 2–3% of hemoglobin in the normal adult, contains two α chains and two δ chains, the latter having β-like sequences. The δ chain differs from the β chain in only 10 of its 146 amino acids. The formula for Hb A_2 is $\alpha_2\delta_2$. The predominant hemoglobin from the eighth week of development until birth is fetal hemoglobin (Hb F). Hb F contains two α chains and two γ chains, the latter being analogous to the β chains. The γ chain differs from the β chain in 39 of its 146 amino acids. Hb F can be represented as $\alpha_2\gamma_2$. By the time a normal infant is about six months old, very little Hb F remains in the blood. Only in individuals with certain inherited blood disorders in which the β chain is not synthesized is Hb F still produced in appreciable quantities throughout adult life.

The first abnormal hemoglobin to be studied at the molecular level was sickle-cell hemoglobin (Hb S), which is responsible for sickle-cell anemia, a serious heritable disease that occurs primarily in individuals of African ancestry. In afflicted individuals, the red blood cells have an abnormal morphology; instead of being biconcave disks, the erythrocytes are crescent- or sickle-shaped. The misshapen cells block small blood vessels, damaging internal organs, and are short-lived, resulting in anemia. At the protein level, the difference between Hb A and Hb S is but a single amino acid in each β chain. Specifically, at the sixth position from the α-amino end, glutamic acid is replaced by valine. If we designate the abnormal β chain as β^s, the Hb S tetramer can be written as $\alpha_2\beta^s_2$. A much rarer variant is hemoglobin C (Hb C), which is responsible for hemoglobin C disease, a less serious condition than sickle-cell anemia. The molecular basis for Hb C also involves a change at the sixth position of each β chain; instead of a glutamic acid, there is a lysine. The Hb C tetramer can be written as $\alpha_2\beta^c_2$.

The table below gives the tetrameric formulas of the aforementioned hemoglobins and summarizes differences in the primary structure of the β chains and differences in isoelectric points.

Hemoglobin	Chain Formula	β_6 position	pI
Hb A	$\alpha_2\beta_2$	Glutamic acid	6.93
Hb A_2	$\alpha_2\delta_2$	Glutamic acid	7.22
Hb F	$\alpha_2\gamma_2$	Glutamic acid	7.00
Hb S	$\alpha_2\beta^s_2$	Valine	7.10
Hb C	$\alpha_2\beta^c_2$	Lysine	7.28

Table 1 Comparison of various characteristics of different types of hemoglobin

A medical student runs a gel electrophoresis on three different samples of patient's blood in order to determine the various hemoglobins present in these samples. The results are shown below.

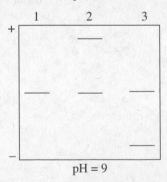

Figure 2 Student-run gel electrophoresis of the hemoglobins found in three different patients

1. Which of the following is true regarding hemoglobin?

   A. It exhibits quaternary protein structure.
   B. It carries one molecule of oxygen.
   C. It is found in both red blood cells and skeletal muscle cells.
   D. Its central iron atom is oxidized from 3^+ to 2^+ when oxygen binds.

2. Which of the following describes the mutation that creates Hb C instead of Hb A?

   A. Conversion from a non-polar to a polar amino acid
   B. Conversion from a polar to a non-polar amino acid
   C. Conversion from a non-polar to another non-polar amino acid
   D. Conversion from a polar to another polar amino acid

3. Which of the following accurately explains the difference between the gel electrophoreses in pH of 9 and pH of 2?

   A. Hb A has an acidic side chain which is deprotonated at pH of 9 and therefore migrates toward the cathode.
   B. Hb S has an acidic side chain which is neutral at pH of 9 and therefore does not migrate to either pole.
   C. Hb C has an alkaline side chain which is protonated at pH of 2 and therefore migrates to the anode.
   D. Hb A is less acidic at pH of 2 and therefore is neutral and does not migrate to either pole.

4. During oxidative stresses, Hb S can cause the affected red blood cells to sickle. The spleen is very vascular and is responsible for removing old or damaged red blood cells. Recurrent sickling can cause blockage of blood flow in the spleen, resulting ultimately in death of splenic cells. Which of the following would result from destruction of the spleen?

   A. Impaired ability to synthesize red blood cells
   B. Impaired ability to fight off encapsulated bacteria
   C. Impaired digestion
   D. Increased red blood cell destruction

5. Based on the electrophoresis gels run on the patients' blood specimens, which type of hemoglobin is present in patient 2?

   I. Hb A
   II. Hb S
   III. Hb C

   A. I and II only
   B. I and III only
   C. II and III only
   D. I, II, and III

6. Hydroxyurea is a medication that can increase the concentration of Hb F made in an adult. Would this medication be useful to a patient with sickle cell disease?

   A. No, because the defect in sickle cell disease affects the β-chain of hemoglobin and consequently, Hb F will sickle also.
   B. No, because unlike Hb A, the Hb F would not carry oxygen.
   C. Yes, because the Hb F, which can carry oxygen, will not sickle.
   D. Yes, because Hb F will carry more oxygen than Hb A.

7. In which of the following diseases would an increase in Hb F concentration be expected in the adult?

   A. α-thalassemia, where there is a genetic defect in the production of α-chains of hemoglobin
   B. β-thalassemia, where there is a genetic defect in the production of β-chains of hemoglobin
   C. Chronic kidney disease, where there is a decrease in the production of erythropoietin
   D. Pernicious anemia, where a deficiency in vitamin B_{12} causes abnormal red blood cell production

Passage II (Questions 8–13)

The Human Immunodfeciency Virus (HIV) is an example of an enveloped retrovirus. The envelope is studded with two main glycoproteins: gp120 and gp41. These glycoproteins facilitate fusion and entry into a new cell with the assistance of a cell receptor, the CD4 receptor. Once HIV has entered the new cell, the viral RNA genome must be converted to DNA. HIV must carry its own copy of reverse transcriptase, the enzyme that converts RNA to DNA, since reverse transcription is not a normal part of the human cell's genetic processes. The nucleotides used to form the new DNA came from the host's pool of nucleotides. After reverse transcription, the DNA is then integrated into the host's genome through the use of the viral enzyme integrase. The viral genome is now a part of the host's genome, and it is now subjected to transcription and translation, as these are normal cellular processes for the host cell. New viral proteins are made and then cleaved into smaller, functional proteins—such as glycoprotein (gp) 120 and gp41—by the viral enzyme protease. New viral particles are assembled in the host's cytoplasm, and then the new particles bud off, encasing themselves in host plasma membrane.

There are several medications that target different parts of the HIV life cycle. One main class of antiretrovirals is reverse transcriptase inhibitors. This class can be further subdivided into nucleoside and non-nucleoside based on their structures. An example of a nucleoside reverse transcription inhibitor is 3'-Azidothymidine (AZT). AZT is a thymidine analogue that is lacking the 3' hydroxyl group necessary for elongation of the growing DNA chain. Because AZT is a thymidine analogue, it could also be utilized during the host cell's normal replication. This would result in arrest of host replication, ultimately resulting in the death of the cell. This cellular death is responsible for some of the side effects seen with the administration of AZT, namely suppression of bone marrow cellular development. Efavirenz is a non-nucleoside reverse transcriptase inhibitor because it binds at an allosteric site on the reverse transcriptase to inhibit its function. Efavirenz is not a nucleoside analogue. Therefore, it cannot be utilized in the normal host cell's DNA replication process. As a result, the main side effect associated with efavirenz is vivid hallucinations, a consequence of the drug's ability to cross the blood-brain barrier.

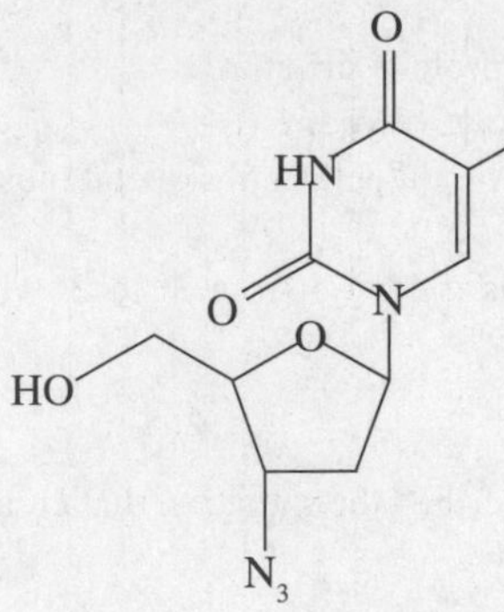

Azidothymidine (AZT) 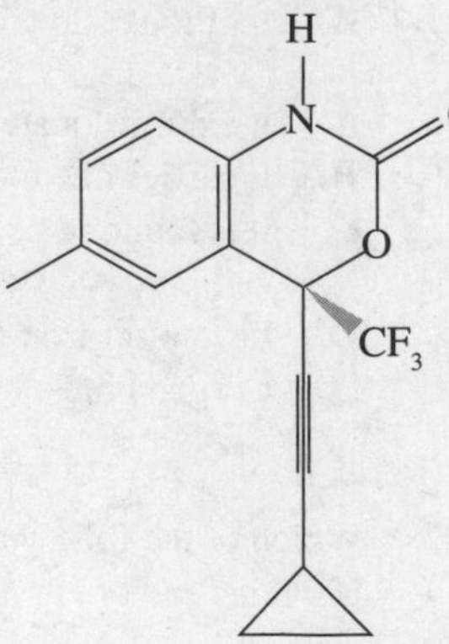   Efavirenz

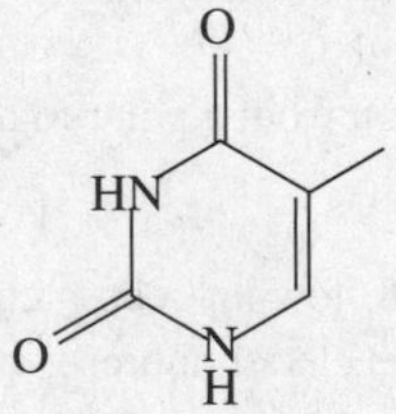

Thymine

Figure 1 Diagrams of HIV Drugs

8. Which of the following is reverse transcriptase?

   A. DNA-dependent DNA polymerase
   B. DNA-dependent RNA polymerase
   C. RNA-dependent DNA polymerase
   D. RNA-dependent RNA polymerase

9. Nevirapine is an example of a non-nucleoside reverse transcriptase inhibitor. Which of the following is true of nevirapine?

   A. It is a competitive antagonist of reverse transcriptase.
   B. It is a noncompetitive antagonist of reverse transcriptase.
   C. It is an uncompetitive antagonist of reverse transcriptase.
   D. Its effect on reverse transcriptase can be reversed with increasing concentrations of adenine, thymine, cytosine, and guanine.

10. Human T-cell Lymphotropic Virus (HTLV) is very similar to HIV. Which of the following would be true regarding HTLV?

   I. HTLV exhibits a lysogenic life cycle.
  II. HTLV is a retrovirus.
 III. HTLV destroys the antibody-producing cells.

  A. I and II only
  B. I and III only
  C. II and III only
  D. I, II, and III

11. Atazanavir is an example of a protease inhibitor. It causes all the following events in cells that take it up EXCEPT:

  A. cessation of HIV replication.
  B. fewer helper T-lymphocytes being killed.
  C. direct inhibition of the enzyme that incorporates the viral DNA into the host's DNA.
  D. lack of gp120 and gp41.

12. Which of the following is the product of reverse transcriptase activity on the following piece of RNA?

5'-AUGGUACAUACUUGC-3'

  A. 5'-UACCAUGUAUGAACG-3'
  B. 5'-GCAAGUAUGUACCAU-3'
  C. 5'-TACCATGTATGAACG-3'
  D. 5'-GCAAGTATGTACCAT-3'

13. The molecular structure of stavudine, another HIV medication, is shown below.

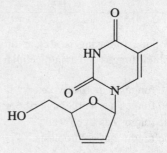

Stavudine

Which of the following is true regarding stavudine?

  A. It is a non-nucleoside antagonist.
  B. It is a nucleoside antagonist.
  C. It will block viral RNA synthesis.
  D. It will not affect mammalian cell replication.

_____

Questions 14 through 18 are NOT based on a descriptive passage.

14. Which of the following is a clear difference between a multicellular fungus and a multicellular animal?

    A. The fungus is a prokaryote.
    B. The fungus has a 50S large ribosome subunit.
    C. The fungus has a cell wall.
    D. The fungus has chloroplasts.

15. Cyanide is a poison that inhibits complex IV of the electron transport chain. Which of the following occurs as a result of cyanide poisoning?

    A. Energy formation from the oxidation of $FADH_2$ but not from NADH
    B. Transfer of the final pair of electrons to oxygen to form water
    C. Components of the electron transport chain will ultimately be in their reduced forms
    D. Uncoupling of the resolution of the proton gradient and ATP synthesis

16. Which of the following is/are derived from ectoderm?

    I. Cornea
    II. Adrenal medulla
    III. Cerebellum

    A. III only
    B. I and II only
    C. II and III only
    D. I, II, and III

17. The smooth muscle that encircles arteries and arterioles contains α_1-adrenergic receptors. Which of the following would be expected if an α_1-adrenergic antagonist is administered?

    A. Increased systemic blood pressure
    B. Decreased systemic blood pressure
    C. Decreased cardiac muscle contraction
    D. Decreased stroke volume

18. The fetal great vessels, the aorta and pulmonary artery, are connected via a structure known as the ductus arteriosus. Which of the following is a correct explanation for fetal circulation through the ductus arteriosus?

    A. Blood flows from the pulmonary artery to the aorta because of greater systemic arterial pressure.
    B. Blood flows from the aorta to the pulmonary artery because of greater systemic arterial pressure.
    C. Blood flows from the pulmonary artery to the aorta because of greater pulmonary artery pressure.
    D. Blood flows from the aorta to the pulmonary artery because of greater pulmonary blood pressure.

Passage III (Questions 19–25)

The most common abnormalities of chromosome number are trisomies. These occur when there are three representatives of a particular chromosome instead of the usual two. Trisomy can be present in all cells or may occur in mosaic form. Most people with trisomies exhibit a consistent and specific phenotype depending on the chromosome involved. The most common trisomy is trisomy 21, also known as Down syndrome. Trisomy 21 occurs with a frequency of about 1 in 625. Some of the characteristic clinical findings include mental retardation, hypotonia, blind-ending jejunum, and heart malformations, including a common arterial trunk coming off both the left and right ventricles. There is also an increased risk of developing leukemia and early-onset Alzheimer's dementia.

Trisomy 13, also known as Patau syndrome, occurs with a frequency of 1 in 10,000 births. Clinical features include a midline cleft lip, holoprosencephaly (a brain malformation characterized by failure of the forebrain to develop in the embryo), and cardiac malformations including a defect in the interventricular septum. Trisomy 18, also known as Edwards syndrome, occurs with a frequency of 1 in 6,000 births. Characteristic clinical features include underdeveloped cranium, small recessed chin, small kidneys, and cardiac malformations including pulmonic valvular stenosis.

Turner's syndrome and Klinefelter's syndrome are examples of abnormal numbers of the sex chromosomes. In Turner's syndrome, there is only one X chromosome. Given the absence of the Y chromosome, there is no testicular development, and the child will consequently develop as a female. Clinical characteristics include underdevelopment of the ovaries, a fluid-filled cyst in the neck (cystic hygroma), and a narrowing of the aoric arch (coarctation). Klinefelter's syndrome has an extra X chromosome. Since a Y chromosome is present, testes will develop. The testes produce the Mullerian inhibitory substance, which causes the regression of the internal female genital structures. The testes produce testosterone which will stimulate androgen receptors and promote the development of internal and external male genital structures. Clinical features of Klinefelter's syndrome include tall stature, small testes, and gynecomastia (the increased growth of breast tissue in men).

19. Which of the following is the most likely explanation for the occurrence of trisomies?

- **A.** Nondisjunction
- **B.** Incomplete dominance
- **C.** Deletion
- **D.** Mutation

20. In a given population, what is the frequency of carriers of Patau syndrome?

- **A.** 1/100
- **B.** 198/10000
- **C.** 9801/10000
- **D.** None of the above.

21. Which of the following is expected to be true of children with Down syndrome?

- **A.** Aortic arterial blood carbon dioxide concentration is normal.
- **B.** Aortic arterial blood oxygen saturation is lower than normal.
- **C.** Pulmonary arterial blood pressure is lower than normal.
- **D.** Pulmonary arterial blood oxygen saturation is lower than normal.

22. A woman who is 20 weeks pregnant presents for an amniocentesis. With a needle and ultrasound guidance, the physician withdraws some of the amniotic fluid for genetic analysis. A karyotype analysis performed on the amnioitic fluid reveals an extra copy of chromosome 21. Which of the following is true of the child after birth?

- **A.** Kidney function will be impaired since the kidneys are underdeveloped.
- **B.** Digestion will be impaired since there is no communication between the small and large intestines.
- **C.** Sensory neural input will be diminished since there is no development of the sensory cortex.
- **D.** Muscle tone will be greater than expected.

23. Which of the following karyotypes is characteristic for Klinefelter's syndrome?

- **A.** 46, XY
- **B.** 45, XO
- **C.** 47, XYY
- **D.** 47, XXY

24. Which of the following structures is/are part of the Mullerian system?

    I. Ovaries
   II. Uterus
  III. Urethra

    A. II only
    B. I and II only
    C. I and III only
    D. I, II, and III

25. Which of the following is a common feature of people with Down, Patau, Edwards, and Klinefelter's syndromes?

    A. They all have heart defects.
    B. They all have 47 chromosomes.
    C. They are all male.
    D. They all have a low life expectancy.

_____

Passage IV (Questions 26–30)

The kidneys and lungs play a critical role in regulating the acid-base status of the body. The pH of the blood must be tightly controlled to maintain a narrow physiological range of 7.35 to 7.45. Acidemia refers to a pH of blood that is more acidic than normal, and alkalemia refers to a pH of blood that is more basic than normal. Acidosis refers to the process by which an acidemia is created, and alkalosis refers to the process that creates an alkalemia. Acidoses and alkaloses are classified based on the primary defect that causes those situations. A *respiratory acidosis* occurs when there is a decreased rate of breathing that causes a buildup of CO_2 in the blood. Increased concentrations of CO_2 in the blood cause more acid production, as evidenced by equation 1 below. Consequently, a *respiratory alkalosis* is caused by an increased rate of breathing which causes a decrease in CO_2 in the blood.

$$H_2O + CO_2 \longleftrightarrow H_2CO_3 \longleftrightarrow H^+ + HCO_3^-$$

Equation 1

The administration of opiate medications, such as morphine, can induce a respiratory acidosis.

The bicarbonate ions (HCO_3^-) are conjugate bases of the carbonic acid. Therefore, if the kidneys reabsorb more HCO_3^-, then a *metabolic alkalosis* may result. When the kidneys increase the secretion of HCO_3^-, a *metabolic acidosis* results. A metabolic acidosis can also occur if the body increases the production of acids in the blood, such as in ketoacidosis from either diabetes or from a carbohydrate-free diet. Ingestion of ethylene glycol, the compound found in antifreeze, can cause a metabolic acidosis. Diarrhea is an example of a cause of metabolic alkalosis.

The compensatory efforts of the lungs and kidneys counter the primary defect that caused the alkalosis or acidosis. If the primary cause was respiratory, the kidneys will compensate by either secreting more or reabsorbing more HCO_3^-. If the primary defect was metabolic, the lungs will compensate by either hyperventilating or hypoventilating. The respiratory compensation is more rapid, occurring within minutes as compared to hours to days for the kidneys.

26. Which portion of the nephron is permeable only to water?

A. Proximal convoluted tubule
B. Descending loop of Henle
C. Ascending loop of Henle
D. Distal convoluted tubule

27. During strenuous exercise, aerobic metabolism often converts to anaerobic metabolism with the consequent buildup of lactate. Which of the following will result?

A. Respiratory acidosis
B. Respiratory alkalosis
C. Metabolic acidosis
D. Metabolic alkalosis

28. Meperidine is an opioid-like medication used for pain control. Which of the following compensatory effects would be expected after long-term consistent use of meperidine?

A. Hyperventilation
B. Hypoventilation
C. Increased HCO_3^- secretion
D. Increased HCO_3^- reabsorption

29. Which of the following could cause a metabolic acidosis?

I. Anaerobic metabolism
II. Vomiting
III. Ethylene glycol

A. III only
B. I and II only
C. I and III only
D. I, II, and III

30. Overdosing on acetylsalicylic acid can cause a metabolic acidosis as well as hyperventilation. Which of the following is true?

A. Blood pH will likely be 7.2.
B. Little compensation is needed to correct the acid-base disturbance.
C. Blood pH will likely be 7.6.
D. The kidneys will need to secrete more HCO_3^- to compensate for the acid-base disturbance.

31. Folic acid is essential in the proper normal development of the neural tube in utero. Which of the following would be impaired if there was a deficiency in folic acid?

    I. Development of the spinal column
    II. Development of the cerebrum
    III. Development of the medulla oblongata

    A. I and II only
    B. I and III only
    C. II and III only
    D. I, II, and III

32. Angiotensin II causes selective vasoconstriction of the efferent arteriole in the kidney. Which of the following would be expected to occur if there was an increase in concentration of angiotensin II?

    A. Increased glomerular filtration
    B. Decreased glomerular filtration
    C. Increased red blood cells in the proximal convoluted tubule
    D. Decreased red blood cells in the proximal convoluted tubule

33. In the autoimmune disease Grave's disease, the body produces antibodies that bind and stimulate the thyroid stimulating hormone (TSH) receptors located on the thyroid gland. Which of the following physiologic processes would you expect to occur in someone with Grave's disease?

    A. Increased skeletal muscle activity
    B. Increased basal metabolic rate
    C. Decreased basal metabolic rate
    D. Decreased skeletal muscle activity

34. Which of the following is NOT a possible blood type of a child born to parents who both have blood type AB?

    A. A
    B. AB
    C. O
    D. None, all of the blood types are possible

35. The frequency of the dominant black fur allele in a population of guinea pigs is 0.6, while the frequency of the recessive white fur is 0.4. The frequency of the recessive allele short whiskers is 0.2. What is the probability of having a guinea pig with short whiskers and white fur?

    A. 0.0064
    B. 0.08
    C. 0.16
    D. 0.20

Passage V (Questions 36–41)

Cystic fibrosis is a disease caused by a defect in the chloride ion channel in cell membranes. The gene is located on chromosome 7, and the gene codes for the cystic fibrosis transmembrane regulator protein (CFTR). The protein allows for the exchange of chloride ions into a cell. A defective protein, as can occur with a missense mutation at the 508 position, will result in thick mucous or overly salty sweat. Thickened mucous can cause plugging in areas such as the lungs, resulting in impaired air exchange at the level of the alveoli. Thickened mucous in the respiratory tree not only causes decreased oxygen transfer but can also provide a growth media for certain bacteria, such as *Pseudomonas aeruginosa*. Recurrent bacterial infections result in further impaired pulmonary function, and they serve as one of the primary causes of death in those suffering from cystic fibrosis. Thickened mucous can also collect in the exocrine ducts of the pancreas. As a result, the digestive enzymes may result in autodestruction of the pancreas, ultimately rendering the individual malnourished. Pancreatic destruction also causes dysregulation of glucose homeostasis. Without adequate nutrition and glucose metabolism, overall growth tends to be stunted.

Cystic fibrosis is the most common inherited lethal disease of Caucasians. It is an autosomal recessive disorder, occurring with a frequency of 1 in 3600. The persistence of the diseased allele is due to the protection from cholera. Cholera occurs secondary to an exotoxin that is elaborated by the bacterium *Vibrio cholerae*. The exotoxin causes an overstimulation of a sodium-chlorine symport channel on the surface of intestinal cells. Activation of this channel causes massive efflux of sodium and chlorine into the lumen of the intestines. This high osmolar concentration of salt induces the secretion of water into the intestinal tract. The high osmolar concentration and amounts of water lead to massive watery diarrhea. With continued secretion of sodium chloride and watery diarrhea, an affected person is at great risk for dehydration. In cystic fibrosis, since there is a defective chloride ion channel, the cholera toxin cannot exert its effects. This results in protection for people living in those areas where the prevalence of cholera is quite high.

Two medical students, who are interested in microbiology, conducted a retrospective analysis of sputum cultures of patients with cystic fibrosis who were admitted to their hospital over the past six months. Their data appears next.

Organism	Number of Positive Cultures
Gram-Positive	160
Staphylococcus aureus	120
Methicillin-susceptible	5
Methicillin-resistant	115
Streptococcus pneumoniae	20
Gram-Negative	180
Pseudomonas aeruginosa	130
Acinetobacter baumanii	20
Klebsiella pneumoniae	20
Serratia marcescens	10
Fungi	5

Table 1 Number of positive sputum cultures based on mircoorganism detected

36. Which of the following is characteristic of Gram-negative bacteria?

 A. Their cell wall has no peptidoglycan.
 B. They always have flagella.
 C. They have a periplasmic "intermembrane space" between their outer and inner membranes.
 D. They have multiple copies of their circular DNA to facilitate genetic transfer of resistance to other bacteria.

37. In a population of 18,000 Caucasians, how many are expected to be carriers of cystic fibrosis?

 A. 50
 B. 295
 C. 590
 D. 1180

38. After an adult with cystic fibrosis ingests a carbohydrate-rich meal, which of the following would you expect to occur?

 A. High intracellular concentration of glucose
 B. Increased secretion of insulin
 C. Increased secretion of glucagon
 D. High extracellular concentration of glucose

39. Based on the data collected from the medical students' study, what percentage of the isolates were methicillin-resistant *Staphylococcus aureus*?

- **A.** 115/120
- **B.** 115/160
- **C.** 115/345
- **D.** 115/785

40. If a patient with cystic fibrosis receives a double-lung transplant from a non-cystic fibrosis donor, would the new lungs be expected to develop cystic fibrosis?

- **A.** Yes, once you have cystic fibrosis, it develops in every organ of the body.
- **B.** Yes, since the primary defect is with respiratory secretions.
- **C.** No, because the infectious causes of the disease will be removed when the old lungs are taken out.
- **D.** No, since cystic fibrosis is due to a gene defect, the cells of the new lungs will have the normal CFTR gene.

41. There is no known pharmacologic therapy for cholera. One of the supportive therapies is oral rehydration solution of simple sugar and salt water. Which of the following is an accurate explanation as to the benefit of oral rehydration?

- **A.** The intestines are secreting large amounts of salt and water, and the cells are salt-deprived; therefore, ingested salt will be avidly absorbed by cells, and water will naturally follow.
- **B.** The intestines cannot absorb proteins without salt; therefore, ingestion of salt will allow proper balanced nutrition.
- **C.** The massive loss of water causes the body to be dehydrated; any solution containing water will be absorbed, but adding sugar and salt improve the taste of the solution.
- **D.** Salt and sugar will provide the additional calories needed during the acute infection because the cholera bacteria are depleting the host's energy supply.

Passage VI (Questions 42–47)

There are several forms of androgen insensitivity syndrome (AIS) resulting in male pseudo-hermaphroditism, one of which is an X-linked defect of receptor function known as complete AIS. In this disorder, affected persons are chromosomal males with apparently normal female external genitalia but no internal genitalia. The incidence of AIS is about 2 in 20,000 live births. Axillary and pubic hair is sparse. As the alternative name "testicular feminization" indicates, testes are present either within the abdomen or in the inguinal canal, where they are sometimes mistaken for hernias in infants who otherwise appear to be normal females. Although the testes secrete androgen normally, there is end-organ unresponsiveness to androgens resulting from absence of androgen receptors in the appropriate target cells. The receptor protein, specified by the normal allele at the X-linked receptor locus, has the role of forming a complex with testosterone and dihydrotestosterone. If the complex fails to form, the hormone cannot enter the nucleus, become attached to chromatin, and stimulate the transcription of the messenger RNAs required for differentiation in the male direction.

Several variants of AIS, some with milder expression, may be allelic to the classical form. The molecular defect has been determined in several cases and ranges from a complete deletion of the gene on the X-chromosome to point mutations in the steroid-binding domain of the androgen receptor protein.

In contrast to "testicular feminization," congenital adrenal hyperplasia (CAH) may be a cause of female pseudo-hermaphroditism, a "masculinization syndrome." Since the adrenal glands normally contribute a small amount to the homeostatic levels of sex hormones in the body, overproduction of these glands has the potential to alter the normal genetically-determined development. Girls born with CAH may appear to have slightly male or ambiguous genitalia, since an overproduction of androgens from the adrenal glands can "masculinize" the peripheral tissues. In Figure 1, the adrenal hormone synthesis pathways are outlined, with the respective catalyzing enzymes. Most biochemical defects in the synthesis pathways arise from enzyme deficiencies. When a specific enzyme is deficient, then the substrate must opt for another pathway, thereby increasing the concentration of other hormones. The most common enzymatic deficiency causing CAH is 21-hydroxylase. This results in an overproduction of androgens. Consequently, the clinical features characteristic of CAH due to 21-hydroxylase deficiency includes masculinization of peripheral tissues.

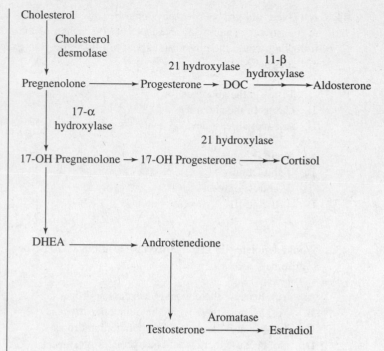

DHEA = Dehydroepiandrosterone
DOC = Deoxycorticosterone

Figure 1 Pathway for the biosynthesis of endogenous steroid hormones in the adrenal gland

42. Which of the following is true regarding the menstrual cycle and hormones in the female?

   A. A spike in estrogen directly causes the ovulation of the egg cell from the ovary.
   B. Progesterone peaks immediately prior to ovulation.
   C. Follicle-stimulating hormone levels are highest following menses.
   D. Luteinizing hormone levels peak as a result of ovulation.

43. What is the probability that a normal woman who has a son with AIS gives birth to a daughter with AIS if the father is normal?

   A. 0%
   B. 25%
   C. 50%
   D. 100%

44. A 17-year-old girl sees her physician because she has yet to menstruate. The physician suspects AIS. Which of the following would the physician expect to find if the young girl does have AIS?

    I.   Testes in the abdomen
   II. Uterus in the abdomen
 III. Adequate breast development

    A.   I and II only
    B.   I and III only
    C.   II and III only
    D.   I, II, and III

45. Would deficiency in 11β-hydroxylase result in a CAH-type syndrome?

    A.   Yes, because there would be excess androgens.
    B.   Yes, because there would be deficient estrogens.
    C.   No, because there would be deficient androgens.
    D.   No, because there would be excess progestins.

46. Based on the information presented in the passage, which of the following receptors are most responsible for the development of external genitalia?

    A.   Dihydrotestosterone
    B.   17β-estradiol
    C.   Progesterone
    D.   Aldosterone

47. Which of the following is most responsible for the hypokalemia associated with 17α-hydroxylase deficiency?

    A.   Higher than normal levels of cortisol
    B.   Higher than normal levels of aldosterone
    C.   Lower than normal levels of aldosterone
    D.   Lower than normal levels of cortisol

Questions 48 through 52 are NOT based on a descriptive passage.

48. Furosemide is a diuretic that acts on the ascending loop of Henle. Which of the following effects is expected in a person who was taking furosemide?

    A.   Increased reabsorption of water in the ascending loop of Henle
    B.   Increased reabsorption of water in the collecting duct
    C.   Decreased reabsorption of sodium ions in the ascending loop of Henle
    D.   Decreased excretion of sodium ions in the ascending loop of Henle

49. Which of the following neurotransmitter and receptor combinations on a post-synaptic neuron would elicit an action potential?

    A.   Acetylcholine opening a potassium ion channel
    B.   Gamma-aminobutyric acid opening a chloride ion channel
    C.   Dopamine opening a sodium channel
    D.   Serotonin preventing the opening of a calcium channel

50. Captopril is a medication that inhibits angiotensin-converting enzyme. Which of the following series of effects would be expected with the administration of captopril?

	Angiotensin I	Angiotensin II	Vascular Smooth Muscle
A.	Increased	Increased	Contraction
B.	Increased	Decreased	Contraction
C.	Increased	Decreased	Relaxation
D.	Decreased	Decreased	Relaxation

51. A penetrating knife injury to the thoracic cavity results in a pneumothorax where atmospheric air enters the cavity and compresses the lung. Which of the following is the best explanation for the development of a pneumothorax?

A. The injury causes a greater negative pressure in the pleural cavity causing the lungs to collapse.

B. The injury causes a greater positive pressure in the pleural cavity causing the lungs to expand.

C. The injury destroys the negative pressure within the pleural space causing the lung to collapse.

D. The injury destroys the positive pressure within the pleural space causing the lung to collapse.

52. What stages of meiosis has an egg cell completed when it is finally ovulated?

A. Up to prophase I
B. Up to anaphase I
C. Complete meiosis I
D. Complete meiosis II

_____

Passage VII (Questions 53–58)

The excretory system of a vertebrate is comprised of a pair of kidneys, each connected by a ureter to the urinary bladder, which is connected to a urethra through which the stored urine is eliminated. The excretory system functions to maintain homeostasis of the body through regulation of the composition and volume of blood. Consequently, the kidneys are highly vascularized. Solutes are selectively removed from the blood by filtration and secretion, and then they are carried from the body in varying amounts of water as urine.

The functional unit of a kidney is the nephron. Collectively, the nephrons of an adult human produce about 175 liters of filtrate daily. This is accomplished by forcing fluid out of glomerular capillaries and into glomerular (Bowman's) capsules using the hydrostatic pressure of the arterial system. The vast majority (99%) of this filtrate is returned to the circulatory system and the remaining small volume of fluid containing concentrated solute is continuously delivered to the urinary bladder.

Concentration of glomerular filtrate into a hypertonic urine involves establishment of an osmotic gradient within the tissues of the kidney. This is accomplished by active pumping of ions (sodium and/or chloride) through the wall of certain portions of the nephron. As filtrate flows through the collecting tubules on its way into the renal pelvis, it encounters increasingly hypertonic tissue fluids in the medulla of the kidney. Water osmotically moves through the walls of collecting tubules into this surrounding tissue, and the filtrate thus becomes concentrated into urine. Capillaries associated with the tubules of the nephron reabsorb water, as well as some ions and small molecules, to return it to the circulatory system. The urine formed by this process travels to the urinary bladder via the ureter.

Because they are critical in maintaining homeostasis of the osmolarity of the blood and blood pressure, the kidneys are subject to hormonal regulation. Parathormone (PTH) acts on the distal convoluted tubule to increase calcium reabsorption, thereby increasing the serum concentration of calcium. Aldosterone acts on the distal tubule and essentially reverses the sodium-potassium pump, causing potassium to be secreted into the tubule and sodium to be reabsorbed into the tubular cell. As sodium is reabsorbed, the osmolarity of the blood increases; this, in turn, stimulates the secretion of vasopressin. Vasopressin acts on the collecting duct to mobilize water channels to the tubular surface and thus enhance water reabsorption to counter the increase in serum osmolarity.

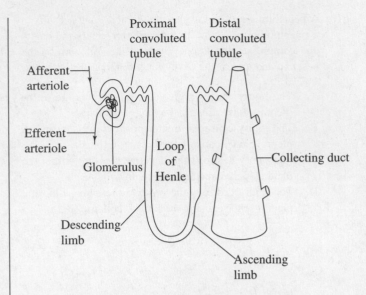

Figure 1 Diagram of the anatomical segments of the nephron in the kidney

53. The ion pumps for sodium and chlorine that establish the countercurrent multiplier system in the medulla of a vertebrate kidney are located in the cell membrane of the:

A. proximal convoluted tubules.
B. distal convoluted tubules.
C. descending loops of Henle.
D. ascending loops of Henle.

54. The process by which the nitrogen metabolism by-product urea is removed from the blood in the glomerulus is known as:

A. tubular secretion.
B. reabsorption.
C. ultrafiltration.
D. osmosis.

55. Which of the following would be LEAST likely to be present in the glomerular filtrate entering the proximal convoluted tubule?

A. Glucose
B. Platelets
C. Amino acids
D. Urea

56. Abnormally low blood pressure in a human causes a decrease in the production of urine because there would also be a(n):

A. decrease in the osmotic concentration of the blood plasma.
B. decrease in hydrostatic pressure in the glomerulus.
C. increase in osmotic concentration of the blood plasma.
D. decrease in the concentration of urea in the blood plasma.

57. Spironolactone is an aldosterone antagonist. Which of the following would be expected in someone who was given spironolactone?

	[Na$^+$]blood	[Na$^+$]urine	[K$^+$]blood	[K$^+$]urine
A.	Increased	Decreased	Increased	Decreased
B.	Decreased	Increased	Increased	Decreased
C.	Increased	Decreased	Decreased	Increased
D.	Decreased	Increased	Decreased	Increased

58. In which of the following situations would you expect an increase in PTH activity?

A. A person whose thyroid gland has been removed
B. A person with increased osteoclastic activity
C. A person with increased osteocytic activity
D. A person with higher than normal urinary calcium concentration

Passage VIII (Questions 59–63)

Defects in DNA repair may lead to a number of diseases including xeroderma pigmentosum, ataxia telangiectasia, hereditary retinoblastoma, and Fanconi's anemia. Xeroderma pigmentosum (XP) is the best understood of these conditions. Those suffering from this affliction are particularly sensitive to the effects of sunlight. Exposure to the sun creates severe skin reactions that range initially from excessive freckling and skin ulceration to the eventual development of skin cancers. Some forms of the disease are also accompanied by various neurological abnormalities.

Normal mammalian cells can carry out excision repair of DNA. In contrast, skin cells from XP patients are unable to repair the DNA damage produced by ultraviolet light. This defect originates from a reduced effectiveness of the first step of the repair mechanism, the step at which an endocnuclease nicks the DNA undergoing repair near a pyrimidine dimer. It has been suggested, based on indirect evidence, that this enzyme is defective in XP patients. At present, the exact genetic basis for defective DNA repair is unknown.

One particularly intriguing aspect of diseases related to defective DNA repair is the possible relationship to carcinogenesis (the development of cancer). Although these diseases are rare autosomal recessive conditions, the carriers of the defective genes are relatively common; the frequency of the XP allele is 1% in the general population. An interesting finding is that not only are those who are afflicted by XP susceptible to cancer, but the carriers of the gene have a higher incidence of skin cancer as well. These and other similar findings suggest the presence of some subtle defect in DNA repair among the carriers of these genes. Further research on the predisposition of these carriers to cancer might provide some clues regarding the mechanism of carcinogenesis for some types of cancer.

Researchers have theorized that the extent of the disease XP can be ameliorated to some degree through recombinant DNA gene replacement therapy. By providing cells with the enzymes necessary for DNA repair, then those cells will be less susceptible to the development of cancers. A study was conducted to determine if there was any benefit to gene replacement in patients with XP. The study group consisted of 100 patients with XP, ranging in age from 6 to 22 years. Half of the group was randomized to the control arm, and the remaining half was in the experimental arm. Patients in the experimental arm received daily injections of an adenoviral vector containing the DNA that would encode for one of the endonucleases used in the nucleotide excision repair of damaged DNA. The patients were followed for six months and monitored for the development of skin lesions. The data are presented below, including a Kaplan-Meier curve demonstrating the remaining number of patients in each group that did not develop skin lesions.

	Control Group	Experimental Group
Original Number	50	50
New lesions at 1 mo.	12	10
New lesions at 3 mos.	15	12
New lesions at 6 mos.	20	20

Table 1 Data table describing the number of patients in each group with new lesion at beginning, 1 month, 3 months, and 6 months

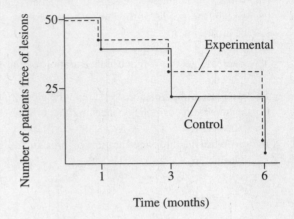

Figure 1 Kaplan-Meier curve representing the number of patients in both groups who never developed lesions

59. During DNA replication, which of the following enzymes is necessary for completion of the lagging strand?

    A. Helicase
    B. DNA ligase
    C. Topoisomerase II
    D. Primase

60. Which of the following is an example of the type of defect that XP patients cannot repair?

    A. Guanine-guanine
    B. Cytosine-guanine
    C. Adenine-thymine
    D. Thymine-thymine

61. In a population of 10,000 people, how many carriers of XP are there?

A. 99
B. 198
C. 900
D. 1,800

62. In the disease hereditary retinoblastoma, which of the following cells would most likely exhibit a defect in DNA repair similar to XP?

A. Cerebellar neurons
B. Ophthalmic artery endothelial cells
C. Red blood cells
D. Cone cells

63. Which of the following is an accurate interpretation of the data from the experiment?

A. There is significant improvement in survival of patients who received the gene replacement.
B. There is no significant difference between the two groups in the incidence of new lesions.
C. The experimental group had fewer new skin lesions at each measured interval.
D. There are more patients who are lesion-free in the experimental group than in the control group.

Questions 64 through 74 are NOT based on a descriptive passage.

64. Which of the following is an example of tertiary protein structure?

A. The α-helix conformation of collagen
B. The disulfide bridge that connects amino acid 24 and amino acid 254 in insulin
C. The complex structural form of hemoglobin, created by the interaction of four polypeptide chains and a central heme group
D. The solenoid conformation of DNA in a cell

65. Which of the following is NOT a function of the liver?

A. Conversion of glucose to glycogen
B. Detoxification of drugs in the body
C. Ability to produce red and white blood cells
D. Release of bile from the gallbladder

66. Which of the following is the expected ratio for a color-blind man and his normal wife whose father is also color-blind?

A. 100% of males are color-blind.
B. 25% of females are color-blind.
C. 50% of all children are color-blind.
D. 25% of all children are color-blind.

67. Which of the following indicates a problem with the kidney?

A. A concentrated urine output with increased levels of ADH
B. A dilute urine output with decreased levels of aldosterone
C. A concentrated urine output with decreased intake of water
D. A dilute urine output with secretion of renin

68. Which of the following is true regarding the stomach?

   A. It is lined with many epithelial cells thrown into folds, similar to the small intestines.
   B. The parietal cells secrete mucous to aid in protection of the stomach.
   C. The chief cells secrete hydrochloric acid to aid in digestion.
   D. Pepsin is secreted to begin the digestion of polypeptides.

69. Two bacteria are grown on separate nutrient agar plates. Each plate contains both erythromycin and penicillin, each on one half of the plate. The microorganism on plate A grows on the penicillin side, appears to have spherical shape under the microscope, and grows only in environments rich in oxygen. The microorganism on plate B grows on the erythromycin side, resembles little rods under the microscope, and can grow with or without oxygen. Which of the following is a correct identification of the organism?

   A. Plate A is growing *Peptostreptococcus* species, a Gram-positive microaerophilic organism.
   B. Plate B is growing *Escherichia coli*, a Gram-negative facultative bacillus.
   C. Plate A is growing *Neisseria gonorrhoeae*, a Gram-negative anaerobic diplococcus organism.
   D. Plate B is growing *Clostridium botulinum*, a Gram-positive motile anaerobic bacillus.

70. Which of the following changes in the blood would you expect to increase the respiratory rate of an individual?

   I. Increased concentration of bicarbonate ions
   II. Increased concentration of carbon dioxide
   III. Lowered pH

   A. I and II only
   B. I and III only
   C. II and III only
   D. I, II, and III

71. In sickle cell anemia, simple substitution of a valine for a glutamic acid at the sixth position of the β-chain of hemoglobin causes a severe disturbance in the shape of the red blood cell under times of deoxygenation. Which of the following is the genetic cause of sickle cell anemia?

   A. Nonsense mutation
   B. Missense mutation
   C. Silent mutation
   D. Null mutation

72. Which of the following is a consequence of removing the adrenal cortex in a person?

   A. Inability to concentrate urine
   B. Inability to increase serum glucose
   C. Inability to reduce serum potassium
   D. Inability to increase blood pressure

73. Multiple sclerosis is a slowly progressive central nervous system (CNS) disease characterized by disseminated patches of demyelination in the brain and spinal cord. This results in multiple and varied neurology symptoms and signs, usually with remissions and exacerbations. Which of the following would you NOT expect to see in a person with multiple sclerosis?

   A. Slowed conduction of action potentials through affected nerves
   B. Decreased number of oligodendrocytes surrounding axons in the CNS
   C. Normal depolarization of the soma upon opening ligand-gated Na^+ channels
   D. Saltatory conduction of action potentials through affected nerves

74. Methotrexate is an analogue of folic acid that has been used with great success in the treatment of childhood leukemias. Its mechanism of action is based on its competition with dihydrofolate for the enzyme dihydrofolate reductase (DHFR). Which of the following changes in enzyme kinetics would you expect to see as a result of adding methotrexate to a system containing dihydrofolate and DHFR?

   A. The K_m would increase.
   B. The V_{max} would decrease.
   C. The K_m would increase and the V_{max} would decrease.
   D. The order of kinetics would change from first-order to zero-order.

Chapter 22
Biology Practice:
Answers and Explanations

The key features of this passage include: the structure of hemoglobin, the structure of amino acids, and the concept of pH. The passage provides a nice background on the different hemoglobin molecules you can come across in the adult human. You need to remember that since hemoglobin is a tetramer of globin chains, it has quarternary structure. The quarternary structure is formed by the heme center connecting to each of the four chains. Each chain can bind an oxygen, and therefore, four molecules are bound to a hemoglobin. Oxygen binding to hemoglobin exhibits a unique phenomenon called "cooperativity," where the binding of one molecule of oxygen enhances the affinity for binding other molecules of oxygen.

Amino acids are broadly classified as polar or nonpolar. Within the nonpolar, they are broken down further into aliphatic, aromatic, and "other" categories. The polar amino acids are divided into acidic, basic, and neutral. This classification scheme is derived from the different R groups attached to each amino acid. Glutamic acid, for instance, has a $-CH_2CH_2COOH$ side chain, and it will therefore be deprotonated at a higher pH (typically >2.8). Valine, a nonpolar aliphatic amino acid, will not be protonated or deprotonated at any pH because its side chain is just hydrocarbons. Lysine, an alkaline amino acid, will be protonated at a low pH given it has a polar nitrogen on its side chain.

1. A   The passage states that hemoglobin is a tetramer of 2 α-chains and 2 β-chains. Quaternary structure is only present in proteins that consist of more than 1 polypeptide chain. The passage states that each chain can carry a molecule of oxygen; therefore, each hemoglobin can carry four molecules of oxygen (B is incorrect). Hemoglobin is only found in red blood cells (hence the prefix *hemo-*); its equivalent, myoglobin, is found in skeletal muscle cells (C is incorrect). The heme center is oxidized from 2^+ to 3^+ when oxygen binds; 3^+ to 2^+ represents a reduction (D is incorrect).

2. D   The primary defect in Hb C is a change in the sixth position from the normal glutamic acid to lysine. Glutamic acid is a polar acidic amino acid. Lysine is a polar basic amino acid. Therefore, the defect is changing from a polar acidic amino acid to a polar basic one.

3. A   The acidic amino acid is deprotonated at an alkaline pH. The deprotonated form carries a negative charge. This would then migrate toward the positive pole, the anode (in electrolytic cells the anode is positive and the cathode is negative). Hb S has a neutral side chain (valine is a non-polar amino acid) and would therefore not migrate significantly during electrophoresis (B is incorrect). Hb C has a basic amino acid which is protonated at an acidic pH, but it is also protonated at a pH of 9 and therefore does not represent a difference (C is incorrect). At an acidic pH, the acidic side chain is protonated and carries no charge. If it is protonated, it is not "less acidic" than if deprotonated (D is incorrect).

4. B   The spleen is one of the major organs of the immune system. It is rich with lymphocytes, both B and T, and serves a major resource in the body's natural defenses against pathogens, especially encapsulated bacteria. The spleen is not the site of red blood cell synthesis; the bone

marrow is (A is incorrect). The spleen is not involved in digestion (C is incorrect). The spleen also removes damaged or old red blood cells. If the spleen is damaged, or infarcted, then there will be less destruction of red blood cells (D is incorrect).

5. **A** The gel electrophoresis shows two bands: one near the anode and one stationary in the middle. This indicates a neutral hemoglobin and a negatively charged hemoglobin. Since the gel is run at a pH of 9, the negatively charged hemoglobin must be the acidic deprotonated Hb A (statement I is true; eliminate C). The neutral hemoglobin must be the nonpolar Hb S (statement II is true; eliminate B). Hb C is positively charged at an alkaline pH, so it should migrate to the negative cathode. There is no band near the cathode. Therefore, there is no Hb C (statement III is false; eliminate D).

6. **C** Hb F actually has a greater affinity for oxygen than Hb A does (B is incorrect). This is the way that fetal hemoglobin can extract oxygen from the maternal circulation through the placenta. Because Hb F does not contain b chains, it is not subject to sickling (A is incorrect). Hb F can only carry four molecules of oxygen, the same as Hb A (D is incorrect).

7. **B** Per the passage, adult production of Hb F increases in hematologic conditions where there is decreased β-chain synthesis. β-thalassemia affects the β-chain synthesis and thus will cause the production of Hb F into adult life.

Passage II (Questions 8–13)

This is a typical passage on Microbiology, integrating Molecular Biology. You need to have some grasp on normal cellular processes, such as DNA replication, transcription, and translation. Understanding that HIV is a retrovirus and that it needs to undergo reverse transcription to form DNA will help you answer the questions that follow. The molecule AZT looks a lot like thymine; the only difference is an azido group at the 3' carbon. This prevents elongation of the polymerizing chain, and hence, reverse transcription comes to a halt. If the genome cannot be reversely transcribed, then it cannot become DNA and therefore cannot integrate into the host's genome. Therefore, AZT is a competitive antagonist. Efavirenz, on the other hand, is an example of a noncompetitive antagonist. As you can see from the structure, it does not resemble any nitrogenous base. It must bind outside of the active site of reverse transcriptase in order for it to exert its effects.

8. **C** The passage states that reverse transcriptase is the enzyme that converts viral RNA into DNA. The synthesis of DNA requires a DNA polymerase. The template being used is RNA; therefore, it is RNA-dependent.

9. **B** Nevirapine is a non-nucleoside antagonist. As the passage states, the non-nucleosides are allosteric inhibitors. As a result, they must be noncompetitive inhibitors of reverse transcriptase. Noncompetitive inhibitors cannot be reversed by increasing the concentration of substrate; that would work only for a competitive inhibitor.

10. **A** If HTLV-1 is similar to HIV, then it must also be a retrovirus (statement II is true; eliminate B). HIV also exhibits a lysogenic life cycle since it integrates into the host's genome (statement I is true; eliminate C). HIV and HTLV-1 infect the host's T-cells. The B-cells are the antibody-producing cells of the body. There is no discussion of HIV infecting B cells. Therefore, statement III is false (eliminate D).

11. **C** The integration of viral DNA into the host's DNA is mediated by the enzyme integrase, not protease. The protease enzyme is used to cut larger proteins into smaller functional proteins, such as gp160 into gp41 and gp120 (D is a correct statement). Without these functional proteins, viral replication comes to a halt (A is a correct statement). If viral replication stops, then fewer helper T-cells will be infected (B is a correct statement).

12. **D** Reverse transcriptase will make DNA. Therefore, eliminate A and B since they contain uracil. The resultant strand of DNA will be anti-complementary to the template strand. Therefore, the 3' end of the template corresponds to the 5' end of the newly synthesized strand. Cytosine pairs with guanine and thus, D is correct.

13. **B** Stavudine has a molecular structure very similar to AZT. Therefore, it is expected that stavudine will also be a nucleoside antagonist. As such, it will block DNA synthesis, not RNA synthesis, since it is a thymidine analogue (C is incorrect). Because mammalian DNA contains thymine, stavudine would be expected to affect mammalian cell replication as well (D is incorrect).

Freestanding Questions 14–18

14. **C** Multicellular fungi are eukaryotes, not prokaryotes (A is incorrect). The sizes of the small and large subunits of the ribosomes in prokaryotes are 30S and 50S respectively, whereas 40S and 60S are the small and large subunits, respectively, in eukaryotes (B is incorrect). Fungi have cell walls which contain a characteristic molecule called chitin. Chitin is what helps provide structure and integrity to the exterior of fungi. Fungi do not contain chloroplasts (D is incorrect).

15. **C** Complex IV is the terminal component of the electron transport chain (ETC). It requires O_2 as the final electron pair acceptor, thereby creating water. Since the entire electron transport chain is a series of redox reactions, if one terminal step is faulty, then electrons cannot be passed on to those intermediates which are in the oxidized state. If electrons cannot be passed on, then electron carriers are not able to be emptied and recycled. All preceding reactions come to a halt because electrons cannot be passed on to those intermediates which still have electrons—those that are reduced.

    $FADH_2$ enters the ETC at Complex II, whereas NADH enters at Complex I. Both complexes transfer their electrons to ubiquinone, which then continues to pass the electrons on ultimately to Complex IV. Therefore, neither $FADH_2$ nor NADH will be able to generate ATP (A is incorrect). If Complex IV is poisoned, then electrons will not be transferred to oxygen (B is incorrect). Damage to the inner mitochondrial membrane would allow the protons in the intermembrane space access to the matrix without having to utilize the ATP synthase complex. Cyanide inhibits Complex IV, which does not destroy the integrity of the inner mitochondrial membrane. As a result, uncoupling would not be expected (D is incorrect).

16. **D** The ectoderm is responsible for the development of the entire nervous system, the adrenal medulla (II is true), the retina and the cornea of the eye (III is true). The cerebellum is the part of the brain that is responsible for coordinating fine motor movements and overall balance (I is true).

17. **B** If stimulation of the a1-adrenergic receptors results in vasoconstriction, then inhibiting these receptors will cause vasodilation. Dilation of the blood vessels will ultimately result in lower blood pressure (A is incorrect). Cardiac muscle contraction and stroke volume are directly related; if the cardiac muscle has a greater force of contraction, then more blood will be ejected. Cardiac muscle is different than smooth muscle based on several features, namely being striated. The antagonist affects smooth muscle, not striated muscle (C and D are incorrect).

18. **C** In utero, the fetus derives its oxygenated blood from the mother via the placenta. There is a countercurrent exchange of gases, O_2 and CO_2. Blood traveling from the fetus to the placenta is poor in oxygen. While in the placenta, the blood from the fetus and the blood from the mother will course near each other and allow countercurrent exchange of gases. The blood returning to the fetus through the umbilical cord will now be rich in oxygen. Because the blood is returning to the baby, it will ultimately arrive at the right ventricle. The blood will then enter the pulmonary artery. Since the lungs will not oxygenate the already-oxygenated blood, the blood will be shunted through the ductus arteriosus to the aorta due to higher arterial pressure in the pulmonary artery. The oxygenated blood will then be circulated throughout the fetal body.

Passage III (Questions 19–25)

This genetics passage tests more of what happens in genetics and meioisis and fertilization rather than focusing on Mendelian laws. If a trisomy had occurred, then there must have been a mistake with some part of meiosis that caused one extra chromosome to be a part of the fertilized egg, whether it be from the sperm or the egg cell. This is typically secondary to nondisjunction, when one chromosome "sticks" to its homologue (or if a sister chromatid fails to separate in Meiosis II) instead of segregating individually.

19. **A** Trisomies and monosomies occur because of improper segregation of homologous chromosomes in Meiosis I or sister chromatids in Meiosis II. As a result, one daughter cell will receive 2 copies of a chromosome, whereas the other will receive no copies of that chromosome. This process is called non-disjunction. Incomplete dominance refers to the fact that the dominant

allele cannot overpower the expression of a recessive allele in a heterozygous form, and therefore a blend of the dominant and recessive alleles is the resultant phenotype (B is incorrect). A deletion of an entire chromosome would cause a monosomy, not a trisomy (C is incorrect). A mutation would only potentially affect one gene on a chromosome, not increase the number of chromosomes (D is incorrect).

20.   D   The Hardy-Weinberg equation can only be used to describe the frequencies of autosomal recessive or dominant traits or conditions, not changes in chromosome number. Because trisomies are not autosomal recessive conditions, the Hardy-Weinberg equation cannot be used, and one cannot predict the occurrence of the carriers in a population. Also, because trisomies are not based on dominant or recessive expressions, there is no "carrier" state.

21.   B   In children with Down syndrome, one of the primary cardiac defects is a truncus arteriosus, a common arterial trunk coming off both the left and right ventricles. This allows for mixing of blood from the left and right circulations. Because the right circulation is relatively deoxygenated and the left circulation is well-oxygenated, the resultant mix will be somewhere between. As such, the overall aortic arterial oxygen saturation will be less than normal.

Carbon dioxide concentration is dependent on cellular respiration. If there is less oxygen reaching the tissues (since less saturation), then the rate of anaerobic respiration may increase, thereby increasing the concentration of carbon dioxide (A is incorrect). Because a common arterial trunk is receiving blood from both the right and left ventricles, the pulmonary artery will be receiving more blood than usual and therefore will have a higher than normal blood pressure (C is incorrect). Given the mixing of well-oxygenated and poorly-oxygenated blood in the common arterial trunk, the pulmonary arterial oxygen concentration will be higher than it is normally (D is incorrect).

22.   B   As per the passage, the child with Trisomy 21 may suffer from prematurely ending small intestines, and therefore, digestion will be impaired if not surgically corrected. The passage does not describe kidney dysfunction in Trisomy 21 (A is incorrect) or underdeveloped sensory cortex (C is incorrect). The passage says hypotonia is involved, which is a decrease in muscle (D is incorrect).

23.   D   The passage states that in Klinefelter's syndrome, there is an extra X chromosome and a Y chromosome is also present. This totals 47 chromosomes, instead of the normal 46. Turner's syndrome has the karyotype of 45, XO.

24.   A   The passage refers to the Mullerian ductal system as part of the internal female genitalia. The urethra is not a part of the internal female genitalia (statement III is false; eliminate C and D). The ovaries and testes are coexistent for the first 10 weeks of gestation (known as bipotentiality). The presence of the Y chromosome and the product from the SRY (sexual response element on the Y chromosome) gene allow the differentiation into testes. The testes produce the Mullerian

inhibiting substance which inhibits the growth of the fallopian tubes, uterus, and distal 2/3 of the vagina. The ovaries are not a part of the Mullerian system (statement I is false; eliminate B).

25. **B** All of the listed syndromes are trisomies: Down-21, Patau-13, Edwards-18, Klinefelter's-sex. There is no mention of heart defects in Klinefelter's syndrome (A is incorrect). There is no gender difference in the autosomal trisomies (C is incorrect). There is no mention of life expectancy in any of the diseases (D is incorrect).

Passage IV (Questions 26–30)

The main concept of the passage is that the delicate acid-base balance of the body is under strict control by both the kidneys and the lungs. The kidneys take longer to exert their effect on acid-base homeostasis, whereas the lungs modify the acid-base balance very quickly. The other key concept to remember is that a high concentration of CO_2 means a high concentration of H^+, thereby creating acidemia.

26. **B** This is a fact-based, know-something type of question. The answer cannot be found in the passage. The proximal convoluted tubule is permeable to nearly all substances, and it serves as the part of the nephron where the greatest amount of reabsorption takes place. The ascending loop of Henle is impermeable to water and permeable only to salt ions, such as Na^+, K^+, and Cl^-. The distal convoluted tubule actively reabsorbs and secretes salt ions.

27. **C** Lactate is the ionized/deprotonated form of lactic acid. Therefore, an acidosis is expected to develop. Since lactate is generated through a metabolic process and not a function of breathing rate, it is expected to cause a metabolic acidosis. Respiratory acidosis is secondary to an increased CO_2 concentration, typified by decreased respiratory rate. An alkalosis would result in increasing the pH of the blood. If it is metabolic in origin, then there is an increased concentration of HCO_3^-, whereas if it is respiratory, then there is a decreased concentration of CO_2.

28. **D** According to the passage, "the administration of opiate medications…can induce a respiratory acidosis." The passage also states that if the primary cause of acidosis is respiratory, the kidneys will compensate by adjusting secretion of HCO_3^-, so answers A and B can be eliminated. Because the pH is too acidic, increasing reabsorption of HCO_3^- would be necessary to increase the pH.

29. **C** Anaerobic metabolism results in the formation of lactic acid. This creates a metabolic acidosis (see question 2). Therefore, statement I is true and answer A can be eliminated. The passage states that ethylene glycol (antifreeze) can cause a metabolic acidosis, so statement III is true and B can be eliminated. Vomiting causes the loss of hydrochloric acid from the stomach. This in turn causes the parietal cells to avidly take H^+ from the blood-side of the cell to create new HCl. By removing H^+ from the blood, an imbalance between H^+ and HCO_3^- exists, with greater HCO_3^- than normal. This results in a metabolic alkalosis, and therefore, statement II is false, eliminating answer choice D.

30. B A metabolic acidosis is caused by a decrease in HCO_3^- concentration, resulting in a comparatively higher than normal H^+ concentration. Hyperventilation causes a decrease in CO_2 concentration. Remembering that CO_2 is acid (since H^+ are formed from Equation 1), hyperventilation creates a respiratory alkalosis. The combination of both respiratory alkalosis (which results in a higher blood pH) and metabolic acidosis (which results in a lower blood pH) would result in a near normal blood pH. As a consequence, there will be little compensation required to maintain a normal level pH in the blood.

A pH of 7.2 indicates acidemia, typically caused by an acidosis, or potentially two acidoses (respiratory and metabolic). A pH of 7.6 represents an alkalemia, caused by one or two alkaloses. If the kidneys secreted HCO_3^-, then the blood pH would become lower since the body is ridding itself of HCO_3^-, a base. This compensation would only be necessary if there was an alkalemia to correct.

Freestanding Questions 31–35

31. C The neural tube will develop into the entire central nervous system. The central nervous system consists of the brain and the spinal cord. The medulla oblongata and the cerebrum are both parts of the brain (statements II and III are both true). The spinal column, however, is the series of verebrae that encircle and protect the spinal cord. The spinal column, consisting of bone, is derived from mesoderm (statement I is false).

32. A Glomerular filtration is directly proportional to the glomerular capillary pressure generated. With selective vasoconstriction of the efferent arteriole, there will be more blood pooling in the glomerular capillaries, thereby increasing overall glomerular pressure. This increase in pressure will result in greater filtration across the glomerular basement membrane (B is incorrect). Typically, red blood cells only appear in the urine sediment when there is damage to the glomerular basement membrane. Selective vasoconstriction of the efferent arteriole will not damage the glomerular basement membrane (C and D are incorrect).

33. B Since the autoantibodies stimulate the TSH receptor, the effect would be similar to excess TSH. TSH causes the release of thyroid hormone from the thyroid gland. The thyroid hormone is related to basal metabolic rate. Having greater than normal concentration of thyroid hormone will result in an increase in basal metabolic rate (C is incorrect). Thyroid hormone does not have any direct effect on skeletal muscle activity (A and D are incorrect).

34. C The ABO blood typing system is an example of co-dominance. The alleles determining A blood type and B blood type are both dominant to the recessive allele. Therefore, AB blood type is a result of having both dominant A and B alleles. Blood type O is formed from two recessive alleles. If two parents are AB blood types, then they only have dominant alleles, and the homozygous recessive blood type O is impossible to have as a child.

35.   A   In order to determine the probability of having a guinea pig with short whiskers AND white fur, we must multiply the probabilities of each individual trait. The frequency of the recessive white fur allele, q, is 0.4. Therefore, the probability of having a guinea pig with white fur, q^2, is 0.16. If the frequency of the recessive short whiskers allele, q, is 0.2, then the probability of having short whiskers will be q^2, or 0.04. Therefore, the probability of having two simultaneous unlinked traits occurring is (0.04)(0.16), which is 0.0064.

Passage V (Questions 36–41)

This passage helps you integrate more than one Biology topic into an overall passage. The passage requires you to be familiar with bacterial genetics and growth, genetics with regards to autosomal recessive disorders and normal physiology of the body. Remember that the MCAT likes to ask you to differentiate major topics, like Gram-positive from Gram-negative bacteria, so, it would behoove you to know some of these differences going into the exam.

36.   C   Bacteria are described as Gram-negative if they do not avidly hold the Gram stain. The Gram stain complexes with significant amounts of peptidoglycan. All bacteria with cell walls contain peptidoglycan; however, there are varying amounts of peptidoglycan in cell walls. Gram-negative bacteria have a thin layer of peptidoglycan in their cell wall within their outer membrane (A is incorrect). Their outer membrane is separated from the inner membrane by a periplasmic space. This periplasmic space contains proteins that can inhibit certain antimicrobial medications, such as penicillin. Only motile bacteria possess a flagellum (B is incorrect). Bacteria only possess one copy of their genomic circular DNA. Resistance tends to be transmitted via plasmids, extrachromosomal pieces of DNA (D is incorrect).

37.   C   The passage states that the frequency of the autosomal recessive condition Cystic Fibrosis, q2, is 1 in 3600. The frequency of the recessive allele, q, then is 1 in 60. The frequency of the dominant non-disease producing allele, p, is 59 in 60. The carriers of a population are determined by the expression 2pq. In the given population, the number of carriers would be (2)(1/60)(59/60)(18000) or 590.

38.   D   The passage states that people with Cystic Fibrosis tend to have autodestruction of the pancreas. Autodestruction would eliminate the Islets of Langerhans which secrete both glucagon and insulin (B and C are incorrect). After a carbohydrate-rich meal, the serum glucose concentration should rise. In the absence of insulin, the serum glucose concentration will remain high until it can be cleared from the blood by the kidney (A is incorrect).

39.   C   The table lists the number of cultures of each type of organism. The number of positive isolates for methicillin-resistant *Staphylococcus aureus* is 115. The total number of cultures reported is the total Gram-Positive plus the total Gram-negative plus the fungal cultures:
160 + 180 + 5 = 345.

40. **D** Cystic Fibrosis is a genetic disease based on the abnormal protein CFTR. In a set of lungs from a non-Cystic Fibrosis person, the lung cells presumably have normal-functioning CFTRs. Therefore, the new lungs should not be subject to the development of Cystic Fibrosis (eliminate answers A and B). Cystic Fibrosis is a multi-organ disease since the CFTR is used in secretions from several glands, but this does not cause normal CFTRs to become abnormal. The primary defect is the protein CFTR, not the pulmonary secretions or an infectious cause (C is incorrect).

41. **A** With the vast amounts of salt and water wasting in *Cholera* infection, the intestinal cells become highly salt- and water-deprived. Because the large intestinal cells, not the small intestinal cells, are the cells that typically reabsorb water, the only way water can be reabsorbed is osmotically with salt. By providing salt and sugar, the small intestinal cells will reabsorb the salt and sugar and exert an osmotic force to cause the reabsorption of water. Protein absorption in the small intestines is independent of salt concentration (B is incorrect). The addition of salt and sugar are for increasing the osmotic concentration, not for taste (C is incorrect). The *Cholera* bacteria are not depleting the body's energy supply. Therefore, extra calories are not the reason for the salt and sugar solution (D is incorrect).

Passage VI (Questions 42–47)

The main concept of this passage is that there are genetic defects that can result in altering the phenotypic expression of the genotypic sex. It requires a familiarity with hormones and how they behave in the body. The diagram provided illustrates the steroid biosynthesis pathway that occurs in the adrenal cortex. This will be used to answer at least one of the questions for the passage.

42. **C** This is a knowledge-based question. FSH initiates the follicular growth phase of the ovary. FSH is released by the anterior pituitary after menses has occurred. This allows for the ovarian follicle to develop prior to ovulation. The spike in estrogen levels immediately before ovulation is not directly responsible for ovulation. The spike in estrogen changes the typical negative feedback system to a positive feedback system, so the estrogen spike causes a spike in LH. The LH surge is directly responsible for ovulation. After ovulation, the LH levels plummet. Progesterone peaks immediately after ovulation.

43. **A** This is a tricky question. The passage discusses AIS as an X-linked disorder but does not tell you if it is dominant or recessive. If the normal woman has an affected son with AIS, she must be a carrier for the disorder, and since she does not have AIS, the disease is recessive. If she has a child with a normal male, then her daughters would have a 50/50 chance of being carriers and would all have normal phenotypes. Thus, the correct answer is A.

44. **B** A girl with AIS is genetically male by possessing a Y chromosome. This results in the development of testes. With the lack of response to androgens, the testes fail to descend from the abdomen to the scrotum. Therefore, statement I is true, eliminating answer choice C. Because she has a Y chromosome with an intact SRY gene, the Mullerian-Inhibiting Substance will be

secreted, thereby causing the regression of female internal sexual structures, including the uterus. Statement II is therefore false and eliminates answer choices A and D, leaving B as the only correct answer. There is no need to fret over statement III because it has to be true. There will be adequate breast development since the default for peripheral sexual development is female in the absence of androgens or in the inability to respond to androgens, as is the case in AIS.

45. **A** CAH can be caused by an excess of androgens, not a deficiency in female sex hormones. According to the steroid biosynthesis pathway, a deficiency in 11β-hydroxylase results in a shunting of the pathway to form more testosterone, so a deficiency in 11β-hydroxylase should result in a CAH-type syndrome in women. Therefore, answers C and D can be eliminated. Because the syndrome is caused by an excess of androgens, answer B is incorrect.

46. **A** The development of male external genitalia is dependent on the presence of androgens and androgen receptors in peripheral tissues. Dihydrotestosterone is an androgen and therefore is the correct answer. 17β-estradiol is the most common estrogen found in the body. Progesterone is a progestin. Aldosterone has no effect on the development of genitalia.

47. **B** According to the biosynthesis pathway, a deficiency in 17α-hydroxylase causes a shunting to the production of aldosterone. Aldosterone exerts its effects on the distal convoluted tubule to increase Na^+ reabsorption and K^+ secretion into the tubule. This results in hypokalemia, a lower-than-normal concentration of K^+ in the blood. Cortisol has no influence on the homeostasis of K^+ in the blood (eliminate answer choices A and D). A lower-than-normal concentration of aldosterone would result in a higher-than-normal concentration of K^+, hyperkalemia.

Freestanding Questions 48–52

48. **C** Furosemide blocks the ascending loop of Henle and causes an increase in urine formation. The increase in urine formation results from increased water content in the tubular filtrate. If there is a higher solute concentration in the loop of Henle, then less water will be reabsorbed. If furosemide acts on the ascending loop of Henle, which is permeable only to salts, then the direct action is to inhibit the reabsorption of salts. This results in an increased solute concentration in the tubular filtrate, and water will remain in the tubular filtrate due to osmolar concentrations. Water is not reabsorbed in the ascending loop of Henle (A is incorrect). Water will remain in the tubular fluid due to the hyperosmolar concentration of solute and therefore will not be reabsorbed in the collecting duct (B is incorrect). Sodium ions are reabsorbed, not excreted, in the ascending loop of Henle (D is incorrect).

49. **C** An action potential in a post-synaptic neuron will be stimulated if there is a depolarization of the resting membrane potential to reach the threshold potential. If a potassium ion channel opens, then potassium will leave the neuronal cytoplasm, resulting in a hyperpolarization of the membrane potential (A is incorrect). If a chloride ion channel opens, then chloride ions will enter the post-synaptic neuron and cause a hyperpolarization of the membrane (B is incor-

rect). Opening a calcium ion channel will result in calcium influx and consequently depolarizing the membrane; therefore, if calcium ions are prevented from entering the post-synaptic neuron, depolarization will not occur (D is incorrect).

50.   C   Angiotensin-converting enzyme (ACE) is the enzyme that catalyzes the conversion of angiotensin I to angiotensin II. An inhibitor of the enzyme would therefore cause a decreased level of angiotensin II (A is incorrect). Also, the inhibition of the enzyme results in an increase in the level of the substrate, angiotensin I (D is incorrect). Angiotensin II is the most potent vasoconstrictor in the human body and therefore, vascular smooth muscle relaxation would be expected if there were decreased angiotensin II levels (B is incorrect).

51.   C   Normally, the intrapleural space (the space that separates the parietal pleura coating the thoracic wall from the visceral pleura on the outside of the lung) is under negative pressure (D is incorrect). The negative pressure is what allows the lungs to expand when the thoracic cavity expands during inhalation. A penetrating chest wall injury allows communication between the atmosphere and the intrapleural space. Because the intrapleural space is under negative pressure and the atmosphere has positive pressure, air will rush into the intrapleural space. This destroys the negative pressure, making the intrapleural space now with positive pressure (A is incorrect), thereby collapsing the lung (B is incorrect).

52.   C   During embryonic development, the ovary undergoes significant follicle atresia. At birth, the ovary contains follicles with gametic cells frozen in late prophase I. During puberty, the follicles are stimulated to develop further and eventually ovulate. The ovulated egg cell, however, is frozen in prophase II, awaiting fertilization. Upon fertilization, the egg cell quickly completes meiosis II prior to fusion of the sperm and egg nuclei.

Passage VII (Questions 53–58)

Understanding the passage requires familiarity with the physiological properties and actions of the kidney. The kidney is an important subject tested frequently on the MCAT. You should be familiar with what substances are absorbed in the different parts of the kidney tubule. The passage also discusses some of the hormonal influences on the kidney.

53.   D   Ion pumps for Na^+ and Cl^- must exist in a part of the nephron that is permeable to those ions. As a result, answer C can be eliminated since the descending loop of Henle is permeable ONLY to water. Answer choices A and B can be eliminated based on knowledge of the anatomy of the nephron and kidney. The convoluted tubules are located in the cortex of the kidney. The question specifically asks "in the medulla of a vertebrate kidney." The loop of Henle is the only part of the nephron, aside from the collecting ducts, that delves into the medulla of the kidney. The deeper into the medulla the loop travels, the greater the countercurrent multiplier concentration that can be established, creating more highly concentrated urine.

54. **C** The passage states that filtration occurs at the glomerulus in Bowman's capsule. This allows small substances to travel into the proximal convoluted tubule. Tubular secretion occurs for ions such as K^+ in the distal convoluted tubule (A is incorrect). Reabsorption is the process by which substances in the tubular filtrate are brought back into the blood (B is incorrect). Osmosis refers to the movement of water down its concentration gradient (D is incorrect).

55. **B** The filtration system located in the glomerulus is restricted to the movement of small molecules and ions. Larger molecules and cells are not filtered out since they are too large to pass through the filtration slits. The presence of medium-large proteins or cells in the urine indicates damage of the integrity of the filtration barrier.

56. **B** The production of urine, as the passage states, is a function of filtration at the level of the glomerulus. Filtration is dependent on the blood pressure created by blood flow through the afferent and efferent arterioles entering and exiting the glomerulus, respectively. Abnormally low blood pressure, therefore, would result in lower pressure transmitted to the glomerulus. This will cause less filtration and hence a decrease in the production of urine. The osmotic concentration of the plasma is not affected by low blood pressure (A and C are incorrect). The concentration of urea has no influence on the blood pressure (D is incorrect).

57. **B** Because the actions of aldosterone are being inhibited by spironolactone, we would expect the Na^+ concentration in the blood to be lower than normal and K^+ concentration in the blood to be higher than normal. Since Na^+ is not being reabsorbed from the tubular fluid, the concentration of Na^+ in the urine should be higher than normal, and K^+ concentration in the urine should be lower than normal since it is not being secreted into the fluid.

58. **B** PTH is secreted by the thyroid gland in response to low serum levels of calcium. If the thyroid gland is removed, then PTH is not found in the blood (eliminate A). PTH increases osteoclastic activity in order to release calcium into the blood. PTH also, as the passage states, reabsorbs calcium from the distal convoluted tubule. If calcium is being reabsorbed from the distal convoluted tubule, then a lower than normal urinary calcium concentration would be expected (eliminate D). An increase in osteoblastic activity causes new bone formation. New bone formation requires calcium, which is removed from the blood and deposited into the bone. Osteocytes, however, do not form or remodel bone, and therefore, they have no influence on calcium homeostasis (C is incorrect).

Passage VIII (Questions 59–63)

Here is a passage regarding a medical illness rooted in a biochemical defect. There are several diseases of the human body that are due to some genetic defect in an important cellular protein or enzyme. Deficiency in this protein forces the body to create other ways of bypassing that defect. If, however, the body has no sufficient way of bypassing the step, then disease will manifest itself.

59.   **B**   In DNA replication, the lagging strand is a result of the discontinuous 5'->3' synthesis on the template strand of DNA. These *Okazaki fragments* need to be joined together to make one continuous strand of DNA. DNA ligase is the enzyme that will connect the Okazaki fragments. Helicase is used to unzip the double-helix structure of DNA to allow for DNA polymerase to enter. Topoisomerase II (DNA gyrase) is the enzyme that relieves supercoiling of DNA that typically occurs with circular DNA, not linear DNA. It relieves the supercoiling by making nicks in both strands of DNA to allow uncoiling and then reconnecting those strands. Primase is the enzyme that is necessary to generate an RNA primer upon which DNA polymerase can latch to begin DNA polymerization.

60.   **D**   The passage states that the problem with XP is the inability to repair pyrimidine dimers created by ultraviolet radiation. Cytosine, uracil, and thymine are the pyrimidines. Therefore, thymine-thymine is the only pyrimidine dimer listed in the answer choices.

61.   **B**   The passage states that the frequency of the recessive XP allele, q, is 1% (0.01). Therefore, the frequency of the dominant non-disease expressing allele, p, is 0.99. The number of carriers is determined by the expression 2pq. Therefore, in a population of 10,000 people, the number of carriers would be 2(0.01)(0.99)(10000), or 198.

62.   **D**   The disorder retinoblastoma affects the retina of the eye. The cones are the color-identifying neurons of the retina. Cerebellar neurons and red blood cells are not related to the retina. Ophthalmic artery endothelial cells are those cells that line the artery vessel wall. These are not part of the retina and therefore, they would not be expected to be affected.

63.   **B**   Per the table, the numbers of new lesions in the two groups are extraordinarily similar. This indicates that there is no real difference between the two groups. There are several reasons as to why this may have occurred: (1) not all cells took up the adenovirus with the DNA, (2) those cells that did take up the adenovirus may not have expressed the DNA, and (3) more than one enzyme may play a role in excision repair. The survival curve shown illustrates that the two groups approach the same lesion-free percentage, so there is no survival benefit.

64.   **B**   Proteins have four levels of structure. Primary structure refers to the sequence of amino acids that creates that specific protein. Secondary structure refers to the interaction of nearby amino acids, thus creating either an α-helix or a β-pleated sheet. Tertiary structure refers to the interaction of distant amino acids. This interaction can consist of hydrophobic interactions, hydrogen bonding, ionic bonding, or even covalent bonding. Disulfide bridges are covalent bonds formed from two cysteine residues. The tertiary structure can create domains in a protein, such as an active site in an enzyme. All proteins have these structures. Quaternary structure refers to the interaction of more than one polypeptide chain. Therefore, only certain multimeric proteins will have quaternary structure. The α-helix conformation of collagen is a quaternary structure because it requires the interaction of three polypeptide chains. Hemoglobin is formed by the interaction of four globin chains and is therefore an example of quaternary structure. The solenoid conformation of DNA is an interaction of nucleosomes, and it represents a structural configuration rather than a protein structure.

65.   **D**   The liver has various functions in the human body. It is the primary location for the storage of glucose in the form of glycogen. It has the ability to detoxify chemical compounds (e.g., medications) through the use of a cytochrome oxidation system. In fetal life and sometimes in post-natal life, the liver has the ability to synthesize red and white blood cells. The liver also constitutively manufactures bile. The bile is transferred to the gallbladder for storage. The gallbladder releases bile in response to the hormone cholecystokinin, which is secreted by intestinal cells during digestion.

66.   **C**   Color-blindness is an X-linked recessive trait. The color-blind man, therefore, has a genotype of X^*Y. The normal wife whose father is color-blind must be heterozygous since her color-blind father could only give her the affected X chromosome. Thus, the potential progeny from this couple is outlined in the Punnett square below.

	X	X*
X*	XX*	X*X*
Y	XY	X*Y

As you can see, two of the four possible genotypes will demonstrate the color-blindness trait. This ratio corresponds to 50% of all children (50% of males and 50% of females).

67. D Renin is secreted by the juxtaglomerular apparatus of the nephron in response to low blood pressure. Renin converts angiotensinogen from the liver to angiotensin I. Angiotensin I is converted to angiotensin II by the angiotensin converting enzyme. Angiotensin II causes constriction of blood vessels and the release of aldosterone from the adrenal cortex and vasopressin from the posterior pituitary. Aldosterone will reabsorb sodium from the distal convoluted tubule and cortical collecting duct, and vasopressin will enhance water reabsorption from the collecting duct. As a result, the urine will be water-deficient and concentrated. Therefore, dilute urine in the face of renin secretion indicates a problem with the kidney.

68. A In order to expand to accommodate a meal, the stomach must have folds, similar to the small intestines. The villi in the small intestines serve to increase the surface area across which absorption can take place. Since there is no absorption occurring in the stomach, the *rugae* of the stomach serve to increase the surface area for expansion of the stomach. The parietal cells secrete hydrochloric acid (C is incorrect). Goblet cells secrete mucous to aid in protecting the stomach (B is incorrect). Pepsin is created from the secreted zymogen pepsinogen with the assistance of the hydrochloric acid in the stomach (D is incorrect).

69. B Spherical-shaped bacteria are termed *cocci*, and rod-shaped bacteria are termed *bacilli*. If the bacteria can only grow in an environment rich in oxygen, they are considered obligate aerobes. If they cannot grow at all in the presence of oxygen, they are termed obligate anaerobes (C and D are incorrect). Facultative anaerobes are bacteria that can grow in the presence or absence of oxygen. Microaerophilic refers to an environment with low concentration of oxygen where bacteria grow (A is incorrect).

70. C An increased respiratory rate is a compensatory mechanism for the body to re-establish acid-base homeostasis. An increased respiratory rate serves to decrease CO_2 concentration in the blood. CO_2 in the blood is easily converted to carbonic acid and subsequently dissociates to form a proton (acid) and bicarbonate ion (conjugate base). Therefore, there must be an elevated amount of protons or CO_2 in the blood, if the body is compensating by increasing the respiratory rate (statements II and III are correct, so eliminate A and B). An increase in the concentration of bicarbonate ions results in an alkalemia, more alkaline pH of the blood. The body compensates by increasing the acid content of the blood. This is manifested as decreasing the respiratory rate in order to increase CO_2 concentration in the blood, thereby increasing acid content of the blood (statement I is false).

71. B A silent mutation describes a mutation in the genetic code that does not influence the translated amino acid. A missense mutation refers to a mutation in the genetic code that causes a change in the translated amino acid (e.g., converting glutamic acid to valine). A nonsense mutation is a mutation that results in a premature stop codon. A null mutation is a mutation which renders the protein non-functional.

72.   C   There are a few hormones that can perform the same physiologic function in the human body. Both aldosterone and vasopressin can concentrate the urine. Since vasopressin is secreted by the posterior pituitary, there is still a way to concentrate the urine. Serum glucose can be raised by the actions of cortisol and glucagon, neither of which is secreted by the adrenal cortex. Angiotensin II and vasopressin can both be used to raise blood pressure. Neither of them is produced by the adrenal cortex.

73.   D   The purpose of myelin is to increase the speed with which nerve impulses can travel. By having periodic spaces where there is no myelin (nodes of Ranvier), the nerve impulse appears to "jump" along the axon. This is termed salutatory conduction. In a demyelinating disorder, the nerve impulse signal cannot "jump" along the length of the axon. Therefore, salutatory conduction is not expected in individuals with demyelinating diease. With less myelination, nerve conduction will not be as fast and efficient. This is manifested as slower action potentials (A is a correct statement). Oligodendrocytes are neuronal cells that are responsible for synthesizing myelin in the CNS (B is a correct statement). Because myelin wraps around the axon of the neuron, only voltage-gated channels will be affected. Ligand-gated ion channels will not be affected (C is a correct statement)

74.   A   A competitive inhibitor binds to the same active site as the desired substrate. This inhibition, however, can be overcome by increasing the concentration of substrate, as if "flooding" the enzyme with substrate. Therefore, the Vmax will remain the same for a competitive inhibitor (B and C are incorrect). If it takes more substrate to reach the same Vmax, then, by definition, the Km must increase, since the Km is the substrate concentration when 50% of the Vmax has been reached. Zero-order kinetics refers to a constant rate of reaction no matter the concentration of substrate; this occurs once the Vmax has been reached. Until the Vmax is reached, the kinetics usually are first-order (D is incorrect).

About the Authors

Matthew Patterson, M.D. received his medical degree from Columbia University College of Physicians & Surgeons. Over the past decade, he has been a regular contributor to The Princeton Review's MCAT books and instructional courses as an author, trainer, and teacher.

Jennifer Wooddell received her undergraduate degree in History and Literature from Harvard University. She has been teaching, training teachers, and training trainers for The Princeton Review LSAT and MCAT courses for the last fifteen years. She is the Senior Editor for MCAT Verbal Reasoning and Writing course materials for The Princeton Review.

Jason Faulhaber, M.D. has worked with The Princeton Review since 1993 as a teacher and tutor for MCAT, USMLE, and SAT Subject Tests, and as a Master Trainer for MCAT and USMLE since 1997. He has contributed to preparation materials for the USMLE and SAT Subject Tests in Chemistry and Biology. He currently practices medicine in Boston, MA.

NOTES

NOTES

NOTES

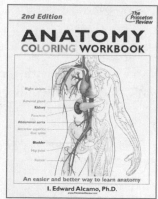